D1483774

Confederate Industry

Confederate Industry

MANUFACTURERS AND QUARTERMASTERS
IN THE CIVIL WAR

Harold S. Wilson

University Press of Mississippi   *Jackson*

www.upress.state.ms.us

Copyright © 2002 by University Press of Mississippi
All rights reserved
Manufactured in the United States of America

Paperback Edition

10 09 08 07 06 05 04 03 02   4 3 2 1

⊗

Library of Congress Cataloging-in-Publication Data

Wilson, Harold S., 1935–

   Confederate industry : manufacturers and quartermasters in the Civil War / Harold
S. Wilson.

      p. cm.

   Includes bibliographical references and index.

   ISBN 1-57806-462-7 (cloth : alk. paper)

      1. Manufacturing industries—United States—History—19th century. 2. United
States—History—Civil War, 1861–1865. 3. Quartermasters. I. Title.

HD9725 .W546 2002

973.7'1—dc21   2002000633

British Library Cataloging-in-Publication Data available

CONTENTS

PREFACE

The Civil War brought an end to slavery; it also brought an end to an antebellum renaissance in Southern manufacturing. On the eve of the Civil War, the slave states ranked among the industrial nations of the world in miles of railroads, numbers of steamboats, annual production of pig iron and coal, and the extent of telegraph connections. Tanneries, foundries, slaughterhouses, and flour mills added greatly to the material capacity available to the nascent Confederacy. Only England, France, two other European powers, and the North possessed more cotton and woolen spindles than the slave states, which had several hundred cotton and woolen mills. While the Confederacy mobilized these resources, the Union systematically endeavored to destroy them.

A study of manufacturing within the Confederacy offers illumination on a number of important issues, including the extent of the Southern factory system. Some historians, such as Charles Ramsdell, have questioned whether state and Confederate industrial policies contributed to or inhibited the general war effort. Recent writers have asked whether businesspeople were predators or patriots to the new cause. How did economic risks balance with opportunities after secession? Did the Confederacy effectively exploit manufacturing and material resources? Despite the overwhelming testimony to the contrary, were Confederate forces reasonably clothed and shod? Further, and more important, what were the immediate and long-term impacts of the destructiveness of the war? What insights into the origins of the New South can be gained by investigating the war experiences of Southern manufacturers?

Numerous studies have demonstrated that the antebellum South produced a large class of manufacturers who opposed extreme states' rights dogmas and supported the importation and exploitation of technology.[1] Alexis de Tocqueville, on his American visit, astutely observed that "as the mass of the nation turns to democracy, that particular class which is engaged in manufactures becomes more aristocratic" (*Democracy in America* 2:158–61). He particularly referenced Northerners who brought business skills to the slave states. In the South, manufacturers amassed wealth, utilized both free and slave laborers, adapted to free markets, and emerged as a "new aristocracy." Swept into war by a secession movement they opposed, this group nevertheless rendered highly effective service to the Confederate cause. Ever suspicious of the agrarian propensities of Confederate authorities, manufacturers ably utilized domestic resources in clothing and sheltering the armies. As a consequence, they were caught between two fires, an onerous and draconian Confederate military governance fostered in part by public suspicion of corporations and their profits and a Union military policy of extreme retribution.

The literature on Confederate manufacturing is surprisingly meager. There is no study of Colonel Abraham C. Myers or General Alexander R. Lawton, Confederate quartermaster generals, comparable to Russell Frank Weigley's *Quartermaster General of the Union Army: A Biography of M. C. Meigs*. Although Richard D. Goff's *Confederate Supply* and James Lynn Nichols's *The Confederate Quartermaster in the Trans-Mississippi* represent important contributions to the study of logistics, neither emphasizes manufacturing. The view of most historians is that Southern troops probably were boldly led and poorly fed, that Confederate logistics was in fact a misnomer. Charles W. Ramsdell's *Behind the Lines in the Southern Confederacy* and his companion article, "The Control of Manufacturing by the Confederate Government," graphically describe Southern deprivations and desperate attempts at state action and probably represent the historical consensus. There is acknowledged to be one sterling exception within the Confederate battlement: the Ordnance Bureau and its associated suppliers. These operations were effectively described by Frank E. Vandiver in *Ploughshares into Swords: Josiah Gorgas and Confederate Ordnance* and by Charles R. Dew in *Ironmaker to the Confederacy: Joseph R. Anderson and the Tredegar Iron Works*. Mary A. DeCredico's study of urban entrepreneurs in four Georgia cities during the Civil War, *Patriotism for Profit*, ably expands upon Emory Thomas's thesis that the war stimulated centralization, urbanization, and industry in central Georgia. Bess Beatty's *Alamance* shows the ambiguities and ironies of war in an important manufacturing community in North Carolina.[2] These books suggest that a substantial manufacturing effort was mounted to reinforce the Confederate movement for independence, and that endeavor is the focus of this study. By secession, Old South manufacturing was brought to its pinnacle of development and then to a great extent perished in the holocaust of the war.

Recently, colonialist, postcolonialist, and postmodernist critics have begun to apply to Southern society the criteria used in evaluating non-Western societies, specifically the judgment that technological supremacy creates a power arrangement in which mechanical technology can force a rearrangement of society and its values. Mark M. Smith, in *Mastered by the Clock: Time, Slavery, and Freedom in the American South*, argues that the importation of cheap clocks into the South and the growth of time-consciousness, time-discipline, and time-obedience reshaped the contours of plantation life into a semblance of Northern factories with their pressed, if not oppressed, workers. In Reconstruction, the master class utilized this imported Northern tool to discipline free workers. Scott Reynolds Nelson, in *Iron Confederacies: Southern Railways, Klan Violence, and Reconstruction*, looks at the imperialism of space, the exploitation of Confederate rhetoric by Northern railway leaders who established control over Southern trunk lines after the war. Both Nelson and Alexander C. Lichtenstein, in *Twice the Work of Free Labor: The Political Economy of Convict Labor in the New South*, argue that Northern railroaders and other capitalists were the chief instigators of racial violence and the beneficiaries of the growing prison population in the postwar South, especially the convict lease system which, they argue, was at the core of New South development.

The findings in this study suggest some limits to these generalizations. Other machines besides clocks reshaped the Southern landscape; there were also railroads, telegraph lines, steamboats, and cotton mills. Individuals willingly acquired the precise discipline necessary to maintain these technological systems. Although Southern manufacturers were strict devotees of the clock, with time often measured in ticks per minutes on the looms, free workers maintained the option of returning to the routines of the agricultural cycles. The conditions of war seem to have especially militated against the strict exploitation of scientific measures of efficiency; for their part, white and black workers, who suffered much in the war, proved remarkably reluctant to suborn themselves entirely to the demands of the machinery. Railroad trunk lines, as Nelson shows, were an indigenous creation of the Confederacy during the war, not imposed from the outside, and the convict labor system antedated Reconstruction by decades. The convict lease system, railroad trunk lines, and scientific efficiency were hardly the original sins of the Reconstruction South.

One consequence of the modernization wrought by the Civil War, however, was a painful reinterpretation of the traditional concepts of freedom, progress, states' rights, secession, and union. This process of transformation did not come to the South as a result of Union conquests. The antebellum arguments of Southern manufacturers that abundant and inexpensive water power, labor, and raw materials made the region ripe for development took on significant new meaning when the armies in Virginia and Tennessee were facing extreme deprivation. War necessities and an economy of scarcity forced a reevaluation of the prewar industrial gospel and prepared the public mind for the acceptance of a new industrial South.

While many manufacturers lost their estates in the rebellion, they profited politically in Presidential Reconstruction. The war vividly demonstrated the values of technology to an agrarian public, and afterward manufacturers, editors, and Confederate veterans united in explaining that the "Lost Cause" failed because of the superior technologies of the North. As proto-Unionists and purveyors of technology and market economics, the Southern manufacturing class became an important arm of Andrew Johnson's attempt to construct new loyal governments in the South. Although these efforts were thwarted by congressional Radicals, manufacturers and their spokespersons—such as Henry Grady, Henry Watterson, and Daniel Tompkins—later reemerged as leaders of the New South. The Confederate defeat inspired a large effort at rebuilding, and with broad public acquiescence and political patronage a New South arose on the foundations firmly laid down in the old. The stone rejected by the builders became the cornerstone.

This study is indebted to the encouragement of Richard W. Griffin, who guided the Textile History Society for many years, and to other officers of that society, especially Jack Blicksilver and Ernest Lander. Many history colleagues deserve special acknowledgment, especially James Bugg, Peter Stewart, Thomas Alexander, Bell Wiley, Louis Harlan, Willie

Lee Rose, and Charles Simmons. Those who served as external readers for the press rendered an invaluable service with their helpful and insightful criticisms. I owe a permanent debt of gratitude to two brilliant teachers, scholars, and gentlemen, James Harvey Young and C. Vann Woodward.

It is a pleasure to acknowledge the aid of librarians and archivists at approximately fifty depositories where research was conducted. Especially helpful were the able staff at the Moravian Archives at Old Salem, Claire Bishop and Robert Lovett at the Baker Library of Harvard University, Mattie Read of the Perkins Library at Duke University, and Cynthia Duncan and Jean Major of the Perry Library at Old Dominion University. The National Archives is a national treasure. The excellent staffs at the Wilson Library at the University of North Carolina, the Lilly Library at the University of Indiana, the Caroliniana Library at the University of South Carolina, and the Library of Congress were always exemplary in their professionalism. Among the state historical societies, those of Virginia and Massachusetts were models of courtesy and efficiency. The Merrimac Valley Textile Museum of North Andover, Massachusetts, and the Smithsonian Institution in Washington, D.C., were helpful on technical questions.

Elaine Dawson of Old Dominion University capably and professionally formatted the entire manuscript. Robert Burchfield, copyeditor, rendered excellent service in winnowing out many egregious technical errors and clarifying larger issues. Craig Gill and Anne Stascavage, editors, supervised the whole project with good humor and aplomb. Finally, I wish to thank my wife, Rhetta Fair Wilson, who patiently endured this project, proofread the entire manuscript several times, and made many valuable suggestions, and Katherine and Kyle, who missed a trip west because their father communed with the muses.

INTRODUCTION:

SOUTHERN MANUFACTURING CIRCA 1860

The statistical war between the sections began before the first shots sounded at Fort Sumter. James D. B. DeBow, superintendent of the national census in 1850, devoted most of three volumes on industrial resources to a benevolent analysis of cotton and slavery in the South. His successor, Joseph C. G. Kennedy, superintendent of the 1860 census, was the alleged author of a polemic against the "King Cotton" theorists that favorably compared the economy of New York to that of the Gulf states (Colwell; Elliott). Drawing freely upon the decennial reports and other sources, abolitionist Hinton Rowan Helper in *The Impending Crisis* and Southern apologist Thomas P. Kettell in *Southern Wealth and Northern Profits* applied statistics to larger theoretical constructs about the impacts of slavery upon economic development. Gilbert J. Beebe and Samuel M. Wolfe promptly wrote refutations of Helper, while Henry Chase and Charles W. Sanborn, in *The North and the South*, defended him. These publications in turn fueled debates in Congress and in the press. Although marked by inevitable disagreements, misstatements, and inaccuracies, the controversy disclosed much about the quantity of war-related industries in the South.

Such a revealing exchange took place in March 1860 between Senator Daniel Clark of New Hampshire and Senator Andrew Johnson of Tennessee. Clark's offending remark was that "Tennessee had both coal and copper, but she lacked the energy to develop her resources . . . and he had himself seen copper taken from the mines there and sent to New York to be smelted by the 'mud sills' of society, because there were not energy and enterprise enough in Tennessee to do it" (Johnson 3: 491). The east Tennessee commoner was instantly on his feet. The Ducktown copper mines, discovered in 1851, were in an inaccessible area, and Tennesseans had shown "a sufficient amount of enterprise and energy to dig down the hills, fill up the valleys, make good roads, and extract large amounts of ore from the mines" that kept seven smelting furnaces in constant operation (492). Johnson then turned to the inevitable comparison, Tennessee and New Hampshire. Using DeBow's figures, Johnson enumerated in each state the number and value of farms and the number of miners and found "the number of persons engaged in manufacturing in Tennessee was 17,815; in New Hampshire 17,826" (493). The Niagara of figures rolled on: more wool in Tennessee, where the national crop was migrating and where a resident won the best fleece award at the Crystal Palace exhibit in 1851, ten times the bushels of wheat, fifty times as much corn, a million times as much tobacco. Of pig iron, the Tennesseans made 30,000 tons, New Hampshire 200, and the Southern state boasted 1,110 miles of railroad, with more being built every day.

A similar exchange in the House of Representatives pitted Alexander Stephens of Georgia against representatives from Ohio. Stung by remarks on Southern backwardness, the Georgian announced that he had "looked a little into the statistics of Georgia," which he compared favorably with "the State of Ohio, . . . one of the most prosperous of the North" (Cleveland 430). By his figures, with half the population, Georgia produced agricultural products worth more than those of Ohio and, even excluding cotton, of far more value per capita. His state grazed about as many "neat cattle" and far more swine than the Northern state. With thirty-eight cotton and woolen factories, Georgia's investment in manufacturing was about double that of Ohio, while the state's railroad mileage exceeded 1,000 miles (451). Data on colleges, churches, and newspapers were also thrown into the fray. Such forays were common enough in the heated days of sectional frenzy.

The press and pamphlet war accelerated with the publication of Thomas J. Kettell's *Southern Wealth and Northern Profits* in 1860 and Joseph Kennedy's new federal census soon thereafter. These enumerators presented fresh materials concerning the relative economic strength of the sections. Kettell's findings bore special relevance to logistics and, along with DeBow's work, provided an important text for mental war games at Southern military academies. He calculated that the slave states possessed half of the millions of horses and milk cows in the country and over two-thirds of the mules, oxen, meat cattle, and swine. These animals provided a plenitude of skins for tanning. The pork was cured in brine, and Virginia was the second largest producer of salt in the Union. He found that the most serious Southern deficit was in sheep, two-thirds of which were in the North and West (Kettell 43). Southerners raised, per capita, two times the foodstuffs of the Northern commercial states, which amounted to thirty-seven bushels of corn and four and one-half bushels of wheat per person. Virginia ranked fourth nationally in flour production, with two of the three largest flour mills in the country located in Richmond. Kettell generously calculated that the South, with more area and less population than Europe, had 9,058 miles of railroad, compared to 6,426 in England and Wales, 3,712 in France, and 2,309 in Prussia (Kettell 51; Flint et al. 224). Thirty-one canals and two major harbors enhanced Southern communication: over 70,000 tons of vessels were ported at New Orleans and more upriver at St. Louis and Louisville. Three telegraph lines linked Baltimore to New Orleans, and all major Southern cities were connected. The cost for raising twenty-five oak poles carrying one mile of galvanized iron wire was only $150, and in 1852 the nation was connected with 23,283 miles of line. This amount of cable likely doubled by 1860, with the South having about one-third or some 15,000 miles, more than continental Europe.[1] By use of ten repeaters, an operator in Baltimore could quickly rouse New Orleans.

Southern cotton manufacturing was also growing. Relying primarily on the 1850 census, Kettell credited the slave states with having 180 cotton factories and 249 woolen mills, "but it is shown that in 1859 the spinners of that section took 98,000 [198,000] bales of cotton, or an increase of 50 percent, over the quantity used in 1850" (Kettell 55). This amounted to over one-quarter of the national total. As he noted, "the rate of progression [in the South] was far greater than in the North or East," and the South "is fast supplanting Northern and imported goods with its own industry" (55, 62).

In *Eighty Years' Progress*, a compelling essay for the compendium, Kettell expanded on the nature of Southern mill production. Slave labor was extensively used in Alabama and South Carolina mills; otherwise, white adults and children aged twelve to fifteen were employed. The average hours of labor were twelve but varied according to the season. A dozen large mills operated in central Virginia, where the principal product was three million pounds of coarse cottons, which averaged about two and one-half yards to the pound. This included heavy water-resistant shirting, pantaloon cloth for slaves, and bagging. This bagging was used by local flour mills and exported "to Brazil for sugar bags" (Flint 284). Kettell cited the *New York Herald,* which counted more than twenty-eight mills near Columbus, Georgia, manufacturing millions of yards of both cotton and woolen goods (Kettell 68). Similar clusters of mills operated in central North Carolina, along the tributaries of the Tennessee and Cumberland Rivers in Tennessee, and elsewhere throughout the South.

The federal census of 1860, superintended by Joseph Kennedy, enlarged upon Kettell's findings and credited the slave states and the Federal District with having 200 cotton mills, or 22 percent of those counted (Kennedy 180). Many rural mills went uncounted, and a modern historian has calculated that there were at least 250 cotton mills, encompassing nearly half a million spindles, in operation within the slave states.[2] By Kennedy's count, the slave states also possessed 153 woolen factories and most of the carding and fulling mills in the country, or 479 out of 722 (Superintendent of the Census xxxv). The woolen mills made nearly nine million yards of goods in 1860, but almost half of this spindleage lay in the vulnerable border states of the Upper South. However, Virginia alone had forty-five woolen mills and sixty-three carding mills, the latter being mostly in the mountains and lower Valley. These produced annually over one million yards of goods, enough for 200,000 suits of clothing. Other states such as Georgia and North Carolina also had a significant woolen industry. Lower South carding mills cleaned over one million pounds of wool for a thriving home industry of country spinners and weavers.

As a cotton manufacturing region, in pounds of cotton consumed, the slave states ranked behind the North, England, and France but above Austria-Hungary, Belgium, Spain, and Finland.[3] The region's carding and fulling mills, plantation spinning houses, rope walks, jute and burlap weavers, and home industries were a vital element in domestic supply. While Southern spindles were far fewer than those of the North, they were generally newer and more cheaply operated. A contrast with Britain in 1860 is instructive. British mills held about eight times as many spindles as those of the United States but produced only about four times as much cloth (Adams 2: 6).[4] The South held about the same relationship with the North.

The growth of cotton manufacturing stimulated other industries. Paper production and thus publishing used rags and waste, a byproduct of cotton manufacturing, as the basic raw material for making pulp. The Kennedy census enumerated fifty-two paper mills in the slave states, which produced annually in excess of 12 million pounds of paper, equivalent to about sixty million newspapers (Superintendent of the Census cxxxi). By contrast, Europe's leading producer and exporter—England—made 105 million pounds of paper in 1850, mostly from Southern cotton (Tomlinson 2: 374). Most Southern paper mills lay near cotton factories on the fall line between the Upper South and the Black Belt. Nine Virginia mills produced 1.9 million pounds of paper and newsprint, and six North Carolina mills located mostly in Cleveland, Lincoln, and Wake Counties made 1.4 million pounds, about the same quantity as produced by the four mills in Georgia. The Bath paper mill at Augusta was the largest in the Lower South, and, like the Rock Island paper mills at Columbus and Lister and Sons at Greenville, did a large regional business with publishers and newspapers (Parrish and Willingham 13).

Cotton mills and railroads stimulated the growth of an iron industry. Over a hundred iron furnaces and bloomeries, which refined ore, were scattered across the slave states, and in practically every locality iron works fabricated water wheels, gears, and parts. The Virginia Iron Works at Wheeling and the Canton Iron Works at Baltimore, the latter founded by Peter Cooper, were two of the premier iron manufacturers in the country. The Wheeling mill made 1,000 kegs of nails a week, while five adjacent rolling mills had a capacity of 20,000 tons of rails a year. The Canton works in Baltimore possessed a rolling mill capable of making four-inch iron plates. Farther south, a few mills made nails, locomotives, wire, and steam engines. Fifty-four foundries in Virginia did casting, and across the Lower South 115 establishments performed precision machine tooling. Most of the large mills and railroads operated their own machine shops. Precise figures on blast furnaces and charcoal production were not accessioned; however, the Montgomery Iron Works in Alabama, King's Mountain in South Carolina, East Tennessee Manufacturing, and Tredegar Iron Works in Virginia were large and successful establishments. By 1860, the Etowah Manufacturing and Mining Company in Georgia, a pioneer in the iron and coal business in that region, consisted of a factory village sited on 12,000 acres of land fronting five miles of river in Cass County. The company operated a nail factory, a drilling mill, a blast furnace and rolling mill, a charcoal smelting furnace, an iron mine, a flouring mill, two gristmills, a sawmill, boarding- and operative houses, churches, schools, prosperous merchant houses, and four miles of railroad track.[5] A student of the Southern iron industry writes that "the Tredegar works and other private and government establishments had the capacity to turn out large quantities of high quality ordnance, munitions, gunboat plates, railroad supplies, and other strategic and badly needed items" and suffered only from a want of pig iron (Dew 177–78). In 1860, both Tredegar and the neighboring Richmond foundry, Balonna, did a heavy business casting cannon for the War Department. At Harpers Ferry stood the model arsenal of the United States with two complete sets of rifle-making machinery. Fifty-four Southern cotton gin factories drew upon Southern iron resources. There were only three gin companies outside the Lower South. The best-known manufacturers were Daniel Pratt, whose foundry and factory were located at Prattville, in central Alabama, and produced 500 fifty-tooth gins a year, and Samuel Griswold, who operated a large manufacturing village near Macon, Georgia. These establishments possessed sophisticated casting and tooling capacity with great military potential.

The South also had 1,246 leather shops and tanneries which manufactured about four million pairs of shoes and boots annually, about half of the region's needs. Massachusetts alone produced over forty million pairs for internal distribution and export, and Baltimore, St. Louis, and New Orleans each imported about one million pairs each year from the North. Many of these Northern shoes were of modern construction, with soles attached to the upper leather by means of wooden pegs, a design of dubious military value. The Southern artisans fashioned a very sturdy and serviceable article but generally without utilizing either leather-splitting devices or powered sewing machines. An exception was the Southern Shoe Factory in New Orleans, established in 1861, which used the most modern machinery to produce 65,000 pairs of plantation brogans a year, a number easily doubled with additional machinery (Albert Richardson 63). A great advantage to the South in shoe manufacturing lay in the abundance of hides secured from the slaughter of livestock; the forests rich in the bark of oak and hemlock, which provided tannin for processing; and the possession of a corps of experienced personnel who knew how to cure hides in vats for five months to make leather (Superintendent of the Census lxxii, 716; Flint 324; Tomlinson 125–40).

Although the South had some deficiencies in powder mills and lead mines, in many critical areas the slave states possessed the sinews of war: a manufacturing base, a transportation and communication infrastructure, and an educated and politically aware leadership. There was a sufficiency of manufacturers and railroaders, of skilled workers and engineers, to support a military mobilization. A statistical study of the Southern economy has noted, "if we treat the North and South as separate nations and rank them along the countries of the world, the South would stand as the fourth richest nation of the world in 1860" (Fogel and Engerman 249). Not only was the South more developed than contemporary Japan or India, but Southerners possessed more wealth than France, Germany, or Denmark. Not all of this wealth was in the form of cotton lands and slaves, for in every Southern state manufacturers were at the forefront of economic life.

Contemporary literature has enriched our knowledge of these men. Archibald Graham McIlwaine was the dean of mill owners in Virginia. After emigrating from Ireland to Petersburg as a youth, McIlwaine first became a successful merchant, then an entrepreneur. He served as principal financial backer and president of four local factories—Merchants, Ettrick, Battersea, and Matoaca.[6] These mills imported 200,000 pounds of cotton a month from the Lower South by rail and marketed their yarns and cloths in Virginia, Baltimore, Philadelphia, New York, and Brazil. By 1860, McIlwaine, a staunch Whig and Unionist, passed the active management of these mills into other hands. In that year, a large woolen factory in Richmond—the city's second—was erected by Joseph, William, and Louis Crenshaw, successful commission merchants and real estate investors. The four-story mill was raised near the Tredegar Iron Works on the James River where a previous mill had burned. The Crenshaws equipped their factory with both narrow and broad looms in order to manufacture suit cloth and blankets (Mordecai 327).

In North Carolina, Francis Levin Fries of Salem and Edwin Michael Holt of Alamance County were representative of the manufacturing class. Often called Frank, Fries belonged to the old German Moravian community, where he erected in succession three mills: one for the Gemein Diaconie, the religious governing council, and two for himself.[7] His mills, powered by steam, held 1,026 modern spindles and twenty-six looms, a powerful assemblage of machinery in his hands. Edwin Holt, his friend, was a pioneer manufacturer in North Carolina who raised a mill—the first of five—in Alamance County, at the site of a gristmill. He quickly acquired an estate worth over $100,000, with property including two factories; substantial acreage; fifty-one slaves; a sawmill, which he operated with his sons; and several general stores, where he marketed his dry goods and yarns.[8] By 1860, Holt presided over the affairs of a local bank and made "between 2 & 3000 bushels of wheat per annum."[9] His cotton mills made some of the best plaid cloth in North Carolina, and the owner successfully blended the life of a small planter with that of a merchant manufacturer.

Perhaps the most renowned manufacturer in the Lower South was William Gregg of Edgefield District, South Carolina.[10] A Virginian by birth, Gregg and his son, James, were the principal shareholders in two mills, the Vaucluse factory and the Graniteville Manufacturing Company. On 9,000 acres of land at Graniteville, Gregg constructed the larger mill, designed to hold 12,000 spindles, eighty-three dwellings, two dams, a race one mile long, two churches, a school, a hotel, and a sawmill and gristmill (*American Agriculturalist*, May 6, 1849). Theodore D. Wagner, a partner in the commission house of John Fraser and Company of Charleston, New York, and Liverpool, was a partner.[11] By 1860, with all spindles in operation, the Graniteville factory was the center of a considerable manufacturing town of 830 persons.[12] Although Gregg took little interest in paper manufacturing, he sold large quantities of waste cotton to John G. Winter's Bath paper mill, also located on Horse Creek.[13]

Manufacturer James Barrington King ran three mills at Roswell, near Atlanta, and in many respects typifies other Georgia manufacturers. He commenced with an original small structure, raised in 1838, then expanded. He added a second factory by 1850, then built Ivy woolen factory and established Lebanon Mills, a large flouring concern (White 402). As at Graniteville and elsewhere, a regular village developed around the mills, warehouses, company stores, churches, schools, and boardinghouses.[14] By 1860, Georgia had fifty-nine other mills operating under similar conditions. King freely recruited Northern and foreign mechanics and workers, one of whom was Henry Merrell from New York, who spent five years at Roswell before launching a career for himself as a manufacturer in central Georgia and Arkansas.

After migrating to Royston in Pike County, Arkansas, Merrell achieved a measure of success by establishing a manufacturing village around his mill of 400 spindles. He spun cotton and carded wool and sometimes made 550 pounds of yarn and carded 700 pounds of wool in a day and a night. His hands worked from sunup to dusk and were paid, when possible, in goods from the company store. Since few mills operated west of the Mississippi, competition was rare (Merrell 297).

Daniel Pratt's town of Prattville, on a tributary of the Alabama River, was also a center of manufacturing. Pratt, a native of New Hampshire, was a large slaveholder who ran a manufacturing complex that included a gin factory, foundry, sawmill, and gristmill. His cotton mill, built originally for 2,800 spindles, was considerably enlarged by 1860, and he added a second mill, a woolen factory.[15] The manufacturer presided over an improved village with public plank roads, museums, vineyards, schools, and churches. Across northern Alabama and central Tennessee, and indeed the entire South, rested several hundred manufacturing communities that resembled Prattville, Royston, Roswell, or Graniteville.

Men such as McIlwaine, Pratt, and Gregg had much in common with each other and the entire fraternity of manufacturers across the South. They maintained steady business communications with the North; in their employ were a disproportionately high number of immigrants from the Northern states; they took a Whiggist perspective on national economic issues such as the tariff, banking, and railroad development; and they vigorously opposed the violent rhetoric of nullification and secession. And yet they held in their hands the very tools by which Southern independence might be established. The prospect of prolonged civil strife meant an entirely new status of manufacturing within a Southern nation. "No people on earth," stated a writer for the *Southern Cultivator*, "are better prepared to make almost everything we need for ourselves, and among ourselves."[16] The editor wanted more machine shops, tanneries and shoe businesses, fabrication of clothing, soap and starch manufactories, paper mills, authors, and Southern books, for "now is the time for manufacturers to let themselves and their businesses be known all over the land" (Parrish and Willingham 9).

On October 5, 1860, Governor William Henry Gist of South Carolina dispatched by special messenger a confidential circular letter to all the governors of the cotton states except Texas, announcing that his state would probably secede because of Lincoln's impending election. He requested their cooperation. Along with this letter each governor received a large columned paper of broadside dimensions listing the resources of the North and the South. Arranged in neat parallel rows were the familiar categories of comparison between the sections: the number of acres, livestock, slaves, cotton, food crops, population, males of military age, and manufacturers. With secession, the quest for Southern independence hung on such statistical realities.

Confederate Industry

1

The Advent of Abraham C. Myers, Quartermaster General of the Confederacy

Southern manufacturers did not sleep through the long secession winter of 1860–61. They resolutely resisted the states' rights zealots at every turn. Francis Fries and Edwin Holt in North Carolina, James Simmons in Georgia, William Gregg in South Carolina, Daniel Pratt in Alabama, and Henry Merrell in Arkansas were simply the better known of a large number of manufacturers who unsuccessfully attempted to stay the hand of secession in their states (Beatty 77–78; Merrell 292–93; Evans 457, 466). Allies for the manufacturing class reached deeply into the old Whig leadership with its national perspective on economic development: tariffs; the state's fostering care of roads, railroads, and harbors; and national banking. The Southern corporate community, as a class, held a national perspective on politics, did business with the North, bought tools and machinery there, and disposed of surplus goods in Baltimore, Philadelphia, or New York.

By contrast, the Southern Confederate constitution drafted in Montgomery in February 1861 ominously called for "no encouragement to domestic industry," indicating that manufacturers were faced with both an external and an internal foe in a revolutionary economic situation: a militant enemy abroad and political hostility at home.[1] A Union economic blockade quickly followed upon secession. Southern access to Northern markets ended, the avenues of regional commerce were paralyzed by uncertainty, and banks, except for Louisiana, quickly suspended specie payments. The Confederate leadership, dominated by planter aris-tocrats with a long antagonism toward the commercial North, only re-luctantly acknowledged these problems. However, material scarcity within the army, evident in the logistical chaos that accompanied the early campaigns in Virginia, encouraged editors, field commanders, and governors to demand a reassessment of the Confederacy's ability to feed and clothe the troops. One result was the enactment of increasingly stringent regulations governing Southern manufacturers. The principal architect of the early Confederate industrial policy was Abraham Charles Myers, the first quartermaster general.

When appointed, Myers faced the daunting task of equipping a grow-ing field army from the limited resources of the South. As quartermaster general, he successfully cultivated warm support in the Confederate Congress; however, his every action was critically scrutinized by the mili-tary, which found supplies inadequate, and by business leaders, who found his controls too stringent and arbitrary. His more astute contem-porary critics also faulted him on other fronts: he was an obstacle to full and efficient mobilization of the Confederate economy; within his bureau, he failed to grasp the modern notions of efficiency and system that Josiah Gorgas and his Ordnance Bureau team so readily embraced; and he lacked ability to plan.[2] His failure to anticipate critical shortages, for example, contributed to a wool famine that paralyzed Southern mili-tary production of field uniforms by the second winter of the war.

The Confederate Congress created the position of quartermaster general on February 26, 1861, a few days following the drafting of a pro-visional constitution and the appointment of Jefferson Davis as provi-sional president. This officer was designated to disburse most of the billions expended by the Confederate government in the war. Under the terms of the legislation, the secretary of war (initially Leroy Pope Walker of Alabama) was permitted one colonel and six majors to serve as bureau quartermasters at the seat of government. Their charge was to equip the army of 100,000 men requested by Davis in his inaugural ad-dress. Subordinate quartermasters could be appointed across the South as needed for specialized duties, such as running regional depots or ware-houses where goods might accumulate. Through the machinery of the armies within the various military districts, these men would respond to requisitions of quartermasters in the regiments.

The government, acknowledging its limited ability to clothe troops, adopted on March 6, 1861, the *Regulations of the United States Army, 1857*, as a guide.[3] Until the law was rescinded in October 1862, the Confederate government paid commutation money "to the sum of twenty one dollars in lieu of six months clothing" to every volunteer.[4] Instead of actually supplying the soldiers with at least two complete outfits a year, the chief quartermaster was authorized to discharge his obligation by giving the soldiers $3.50 a month in Confederate currency. Soldiers could buy needed items from the government or secure them from private sources. In reality, at the beginning of the war nongovernment resources were more available. As Abraham Myers later explained, for the first two years of the war "no arrangements had been completed, by which clothing could be supplied to the troops, and it was necessary to rely upon the private sources of the country to have volunteers sent into the field properly clothed."[5] As the war progressed and scarcity grew, this old-army peacetime policy of commutation wrought great hardship upon the soldiers. It placed Myers in the difficult position of either letting troops clothe themselves from very limited private resources or having the government exact supplies for them from the factories. Further, should the quartermaster general seek close working relationships with manufacturers, critics could charge that he was fostering domestic industry.

Jefferson Davis's appointment of Abraham Myers became one of the most controversial appointments in the Confederate government, and the designation of the fastidious staff officer, owner of a Louisiana plantation and slaves, as acting quartermaster was not made until March 25, 1861. Davis weighed several other options before appointing a man destined to become his, and the army's, nemesis. Myers, born in 1811, the son of a lawyer and grandson of Charleston's first rabbi, chose the life of a cavalier aristocrat. He graduated from West Point in 1833, ranked thirty-second in his class, and received a first lieutenant's commission in the Fourth Infantry and appointment as assistant quartermaster before the Mexican War. He served in Mexico, where his mastery of severe logistical problems brought him the brevet ranks of major and lieutenant colonel, but after the war Myers returned to service as a post quartermaster and plantation manager (Hamersly 657). On post in New Orleans when South Carolina seceded on December 20, 1860, Myers immediately surrendered his military property to Louisiana Confederate authorities and accepted an appointment as state quartermaster from Governor Thomas O. Moore.[6] Undoubtedly, Myers's wife, a daughter of General David Emanuel Twiggs and heiress to a sizeable Louisiana plantation, influenced him in this decision. Twiggs, commander of the Department of Texas, followed Myers's example and surrendered his supplies and troops to Confederate general Ben McCulloch, an act that merited his dishonorable dismissal from the U.S. Army and subsequent appointment to the Confederate service as commander of the Military District 1, which included the state of Louisiana.

Encouraged by his friends William Porcher Miles from Charleston and Charles Magill Conrad of New Orleans, both members of the Confederate Congress, Myers quickly and quietly pressed his case for appointment as quartermaster general before the Confederate government at Montgomery. In addition to Miles and Conrad, Myers secured endorsements from General Pierre T. G. Beauregard, Davis's newly appointed commander at Charleston; Judah P. Benjamin, the new Confederate attorney general; and Richard Taylor, son of Zachary Taylor.[7] Beauregard, whose appointment was also endorsed by the powerful New Orleans political faction headed by Benjamin and John Slidell, paused in Montgomery en route to Charleston to lobby Secretary of War Walker on Myers's behalf. The Creole commander explained in a meeting on February 27, 1861, that Myers had earned "two brevets in Mexico, & is most intelligent, zealous."[8] Soon after Davis's inauguration on February 18, 1861, Myers himself traveled to Montgomery to present his case.[9] Although the quartermaster and Davis had served together on the Mexican front, there was no spark of affection between them. Davis, who offered the position to several others before seriously considering Myers, probably shared the line officers' disdain for a career staff functionary. After a lengthy interview with the Confederate president, Myers confided to Twiggs that Davis "don't want me as Quarter master General."[10] The affair could have ended there, but as capable people flowed into the Confederate Army, few coveted the challenge of supplying the army from dwindling resources. Finally, Davis bowed to necessity and appointed Myers on March 25, 1861; the selection of Colonels Josiah Gorgas at the Ordnance Bureau and Lucius Northrop at the Commissary Bureau soon followed.[11] These men administered their important bureaus under the secretary of war.

Myers was fatalistic about his own elevation. In addition to the ire of the president, there was a prospect under the enabling legislation that a brigadier general would be appointed to command over him, and, in fact, he held office only as a colonel and an acting quartermaster general until the next winter. The whole proceedings boded ill for the future, he believed; Myers wrote Miles that if "they attempt to put some one in over me . . . then I will resign if the attempt succeeds."[12] "They" were Jefferson Davis and the line officers. The provisional nature of his appointment gave no indications of the important role he was to occupy.

Myers had twenty-five years of military service, mostly at the rank of first lieutenant. He had many political friends but possessed only limited knowledge of the manufacturing resources within the Confederacy, and although he easily assumed the mantle of power bestowed by the office, he began with limited funds and staff. With one lieutenant colonel, four majors, and a small assortment of lieutenants, Myers was charged with clothing and equipping one hundred regiments of infantry and proportionate units of cavalry and artillery, an army of 100,000 men. For this he initially budgeted $128 million, a figure quickly pared by a parsimonious Confederate Congress.

Myers also had other extensive responsibilities. Most of the funds expended by the Confederate government flowed through his hands. All military contracts with cotton factories had to be validated by his office. He distributed the entire military payroll, contracted for and controlled all rail- and water-borne transportation, secured all prisoners of war, provided forage for all military horses and mules, and stored all commissary stores. In addition to procuring all garrison and field equipage, which included everything from tents to pots and axes, Myers's office was responsible for inspecting all impressed materials prior to payments by the Second Auditor's Office. The war necessitated further augmentation of Myers's responsibilities until he presided over the largest bureaucracy within the South, a veritable army of depot quartermasters, transportation clerks, mill workers, seamstresses, mechanics, and detailed soldiers.

The future czar of Southern manufacturing struck many as a dandy. From his pictures, he was of average height, slender, and delicate in his dark features. At the Montgomery capital, Myers affected a lifestyle of opulence that inspired criticism. While Jefferson Davis cowered in a Montgomery hotel room besieged by legends of office-seekers, many of whom were refugees from the late Buchanan administration, received official delegations, and made critical civil and military appointments, Myers, with mess mates Adjutant General Samuel Cooper and Surgeon General David C. De Leon, presided over "the favorite lounging-place in the evenings of the better and brighter elements of the floating population" (De Leon 28). Myers's affluent salon, with its well-stocked tables, attracted "the newest arrival, if he were worth knowing" (28). The Quartermaster Bureau, wrote Thomas De Leon, the surgeon general's brother, "is the life of the army—the supplies of every description must be received through its hands" (115). De Leon, soon en route to Europe to procure military supplies himself, surmised that if Myers's bureau were "efficiently directed, it can contribute to the most brilliant results, and badly handled, can thwart the most perfectly matured plans of genius, or generalship" (115). Myers had hardly begun to deal with these awesome responsibilities when the Confederate government moved to Richmond, Virginia, in the last week of May 1861.

At Richmond, Myers quickly rented an old warehouse at 15th and Cary Streets, soon named the Clothing Bureau, which housed assorted manufacturing operations; he established administrative headquarters in an office building at the corner of 9th and Main Streets.[13] As the bureau grew, he requisitioned additional warehouse space and private homes around the city. Even before leaving Montgomery, Myers appointed a rudimentary field staff and began structuring a basic system of supply. Most of the available goods within the Confederacy remained on store shelves, and starting on April 2, 1861, Myers appointed assistant quartermasters at Charleston, Montgomery, New Orleans, and San Antonio and charged them with purchasing and manufacturing military accouterments or supplies.[14] Quartermasters could either contract for military necessities or purchase the raw materials and fabricate the items themselves. On April 30, Myers established offices in fifteen additional cities, including Richmond and Baton Rouge. His plans for supplying the Confederacy represented his West Point training, his years of experience in the old army, and classic military doctrine concerning the establishment of "bases of operation." As he explained to Judah P. Benjamin, military depots to the rear of the armies should be established "similar to that of Richmond to the armies of Manassas, Yorktown, &c."[15] Depots at Charleston, Savannah, and Columbus would supply "troops serving upon the Atlantic." New Orleans would be the principal depot for troops gathering in Texas, Arkansas, and Missouri, while Nashville and Memphis would serve the armies in Tennessee and Kentucky. Anticipating the heavy importation of military supplies once domestic resources were exhausted, Myers gave particular attention to the quartermasters at port cities. Some of his depots, such as the Richmond Clothing Bureau, employed large numbers of white and black laborers to manufacture goods; others served simply as distribution points. Although the vicissitudes of war forced periodic relocation of some depots, the basic structure of procurement remained in place throughout the war.

To staff his emerging bureau, Myers drew personnel "both from the old service and from the active business men of the South" (115). In Richmond, the quartermaster's staff quickly grew to some forty-eight officers. William B. B. Cross, at the pinnacle of this hierarchy, became Myers's principal administrative aide. Before appointment as a quartermaster major, Cross was a successful Washington lawyer married to a daughter of Thomas Ritchie, editor of the *Richmond Enquirer*. In the waning days of the Buchanan administration, Cross served as judge advocate in the court martial proceedings against Captain James Armstrong, the Federal officer who had surrendered the Pensacola naval yard to Confederate forces in early 1861. After Armstrong was cashiered, Virginia seceded, and Cross moved to Richmond to work with Myers.[16] Lieutenant Colonel Larkin Smith presided over the Richmond depot, the main source of supplies for troops in Virginia. Smith, a native Virginian and a graduate of West Point, class of 1835, served with Myers in the Mexican War, rising to the rank of brevet major (Hamersly 769). Major Richard P. Waller, apparently a former businessperson, administered the Richmond Clothing Bureau, which fabricated tents, shoes, clothes, and hospital supplies. Under the oversight of Jefferson Davis and the secretary of war, Myers and his three subordinates, after negotiation with Congress and generals in the field, formulated and administered bureau policy.

Two subordinates in Waller's Clothing Bureau held important responsibilities for activities around Richmond. Lieutenant Aurelius F. Cone, a Georgian who graduated from West Point in 1857, served as an administrative assistant, and Captain James B. Ferguson Jr., formerly the proprietor of a large export-import business in Richmond and Petersburg, worked with the factories.[17] Ferguson, along with his brother, William, shared responsibility for "all contracts, purchases, and general supervision of the whole."[18] They became Myers's direct liaison to manufacturers. Through their efforts, Waller's Clothing Bureau received all foreign goods shipped to Richmond and "all domestic goods manufactured in Virginia."[19] This depot quickly became the principal supply facility for the armies on the Virginia front.

Throughout the summer of 1861 Myers's list of field appointments grew, many of them drawn from his large collection of old acquaintances. The port cities received special attention. As assistant quartermaster authorized to secure and manufacture imported goods, Myers placed Isaac T. Winnemore, an old friend, at New Orleans. An accounting of Winnemore's assets in a subsequent investigation revealed that he was only marginally a member of Myers's aristocratic slaveholding class. The New Orleans major owned one Negro woman, bank stock, gold valued at $5,000, and Texas real estate worth $6,500. Of Winnemore's character, one contemporary wrote, "no reports have reached me . . . except the most *indefinite* character."[20] Much the same was true of the other men Myers posted to port cities. Julius Hessee at Mobile was a member of the firm of Cox, Brainard, and Company and a state quartermaster.[21] Other appointees were probably local business clerks: Herman Hirsch at Savannah, Hutson Lee at Charleston, James Seixas at Wilmington, and Benjamin Bloomfield at Yorktown.[22] None were graduates of West Point. These men exercised important responsibilities as depot supply officers, expending hundreds of thousands of dollars. Three—Hessee, Seixas, and Hirsch—were subsequently investigated for ineptitude and fraud but exonerated. All served through the war, if not with distinction at least to the satisfaction of demanding local field commanders.

In the Tennessee military district, the Confederates' critical western front, appointments came from the ranks of the local business elite. On September 10, 1861, Myers named Vernon K. Stevenson, a professional railroad builder, president of the Nashville and Chattanooga Railroad, and proponent of cotton mills, as chief quartermaster for General Albert Sidney Johnson's army. Stevenson established a major depot at Nashville and subdepots at Memphis and other towns across the state. Like other quartermasters, Myers instructed Stevenson to acquire a "perfect familiarity with the resources of the States in which your operations will be conducted."[23] Stevenson's activities required him to buy supplies on the open market or fabricate them when necessary. Along with tents, pans, spades, cartridge boxes, knapsacks, and saddles, Stevenson was reminded, "the clothing for the army in sufficient quantities for the several commands is an object of the utmost solicitude."[24] Stevenson in turn recruited Tennessee merchants, such as George W. Cunningham at Nashville and William Anderson at Memphis, as subordinates. These men contracted for supplies "of every description" and forwarded the bills to Richmond.[25]

With supplies dispersed across the Confederacy and transportation facilities limited, Myers allowed the fabricating activities of his command to expand quickly. He established depots to manufacture supplies in San Antonio, Texas; Fort Smith, Arkansas; Enterprise and Columbus, Mississippi; Huntsville and Montgomery, Alabama; and Atlanta and Augusta, Georgia. These were sites seemingly secure from enemy threats and conveniently adjacent to factories and transportation facilities.[26]

In Richmond, Myers charted a steady course between demands of the army and those of private business. His fondness for the bureaucratic style of the old army became his best defense. Even as the Confederates marshaled large military forces before the Federal capital in June 1861, he remained a steadfast devotee of military regulations in all their complexity, and he often saw his civilian superiors as mere impediments to his administration.

John B. Jones, a clerk in the War Department and one of Myers's staunchest critics, wrote in his diary that the quartermaster general "hated" Secretary of War Walker. Scarcity of supplies and disorder of distribution undoubtedly contributed to the strained relationship, but the men held different views of the bureaucracy. A revealing case developed regarding George Schley's Richmond factory near Augusta.

In April 1861, Schley, manufacturer of the famous Sibley tents, offered to supply 2,000 yards of duck cloth a day to the Quartermaster Department, as he had previously to the U.S. government. Schley provided an imposing list of references. Alexander Stephens, the vice president, found him to be "a gentleman of high character," and General William Henry Walker of Georgia wrote that Schley possessed "a first rate factory and his acts will come up to his promise."[27] The manufacturer held contracts with the South Carolina government and had the endorsement of Governor Joseph E. Brown of Georgia, for whom he had agreed "to make anything wanted in cotton goods.''[28] But such unsolicited proposals were outside the Confederate military regulations at that time, and, as a consequence, Myers rejected them with a stock response. He wrote Schley that "you may be satisfied that when an opportunity offers, your offer will be favorably considered."[29] Similar replies were sent to other Confederate manufacturers as the contending armies marshaled at Manassas.

The impending war generated no great sense of urgency within Myers's fledgling bureau. General Walker, a close friend to both Governor Joseph E. Brown and George Schley, discovered this when he visited the War Department in July. Walker held a long and unsatisfactory conversation with Myers that apparently dealt with the mounting supply problems both in Virginia and on the Georgia coast. Some troops at Manassas were without shelter while the quartermaster general systematically rejected contracts with Georgia factories. Myers frequently dealt with complaining officers by citing the authoritative regulations in detail: soldiers were paid commutation money to buy their own uniforms. Their officers took these funds and made the necessary purchases from either private or government stores. Of course, soldiers who were not paid could not purchase clothing. Bewildered field commanders, many with little previous military experience, constantly demanded supplies from the secretary of war.

After the Georgia general's unsatisfactory interview, Jones wrote, the general demanded to see Secretary of War Walker. However, the secretary was not available, and the general's entry was barred by the assistant secretary, Colonel Albert T. Bledsoe, in civilian life a noted proslavery writer and mathematics professor at the University of Virginia. A vigorous altercation ensued between the general and Bledsoe, after which Bledsoe "fumed and fretted like an angry volcano" because he "disliked Col. Myers, and believed he had sent the general in under prompting" (John Jones 1: 61). The event underscored the rising opposition to the War Department by Georgia leaders such as Governor Brown, General Walker, and Schley.[30]

Such disputes sometimes surfaced in the press, to the discredit of the War Department. Officers like Walker, left to their own devices, usually sought aid from the states or private sources. Richmond was filled with stories of how private individuals, governors, and business leaders equipped troops when the bureau could not.[31] At the culmination of this episode, Jones wrote on July 12, 1861, "To-day for the first time, I detected a smile on the lip of Col. Myers, the quartermaster general, as he passed through the office" (John Jones 1: 61). In Jones's estimation, Myers was a superb master of military regulations as well as of department polity. By the battle of First Bull Run on July 21, 1861, the Quartermaster Department had a complement of staff but was still unprepared to make substantial issues to the troops.

The rapid growth of the army in the summer of 1861 overwhelmed all efforts at central planning and control. The 100 regiments authorized in April grew to 198 regiments and thirty-four battalions by mid-July.[32] Since each regulation regiment held 1,000 men, the army effectively doubled in size from 100,000 to 200,000 men. Soldiers were more plentiful than arms or accouterments. When the Confederate Congress slashed Myers's initial budget request of $128 million to $39 million, "a sum inadequate to the necessities of the service," he retaliated by inflating the estimated number of full regiments needing supplies to 400, or 400,000 men, in the fall.[33] Since Secretary Christopher Memminger's Treasury Department did not promptly remit even budgeted and approved funds, Myers's bureau quickly became the Confederacy's most chronic debtor.[34]

Under the Confederate system, the initial responsibility for securing soldiers' clothing fell upon company commanders, who were obliged by regulation to expend, twice a year, the commutation funds by making requisitions upon the Quartermaster Department or other sources, such as state authorities. Each soldier in the first year of service was due one blanket and great coat; two caps and field jackets; three shirts, drawers, and pairs of trousers; four pairs of shoes and stockings; and other items in proportion.[35] Regulation field shirts were blue, and trousers were gray.[36] The trim was light blue for infantry, yellow for cavalry, red for artillery, and black for the medical corps. For long-term encampment, single tents were allotted to each captain, two lieutenants, or fifteen men. The conical or tepee-shaped Sibley tents were generally issued for camp use, while wall tents were provided for hospitals. Tent flies, or canvas strips that could be attached to make two-person dog tents, were usually used in the field. Soldiers were personally accountable for government-issued property, and military regulations made no provision for replacement of clothing, even clothing lost or destroyed as a consequence of battle or accident. Myers's strict adherence to these antiquated regulations earned few friends among field officers.

The chief quartermaster's plan of supply was to invite business competition for military contracts, as had been done in the old army, and duly on May 16, 1861, he mailed a circular to selected mills inviting bids for cadet gray uniforms.[37] In addition to manufacturing the cloth, Myers assumed that mills receiving contracts would generally hire local workers to fabricate the complete uniforms; if not, the army depots would do so. The quartermaster general had an imperfect grasp of the capacity or extent of Confederate manufacturing. In his initial circular, Myers adhered to the conventional prewar practice of requiring businesses to submit samples and closed bids, after which his inspectors in Richmond conducted an evaluation of the quality of the work. The awarding of contracts gave Myers an obvious way to reward partisan supporters of the government and punish those who opposed secession.

The circular of May 16 found Confederate manufacturers in dire circumstances. The economic conditions were unparalleled since the Revolution. All trade with the North was interdicted, Confederate currency and credit remained untested, alien debts were under imminent threat of sequestration, and critical personnel deserted the factory floor for the army. Despite the commercial paralysis, in which buying and selling of goods practically ceased in the late spring, some manufacturers attempted to maintain trade connections with the North. Georgia's Roswell company still had "in Phil[adelphia] unsold, over 480 bales" of cotton, with 123 more at Savannah, "afraid to ship it."[38] Notions of a Northern trade died hard in the commercial community. George Camp of Roswell queried the president of the East Tennessee and Georgia Railroad in mid-April: "[C]an I make an arrangement with you, and your northern connexion by rail to take cotton yarn through to Phila.?"[39] Isaac Scott of Macon, soon to be named a vice president of the Manufacturing and Direct Trade Association of the Confederate States, petitioned the Confederate government in March to permit the passage of duty-free goods through Georgia to alleviate the business collapse.[40] Getting currency through the lines was a less vexatious possibility. Hay and McDevitt, the Philadelphia agents for the Roswell and Curtwright factories in Georgia, attempted to circumvent governmental regulations by exchanging Southern and Northern due notes in St. Louis.[41] Despite some successes, manufacturers suffered heavy losses. William Gregg, president of the Graniteville Manufacturing Company, wrote that a bankruptcy caused by the secession panic "just sunk me a considerable sum" (*Proceedings* 13).

Astute manufacturers desperately sought parts, dyes, card clothing (strips of leather with embedded staples of wire designed to comb and straighten cotton fibers), oil, machinery, and other essentials before the armies closed all trade. William Gregg ordered fifty new looms from John C. Whiten in Massachusetts, which were never delivered. However, James J. Gregg, William's son, successfully refitted the nearby Vaucluse factory in the crisis, but in so doing he was "totally unprepared to work for the Southern trade."[42] He gambled on selling his product on national markets. Many manufacturers, like George Camp of Roswell, saw that "we are all likely to suffer for supplies of one kind and another" and hoarded stores of card clothing, oil, and other necessities.[43] Henry Merrell, who operated 400 new Danforth spindles in Pike County, Arkansas, wrote, "In anticipation of the War, I had laid in at least three years supply of 'findings' necessary to keep our works in order" (Merrell 307). In North Carolina, manufacturers Francis Fries and Wilfred Turner conducted a Southwide search for sperm oil for their machines.[44]

Despite Abraham Lincoln's official closing of Southern ports on April 19, 1861, some manufacturers turned to imports. The Crenshaw Woolen Mill in Richmond found relief when the *Tropic Winds* ran the blockade with a large supply of logwood—a water-soluble purple-black dye made from the heart of a South American tree—salvaged from a wreck on the Cuban coast, thus permitting woolen dyeing operations to resume. The company offered "to furnish their less fortunate friends throughout the South with as much logwood as can be needed for months to come."[45] Francis Fries of Salem conferred with John A. Young of Charlotte on "a list of articles most needed to send [in] an order to England." The Salem manufacturer believed that "on several trials we may succeed in getting our lot through, have made the arrangements to that affect, & will risk it."[46] John A. Fraser, the Charleston importer, got Fries's business. Barrington King of North Georgia, in the market for 200 looms, patronized the same firm, "under the impression that England can supply on better terms, than the north."[47]

Throughout May, June, and July 1861, as Abraham Myers transferred his office from Montgomery to Richmond and organized the quarter-master corps, Southern mills suffered hard times reminiscent of the Panic of 1857. At the Vaucluse factory, James Gregg, like many manufacturers, had concentrated on making warps for Northern mills and now had no market.[48] For lack of orders, the Roswell factory near Atlanta was reduced to three-quarter time and on July 23, the week of the battle of Bull Run, had "idle 7000 spindles."[49] The company soon discharged thirty hands and put the spinning room on half-time; this, wrote King, was "merely to feed our hands, we have about 750 mouths to provide for."[50] But even with only 3,000 spindles turning, the Roswell mill was merely piling *"up our production* waiting for better times."[51] Across Georgia, George Camp observed that "many spindles and looms are now idle from the effect of hard times and very few goods are in the country."[52]

While the secession crisis panic persisted, prices declined and the inventories of unsold goods rose. "Such has been the depression of late," declared William Gregg, "that a pound of cloth, when reduced to cash, will fall far short of purchasing two pounds of cotton, and in many instances not more than a pound and a half, when it ought to bring 2½ pounds" (*Proceedings* 12). Nevertheless, Camp wrote, "I want the blockade to last one full year yet, for it would take that long to convince the South of the need for manufacturing and to 'wean her' from the North."[53] Frank Fries also saw long-range benefits in the crisis, believing that "now is the time for our Southern manufactories to build up a trade," for "by making a *good* article we can run the trifling Northern stuff out of the markets."[54] The *Richmond Enquirer* advised that "a speedy peace, we very much fear, would throw us commercially into the hands of the Yankees again" (November 14, 1862).

The secession panic dramatically changed the way companies did business. The Roswell mill, and probably others, "inaugurated a policy of diversity production," whereby the company offered local merchants a large variety of threads, wrapping twine, ropes, tent duck, checks, and woolens.[55] James Gregg toured Georgia stores in a vigorous effort "to transfer our business to a southern house and market."[56] King offered Roswell yarns and warps to the merchants and woolen mills at Richmond in an attempt to find a new market in Virginia.[57]

Richmond's Crenshaw mills often used cotton warps from England but now secured "an ample supply, nearly as excellent in quality," from the Cedar Shoals factory at Franklinsville, North Carolina.[58] The Roswell mill tested other markets in New Orleans, Memphis, Nashville, and Charleston as well as across Georgia. The company dispatched 130 bales of yarn to Savannah, principally for use "by our patriotic farmers turning their own hands to making woolen goods at home."[59] Many of these goods ultimately went to the use of soldiers equipping for the field.

The economic hard times brought manufacturers into numerous conventions to deliberate on issues of mutual concern, such as the proposed Confederate tariff, finance and currency regulations, and direct trade with Europe. In late December 1860, the Cotton Planters Convention in Macon, Georgia, was a remarkable event, according to the *Charleston Mercury*. The ship *Henry*, from Antwerp, brought a large collection of Belgian and European items for display and sale. Imported marble, glass, and cloth items were housed in a special exhibit hall. The Home Department Building was decorated with a miniature "President's Mansion" of the Southern Confederacy, made of seashells. Domestically produced wax flowers, tapestries, paintings, jewelry, crocheted mats, quilts, shawls, and "Secession Bonnets" competed with the wares of import houses.

Those assembled at Macon heard a keynote address by Dr. Joseph Jones, an eminent chemistry professor at the Augusta Medical College, who instructed the audience that "it is time that Southern manufactories should be established and sustained by Southern money . . . ; the fire and sword with which our Northern enemies threaten us, will prove our ultimate good and their final injury" (Joseph Jones 11).

A similar theme permeated the Confederate Manufacturing and Direct Trade Association organized in Atlanta on February 13, 1861. Called by John J. Gresham and Thaddeus G. Holt, representatives of the Macon cotton mill, the session was chaired by Enoch Steadman, owner of the Gwinette mill and a well-known author of books on manufacturing. Most of the larger mills in the Lower South sent delegates. Being shorn of Northern markets, the gathering deliberated on the best methods of "introducing Southern Spun Cotton Yarns into the markets of France, Belgium, Switzerland, German, and Russia" (*Proceedings* 1).[60] Constantine G. Baylor, former U.S. consul to Brussels and a long-time advocate of direct trade before the Southern commercial conventions, advised that in Europe "there is a profitable demand for the numbers [of yarn] already made in Georgia" (6). The convention charged Baylor with placing these views before the Confederate Congress then assembled in Montgomery. The manufacturers also commissioned a census of manufacturing establishments in the Lower South, with the results to be published in *DeBow's Review* (31: 556–57). At a second session of the association on March 19, 1861, William Gregg served as president; Daniel Pratt, builder of a manufacturing complex in Alabama, and Isaac Scott, a railroader and manufacturer from Macon, were vice presidents; and William J. Russell of the New Manchester factory in north Georgia was secretary.

In a long address to the convention, Gregg reassured planters and farmers that the manufacturers had "not met here to form combinations to put down wages, or raise the price of commodities, but for a general interchange of ideas, as to the best markets the world affords us for our products" (*Proceedings* 12). The Graniteville manufacturer acknowledged that he addressed a skeptical public opinion, for "the impression is pretty general amongst us, that our manufacturers have received large bounties from the government under a tariff odious to all Southerners" (11). Several state secession conventions had cited the tariff as one of the causes of the revolution, and in South Carolina a legislative witness accused Gregg's mill alone of profiting some $80,000 a year from tariff protection. With little discussion, the convention of manufacturers gave universal assent to a resolution submitted by Arnoldus Brumby, cotton manufacturer from Marietta, that the Confederacy place all cotton and woolen machinery on a duty-free list. Within the association there was obvious concern over the free-trade notions of a planter-dominated Confederate government. With regard to the impending war, manufacturers seemed as ill informed as the Quartermaster Department regarding the explosive demands to be met.

Manufacturers also raised questions about the stability of Confederate finances. Secretary of the Treasury Christopher Memminger had made little effort to secure specie, he was very slow to print Confederate notes for currency, and he took uncertain and erratic actions toward funding the national debt. A convention held at Macon in July debated these and other economic issues. John J. Gresham, president of the Macon factory, served as a conference officer. There was support within the convention for an idea presented by Duff Green, a Jacksonian-era editor who held extensive manufacturing interests across the South. Green argued that the Confederate government should purchase the entire cotton crop and use it as collateral to back the new paper currency.[61] This idea appealed to Alexander Stephens and John Schley. Before the convention adjourned, those attending resolved that Governor Joseph E. Brown "place before the people, or their representatives in the Legislature, such information as may serve to promote the development of the cotton yarn interest of the South, with a view to opening a foreign demand for Southern spun cotton yarns."[62]

Elsewhere across the South, groups of business leaders took similar counsel. Many manufacturers, including Alfred T. Harris of Virginia, John D. Williams of North Carolina, and Allen Macfarlan of South Carolina, attended a bankers' convention in Richmond on July 24, where the assembled endorsed Green's proposed produce loan, based principally on cotton, and agreed to accept the new Confederate notes as currency.[63] In Alabama, Daniel Pratt called for a convention of "every manufacturing establishment." Knowing that every standard winter military uniform required five yards of woolens, he was particularly solicitous that the "woolen as well as the cotton business is represented in our convention."[64] The agenda doubtlessly included discussion of mill cooperation and the proposed Confederate policies. In North Carolina, Francis Fries fostered deliberations among manufacturers on similar issues.[65] Informal groups of manufacturers likely met at Nashville, Durham, Fayetteville, Petersburg, and Richmond to weigh collective action. The conventions gave little indication of concern regarding military preparation and factory mobilization.

Military representatives were notably absent at the Commercial and Financial Convention in Macon on October 14, 1861, but present were some of the Confederacy's best political economists. Treasury Secretary Memminger mingled with James D. B. DeBow, former superintendent of the 1850 census and editor of the *Commercial Review* in New Orleans; with Duff Green, the Jacksonian editor who was currently aiding the government of Alabama to equip and clothe its troops; and with William Gregg, the outspoken founder and president of the Graniteville Manufacturing Company. A large contingent of cotton manufacturers represented the mills of middle Georgia. In lengthy sessions, the assembly discussed the Confederacy's current financial exigencies. George Trenholm, who succeeded Memminger as treasury secretary, undoubtedly defended his decision to pay for military purchases with a combination of bonds and currency, an issue of considerable interest to men who had to pay workers and purchase raw materials with acceptable currency. Notably, Abraham Myers was absent. Although he had previously attended conventions of railroad presidents at Montgomery and Augusta, where important agreements were reached on travel charges, neither he nor his associates in the Quartermaster Bureau made presentations to this important body.[66]

Some of these deliberations by manufacturers bore fruit. The tariff approved by the Confederate Congress on May 21 closely resembled the Federal tariff of 1857 and provided for duties ranging from 5 to 25 percent, with cotton and woolen goods in category C, which required an ad valorem tax of 15 percent.[67] Memminger expected to pay a large portion of Confederate expenses out of these proceeds. Through the efforts of Eugenius A. Nisbet, of the Macon mill, the Congress also passed an act "to admit duty free all machinery for the manufacture of cotton, or wool, as necessary for carrying on any of the mechanical arts."[68] With delight William Gregg wrote, "our Southern tariff has been so altered to allow america's [sic] machinery to come in free."[69] With the advent of the blockade, neither the tariff nor the movement for direct trade proved especially important, for few commercial goods either entered or left the Confederacy.

The Federal blockade fleet arrived at Southern ports in May 1861, and many proponents of direct trade turned to the organization of blockade-running companies.[70] Governor Joseph E. Brown commissioned Thomas Butler King of Savannah, a former Whig representative who successfully bought Northern arms for Georgia troops in the secession crisis, as an agent to secure regular steamship service between Antwerp and Savannah. King departed for Europe in the summer of 1861 and circulated among the shippers of Liverpool and Paris a hundred-page book, written by him, on the advantages of direct trade. Especially in Belgium, businesspeople exhibited willingness to contract for a fast steamer service to Savannah to carry out Georgia yarns. Investors in both Savannah and Antwerp offered to advance $40,000 if Georgia would subscribe an additional $40,000, but ultimately the men of capital refused to hazard the blockade, and Governor Brown was forced to charter the *Little Ada* for exclusive state use.[71]

Constantine Baylor carried out in detail his directive from the Confed-

erate Manufacturing and Direct Trade Association. He secured "semi-of-
ficial information from Brussels" with regard to the establishment of
"the steam service between Antwerp and Savannah." In June 1861, Baylor
reported to Governor Brown that he caused "the information obtained
to be disseminated among the manufacturers of the state, and if they
have not taken advantage of it for the public good, the fault is not
mine." To promote the manufacturing cause, Baylor "sent samples of
Georgia spun yarn to Europe, with full information in regard to the individual capacity of the state."[72] Then, securing a commission as the "commercial and financial" agent of Georgia, Baylor sailed to Bermuda en
route to Europe but, seeing the strength of the Federal blockade, relinquished the project and fled north.[73] Gregg's vision that Southern yarns
worth 14 cents a pound in Philadelphia would sell for 20 cents a pound
in Germany was not realized during the war. The principal Southern advantage lay in low production costs, not in transportation savings, for
the sea lanes of the sailing fleets ran fast by New York.

The manufacturers were more successful in striking down state statutes limiting work hours. A Georgia law, originally passed in 1845, limited the working hours for white persons under twenty-one "in all
cotton, woolen, and other manufacturing establishments" to eight in
winter and fourteen in summer.[74] Although some managers like Gregg
found little profit in longer hours, many others used the new gaslight
illumination, which allowed them to maintain the traditional seventy-
hour work week from October through March. As a war measure, the
Georgia legislature sanctioned the longer hours and, in a further concession to manufacturers, outlawed "conspiracies" by laborers to strike (De-
Treville 269).

Abraham Myers's circular of May 16, 1861, inviting bids on cadet gray
uniforms, encouraged manufacturers for the first time to turn to the new
Confederate War Department for contracts, with payment in both bonds
and currency. James Gregg wrote to Myers from the Vaucluse factory asking for a tent contract, hoping to put his new drill looms to use.[75] He
received a military contract for walled hospital tents, some of which were
probably sent on to Manassas, but on July 15 Myers informed him that
"for the present no more [cotton duck] is needed."[76] In June, Martin and
Weakley of Florence offered the quartermaster a large lot of cotton duck,
only to learn that "the Army is not in want of the material a sample of

which you sent."[77] Despairing of the War Department, in July George Camp of Roswell unsuccessfully proffered 40,000 yards of flannels to Christopher Memminger, the secretary of the treasury, and 10,000 pounds of rope to John H. Reagan, the postmaster general.[78] Some disappointed mill owners in Virginia ran newspaper advertisements in an attempt to secure military orders.[79] As Confederate and Federal troops closed at First Bull Run on July 21, Alabama governor Andrew B. Moore angrily wrote the War Department that he was unable to get 3,000 volunteer troops to the front because they lacked uniforms and 600 tents; the cloth had "not even been contracted for." He charged that Myers's bureau was negligent, especially the officer at Montgomery, and concluded, "I would beg leave, to bring to your notice that there are three factories within twenty-five miles of this place which can turn out 5,000 yards a day of tent cloth of an excellent material."[80]

Myers began sending purchasing agents into the field on May 26, instructing Major Larkin Smith to go "to Charlotte North Carolina to visit the Rock Island Wool factory near that place with a view to making arrangements for manufacturing and for the purchase of cloth for the army clothing."[81] The Rock Island factory was owned by John A. Young, a staunch secessionist, and Major Smith bypassed a dozen large mills to call upon him. Although Smith was authorized to visit "any other factory where there is a prospect of obtaining suitable material," he apparently declined to do so.[82] In May, James B. Ferguson, a former Virginia merchant and Myers's principal contracting agent, purchased tent canvas from the Tallassee factory in Alabama, owned by Barnett and Micou, also staunch secessionists; on June 7 Myers invited the manager of the Athens factory, "who has the ability to furnish from one to five thousand suits, to come to this place with samples." He had "no doubt that the Government will enter into arrangements with him to furnish clothing on the terms stated."[83] The battle at Bull Run, however, was a catalyst that escalated the activities of Myers's bureau.

In August 1861, Myers notified the major Virginia mills by circular, offering to take two-thirds of all their product until his new troops were equipped. James Ferguson, who knew numerous mill managers personally, visited them to secure their assent.[84] Many readily cooperated. Duff Green and George P. Scott at Fredericksburg agreed for the duration of the emergency to turn their entire production to military use, and simi-

lar fruitful contracts were made with Crenshaw at Richmond, Jacob Bonsack at Salem, and James Pace at Danville.[85] In four northwestern
counties, Andrew Hunter, a member of the Virginia legislature, "ascer-
tained there were twenty-three considerable woolen factories pouring
out daily 6,000 to 8,000 yards of army cloth."[86] He carried this information to Jefferson Davis and the War Department, neither of whom apparently had any inkling of the bounty. With his Virginia contracts in hand,
Ferguson was ordered to visit "the factories in North Carolina, in South
Carolina, and those in the vicinity of Augusta [Georgia]." Meanwhile,
Myers instructed his subordinate, Richard Waller, to call on Tennessee
mills and "all the woolen mills in western Alabama & Mississippi." He
appointed Francis W. Dillard, a former broker and warehouse manager
at Columbus, Georgia, a regional quartermaster with directions to visit
factories in "Mobile, New Orleans & the southeast portion of Geo & Alabama."[87] Myers still had formulated no general plan for domestic procurement. He undertook no census of available Southern resources and
made no plans for mobilization. Other than purchasing foreign goods,
he clearly intended to draw supplemental supplies from the larger regional mills through his subordinate quartermasters. His agents commonly visited only those factories easily accessible by railroad.

On August 8, 1861, after two weeks' travel, Ferguson reported. His inspections were not very thorough, and his visits were limited to the
larger mills, but he was the first Confederate emissary to call on manufacturers in the Lower South. Ferguson probably met with small groups
of manufacturers at Durham Station, Fayetteville, and Greenville en
route to Georgia, but at Atlanta he paused to see some woolen mills and
then called on "some five in Alabama."[88] At Roswell, George Camp wrote
that "when Major F. was here, I sold him twine and sewing thread."[89] In
fact, Ferguson purchased nineteen bales of warps to be used in the Virginia woolen mills.

At Augusta, on August 1, Adam Johnson of the Richmond factory sold
Ferguson "thirty-five thousand yards of a cotton & wool mixture" for
winter uniforms.[90] Johnson shipped these goods, due in November, to
Richard Waller's Clothing Depot in Richmond for manufacture. At Columbus, Georgia, Ferguson "contracted for 150,000 yards." He also
bought flannel for shirts and another 100,000 yards in "gray donut" for
pants and jackets.[91] On August 7, Ferguson bought coiled rope at Roswell

and brogans in Atlanta, and on August 27 he was at the Tallassee factory in Alabama looking for "tent cloth to the amount of fifty thousand yds."[92] The Florence company of Foster, Fant, and Porter agreed to provide 11,000 yards of "grey tweeds" and "unfinished grey flannel."[93] In North Carolina, Ferguson purchased more warps from Francis Fries to be used by the Virginia woolen mills.[94] Kelley, Tackett, and Ford of Fredericksburg and Harmon and Brother of Montgomery agreed to supply 20,000 army blankets, but there was limited machinery to fabricate them.[95]

Some factories refused to contract with the Confederate authorities. Three mills in Athens claimed to be fully "engaged on work for Contractors for the Army, & for the Country generally." John S. Linton of the Athens factory declined because he was "engaged in making cloth, for the Georgia companies, on the coast." But after equipping General Alexander Lawton's troops, he agreed to work on Myers's account, making "his calculations at what price he will furnish cloth [and] taking wool at 40 cents from the government."[96] In the early months of the war, wool was reasonably abundant in the Virginia mountains, where John Brown had done commerce two years before, but with winter came a growing scarcity.[97]

On August 10, as Ferguson completed his arrangements in the Lower South, Myers determined to secure the majority of his military supplies in England and France. Without much investigation, he subscribed to the prevalent view that Europe was the natural arsenal of the infant Confederacy. As early as May 13, 1861, Myers wrote Secretary Walker that "the resources of the Southern States cannot supply the necessities of the Army of the Confederate States with the essential articles of cloth for uniform clothing, blankets, shoes, stockings, and flannel."[98] To this end Myers made several large contracts with firms in his adopted city, New Orleans.[99] The Crescent City was a promising center for a Confederate import business, since many companies maintained commercial relations in north Mexico, a route around the blockade (Tyler 99, 108). Other importers also received patronage. On August 12, Myers contracted with Gazaway Bugg Lamar of Augusta, Georgia, for 1 million pairs of shoes, 800,000 yards of gray wool cloth, 500,000 flannel shirts, and 500,000 pairs of socks.[100] The Union blockade frustrated the importation of the majority of these goods, designed as a winter supply, and most foreign contracts were eventually abrogated. Only the Mexican border invited easy and relatively unimpeded entrance of supplies; there, along a 200-mile frontier, the pro-Confederate caudillo of north Mexico, Santiago Vidaurri, helped make Matamoros and adjacent ports into the "great thoroughfare" of the South (101).

Meantime, in the private markets of Southern cities, volunteer companies secured available goods, sometimes in competition with the Richmond quartermasters. A military company in Mobile ordered 2,000 yards of cadet gray for uniforms and encouraged the Florence firm of Milner and Wood to run "your looms with lightening speed so that we can furnish our brave soldiers with pants."[101] Soldiers at Cotton Gin, Mississippi, preparing to leave for the seat of war, ordered 600 yards and offered Milner and Wood a military salute: "I hope to meet you again either on the field where strong hearts and arms are marshaled; if not there, in that social realm where brother to brother can tell his whole soul, if in neither where the weary are at rest."[102] The orders to Milner and Wood flowed in, to clothe troops at Fort Pickens who were "almost naked," to furnish three Alabama companies wanting only uniforms for service, to equip North Carolina troops who were emptying the local stores.[103] Daniel Pratt, with a new woolen mill in operation, dressed the Prattville dragoons in resplendent uniforms of black broadcloth trimmed with gold braid (Evans 484).

For manufacturers, such military orders spelled an end to the secession's economic panic. In September, George Camp of the Roswell factory triumphantly wrote, "we are now sold up *one month ahead of production*, and prices have materially advanced."[104] A few months later Barrington King conceded that manufacturers could not "supply half the orders from this state."[105] Henceforth, with no Northern and little foreign competition, the Confederacy was driven by a market of scarcity.

Under the commutation system, volunteer companies might clothe themselves. New units regularly had tailors or numerous ladies' aid societies fashion their uniforms. In Fayetteville, North Carolina, seamstress Sarah Ann Tillinghast wrote that "every now and then a new company was equipped; big bundles of work were sent around" ("Memoirs"). Socks were especially difficult to procure. Since the Confederacy as yet had no machinery for their manufacture, they were knitted by hand. At Fayetteville, "the several factories gave us a 'bunch' of thread a week," and the ladies' societies "employed poor women to double, and twist it, held weekly meetings, distributed yarn and took in socks."[106] Some uniforms also came from homespun. In areas with few mills, such as southern Louisiana and western Arkansas, factory thread was worked up on old hand looms, and the country people made "almost enough cloth to supply the demand."[107]

As the secession depression turned into a wartime boom, Henry Merrell, the manufacturer in Pike County, Arkansas, accelerated his production at his small mill that turned 400 new Danforth cap spindles. From this machinery, the enterprising Merrell spun 550 pounds of cotton yarn per day and, with two double woolen carding machines, made 700 pounds of wool twist in a day and a night. Employing as many as a hundred country weavers and seamstresses, he "could produce materials for about 400 suits of clothes daily" (Merrell 297). By such efforts the Confederate troops were put into the field in the summer of 1861.

Under military regulations, the army usually made special issues in the fall. Civilian groups, not the War Department, first publicly raised questions concerning uniforms for the coming winter. On July 29, a Tennessee society requested the aid of the War Department in forwarding contributions to troops certain to be exposed to the elements in a more northern climate.[108] Myers put little stock in private philanthropy, but Secretary Walker supported these efforts to improve morale and quickly approved the establishment of separate state agencies in Richmond to make distributions to the soldiers. Alabama, Mississippi, Georgia, Florida, and Louisiana proceeded to organize relief headquarters in the capital and appointed supervisors to visit the troops.[109] Fayetteville, Tennessee, organized one of the first drives to secure blankets, quilts, and coats for the absent soldiers, and these efforts shortly stimulated a Southwide effort.[110]

Anticipating a great deficiency in issues of winter clothing, on August 7, 1861, Secretary Walker invited the governors to help provide woolens.[111] State quartermasters quickly responded favorably, especially those with access to local factories. Lawrence O'Bryan Branch, state quartermaster in North Carolina and a former railroad president and congressman, organized a system to supply state troops, as did Georgia quartermaster Ira R. Foster. General George Goldthwaite, the Alabama quartermaster, correctly observed that "the Confederate Government had no clothing and our troops could not be kept on the field without a supply from some quarter, and there was no other source than the State."[112] Myers, with grave misgivings, acquiesced in this plan. Once invited into this new arena of activity, energetic governors would be reluctant to withdraw. Although state involvement was a necessity, it represented an admission that the Quartermaster Bureau could not supply all the troops, that the regulation system of commutation was not working, and that significant foreign importations were unlikely to arrive before winter.

The onset of winter in 1861 placed several hundred thousand Confederate soldiers in precarious circumstances. The store shelves across the South were mostly bare, and private speculators competed with planters, state quartermasters, philanthropic societies, and the Quartermaster Department for the remaining goods. On November 16, the *Vicksburg Sun* threatened to publish the names of "Lincolnite extortioners" who held such goods for higher prices (cited in *Rebellion Record* 3: 391). Public protest meetings against high prices were held in Nashville, Savannah, Macon, and elsewhere to denounce the "monopolies" and buying "on false pretenses." The *Southern Confederacy* protested that those who "have left their homes and their families to fight our battles for us . . . must be clothed, and they have to buy their own clothing." It was a discredit to the Confederacy that "a few men have bought up all the material that could be had, out of which their clothing could be made, and have asked the most exorbitant prices for it."[113]

Although the labor and materials had risen little in cost, drills, a durable cotton fabric in twill weave used as uniform material, rose from 50 cents a yard to $1.25 to $1.50. Under public pressure, the mayor of Augusta, Georgia; the Tennessee legislature; and the governors of Alabama, Mississippi, Louisiana, and Georgia threatened action. One popular notion was to require all manufactured goods to be sold to nonspeculators at a maximum profit of 33.3 percent.

Clothing issues to the army throughout the winter of 1861–62 were late and barely adequate. The army in Virginia was aided by Andrew Hunter, a Virginia official, who found that "our woolen factories . . . (except in one or two instances) have not been destroyed by the enemy even in the lower valley," and he invited the War Department to contract with twenty-three mills in Jefferson, Berkeley, Clarke, and Frederick

Counties.[114] General Thomas J. "Stonewall" Jackson's winter campaign at Romney, Virginia, may have been designed in part to protect these mills. Their product was 5,000 uniforms a week. "This," Hunter wrote, "contributed very largely toward clothing the army."[115] Very few supplies came through Myers's bureau. An investigation by the Confederate Congress showed that for the six months between October 11, 1861, and March 29, 1862, the Quartermaster Department issued to the army in northern Virginia 8,264 tents, 26,214 pairs of shoes, 27,747 blankets, 14,604 uniforms, and 11,475 overcoats.[116] Although there were earlier issues before October, these garments were wholly insufficient for a force that amounted to almost 80,000 men. Most, if not all of these issues, came from Virginia; in 1861, Richmond's Crenshaw Woolen Mill produced 250,000 yards of woolens, including 23,400 army blankets.[117] This represented but a small portion of the regulation. Some regional quartermasters enjoyed a greater success than the Richmond office.

Former railroad president Vernon Stevenson and former merchant George Cunningham, quartermasters at the Nashville depot, were responsible for outfitting Albert Sidney Johnston's army. They announced in October 1861 that "we are now issuing six hundred suits a day & will be receiving that many in a few days & will go up we hope to a thousand suits a day soon."[118] In January 1862, the Tennessee depot secured from manufacturers 153,168 yards of woolens, enough for 25,000 uniforms, and 163,110 yards of cotton goods for shirts. February issues were on the same order.[119] Nashville made more issues in a single month than the Richmond depot did in six. At Memphis, William Anderson, a former Mobile merchant, employed 1,200 workers in a vast manufacturing enterprise and expended for supplies "some six or seven hundred thousand dollars per month."[120] His main suppliers were the mills of the Memphis area. Anderson appointed Ralph C. Brinkley, president of the Wolfe Creek factory, as one of his many agents to manufacture supplies.[121] Anderson reported purchasing in the month of October 1861 "about 150 thousand dollars worth of clothing, and clothing material which will be manufactured into clothing as rapidly as possible."[122]

Farther west in the Trans-Mississippi region during the fall of 1861, Confederate quartermasters at Galveston and San Antonio requisitioned 100,000 yards each of woolens and cotton goods from the Texas prison factory at Huntsville, enough to fabricate 20,000 uniforms "for the use of the Confederate troops."[123] Dutifully, until April 1862, half of the prison's product was sent to Nashville and Memphis for use by the Army of Tennessee, an act that Henry Merrell deprecated because there were "there were at least a hundred factories there to one here" (Merrell 309). The Huntsville mill alone was capable of producing 5,000 winter uniforms a month from a product of 19,334 yards of woolens (*Texas Almanac for 1864* 40).

State aid and private philanthropy omitted, the western troops were better clothed than those in the east. For 1862, the Texas prison factory produced 211,151 yards of woolens and 1.4 million yards of cotton goods, of which the western quartermasters drew 184,241 yards of woolens and 765,791 yards of cotton goods, enough material for 40,000 uniforms and 175,000 each of shirts and pairs of drawers.[124]

At this point a great flaw in Confederate planning became evident. As the winter snows fell in 1861, the Confederate nation underwent a terrible shortage of wool that left much machinery idle. In the prewar period, Southern wool supplies had principally come from Spain, England, and the North, but those sources were no longer available. The incipient wool famine was in large measure Myers's responsibility.

Ostensibly, there were enough sheep in the Confederacy to easily supply the army with winter uniforms, which, counting blankets, required about sixteen pounds of wool per soldier (*New York Herald*, January 3, 1862). But of an initial Southern clip of 13 million pounds in 1860, only about 4.5 million pounds remained available in 1862, and, of this, 1.4 million pounds lay in Texas (McCue 7). The Appalachian Mountains from Virginia to Georgia, Unionist in sentiment, initially held about 1 million sheep, but when the war began the farmers in these areas slaughtered animals in great numbers and used meat for food and the wool for home consumption. Unionist leaders such as Andrew Johnson and William Brownlow of Tennessee encouraged the mountaineers to resist the Confederate leadership and its depreciating currency. Of the 100,000 sheep near Augusta County, Virginia, at the beginning of the war, few could be found two years later.

The wool famine became graphically evident with the onset of winter. In October 1861, John A. Young of Charlotte's Rock Island factory noted, "the supply of Georgia wool that we have heretofore used is exhausted, and . . . we find the market almost barren at an advance of over one hundred percent."[125] Francis Fries of Salem, North Carolina, dispatched his brother to Texas to purchase a lot that was laboriously shipped east by the Memphis and Charleston Railroad.[126] Nevertheless, in December 1861 Fries wrote James Sloan, a state quartermaster, that "really the labor, the annoyance of the uncertainty of pressing the wool business under present circumstances are disgusting me, & it would be a relief to close the mill."[127] In December, a blockade-runner brought a cargo of 48,000 pounds of wool to Wilmington, and Governor Zebulon Vance offered the lot to area manufacturers, but the material was water damaged beyond use.[128]

To the discomfort of Georgia troops, operations at the Roswell factory were interrupted by lack of wool two months after Bull Run.[129] But only when the Crenshaw and Manchester mills at Richmond exhausted their supplies in December did Myers finally order Joseph F. Minter, the assistant quartermaster at San Antonio, to expend $150,000 on Texas wool. Myers wrote Minter to adopt "the most energetic measures to procure an abundant supply and send it forward by special Agent, as fast as you can."[130] In Tennessee, Quartermaster Vernon Stevenson dispatched numerous agents "to hunt wool," and one "went to Texas and other points and bought four hundred and fifty thousand pounds" (Morgan 10). The Federal army and naval forces, however, were already poised at either end of the Mississippi River in an endeavor to split the Confederacy, and opportunities for easy passage were endangered.

The spring clip of 1862 was noticeably deficient in the eastern Confederacy, and additional manufacturers attempted to secure imports from Texas. Allgood, of the Trion factory in Georgia, wrote Judah P. Benjamin that without new supplies "we shall have to stop the wool department of our business."[131] The incapacity of the War Department to help forced Allgood to seek western wool on his own account. John A. Young at Charlotte was also dependent "upon Texas for goods to manufacture," and he wisely pleaded with the state quartermaster to have Texas's "entire crop of wool transported to this side of the Mississippi River."[132] Albert R. Homesley of Shelby, North Carolina, sometimes bought wool in Georgia, but in the summer of 1862 he found the prices advanced several times over the previous winter. Consequently, he canceled his military contract and wrote the state quartermaster, "I know that you will think strang [sic] of this but when I made the contract with you I expected to be able to buy wool in Texas."[133]

The hazards of passing the Mississippi River grew with the ending of spring floods. Francis Fries wrote Governor Vance in April, "the uncertainty of matters in the Valley of the Mississippi, & the almost insurmountable difficulties of getting any freight through from N. Orleans make it impracticable to get our supply of wool from Texas as heretofore." Fries found that "in Virginia, South Carolina, & Georgia we can secure some wool provided we will pay for it in cloth or cotton yarn, when cash will not bring the article."[134] Obviously, many farmers were suspicious of Confederate currency. North Carolina manufacturers John Webb and John A. Young sent wagons laden with cotton yarns across the countryside seeking to barter with reluctant farmers for wool.[135] The Rock Island manufacturer had some success in South Carolina, for "they refuse to sell, but are willing to sell it for cotton yarns" because there were "no cotton mills in that portion of the Country."[136] Mann S. Valentine, on behalf of the Manchester Cotton and Woolen Company at Richmond, found some small lots of wool in Athens and Mobile.[137] Valentine, the Crenshaw brothers of Richmond, and Henry C. Meigs of Columbus, Georgia, who altogether supplied most of the woolens used in Richard Waller's Clothing Bureau in Richmond at this time, were especially forceful in urging the War Department to procure raw wool by extraordinary means.

James Ferguson, the Richmond quartermaster in charge of contracts, investigated the production problem for Myers and reported that wool was "very scarce & many of the mills will I fear have to stop work for the want of it." He recommended that the bureau "make great exertions to get out all the wool that has been bought in the state of Texas—or our supply of clothing for the winter [of 1862] will be short."[138] On May 24, 1862, after much of the Mississippi estuary had been lost to Union forces, Myers committed the bureau to procuring and transporting Texas wools. He designated Vance & Brother at San Antonio as the government agent to secure "the large wool crop of Texas, at fair prices." He divided Texas into four procurement zones, "for the purpose of purchasing wool."[139] As Myers explained to the secretary of war, large supplies were expected from the Trans-Mississippi, "if the Mississippi River can be kept open at any point."[140]

John B. Earle, a Waco manufacturer, served as a government wool agent, and after advertising in the *Dallas Herald* he purchased at half the eastern price 36,273 pounds that were promptly transferred to the quartermaster at Little Rock.[141] Back east this could produce 14,000 uniforms, but only small lots were successfully brought over the river. The same fate befell North Carolina agents sent west by Francis Fries and A. F. Orr of the Rock Island factory. One agent, J. L. Fulkerson, purchased 15,000 pounds, a portion of which he worked as far east as Meridian, Mississippi. The costs and risks were higher than expected, and Fries concluded that "if wool is as high as represented in the interior of Texas, . . . we had as well let some body else buy it, & run the risk of getting it over the Mississippi."[142]

The Federal offensive in the Mississippi Valley in the spring of 1862 greatly increased the risk of securing supplies in the Trans-Mississippi area. Admiral David Farragut passed the forts below New Orleans with his fleet on April 24 and seized New Orleans the following day. Farther north, Fort Pillow fell to Commodore Charles H. Davis and the Union western flotilla on June 3, and Memphis fell on June 6. On July 1, the two victorious fleets held a rendezvous above Vicksburg. Although the Confederacy nominally maintained control of the waters between Port Hudson and Vicksburg for the next year, Union vessels frequently patrolled these waters and menaced civilian shipping.

The interruption of river transportation exposed the Confederate dependency on the vital Trans-Mississippi region. Cloth from Mexican mills, along with other imported goods, could no longer flow freely into the eastern Confederacy, and Texas beef, horses, and leather, along with wool, were interdicted.[143] The virtual closing of the Mississippi left hundreds of thousands of pounds of wool, both government and privately owned, wasting and rotting at depots across Texas. Meanwhile, Confederate soldiers in the east grew more desperate for blankets and overcoats.[144] Fries found the new situation particularly galling. He held 28,401 pounds at Shreveport, Louisiana, and Waxahachee, Texas, which he despaired of obtaining without government aid.[145] Union military activity gave him "endless troubles," but he believed he could have prevailed had Federal forces delayed their advance "to the neighborhood of Vicksburg a few weeks longer." The loss of the Texas wool cost the North

Carolina manufacturer "between 50 & $60,000," an amount far in excess of the year's profits.[146]

Despite Federal audacity, Myers persisted in believing that Texas wool could be procured. In February 1862, Judah P. Benjamin told Jefferson Davis that "the supplies of wool received from Texas and Mexico have proved sufficient to meet the demands of the woolen factories employed in the service of the Department."[147] This was a considerable exaggeration. Benjamin may have anticipated that existing contracts would be fulfilled. Myers forwarded $1 million in currency to the quartermaster at San Antonio to make purchases, and he ordered William Haynes, quartermaster at Shreveport, to ensure that "the wool now reported to be at Alexandria, will be transferred to Major L. Mims, Quarter Master at Jackson, Mississippi, by whom fifty thousand pounds will be sent to Major G. W. Cunningham, Quarter Master, Atlanta, Georgia."[148] Because of uncertainties along the Mississippi River, little wool came forward.

The wool problem grew more serious with each passing month. Woolen mills could not operate without raw material, and Myers seemed helpless in remedying the deficiency. In May 1862, on the eve of the Peninsula campaign, the Richmond Clothing Bureau was bare of woolens. Myers wrote the secretary of war that "the requisitions, representing the complete outfit of 40,000 are necessarily unfilled, of course, greatly to the dissatisfaction of the troops."[149] A few months later a survey by Richard Waller revealed that among the Clothing Bureau's contracting mills, "some are already stopped for want of wool, others can not run over thirty days and none longer than sixty days." Waller concluded that "the resources of this depot, if some remedy is not applied, will very soon be mainly exhausted."[150]

Although the closing of the Mississippi River was the primary reason for persistent scarcity of uniforms in the east, Union military victories in the spring campaigns of 1862 destroyed many factories and large quantities of accumulated military supplies. During the continuing Federal offensive on the Tennessee front, the Confederate army retreated from New Madrid, Bolling Green, Forts Henry and Donelson, Nashville, and Shiloh, abandoning several dozen mills in central and western Tennessee. On the Mississippi, the Union navy occupied the manufacturing centers of New Orleans and Memphis. In Virginia, Confederate troops retired from the Potomac line, vacating Manassas Junction and Gordonsville. Union forces took Yorktown, Norfolk, and Roanoke Island as General George B. McClellan's Peninsula campaign unfolded. These Federal incursions wrecked Myers's forward depots and threatened Richmond itself; factories between Winchester and Charleston, Virginia, fell behind Union lines, as did the mills at Alexandria and Fredericksburg.

The Confederate retreats were precipitous, and large depots of precious supplies near the main armies were abandoned. At New Orleans, little clothing or camp and garrison equipage could be saved; Quartermaster Isaac Winnemore left behind considerable stores and unpaid accounts amounting to almost $2 million.[151] Winnemore moved on to Augusta, Georgia, where he established a new base. At Nashville, one of Myers's officers wrote that "there were quartermaster's and commissary stores here sufficient to clothe and feed the whole army of the Western Department for one year."[152] One cavalry officer remembered chaotic scenes following General Albert Sidney Johnson's precipitous abandonment of the Tennessee capital: "crowds would stand upon the pavements underneath the tall buildings upon the Court House Square, while out of their fourth and fifth-story windows large bales of goods were pitched, which would have crushed any one upon whom they had fallen" (Duke 116). The army slaughtered 15,000 hogs that could not be hauled to Atlanta.[153] Quartermasters Vernon K. Stevenson and George Cunningham hastily left Nashville for Georgia, and William Anderson removed from Memphis to Grenada and Columbus, Mississippi.[154]

In Virginia, General Joseph E. Johnston abandoned Manassas with such rapidity that a tent city, a print shop, a hospital, and boxcars of pork, flour, and molasses were left behind. Entering Federals found burning quartermaster warehouses and smoldering mounds of "new secesh clothes, swords, flags, etc." (*Rebellion Record* 4: 285). At Thoroughfare Gap, 369,000 pounds of Confederate beef and pork were consigned to flames.[155] The invaders burned a few cotton factories and drove Confederate forces from two dozen woolen mills in Virginia's northwest. Myers begged General Thomas "Stonewall" Jackson, then engaged in maneuvering against three Federal armies in the Valley, to accept an order from the Winchester firm of Wood & Brother, owners of Morgan Mills, who "had on hand from fifteen to twenty thousand yards of cloth, part of a supply contracted to be furnished by them."[156] These goods were sufficient to clothe a quarter of the Valley army.

When a committee of the Confederate Senate requested a report on the extent of the spring losses, Myers claimed to be unable to state them "even with approximate accuracy," but he was certain of the "impossibility of replacing this vast amount of supply which have been lost."[157] He wrote Generals Joseph E. Johnston, Pierre T. G. Beauregard, and Robert E. Lee the same tale of lament: Soldiers who had lost equipment or clothing in retreat or capture would not be reprovisioned at government expense. Lee responded that he observed much suffering as soldiers built provisional shelters out of blankets and wore threadbare clothing.[158] Myers's response was to send two inspectors, James Pace and William Browne, into the field to survey the South's manufacturing resources.

The quartermaster ordered James Pace, of the Danville factory, to tour the Upper South seeking out warps for woolen mills and shoe leather. Francis Fries wrote that "we will be glad to see Mr. Pace & have no doubt satisfactory arrangements can be made as to future supplies of warps No. 8 & No. 10."[159] But when Pace arrived in North Carolina, he found that Zebulon Vance, the young war governor, had established a tight rein on state factories. Nevertheless, Pace received a cordial reception in Salem, and, according to Fries, "told us this week that our State would in all probability give over the clothing of our troops to the Confederate authorities."[160] This proved a forlorn hope, for Vance refused to relinquish control. Fries professed neutrality in the contest between the governor and Myers, writing that "we would prefer selling direct to the government, either State or Confederate, as we don't care to realize the high prices offered by speculators."[161]

In South Carolina, Pace found that General Beauregard controlled state mill contracts through two Charleston appointees of his own, Edward Willis and G. S. Crafts, who in turn secured goods from L. D. Childs of Saluda, worked up the sparse cargoes brought though the blockade, and purchased "from parties having small stocks on hand."[162] In an attempt to increase supplies, Willis obtained a military discharge for William Perry of the Grady, Hawthorne, and Perry factory at Greenville on condition that he "put his mill in operation to . . . furnish me with cloth."[163] William A. Finger, of Spartanburg's Valley Falls factory, turned out monthly "on an average of five thousand pounds of cotton yarn of which quantity some three to five thousand of the same material is supplied to the Government."[164] But Finger's mill was soon preempted by an aggressive Augusta quartermaster. From this short tour, James Pace found the regional depots to be in a more thriving condition than the Richmond Clothing Bureau.

A second survey was conducted in the fall of 1862. Following Lee's aborted offensive in Maryland and the repulse of Braxton Bragg's invasion of Kentucky, Jefferson Davis ordered his assistant, English-born William M. Browne, to survey "the probable supplies to be derived from the Lower South for the shoeing and clothing of the Army." This report must have been encouraging to Davis and Myers, for Browne found that "the weekly capacity of the Mills in these States known to the quartermasters at Augusta and Columbus amounts to about 22,000 yards of woolen and 215,000 of cotton goods," sufficient for 20,000 uniforms a month.[165] This was an adequate supply for the retreating Tennessee forces. Browne noted that several Georgia factories worked solely for Governor Joseph E. Brown, and others had no military contracts at all. An additional 1 million yards of cloth, sequestered in Kentucky by General Braxton Bragg during his summer campaign, were in the hands of 1,000 Augusta seamstresses (*Richmond Whig*, November 3, 1862). Francis Dillard, quartermaster at Columbus, held 1 million pounds of shoe leather and contracts with 152 tanneries for more. Dillard was confident that "the Army can be kept well shoed though the agencies which he now has in active employment."[166] Browne's otherwise glowing report cited unnecessary competition between various quartermasters, sometimes "running up the price of articles 50% or 100%."[167] Isaac Winnemore, Myers's close friend and confidant and a former quartermaster at New Orleans now at Augusta, reported that he "heard unofficially, of agents of the several Depts. attending auctions and actually bidding against one another."[168] Often in the Augusta market, Browne discovered, "the Government becomes the only competitor," while in Columbus the "Q M's particularly of regiments, send agents to places where there is a Post Q M who is well acquainted with prices, and, without consulting with him, advance the market very considerably."[169]

In Virginia, a survey by Richard P. Waller on November 7, 1862, showed the general supply situation on the northern front to be less promising than that of Georgia. With 30,000 to 50,000 pounds of wool coming in each week, enough for 15,000 uniforms, Waller believed himself able to contract for cloth sufficient to keep "this Depot going at least during the winter."[170] Beyond that, his prognosis was bleak: "all the former sources of supply in the Valley and Northern Virginia having been directed to Staunton by Gen. Lee's order; the large lot of English goods under contract for this depot, (ordered through Gautherin & Co) having been as I learn, stopped by some officer of the Government near the Mississippi River—few of the goods running the blockade thro' Charleston coming to this point—leave me nothing to rely on except such mills as are under contract with me."[171] The depletion of Virginia wool created stark conditions, for "the alternatives are to get wool at the south, or virtually, to stop." And "to think of stopping in the midst of a snow storm to day with a great army in the field without overcoats, so far as my knowledge extends, and many other comforts in the way of clothing, appalls me."[172]

There remained a plentitude of Confederate cotton cloth, but the scarcity of wool grew constantly worse through the winter of 1862. At Columbus, Dillard was able to amass 200,000 pounds by January 1863, but his case was singular.[173] In Atlanta, George W. Cunningham reported great wool shortages, writing that with the raw material "the number of garments made at this point could be increased at least 33 per cent."[174] This enterprising quartermaster passed such wool as he obtained directly to the factories and hired his own tailors, trimmers, and seamstresses. At Richmond during December, Waller received 29,366 pounds of wool and anticipated from the Virginia spring clip perhaps another 375,000 pounds, barely enough to keep his factories in operation and the army in supply.[175] He outbid speculators and bought everything in the market.[176] But from January 1 to February 7, 1863, not a single yard of woolens was received at the Richmond Clothing Depot, although Waller accessioned 500,000 yards of cotton goods and 1,000 pairs of shoes.[177] Fortunately, most of the troops had already received the winter supply of uniforms.

Under the growing emergency conditions, Myers sought "authority and sanction" to monopolize the wool trade within the constricted Confederacy.[178] Two acts accomplished this. In April 1863, the Confederate Congress enacted a "tax-in-kind," which amounted to one-tenth of all produce. A month later, an impressment act authorized Myers or his agents to seize goods not offered for sale by paying a fixed price. Wool, with a market price of $5 a pound, could be impressed at $3. Although primarily applicable to farmers who were hiding or slaughtering their sheep, these acts also made stocks held by manufacturers liable to seizure.[179]

With this authority, Myers appointed Hutson Lee, quartermaster at Charleston, "to secure all the wool that can be obtained in the State of South Carolina." Lee, like Thornton Washington, Myers's new agent in Texas, was "directed to divide the State into suitable districts," each with a representative of the department.[180] Richard Waller, of the Richmond depot, was made responsible for Virginia, which was also subdivided.[181] In Georgia, George Cunningham accepted responsibility for impressing or buying the clip, while Zebulon Vance in North Carolina and John Milton in Florida assumed authority within their states to appoint county wool agents.[182]

Both new policies, impressment and the tax-in-kind, failed to bring in more wool. In Georgia, which produced an estimated 800,000-pound clip, farmers withheld most from the market.[183] Isaac Winnemore of Augusta, who rarely took exception to Myers's policies, wrote, "I fear we will not be able to purchase much wool, unless we pay the market price for it." For Winnemore, "this impressment business has been a losing one to the Govt, and has caused you, and I as private individuals, to pay higher prices, than we otherwise would."[184] In nine months the Augusta quartermaster was able to secure only 100,000 pounds. In contrast, the Eagle factory at Columbus, which bartered cotton yarn and cloth for wool, obtained 200,000 pounds.[185] Florida agents secured barely enough of the domestic clip to clothe state troops in a single uniform.[186]

Along the Virginia and Tennessee railroads, quartermasters frequently seized wool in transit to manufacturers. Fries, who bartered yarn for Virginia wool, complained that "if these Gov. officials do not stop interfering with business, about which they understand nothing, . . . industry must be stopped." The Salem factory had "been on a dead strain ever since the war & for the last 3 months working day & night to make yarn and pay for wool engaged last Fall, & now the officials seize the wool & will thus stop our mill if in their power."[187] Numerous manufacturers complained that the quartermaster's regulations only inhibited "getting the materials into the State."[188]

The tax-in-kind also produced meager results. One Virginia legislator who examined the receipt books at Myers's office was "satisfied the 10th of wool received by the Confederate States will not clothe the *clerks* in the department" (McCue 9). An inquiry by the Virginia legislature showed that some sheep were being slaughtered for army mess, large numbers of others were killed for home consumption, and 87,547 head were taken by private wool dealers. In consequence, the severity of the wool famine deepened as evidenced by the fact that carpeting, "both of churches and private families, had been cut up and sent to the army," and in places dogs were killed for their pelts (7, 9).

Under these conditions, public criticism of Myers steadily mounted in the press and legislative assemblies, and few contested the view that "we are now destitute of a supply of *blankets* and *overcoats* for our troops this winter, and that there are no factories in the South engaged in the manufacture of blankets" (7). Henry Merrell, an Arkansas manufacturer, was particularly bitter about the inefficiency of local quartermasters, writing that only a modicum of winter clothing reached the troops, and that arrived late, while quartermasters constantly blamed transportation problems. However, he continued, "what I subsequently discovered in the Department of the Clothing Bureau . . . [was a] want of method, if not of zeal as well." He believed that the problem was a Confederate preoccupation with European intervention, which precluded "any timely and adequate provision for anything to be made long in advance." "We had," he noted, "very few men who even realized the magnitude of the undertaking we had in hand" (Merrell 346).

Despite the concession of vast martial powers to the quartermaster, across the Confederacy many factories closed, or worked reduced hours, for want of raw materials. One million pounds of government wool lay rotting in Texas, enough to clothe the entire Confederate army, while Grant's campaign against Vicksburg "prevented its receipt."[189]

In response to the bureau's catastrophes, in 1862 Myers broadened the authority of regional quartermasters to impress and seize supplies. The bureau's correspondence with Major Thornton A. Washington, appointed as quartermaster at San Antonio in December 1862, provides an indication of this change. A graduate of West Point in 1849, Washington served briefly in Virginia before being ordered to the Trans-Mississippi military district. There he was instructed "to let out liberal contracts or to establish government factories according as the one or the other may appear most conducive [*sic*] to the public interest."[190] He had the power to seize private goods at prices, usually below the market value, and pay for them with Confederate notes (Goff 96–104). This gave him great leverage. If bargaining for essential goods such as wool and leather proved unsuccessful, he impressed these items at cheap government prices, an action that immediately yielded 20,000 animal hides much needed back east.

At San Antonio, Washington launched several government enterprises. He erected a tannery, a shoe factory, and a clothing factory on land donated by the city, and he soon reported the construction of a "dam race & building necessary for the reception of machinery which I am about to order from Europe for a woolen factory to be established by the Gov't. near this place."[191] Although Washington posed a competitive threat to local merchants and manufacturers, Myers endorsed such activities, as long as the proper reports were rendered. He wrote approvingly to the secretary of war regarding Washington but urged that the major be cautioned because "the sanction of Congress was necessary to authorize the acquisition of land by the Government."[192]

As western quartermasters assumed a greater sphere of independent action, critics such as Henry Merrell complained: "Did an inefficient officer, in bad repute with the army here & shelved by Head Quarters, yet enjoying personal acquaintance & some influence as a politician, did he above all belong to the old original Secession order of men, he could go to Richmond & become an oracle there . . . until some day, without an accident, he would come back to the department promoted in rank over the heads of those who remained at their posts" (Merrell 340). However, impressment and government-sponsored manufacturing offered some hope of meeting the urgent needs of the army.

Such powers were also creatively used by John S. Cobb, a quartermaster at the Tuscaloosa clothing bureau. By contracting with local cotton mills under the threat of impressment, he drew each week 3,000 to 5,000 yards of osnaburgs and 1,000 pounds of yarn. In apparent violation of department regulations, Cobb bartered with reluctant Alabama farmers for wool, as many Georgia and North Carolina factories were doing. By bartering, Cobb surrendered his right to impress the farmers' wool or seize it for the tax-in-kind. Upon gaining the confidence of the rural folk, he exchanged osnaburgs and yarns "for washed wool (which is costing the government only two dollars per lb), [and] country made jeans [made of] wool & cotton socks." From his proceeds of 2,000 pounds Cobb manufactured "from sixteen to eighteen hundred yards of jeans per week" that, with the aid of local seamstresses, made 400 or 500 uniforms.[193] The creative use of impressment, the construction of manufacturing facilities by quartermasters, and the use of barter to secure critical raw materials offered some hope of keeping the Southern woolen mills in operation as the war passed its second winter.

2

The Reign of Quartermasters

Despite the woolen famine and desultory public clamor about destitute soldiers and improvident quartermasters, Abraham Myers continued to gain influence and authority within the Confederate hierarchy until he held a guardianship over Southern manufacturing that was without precedent. The necessities of the front-line troops, with more men dying from exposure and disease than from bullets, drove Confederate authorities to the brink of military socialism, with Myers as the government's leading actor. With the sanction of the Congress, Myers assumed control of all workers of military age, exempting or detailing back to the factories only such men as he and his agents approved; in return for exempting workers, he compelled manufacturers to accept price and profit controls. Myers's power to impress supplies was unquestioned, and with the repeal of the commutation system in the fall of 1862, he became the acknowledged controlling authority of nearly all military supplies within the Confederacy.

As a consequence, criticism of Myers's administration also mounted. The military complained about exempted men and scarce supplies. Public rumors, fanned by newspapers, abounded that quartermasters were personally profiting from their positions. Manufacturers, chafing under his restrictions and red tape, willingly informed on the suspected malfeasance of local quartermasters and gave testimony against them in military courts, while the press rendered highly colored accounts to the public. The quartermaster general's own self-confident, aloof, and abrasive manner also contributed to the bitterness of these disputes. Finally, when called to account by Jefferson Davis, Myers and his friends responded with a brilliant political *coup de main* that challenged the very

authority of the president himself and embroiled the Confederacy in ac-
rimonious contention.

A main source of Myers's embroilment lay in Confederate enlistment
and conscription policy, which drained workers from the factories. As
labor became scarce, manufacturers were particularly anxious to protect
their workers from the Confederate conscription acts, a power ultimately
vested in the quartermaster general.[1] Even before the draft, volunteering
created special problems. From the onset of the war, mills faced a gradual
depletion of their skilled workforce. After Fort Sumter, at the Cedar Falls
factory in North Carolina, and undoubtedly elsewhere, recruitment officers made hasty appeals to assembled workers. After such an all-day
occasion, on July 10, 1861, the Cedar Falls mill "stood still to see the Randolph Hornets off" to the front.[2] The loss of skilled workers threatened
to erode production. Early in the summer of 1861, Kelly, Tackett, and Ford
of Fredericksburg petitioned the Virginia governor, John Letcher, for the
return of "several of their best hands now in volunteer companies," lest
their operations be "impeded" (Robertson 149). Since the mill was "engaged in the manufacture of woolen cloth for uniforms," Governor Letcher recommended that the men be exempted from the state levy,
"unless drafted and detailed for actual service" (149). In January 1862,
James G. Gibbes, of the Saluda factory, asked the South Carolina convention, then still in session, for military exemptions for his workers. As he
explained, "we are employed in the manufacture of cotton and woolen
goods, and clothing for the State, on quite a large scale, and find our
operations likely to be stopped by the call on our employees for the service of the State." Military recruitment reduced the men in Gibbes's
workforce by "one-half, and those we have left are principally overseers
and foremen." Altogether, he had remaining "nearly one thousand persons employed, and among them not more than forty men, only about
one half of whom are liable to service." On the floor of the South Carolina convention, William Gregg proposed that cotton and woolen factories retain from the military service at least "one overseer for each card-
room, spinning and weave-room, and one driver for each sixty looms,"
but the assembly deferred the matter to Confederate authorities in Richmond and ultimately to Myers.[3]

After the first wave of volunteering ended, the Confederate Conscription Act of April 1862 threatened to take still another levy from the mills.

However, this act superseded state actions and specifically exempted from military service all persons employed in cotton and woolen manufacturing upon their application to Quartermaster General Myers. This law, amended and extended in July and October 1862, essentially gave Myers control of all men of military age, between eighteen and thirty-five, in manufacturing. Even the *New York Herald* (September 16, 1861), reduced to speculating about the Confederacy, reported that "there is an idea afloat in the South to seize all woollen and cotton mills for the use of the government, and that soldiers be employed therein." This was in advance of the truth; however, manufacturers were obviously concerned about the larger implications of the law.

Isaac Powell, of Georgia's High Shoals factory, wrote Governor Joseph E. Brown, inquiring whether "there will be any exemptions under the conscript act of Congress for Superintendents and overseers in cotton & wool factorys [sic]."[4] At High Shoals, Powell feared that "it will be impossible to fill the places of the overseers in each as about half is subject and they do not appear to be disposed to wait for their chances but prefer joining companys [sic] that their friends is in." Andrew Allgood of Trion also wrote Brown "for the information of our men employes [sic] in our Factory."[5]

In Richmond, Myers and George Wythe Randolph, the new secretary of war, were inundated with similar requests for exemptions and details once the terms of the act became public knowledge. The "detailed" were simply drafted soldiers assigned to work in their mills. Francis Fries's workforce at Salem was probably typical. In October 1862, despite the enlistment of many men in the army as volunteers or under the threat of the draft, he calculated that "we have in our employment 79 hands of which there are 29 white males, 36 white females, and 14 black males; of these 13 are between 18 & 35 yrs."[6] John J. Gresham, of the Macon factory, wrote the War Department that "we have in our employment one hundred and thirty hands of whom there are now in the mill sixteen who are between the ages subjecting them to the Conscript Law."[7] Gresham made "about four thousand yards of goods a per day" and considered "if the mill is wholly or even partially stopped should regard it as a serious calamity to the country." Albon Chase, an Athens manufacturer, sought the release of two privates for his auxiliary paper mill because "if their discharge would be granted, the mill would be enabled to supply to a considerable extent, the pressing want of paper now experienced by the Government, as well as individuals."[8]

The labor question grew in significance as conscription was enforced in every county of the Confederacy. Atwood and Rokenbaugh, of the Oconee cotton mill, implored the secretary of war to release ten men from service, for if "taken from us our Factory will be stopped, and between 300 & 400 women & children, many of them soldier's families, will be thrown out of employment and their means of support." The War Department, they assumed, was "aware of the importance to the country of keeping cotton & wool factories in full operation."[9] The mill owners fought desperately to preserve the integrity of their workforce against the powerful hand of the government.

At times that meant securing exemptions for manufacturers and their families. Thomas N. Cooper, of the Eagle mill in North Carolina, turned out 700 pounds of yarn daily and requested two exemptions, one of them for himself "as agnt. & superintendent of cotton factory."[10] As he explained, "we have no contract strictly for gov. but have been [and] are still furnishing woolen factories warp that have contract for Gov of all their product." If drafted, Cooper concluded, "the whole of our machinery will stand still as there is no one left that I could possibly get to operate."[11] Edwin Holt, of the Alamance factory, secured an exemption for his son, William, and requested others for skilled workers (Beatty 81, 101). Sometimes workers and customers requested military exemptions for mill owners. In Coffee County, Alabama, the community presented a letter to the War Department asking for the release of Abram W. Elliott, "the owner of a fine wool carding machine which is of vast utility and convenience, as well as almost indispensable necessity."[12]

Young James J. Gregg of Vaucluse, soon to don the gray himself, lectured the War Department on personnel issues: "we are working on tent cloth, driving our mill night & day, supplying Mr. Schley of Augusta, who is filling a large tent contract for the Government." Even with his military exemptions, young Gregg had "barely enough [men] to keep our machinery in motion." But then "one of our best and most experienced operatives died, which has seriously affected our operations, stopping one half of our night work."[13] In order to continue operations, he desperately requested the return of two men already in active service.

Faced with such a large deluge of exemption requests, Myers resorted to the simple expedient of writing into government contracts a proviso, such as one with the Atwood and Rokenbaugh company, that "it is stipulated and agreed on the part of the Confederate States Government, that the male operatives employed by us, between the ages of 18 & 35 shall be exempt from the conscription law."[14] In General Order No. 50, the secretary of war reluctantly approved this practice, although with regard to details, he required that Myers personally vouch for each case and that deferments be renewed monthly.[15] Companies that did only intermittent work for the Confederate government presented a special problem.

William Gregg's mill at Graniteville brought this issue to a head in the summer of 1862. In a government contract, Gregg requested the release of seven men from one company in the Army of Northern Virginia. James B. Ferguson, the quartermaster who negotiated the agreement, found the military command unyielding on the issue. On Myers's behalf, he "went in person to see Genl. Lee and begged that he would detail the men which he did." But Lee explained that "many of his best men were leaving under the conscript act relieving all over thirty five and he could not consent to give more than half of those asked." Lee released only half the operatives requested by Adam Johnson and William Jackson, manufacturers at Augusta, Georgia, whom he put "on the same footing with . . . others all of whom are going on with their contracts." Believing that he needed troops more than equipage, Lee "requested the Sec of War not to permit any contractor in future to make contacts with the understanding that men were to be detailed from the army to fill."[16]

Myers obviously did not believe that a general commanding in the field could countermand a General Order and contravene the Conscription Act; however, Secretary of War Randolph agreed with Lee and quickly announced that he wanted the practice of making details broken up. Myers had little choice but to order the annulment of Gregg's contracts because they required the detailing "of a number of men now in the service."[17] This left the Quartermaster Bureau in a technical breach of contract. Ferguson pleaded with Gregg not "to take advantage of the situation" and requested that the Graniteville manufacturer and the bureau "arrange this matter without referring it to the Sec of War, as I know he has as much as he can attend to & it belongs properly to our department."[18]

Myers vigorously protested against field commanders nullifying national law and military regulations to the imperilment of supplies. In May 1862, he noted the dire consequences of such a practice. "It has been formally reported to me to day," he wrote Secretary Randolph, "that requisitions representing the complete outfit of 40,000 are necessarily unfilled, of course greatly to the dissatisfaction of the troops." Myers's arrangements with manufacturers were being disrupted by military "interference," factories were "rendered incapable of complying with their contracts," and this "made it impossible to replace the stores which have been issued from the Depots." The quartermaster general urged that "the requisite number of men may be discharged or detailed to enable the various contractors with the Department to fulfill their obligations."[19]

In September 1862, the Confederate Congress modified the exemption law in a manner agreeable to Myers. At the core of the new act was an agreement to give manufacturers relief from conscription only in return for a limitation on profits. Myers would not only arbitrate all personnel allocations but also police the profits of military contractors. Through his friendship with Representative William Porcher Miles of Charleston, the powerful chair of the Military Affairs Committee, Myers helped shape the final legislation.

The movement to make Myers responsible for enforcing Confederate price controls was triggered by a dramatically high inflation rate. On August 26, 1862, Lucius J. Gartrell, a Confederate representative from Atlanta and a member of Governor Brown's inner circle, called upon Miles's committee "to inquire and report to this House what legislation, if any, may be necessary to authorize the Government of the Confederate States to take control during the war of the various establishments within the limits of said Confederate States engaged in the manufacture of woolen and cotton goods, and so to regulate the prices of such goods as to enable the soldiers to clothe themselves and families at reasonable prices" (*Journal of the Congress of the Confederate States of America* 5: 317). Driven by scarcity and a depreciating currency, prices in every branch of manufacturing rose rapidly, and Gartrell believed, as did much of the public, that manufacturers were reaping illicit rewards from the war.

Confederate currency, in general use by the fall of 1862, depreciated at an average rate of almost 10 percent a month. Myers found that within six months following the Fort Sumter engagement, "the prices of materials for clothing . . . advanced about one hundred percent."[20] Critical items in manufacturing such as oils, card clothing, and parts were objects of hoarding and speculation. William Gregg noted that when "it became apparent that the supply on hand was being rapidly exhausted and had to be renewed by running the blockade, everything of the kind advanced in price to such a degree that manufacturers were under the necessity of raising the price of cloth long before cotton or any agricultural product (except bacon) had risen at all" (*Daily South Carolinian*, June 4, 1864). In August 1862, Fries found that card clothing worth $1 a foot before the war cost $7 for a used article.[21] In consequence, the price of finished goods also rose rapidly. In July 1862, Charles T. Haigh, of North Carolina's Rockfish mill, calculated that in North Carolina, ordinary cloth sheeting doubled in price every six months, rising from 10 cents to 40 cents a yard between the battles of First Bull Run and Second Bull Run a year later. A bunch of yarn rose in value from $1 to $5. Haigh explained to the local army quartermaster that "you can form no idea how they are sought after, as I believe principally by speculators, who say they are contractors."[22] As factory prices rose, so did the public outcry.

In October 1862, Francis Fries declined to sell James Chesnut Sr. of South Carolina the usual allotment of plantation cloth for his slaves because of the needs of those "who are in the service & exposed to all kinds of weather."[23] In her diary, Mary Chesnut scorned such a dilemma, writing that the price of osnaburgs—a coarse, heavy cloth—forced planters to lease slaves "to have them fed and clothed" (Chesnut 304–5). Mary Chesnut, whose husband was an aide to Jefferson Davis, reserved a special denunciation for manufacturers: "we, poor fools, who are patriotically ruining ourselves, will see our children in the gutter while treacherous dogs of millionaires go rolling by in their coaches—coaches that were acquired by taking advantage of our necessities."[24] The plaint was a common one. The *Charleston Mercury* (April 14, 1862) applauded the price controls established under martial law in Richmond by Provost Martial General John Henry Winder and recommended that "he ought also to put the iron grip of martial law about the necks of the manufacturers, and force them to charge moderately for their goods." The paper particularly singled out the Manchester Manufacturing Company "for declaring a dividend, the amount of which (25 per cent, for the last quarter), they were afraid to make known to the public." "Do manufactures," the paper rhetorically asked, "invariably turn men into Yankees?"

Another scion of planter aristocracy, Langdon Cheves, proposed dealing with the upstart class of newly rich by imposing "martial law and
making the bloodsuckers disgorge their ill-gotten gains" (Chesnut 197).
William H. Holden, editor of the *North Carolina Standard* and son of a
manufacturer, surmised in an editorial in 1861 that "the manufacturing
community must contain some vampires."[25]

Frank Fries immediately remonstrated to Holden that when "wool advanced to double & three times its former price, cloth of course had to
advance also."[26] Cotton mills raised prices, but "oil had advanced 300
per cent, & when to procure findings (a heavy expense), we must all
resort to England & risk the danger of the blockade, both in remitting
funds & receiving the goods, this is not too much." In August 1862, editor
Holden returned to the attack with a denunciatory piece on cotton manufacturers and tanners entitled "Speculators and Extortioners."[27] Since
cotton was no more expensive than in the prewar period, Holden concluded that the high price of cloth was producing enormous and unjusti-
fied profits. He recommended that "these matters should be regulated by
legislation."[28]

Again Fries responded with alacrity: "in the halcyon days of peace,
when our farmers were glad to furnish us with wheat at $1.00, corn at 50
cts. . . . , they never considered $1.00 for a bunch of yarn at all extrava-
gant." But the parity between a bushel of wheat and a bunch of yarn was
broken when farmers "preferred to hold their produce for higher prices,
at the same time importuning us for yarn for which they wished to pay
the money." The "money" was depreciated Confederate currency. In
order to "bread" 150 workers, Fries established a system of barter, exchanging one bundle of yarn for a bushel of wheat. The result was that
"at first a good many of the dear people who have been taught by the
newspapers & demagogues to abuse 'extortioners' did a good deal of
pious cursing, that we should presume to prescribe in what they should
pay for the yarn."[29] But locally in Salem, North Carolina, Fries's philosophy prevailed, that it was as easy to farm without clothes as it was to
make cloth without food.

Elsewhere Southern newspapers marshaled support for measures to
control prices. The *Spirit of the South* in Eufaula, Alabama, charged that
mills had "raised the prices of their manufactures to such an uncon-
scionable rate, that they have forfeited all claim to the patronage and

support of our people" (cited in the *Macon Telegraph*, April 7, 1862). The editor opined that "our Southern Factories are laying the predicate for their total abandonment as soon as the war closes" and concluded, "we would rather trade with a Yankee after peace is restored, than with the men who take advantage of our necessities at this time, to practice extortion upon us." Even the conservative *Richmond Whig* (November 28, 1862) surmised that "the selfish and unpatriotic policy adhered to by the manufacturers of this State will engender such an account of prejudice against them that at the close of the war the people will prefer to purchase their supplies from any source rather than from those who have taken advantage of the blockade to exact heavy profits from them." The *Washington Telegraph* in Arkansas enlarged upon these views with a discussion of Henry Merrell's well-known factory in Pike County. The newspaper reported (June 4, 1862) that Merrell, a New York native, refused to sell for Treasury warrants, war bonds, or Confederates notes, "for the reason, as we are informed, that gold and silver had been paid for the goods and they must be sold for gold and silver." Charging extortion, the editor warned that "there has been much talk of taking forcible possession of his factory, and running it for the benefit of the community."

Merrell verified this account: "The demand was so great for our products that it appeared as though I could get any prices I chose to ask; and that, said the stump speakers, was too much power to be vested in one man, and should be taken away from him" (Merrell 294). Indignation went further: "Public meetings were held, violent speeches were made, Resolutions passed, Committees appointed to wait upon me, and the measure was greatly discussed whether it was not expedient to take the Factory from me and carry it on for their own benefit—they the people!" (294).

In North Carolina, Fries deprecated such moves. State regulation, he wrote Holden, was fraught with difficulties. Even if "both national & state legislatures are all patriotic & pure, & gifted with more than ordinary common sense, yet it must be admitted that the sad experience of America has been, that legislators with few exceptions are most lamentably ignorant of the laws that govern trade & finance." An immutable law of nature, Adam Smith's invisible hand, set the price of land and slaves as well as cotton goods, and "supply & demand ever will control these matters."[30] The North Carolina manufacturer Thomas Holt almost despaired of making public sales, for "if I sell them all I make, they grumble, because I have not five times as much, if I sell them half I make, they swear I have not sold any, so there is no way to satisfy them."[31] With regard to prices, George Camp of Roswell scolded a Rome merchant, "so your people don't like *our* advancing goods and threaten to put us into the cold—and hold indignative meetings—while they were about it why did they not include Augusta Mills."[32]

In an attempt to delay regulatory legislation such as that proposed by Lucius Gartrell in the Confederate Congress, many mills attempted to reduce prices. By spring 1862, both the Macon and Roswell factories sold goods to merchants with the understanding that the retail price would be advanced no more than 20 percent over the wholesale price.[33] In April 1862, the Georgia, Athens, High Shoals, and Princeton factories announced in the *Athens Southern Watchman* (April 2, 1862) a joint reduction in prices of one-quarter and explained that "when it is considered that many cotton mills have an inadequate supply of card clothing, and other indispensable findings, for over six months' use, and no possibility, during the war of procuring more, it is hoped that the above prices will not be considered unreasonable." Many of the public were convinced that such reductions were evidence that the factories had been gouging in the first place. These experiments in price cutting predictably failed when speculators secured the goods at first sale and hawked them about for higher prices. One editor concluded that "most of the dry goods, medicines and other necessities of life which the country now affords, are in the hands of speculators, who will not part with them except at prices, that many greatly in need of them are utterly unable to give" (*Natchitoches Union*, November 27, 1862).

In June 1862, after a three-month trial, the Georgia factories abandoned their experiment and, as mills at Graniteville and Augusta did, commenced "to make weekly sales by auction or otherwise" (*Athens Southern Watchman*, June 11, 1862). The weekly auction, with each sale usually limited to a few bundles of yarn or yards of cloth, became a common occurrence at mills across the South. These sales invariably attracted large crowds, some of whom came great distances and stayed at local boardinghouses in expectation of getting some lots.

The upward spiral of prices adversely affected the work of the Quartermaster Bureau, which operated on the basis of appropriation bills passed many months earlier. Outrage over prices was commonplace. The managers at the Young, Wriston, and Orr company in Charlotte chastised James Devereux, North Carolina quartermaster, who criticized their charges: "you are laboring under a wrong impression; it is not to make money for ourselves, nor is it that we have the least disposition to control in any way the operations of your department, but simply to give bread to them whom we know must suffer unless they get their work."[34] If mills made no money, how would workers be paid or fed?

A Confederate medical officer at Charlotte searched fruitlessly for goods at "the Factorys in Alemance [Alamance], Randolph, Salem, Catarrus, Mecklenburg, Gaston, & Lincoln," then in despair wrote Governor Vance that "if the people of our country have to pay the prices they are asked by some of our merchants—$10.00 per bunch—they cannot stand it."[35] The Richmond quartermaster James B. Ferguson sought goods at Charlotte in June 1862 and found that "the manufacturers here are asking 50 per cent more for them here than we are paying in Va." Cloth worth 16 cents a yard in Petersburg was marketed for 38 cents, and other goods were priced accordingly.[36] Such reports fed the notion that factories were exploiting both the public and the War Department.

As the Confederate Congress debated relief measures to control price inflation in early 1862, the governors of Georgia and North Carolina moved to action. Governor Joseph E. Brown proposed the seizure of Georgia mills until all state troops were clad, a proposition soon sanctioned in part by the state legislature. In September 1862, Governor Zebulon B. Vance of North Carolina attacked the "inhuman spirit of avarice which is rampant in the land" and called for a reconvening of the state's secession convention in order to deal firmly with manufacturers unhampered "by the forms of the constitution." Having expended $1.5 million on quartermaster stores in the first year of the war, Vance found that "it will be impossible to clothe & shoe our troops this winter without incurring a most enormous outlay & submitting to most outrageous prices." The manufacturers in North Carolina "had advanced their prices to an unheard extent & refuse to make contracts which would prevent them raising next week if they saw proper." The September 1862 price of shirting in North Carolina was 50 cents a yard, while Vance found "by calculations submitted to me by intelligent gentlemen, it appears that 25 cents per yard for cotton cloth will actually pay the mill owners near 300 per cent."[37] To give North Carolina soldiers their winter's allowance of two uniforms, two shirts, and two pairs of drawers required an outlay of $.5 million. Like Georgia's Brown, Vance proposed the seizure of selected mills for state use.

The resolution put before the Confederate Congress in August 1862 by Lucius Gartrell, a political ally of Governor Brown, initiated a month-long debate in Richmond on the manufacturing question. In September 1862, a Senate bill designed as a "Provision Against Extortion" required all factories contracting with the government to submit a detailed statement of costs and profits to Colonel Myers. The quartermaster general was authorized to ensure that manufacturing profits did not exceed 50 percent (*Journal of the Congress of the Confederate States of America* 2: 410).

Only then, and upon receiving a sworn oath of need, was Myers empowered to grant draft exemptions to "superintendents and operatives in wool and cotton factories and paper mills, and superintendents and managers of wool-carding machines."[38] The final measure, passed as the Conscription Act of October 11, 1862, followed the House version of the bill and limited the profits of manufacturers to 75 percent.[39]

In an inflationary economy driven by great scarcity, this measure was not well received in the manufacturing constituency. Henry Atwood, of Georgia's Curtright factory, attacked the measure's vagueness, writing the War Department that, lacking a good bookkeeper, "we do not know what per cent we have been making on our capital since the first of April last." Atwood explained that "from 1856, the time at which we commenced business as cotton manufacturers, up to the date of the last balance sheet the nett profits were less than 7 per ct. on our capital allowing the usual percentage for wear and tear of machinery."[40] But with an exemption for himself and his son, Atwood vowed to meet the requirements of the law.

William Gregg, as was his style, was more caustic. Before an assembly of manufacturers gathered in Augusta, Gregg excoriated the Confederate legislation. He explained that "had it been the design of Congress to restrict the advance of manufacturing industry, and confine it to a limited and sickly existence, they could not have adopted a more certain means of reaching that object than they obtained by the Conscript Act" (*Daily South Carolinian*, June 4, 1864). According to Gregg, the act "undertook to regulate and limit the price of manufactured articles in the hands of the producer, while it left everyone else to speculate on and sell such articles for all the market would offer." It also invited "extravagant expenditure," "profligate outlays," and "enormously high wages" because these costs could be passed on to the government and the public. Gregg noted the popular clamor "with regard to the profits realized by cotton and woolen manufacturers since the war commenced" bred in every legislative body as "a common sentiment with politicians that manufacturers should be made to disgorge their extortionate gains." In reality, manufacturers were faced with inflated prices that rose steadily at 10 percent a month, a growing scarcity of essential parts and supplies, and a hazardous route through the blockade from Nassau. Confronted with Colonel Myers's emerging suzerainty, Gregg could only soberly predict that "the day will come when we will not be at the bid and call of military authority."[41]

An article probably inspired, if not written, by Gregg appeared in the *Charleston Mercury* (June 5, 1863) under the heading "The Productive Power of the South." The Confederacy had political independence, but "what indispensable article," the author asked, "do we lack to render us entirely independent?" It was clothing, for Southern mills could hardly produce what the public demanded. "If Congress and the State Governments desired to limit production," the writer added, "they could not pursue a more certain policy to effect that end, than that of restricting prices, and every such step taken by our rulers will tend to embarrass and ruin our country."

The article continued in a vein reflective of Gregg's views. According to its author, the advance in cloth prices caused by the war "became a theme for newspaper scribblers and politicians, and our industrious, enterprising manufacturers were berated and stigmatized as little better than highway robbers; and such was the rage of warfare, that the public mind was poisoned against them, from the lowest strata of society to the highest circle of politicians." The public was led to believe that cheap cloth could be secured by legislation. The resulting "long discussions in legislative halls set forth in glowing colors the monstrous evil of high prices, devising various modes of restricting them; and Congress wasted time and money enough in such discussions to have paid for importing cards sufficient to supply every working woman in our country." The consequence of "this legal restriction of prices" was to transfer "profits from the hands of the manufacturer to the speculator, and utterly forbade the much needed expansion of manufacturing either by hand or machinery." Restrictive legislation, passed "by Congress and the several State Legislatures," effectively "deterred many who have accumulated money from investing it in English machinery to run the blockade." In the present economic climate, "capitalists will not engage in new manufacturing enterprises unless they have a prospect of great gain; and our prices must be unrestricted by legal enactments, or our factories will be suffered to wear out and burn up without an effort to renew them; and as for new establishments being reared, that is out of the question with the present state of public sentiment, in and out of Congress and our State Legislature."

The writer noted, "if half the amount that has been expended in importing calicoes, brandies, wines, cheese, fancy soaps, and the thousands of jim cracks of Yankee manufacture that load the ships coming through the blockade, had been expended in machinery for manufacture of every needed article, we would now be in a situation to carry on the war." The mistaken public had "sanctioned the idea that he who exchanges our last golden dollar and imports Yankee ten cent calico and sells it for three dollars a yard, is a benefactor to his country"; meanwhile, "the ingenious producer at home is branded with infamy and indicted for extortion for selling a similar article made at home for a dollar and a half." The patron of "Domestic Industry" concluded: "To import machinery now costs from twelve to fifteen prices, and we feel quite well assured that no large establishment in our country has earned money enough in two years past to pay for the importation of machinery that would add twenty percent to their production."

Gregg carried his grievances straight to the War Department, where he received an unsympathetic hearing. According to John Jones, the rebel war clerk, Gregg complained to the secretary of war "that only 75 per ct. profit is allowed by Act of Congress, whose operatives are exempted from military duty, if the law be interpreted to include sales to individuals as well as to the government." Jones calculated that Gregg made 14,000 yards each day, at a cost of 20 cents a yard, and that "75 per ct. will yield, I believe $500,000 profits, which would be equivalent to 32 cts. per yard." But the market price for goods was 68 cents, which would yield $2 million a year. The sardonic war clerk felt "this war is a encour-

ager of domestic manufacturers, truly!" (John Jones [December 4, 1862]
1: 203).

Jones's estimates were not far from the mark. For the first six months
of 1862, the earnings at Graniteville were $225,000, permitting the com-
pany to buy 4,218 bales of cotton and declare a dividend of 10 percent.
Gregg advised his stockholders that dividing the sum would "probably
be imprudent, & it would be more advisable to make a special extra dividend at some other time."[42] At the Augusta factory in June 1862, profits
for six months of operation amounted to $228,000.[43] The company re-
sorted to monthly dividends of 100 percent, and in December 1862 William Jackson, the president, reported that "the business of the company
for the past six months has been profitable beyond all expectation,
showing gross earnings of . . . $796,544.31."[44] The profits at Alabama's
Bell factory in 1862 were also substantial. Robert M. Patton, brother of
the owner, estimated that the mill produced during "present year nett
proffits [sic] of not less than half million dollars." Robert Patton wrote
Governor John Gill Shorter that "it is a great outrage that the Factorys in
Alabama or the South, (whilst the proprietors and laborers by the conscript law are exempt from military duty) should charge for osnaburgs,
tenting, & other goods, 3 or 4 times the price for which they can be
made."[45] However, the war proved for many companies near the front
lines that even high profits were hardly equal to the hazards faced.

Another manufacturer who took exception to the new Confederate
Conscription Act was Francis Fries. He wrote the War Department that
he declined to take the prescribed oath with regard to earnings, for "although we have been doing business for over twenty years & have always
tried to keep strict account of expenses &c., we must say that we could
not tell now what would be the cost of production." Like Gregg, Fries
asked, "how much would we have to count wear & tear of machinery
when some portion of it can not be replaced at *any* price?" Would manufacturers like himself "having some foresight & investing money in stock
at low figures be entitled to but 75 per cent advance while others who
don't care what they pay, are entitled to the same *per* cent on *their* cost of
production?"[46] Manufacturers who paid their laborers $1.00 a day were
entitled to but 75 cents profit, but if they paid $5.00 a day, they could
earn $3.75. The "law is a hard one," Fries wrote North Carolina quarter-
master Charles Garrett, for it passed "profits into the hands of the specu-

lators."[47] Because of the high rate of inflation, the Salem manufacturer calculated that his company could earn more money by buying and selling raw materials than by making cloth.

Despite misgivings, manufacturers from the cotton-producing states met in convention in Augusta in November 1862 to give reluctant assent to the new Confederate legislation. The convention of the Manufacturing Association of the Confederate States adopted, at Gregg's suggestion, a uniform system of calculating costs. The values placed on depreciation, labor, and other production costs were inadequate, Gregg wrote, for "in nine cases out of ten that computation fell short of the reality" (*Daily South Carolinian*, June 4, 1864). In fact, manufacturers frequently computed their profits on current market costs of labor and materials, not the lower costs that existed when cotton was secured and manufactured. In return for granting this favor, Myers received a grudging acceptance of his regulatory authority.

The issue of price controls was not so amicably settled in North Carolina. Governor Vance, who had read a portion of Fries's correspondence with Quartermaster Garrett, responded with "regret and mortification." The youthful governor, in high dudgeon, wrote the Salem manufacturer that "if the standard of patriotism was no higher in the great mass of people, we might treat with the enemy tomorrow and consent to be slaves at once & forever." The governor, a former duelist and Confederate army officer, drew a sorry contrast between the poor soldier earning but $11 a month and his desperate family, "supporting themselves and children God knows how," with the monied "men who stay at home in protected ease to reap a harvest of wealth, which might be called a harvest of blood." Turning the screw still further Vance asked, if the soldier risked all, "cant [sic] you afford to eat food, sleep in a warm bed every night on 75 per cent clear profit for the country's good also?" Having cajoled and shamed, the governor endorsed the principle of the Confederate Conscription Act, that "there is only one remedy to arrest the evil which threatens us; and that is for the civil authorities to permit the military to put forth its strong arm & take what it wants."[48] The governor vowed to deliver North Carolina manufacturers to the Confederate military rather than tolerate extortion.

Frank Fries was not cowed. He responded to Vance, as he had to the bureau in Richmond, that he harbored "some old fashioned notions about taking an oath." Inflation was rampant and pernicious for manufacturers. With vital supplies disappearing from the marketplace and machinery being destroyed by excessive wear, "how any man can conscientiously swear that goods cost just so much is more than we can see." If necessary, Fries threatened to submit to government impressment of his goods and the draft of his men. When a shipment of the Salem mill's cotton was burned at High Point in August 1862, Fries saw the event as evidence of a "fearful spirit of lawlessness" caused by "the teachings men have received, of some of our would-be leading men." Political agitation over the Confederate Conscription Act and "the Union reconstruction" encouraged the public "to take their spite out on us by . . . destroying our property." With a little encouragement, these same reckless spirits would "put the torch to our houses."[49] Had the Confederate revolution come to this? The confrontation between North Carolina manufacturers and the state authorities reached a climax on November 17, 1862, when Governor Vance laid the issue before the legislature. The military situation was dire, the governor reported, for "when a large portion of our army this fall, by the accident of battle and other causes, lost their baggage, it was found impossible at once to replace it." Competition between state and Confederate quartermasters was "stripping bare our markets." Of the factories in the state, only the Rockfish mill gave more than grudging support to the military effort, although "some seven or eight other companies have intimated an intention of following their praise-worthy example." The North Carolina woolen mills seemed particularly "incorrigible."[50] Vance estimated that the co-operating mills would reduce prices by half in response to the new law. The others would suffer the legal penalties of impressment or draft. Fries and the proprietors of four or five other larger North Carolina woolen mills were obviously the intended victims of Vance's attack.

Frank Fries found the governor's assertions "very sweeping." He wrote Quartermaster James Sloan that the millers were "as liberal & patriotic as any & are not more incorrigible than other classes of our citizens."[51] Fellow manufacturer John A. Young, originally a vocal leader of North Carolina's secession movement, challenged Vance on the floor of the state senate and forced the governor into a satisfying "disclaimer" on behalf of Young, Wriston, and Orr, a leading supplier of the state quartermasters. Fries himself prepared a detailed calculation refuting the governor's assertion that the Salem mill "declined entirely to furnish goods at seventy five percent, when asked so to do" and that others were "fixing enormous profits on the cost of the raw material & then adding the seventy five per cent on the finished article."[52] By Fries's calculation, in the week of November 5, 1862, he produced 2,435 yards of woolens at an estimated cost of $4,095.85, which he sold to the Quartermaster Bureau at $2.50 a yard, for a total of $6,087.50. Per pound, wool cost $3.00, cotton 50 cents, and warps $1.00, and these items were worth $3,000. Wages were $500; oil, card-clothing, and incidentals $350; wood $50; the "use of machinery" $100; and there was an unenumerated charge of $95.85, for a total of $4,095.85. The sale price of $6,087.50 gave a profit of 67 percent.[53] Ultimately, however, manufacturers in North Carolina, as in other states, had little choice but to accept the terms of the Confederate Conscription Act. Leviathan would rule Ariadne.

Fries refused to attend a gathering of manufacturers called by the state quartermaster at Greensboro on December 3, 1862, not thinking "it would amount to any thing." He vowed to waste no time validating the Confederate Conscription Act, which was created by "political demagogues" who of necessity "must have something to make capital out of, & with some, manufacturers are now the hobby."[54] But James Sloan, on behalf of the Quartermaster Bureau, attended the conference and negotiated an agreement with manufacturers from the northern part of North Carolina.

As Thomas Holt characterized the affair, "some of us met in the town of Greensboro . . . , & passed a series of resolutions, showing to the world, our willingness to reduce prices, & if possible to bring down our goods from a fictitious to real prices."[55] The agreement validated the government's control of most North Carolina mills. Manufacturers agreed to abide by the Conscription Act, sell the state a quota of goods, and reduce prices. Cotton yarns selling at $6.00 to $8.00 were immediately reduced to $3.50, a genuine bargain since yarns usually sold for ten pounds of cotton then currently worth $5.00.[56]

Another manufacturing conference was held at Fayetteville on October 29. Quartermaster Charles Garrett "required" Charles T. Haigh of the Rockfish Creek factory to "appoint" a meeting for mill men in his counting room. In addition to Haigh, George O'Neill, of the Blount Creek factory, and John Shaw, of Fayetteville Mill, attended, as did others. John

Hall, of Beaver Creek mill, "declined the invitation," and Duncan Murchison, of Manchester factory, "could not make it convenient to come to town."[57] George O'Neill was in good favor with the Confederate authorities and willing to sell the military depots "half, or three-fourths of the goods we make at 75 pcent, say about 25 ct for sheeting & about 30 ct for Osnaburgs, provided, they will let us retain our hands." But O'Neill insisted on the right to sell the "balance of our goods as we choose, we can't control the market." He reiterated the argument used by Fries and Gregg, that "our neighbors would be selling their yarns at $5 & 6 probably, when we would have to take about $2 1/2; for the benefit of out side speculators, when we may as well have the profit as speculators."[58]

O'Neill reminded the Quartermaster Bureau that "our Factory was built & commenced operations in 1848, & up to 1 Sept. we had divided dividends on our cash capital of just 6 pcent p annum."[59] After a brief discussion, probably in the presence of the local quartermaster, the body of manufacturers agreed to abide by the requirements of the Conscription Act and comply "with the requisitions of the State."[60] This meant selling the North Carolina quartermasters one-third of their product at fixed prices, provided other manufacturers in the state did the same.

At least three Fayetteville mills paid "no respect to the Conscript Act."[61] Beaver Creek, Union, and Cross Creek ignored the whole proceedings. But across the state Thomas R. Tate, John Shaw, John Newlin, and John W. Leak signified their acceptance of the law, but usually with the proviso that they could dispose of their own surplus at local market prices.[62]

In the Old Dominion, the *Richmond Whig* took the leadership in calling upon manufacturers to abide by the terms of the new Conscription Act. Noting the acquiescence of conventions held in Georgia and North Carolina, the newspaper believed "a similar suggestion might with propriety be commended to the manufacturers of this state" (*Richmond Whig*, October 28, 1862). How could soldiers "fight with spirit when they reflect that their families at home are suffering from the greedy avarice of speculators and extortioners" (*Richmond Whig*, October 30, 1862). In the same issue, the newspaper lauded Enoch Steadman, the Georgia manufacturer who published a card endorsing the limitation on profits, as a "patriotic manufacturer." The *Richmond Examiner*, usually vitriolic on such matters, debated the issue as well, finding woolens "as precious as golden fleece," and "factory cloth for shirts and drawers, purchased last year at eight and ten cents, is selling for seventy-five, and our country flannel, which last fall was freely sold at thirty cents, is now held at two dollars" (*Richmond Examiner*, November 1, 1862).

But when no meeting of Virginia manufacturers was forthcoming, the *Whig* surmised that "the manufacturers are quietly going on as they have been doing for months past, realizing enormous profits, undisturbed either by compunctions of conscience, or, by apprehensions of a visit from enrolling officers" (*Richmond Whig*, November 28, 1862). Specifically, no enrolling officers called at the Crenshaw Woolen Mill, located near the Tredegar Iron Works on the James River and the War Department's prime contractor for woolens in Richmond. The Crenshaw company, with John Waterhouse as superintendent, employed twenty-five females and "several children ranging in their ages from 10 to 12 years," mostly in filling shuttles (Richmond *Enquirer*, October 17, 1861). According to the *Enquirer* article, the heavier labor was performed by one hundred male employees who were exempt from the draft, being "principally foreigners, from the English, Irish, and German factories," and the mill, which produced 5,000 yards a week, was "superintended by experienced overseers from England."

Antimanufacturing sentiment was quite pronounced in Richmond, perhaps because inflation was greater in the overcrowded city than elsewhere in the South. Sheeting that sold in Fayetteville for 30 cents brought 70 cents in Richmond. A correspondent of the *Whig* noted the common sight that "at every village and crossroad, in shops kept by dealers of foreign and domestic birth, can be found large quantities of ready made clothing, mostly woolen, retailed and retailing to the needy at tremendously extortionate prices" (*Richmond Whig*, October 25, 1862).

Although most Virginia factories operated under the close scrutiny of Colonel Myers and his subordinates, the House of the Virginia legislature established a Committee on Extortion to inquire into the costs and profits of manufacturing. Particular attention centered upon the Crenshaw factory and the Manchester Cotton and Wool Manufacturing Company, both located in Richmond and essential to the Confederate effort. When hearings commenced in January 1863, Alfred T. Harris, president of the Manchester factory, led off with seemingly straightforward testimony. In 1860, his mill declared no dividend "in consequence of losses previously sustained, and the purchase of machinery for the manufacture of woolen goods." But company dividends of 23 percent in 1861 and 120 percent in 1862 left a surplus of $70,000, which was "designed for the purchase of new machinery to supply the place of such as is now, and soon will become, unfit for use." Harris explained that company stock worth $32 in 1861 and $111 in 1862 "would now bring a much higher price."[63]

As to costs, the Manchester company was confronted with the high rate of inflation that prevailed in the Confederate capital. Black hands were hired at "about double the rates of last year; and such has been the advance in prices of food, clothing and fuel, that their labor will probably cost 150 per cent. more than was paid for similar labor last year." White labor was also "fully 150 to 175 per cent. above the rates paid a year ago, with every prospect of a further advance," but raw materials were somewhat cheaper than in North Carolina, with cotton at 23 cents and wool at $2.37 a pound.[64] Nearly all of the product of the mill was sold to Myers's Clothing Depot in Richmond for manufacture into uniforms.[65]

Reluctantly, Harris calculated for the committee that profits for the Manchester company in 1862 "would probably have exceeded 200 per cent." Nevertheless, the mill's machinery was considerably worn, and "the general agent of the company is of the opinion it would require not less than sixty or seventy thousand dollars to restore it to its condition at the time the war commenced."[66]

After hearing Harris acquiesce in the terms of the Conscription Act, the committee turned to the testimony of E. B. Bentley, agent of the James River factory. Bentley was more guarded than Harris but finally agreed to answer "a series of written enquiries."[67] The James River factory declared dividends of 33 percent in 1861 and 140 percent in 1862, and stock values rose from $100 a share to $250.[68] After May 1861, the factory "had been almost exclusively employed upon work for the government, and chiefly in the manufacture of an article not known before, among its productions," namely cotton duck for tents. Bentley's James River company had a cordial and accommodating relationship with Myers's bureau. When the mill lost many of its best employees to the army during the Peninsula campaign in the spring of 1862, Bentley explained to Myers that "the looms would be stopped (for these men were indispensable to the preparation for the beams of weaving), and the mill be changed into one producing cotton yarns only."[69] A detail of the requested men was quickly arranged. In return, Myers's bureau was allowed to purchase goods at low impressment prices.

The Conscription Act changed the bookkeeping at the James River mill. Bentley found it impossible to calculate the exact costs on each delivery "from the fact that the wages paid for labor, as well as the value of every article purchased, advances from day to day." He resorted to a practice common elsewhere of "including several months in the calculation, and averaging the same." The committee was asked especially to note that "during the whole of the last year the government never paid me a price within 25 per cent. of the value of the goods delivered them, in the open markets, and for many months toward its close, the amount received was about one-half their worth in the market." Bentley revealed that the James River mill made substantial profits outside of manufacturing during 1862. It realized a substantial appreciation upon the value of raw materials, due principally "to the fact that a nine months' supply of cotton was laid in early in the year." But this involved considerable risk, for "had the Confederate army evacuated Richmond [in May 1862], or the enemy have obtained possession of it, the whole of this valuable stock of cotton would have been consigned to the flames."[70]

After dismissing Bentley, the legislative committee interviewed Archibald G. McIlwaine and James May, who represented the major Petersburg mills. McIlwaine's Ettrick company prospered by making cloth sacks, which the Confederate army used for grain and sand. Throughout 1862 the company sold "a very large proportion of our production . . . , generally one-third to one-half, at prices very much below market prices."[71] Nevertheless, during the year profits abounded, amounting to $340,000.[72] In December 1862, the Ettrick company auctioned off sheeting at 63 cents a yard in Petersburg while selling the same to the bureau for 25 cents. James May of the Battersea mill demonstrated a government contract that revealed that he accepted the 75 percent profit limitation, got his military exemptions, and sold the entire mill's product to the Clothing Depot. This mill also returned generous wartime profits, amounting to $5,705 in 1860, $15,402 in 1861, and $135,395 in 1862. Other Petersburg mills operated on comparative terms. Matoaca factory had net profits of $17,216 in 1860, $41,231 in 1861, and $318,335 in 1862.[73]

No mill in Virginia was more closely watched than the Crenshaw Woolen Mill, which operated almost solely on behalf of the War Department. The mill mostly employed foreign nationals, then exempt from the draft, and primarily manufactured the "light blue and grey cloths, adopted for the regulation uniform of the Confederacy; [and] broad cloths and blankets" (*Richmond Enquirer*, October 17, 1861). The company operated forty looms in a five-story brick structure fronting the James River, where there were eight dye vats producing 2,000 pounds of indigo-dyed woolens a day. The company's army blankets measured sixty by eighty inches and weighed 3 7/8 pounds.

In testimony before the Virginia legislative committee, Joseph H. Crenshaw told the incredulous gathering that "it is impossible to tell the net profits for the years 1860, 1861, 1862 or during any given time." Nevertheless, in the fall of 1862 the Crenshaw brothers divided $530,000 and added fifteen broad looms valued at $70,000.[74] From a weekly production of over 5,000 yards, Crenshaw provided woolens to the Richmond depot at $7 a yard, while the market price was $14.

The hearings in Richmond precipitated prolonged debates in both the Virginia and Confederate governments and press comments across the South. Some forty speeches were made on the subject in the Virginia Senate alone, while in the Confederate Congress William Porcher Miles's Military Affairs Committee vigorously sought ways to further enlarge Myers's authority over those guilty of "extortion" (*Richmond Enquirer*, January 10 and 31, February 4, 1863). Israel Welch of Mississippi called upon the Confederate Congress to restrict profits further under the Conscription Act because "manufacturers of woolen goods were exempted, while there was an instance in this city, as shown by an official report, where a firm with a capital of $40,000 had realized in one year $200,000."[75]

A measure to limit all profits to 20 percent of the original capital passed the Confederate Senate but failed in the House (*Journal of the Congress of the Confederate States of America 79*, 306). The passage of this measure, Fries calculated, would have permitted his mill, which manufactured over 500 uniforms a week, annual earnings of $58 prewar dollars. If he worked hard for a week, he would then "have to stop, or spin without any profit til the end of the year."[76] The Salem manufacturer wrote North Carolina Senator William Dortch that manufacturers would "cheerfully pay our part, if only other classes of men will be treated the same as manufacturers." Plantation overseers got exemptions and block-ade-runners earned substantial profits, but "Congress & the State legisla-tures seem to have singled out manufacturers as the special objects of legislation restricting their profits, & taxing them in every conceivable way."[77] The planter aristocracy that ran the Confederacy was taking its due.

Upon passage of a 75 percent rule, Quartermaster General Myers strictly enforced the terms of the conscription law upon all manufactur-ers on government contract. Rebellious William Gregg "purchased sub-stitutes and ran our mill six months independent of the conscript law, and sold our goods at market rate" (*Daily South Carolinian*, June 4, 1864). Henry Atwood successfully employed black workers to replace those "kept in the service, some 16 to 18 men, whose services we should other-wise have required to carry on the business of our factory."[78] Fries simply kept the exemptions for his woolen factory, "where more male labor is required," and ran his separate "cotton mill without any conscript assis-tance."[79] This permitted him to sell his cotton goods at market prices while the woolen mill worked on government contracts. For the time being, Myers ruled that "so long as Factories receive no benefit under the Exemption Law and claim no details, there is no way of controlling their prices."[80] But soon the authority of the Confederate quartermaster gen-eral was extended even to these mills through the power of impressment.

William Jackson, whose Augusta factory was an important supplier to both the Atlanta and Richmond military depots, was especially bitter at this new turn of events. When Myers's local quartermaster demanded the entire production of his mill for a month, Jackson assented. But when George W. Evans, Governor Joseph E. Brown's representative, ap-peared at the factory and demanded outfits for 25,000 men, Jackson re-fused to treat with him or even show him the Confederate contract.[81] Jackson was obligated either to operate under the terms of the Conscrip-tion Act or to lose the services of ninety-four valuable workers. If he hired substitutes, Governor Brown had authority under Georgia statutes to seize the mill and limit profits to only 25 percent.[82] Under the circum-stances, Jackson followed Myers's instructions to cease all public auc-tions and submit to the bureau a sworn statement of costs on a quarterly basis.[83] Jackson vigorously protested against the acts that "have been passed by the Confederate Government & State of Georgia, compelling the Augusta Factory to abandon its former policy of selling its goods at auction to the highest bidder & forcing its president (in order to prevent seizure) to contract with said Governments & with charitable associations for its entire production at prices not half of those current in the market, resulting in a loss to its stockholders, on an average of more than $120,000 per month."[84] Under duress, Jackson resorted to subterfuge. Stockholders were given their dividends in cloth, which they in turn sold at the inflated public prices. Although the company had space for 5,000 more spindles and fifty looms, William Gregg observed that the Augusta mill proprietors expended dividends not on machinery but in the futility of blockade-running where profits were not controlled (*Daily South Carolinian*, June 4, 1864). Despite Confederate income taxes, Jackson's mill remained profitable, earning $552,000 in the six months ending in June 1863 and $1.8 million for the same period ending in June 1864.

Other Southern manufacturers also chafed under the military yoke. In North Carolina, Thomas M. Holt found after selling at government prices for five months that "I could buy with what money I had left, very little more cotton than I had at first."[85] His fellow cotton spinner Jasper Stowe believed "the object seems to be, to make this manufacturer subservient to the will of the Quarter Master department without regard to his individual right or relation to the country." Stowe found in his dealings with Myers's department that "perfect obedience to red tape is required" and that "the manufacturing interest is completely subjugated by military authority."[86]

Even individuals within the War Department believed Myers's powers to be excessive. Myers's staunch critic, the clerk John Jones, who often exhibited hostility toward Jewish Confederates, wrote in November 1862 that the people "are now sending ten thousand pairs of shoes to Lee's army in opposition to the will of the Jew Myers, Quartermaster-General, who says everything must be contracted and paid for by his agents, according to red-tape rule and regulations" (John Jones 1: 186). Jones also believed that Myers appointed and protected men both corrupt and incompetent to deal with manufacturers. Even President Davis demanded periodic explanations of Myers over the conduct of his corps of regulators. After a War Department report in November 1862 concluded that Alabama quartermasters were "speculating in food," Jones wrote, "Col.

Myers fails, I think, to make the exhibit required, and it may be the worse for him" (1: 198). Edward A. Pollard also found "a vague impression of the people of the South, that . . . the frauds and peculations of disbursing officers . . . could stagger belief," and that they would "terminate the last breath of confidence in the Davis government" (Pollard 153). That many of Myers's appointees kept poor records, engaged in personal speculations, and lost important financial records to the invading armies was beyond doubt.

In February 1862, one of Myers's first appointees, Major Julius Hessee at Mobile, was brought before an Army Court of Inquiry on twenty-four common charges specified by General Braxton Bragg. Local manufacturers attested that Hessee demanded loans and commissions from vendors, procured shoddy merchandise, lost cash books from his expenditures of several hundred thousand dollars, bought quantities of "double woof" Dog River factory osnaburg and from it fabricated "unfit" tents instead of uniforms, sold government property to private agents, and paid some manufacturers with depreciated Confederate notes while others got more reliable state currency.[87] Major Hessee ably and successfully defended himself against these imputations, which he said were based on mere rumor, slander, and personal enmity. His actions had been fully reported to and approved by Colonel Myers in Richmond, and then he reminded the court of bureau difficulties in supplying the army "in a time of revolution, when new governments were forming; when trade and business were disordered; when former resources were exhausted, and new means of supply to be looked for among a people unaccustomed to manufacture for themselves."[88] Myers was also drawn into other cases.

Major George W. Jones, another Alabama quartermaster, narrowly averted a Court of Inquiry. Jones drew upon the Florence, Huntsville, and Marion County mills and came under scrutiny when a news article under the signature of "Junius" alleged that he secured embargoed cotton, "not on Government account, which is transported from Huntsville to Lawrenceburg, Tennessee, and there exchanged for goods."[89] Through his transactions with factories at Lawrenceburg, Tennessee, Jones acquired "four hundred and seventy five (475) bales of osnaburgs," or 300,000 yards of materials, which he stored in a Tuscaloosa warehouse.[90] "Junius" forwarded his muckraking article to President Davis, who in turn demanded of Myers a "fuller and more specific report on the charges made, as soon as practicable."[91] Jones vigorously defended himself to Myers's satisfaction. The cloth was government property, which he evacuated to a place of safety. Myers made no further inquiry but ordered Jones to deliver the goods to manufacturing quartermasters George Cunningham in Atlanta and Livingston Mims in Mississippi. Then the offending Jones was reassigned to establish a clothing factory at either Tuscaloosa or Scottsville, "as in your discretion you may determine to be the most advantageous location."[92] There the affair ended despite general belief that Jones had intended to profit personally from his cargo.

Isaac T. Winnemore, Myers's personal friend and agent in charge of contracts with the Augusta factories, presented a more complicated case. Winnemore, a native of Pennsylvania, served with Myers in Louisiana at the outbreak of the war, when he was appointed Confederate quartermaster at New Orleans. In the new position, he expended large sums equipping troops, buying steamers, and building fortifications for the Crescent City. In the month of April 1862, his requisitions amounted to some $2.7 million.[93] Upon the evacuation of New Orleans, Myers sent Winnemore to the Augusta post, but the refugee quartermaster left behind in New Orleans a large volume of unpaid bills along with his department's files.[94]

Soon after Winnemore's arrival in Augusta, he found "a report was circulated that I had made a fortune, am living at a rate of great extravagance." A South Carolina general charged "that Mj. Winnemore must have made a large fortune as he was poor before the war, and is now living in great style and magnificently furnished."[95] One temptation for fraud was the pending business claims from New Orleans, some of which were certified by Winnemore and Myers for payment in Richmond while others were not.[96] Suspicions about Winnemore's character were general, perhaps because of his origins. President Davis refused to endorse Winnemore as a permanent officer in the Quartermaster Department, and three times the Confederate Congress rejected his appointment. But Myers loyally continued Winnemore in office as a provisional agent. Winnemore personally wrote Jefferson Davis about the charges of malfeasance, assuming that the rumors "must have reached your ear," and then hastened to Richmond "to lay my case personally before your excellency."[97] But Winnemore was "disappointed in this audience," as Davis refused to interrupt a Cabinet meeting to meet him.

An investigation ordered by Davis was conducted in a superficial manner. Winnemore claimed to have lost large assets "in the hands of the enemy," yet while at Augusta he acquired two slaves and $2,200 in Confederate notes. Apparently, like many quartermasters, he was living out of the provisions of his office. Although he was cleared of all charges, reports "of the most *indefinite* character" came to the War Department.[98] Nevertheless, Winnemore continued to discharge his duties as an Augusta quartermaster.

Another appointee of Myers who came under suspicion was Herman Hirsch, quartermaster at Savannah. Hirsch contracted with the Richmond factory for goods, employed 150 persons to make clothing, and engaged in business on his private account.[99] When the women of Savannah petitioned to sew undergarments for the soldiers, Myers advised Hirsch that "the object the ladies have in view is most commendable; and the subject is referred to your attention with instructions to make an [as] practicable arrangements [as] in your power, to aid the accomplishment of their purpose."[100] Hirsch was soon under investigation. After receiving "reports derogatory to him," the War Department ordered General Hugh W. Mercer, commanding on the Atlantic coast, "to convene a Board of Officers to inquire into the charge." Mercer believed he had a "small hope of proving any thing—for men in Major Hirsch's position, if dishonest, are usually sharp enough to cover up their transactions, so as to defy detection."[101] The matter was soon dropped, although Myers reprimanded Hirsch for some "highly reprehensible" business speculations.[102]

Subsequently, Colonel Eugene McLean, a former chief quartermaster in the Army of Tennessee, reconsidered Hirsch's case. McLean found that "Hirsch having acquired wealth during the war, having previously been in different circumstances, suspicions are directed against him of dishonest application of the funds of the government." As with many of Myers's appointments, Hirsch's "extensive duties, involving the expenditure of large sums of money, which have been entrusted to him, and the fact of his having grown rich, have centered public opinion against him." In this case, Colonel McLean found that "the usual prejudice exists against him in consequence of his Jewish extraction." But McLean discovered no dereliction of duty; rather "the system throughout this entire establishment is excellent, and he has exhibited extraordinary business capacity." Hirsch worked a large number of detailed men and prisoners of war, had recently "manufactured under contract upwards of 1000 hospital tents for the use of the army of Tennessee," built ambulances, produced a substantial number of military undergarments, and was both an excellent post and depot quartermaster.[103]

Even as Hirsch was exonerated a second time, other quartermasters came under scrutiny. In April 1863, Myers recommended the dismissal of Major D. H. Wood, an officer "responsible for military traffic through Richmond" (Kean 48). Wood administered the Richmond transportation office and was guilty of using government boxcars to move fifty barrels of sugar from Augusta to Richmond for private sale.[104] The general state of deprivation and low pay tempted officers such as Wood to violate Section 28 of the Confederate Military Act, which specifically forbade their making private purchases or speculations (*Charleston Mercury*, March 19, 1861). A Wilmington officer, speculating on his private account, was warned that "in the present state of the public mind it is more than any disbursing officer's reputation can stand to accumulate money by buying or selling."[105]

Perhaps no case in the Confederacy created greater anxiety about Myers's loose control over supplies than his patronage of Alfred M. Barbour, the chief quartermaster in Joseph E. Johnston's army. In Virginia, between First Bull Run and the Seven Days' campaign, Barbour was General Johnston's protégé and a bête noire of the press. Out of deference to Johnston, Myers endorsed all of Barbour's vouchers unquestioningly and thereby became an accomplice in the resulting imbroglio. At times Barbour's operations in Virginia rivaled those of the large Richmond depot, for he leased numerous warehouses in the city, maintained a fleet of 104 four-horse wagons and teams, and established at Richmond his own quartermaster staff.[106] From the commencement of the war through September 19, 1862, Myers reimbursed Barbour $6.3 million based upon some incomplete notations in a thin, small "Cash Book."[107] Myers kept Barbour in funds although the officer "never settled his accounts for a single quarter during his long service in the Army of Northern Virginia." Barbour refused to surrender his "Cash Book" during a War Department examination, which concluded that "the reputation for loose management and utter disregard of the public interest, which he has left in Richmond and throughout the country that constituted the field of his operations, is such as attaches to no other disbursing officer in the broad limits of the Confederacy who holds like power and necessarily destroys confidence in his present and future efficiency as a public officer—and the records of this office show that this impression is not made of mere 'public clamor.' "[108]

Nevertheless, Barbour followed General Johnston's command to the West, where he received "twenty millions of money" between April and October 1863, without rendering a single account to the quartermaster general.[109] Myers customarily complied with requests "for five million dollars, without any specification or explanation."[110] Barbour and Johnston, like Kirby Smith in the Trans-Mississippi, simply despaired of getting materials from the War Department. Upon assignment to Johnston's western command in November 1862, Barbour wrote, "I found the supplies of every character collected by these officers [such as Major Julius Hessee] so utterly inadequate to our demands that I never afterward expected any considerable aid from them."[111] Upon this rationale, the chivalrous Barbour forged ahead, making his own contracts with manufacturers.

He appointed his own set of procurement quartermasters, including William H. Browne at Mobile, L. L. Bambridge at Charleston, and W. M. Carey at Montgomery. He pressed them to purchase and manufacture army stores in competition with both state and departmental quartermasters.[112] In Charleston, where Edward Willis and G. S. Crafts manufactured military stores for Beauregard's forces and Hutson Lee procured for the Richmond bureau, Barbour's agent appeared and purchased 20,000 blankets from blockade-runners at an extravagant price of $24 each.[113] Myers's agent, Hutson Lee, pulled rank and impressed the blankets before they could be taken west, and Myers demanded an explanation of Barbour, which was not forthcoming. By one Richmond accounting, there were "perhaps twenty letters addressed to Major Barbour by this Department during this year on important subjects, to which he has made no replies, although all the time within mail communication."[114]

Although Barbour did not interfere with government manufacturing contracts, he moved very quickly to secure the goods being sold in the private market.[115] General Joseph E. Johnston authorized Barbour to "use all means in my power to obtain supplies from the productive States around me."[116] As a result Barbour created further confusion for the quartermaster general.

Eventually an inspecting quartermaster, Colonel McLean, was dispatched to Meridian, Mississippi, to make "a thorough inspection of Major Barbour's affairs, as complaints against him come from all quarters." McLean quickly discovered that Barbour held "large contracts with certain Jew houses for clothing and camp and garrison equipage, which supplies are received through Captain Casey, and Captain J. B. Moore, and which are almost worthless in material and workmanship." Barbour also held "a large amount of supplies stored in Montgomery, while he continues to make heavy estimates upon our other depots for articles scarce and needed."[117] Seemingly with Colonel Myers's approbation, Barbour made substantial contracts with Rosenberg and Company, an exile firm from New Orleans, and Stern and Company of Jackson, Mississippi. The companies manufactured uniforms from cloth secured at public sales or brought goods through the lines. Barbour's transactions with Stern and Company on April 1, 1863, amounted to $1 million, half of which was expended on 78,192 shirts at $48 a dozen and 76,764 pairs of underclothing at $40 per dozen. The costs were exorbitant, and the clothing was poorly made. Barbour paid $4.00 for shirts worth $1.71 at the Atlanta depot and $3.33 for drawers worth $1.09. Inspector McLean concluded that "even had the clothing been good, the contract would have been a bad one."[118]

In May 1863, Stern and Company delivered 14,000 shirts and 8,000 pairs of drawers to Captain Lamson, Barbour's quartermaster at Mobile, who sent them to Demopolis, Alabama, where they were "opened & distributed."[119] There were open complaints among the troops about the issues. Barbour and his local quartermaster insisted "the quality is very good," but General William J. Hardee, corps commander in the Army of Tennessee, appointed a Board of Survey to investigate the matter.[120] In one random lot of shoes, 102 of 137 pairs were "declared unfit for use by reason of being too small, not spiked, & badly made." Of 10,067 pairs of drawers in one shipment, 8,046 pairs were "unserviceable." The undergarments "were by far too small in the waist; whilst others were badly proportioned & shabbily made." A lot of 14,797 shirts was rejected as "all of them are too short & are without collars & waistbands" and were "better suited for 12 year old boys."[121] Soon after the inquiry, McLean found that Stern and Company, the contractors, had "left the Confederacy, and I have no confidence in their returning."[122]

In the early summer of 1863, Barbour expended $4.3 million, mostly in Mobile and Montgomery. In both places, his quartermasters and depots operated in competition with those of the Quartermaster Department. At Montgomery alone, in the last quarter of 1863, Barbour "paid upwards of 2300 vouchers amounting to upwards of $1,600,000."[123] Barbour's total expenditure of $25 million without an accounting rivaled the independent, but more responsible, operations of General Edmund Kirby Smith in the Trans-Mississippi district.

Public notice of Barbour's activity first appeared in the *Mobile Advertiser and Register*. George William Bagby, former editor of the *Southern Literary Messenger*, wrote that "it were policy to say nothing about this, but it is so much talked of on the streets that no advertisement could make it more notorious." The intrepid journalist revealed that a Confederate quartermaster was "discovered to be a defaulter in the small sum of $5,000,000." After military investigations were completed, "it is not improbable that an other cipher will finally have to be added to the shortness of his cash account."[124] A reporter for the *Charleston Mercury* wrote from Richmond that "it is well known here that a certain Quartermaster, or Commissary, who, before the war, could not get credit for five dollars, is now rioting in riches," for the accused "bought $200,000 or $300,000 worth of real estate, and thinks nothing of giving two or three thousand for a young negro" (*Charleston Mercury*, January 21, 1863).

Bagby's article charged that the unnamed Barbour "was living at the rate of five or ten thousand dollars a day; having carriages at his command; everything that was good in the matter of food; ate, like Dives, of the best that the poor markets of this country afford." Barbour was depicted as "clad in raiment of gold, on his sleeves, with wild ducks and pate foi gras on his table: and all this was presumed by innocent people to be derived from the salary of his office, which is equivalent to the purchasing of corn meal and such condiments as may make it palatable."[125] The Confederate War Department quickly ordered General Dabney Maury, then commanding the Gulf District, "to ascertain the name of the officer referred to, and to make an investigation into the matter."[126] Although Barbour forced Bagby into a letter of retraction, the stern Maury proved less tractable.[127] Barbour was ordered to Richmond, where a full investigation revealed a shortage in current accounts of at least $854,791.[128] In a "Statement of Differences Arising upon the Settlement of the Account of A. M. Barbour," the Quartermaster Department passed on the dubious bills to the Treasury Department for final settlement. Barbour's affairs were a public scandal and an embarrassment to the Quartermaster Department, and Myers was certainly damaged by their revelation.

Myers also suffered from scandals among the clothier generals of North Carolina. Again, Myers remitted funds to men who were publicly accused of fraud and extravagance. Two North Carolina quartermasters, Abraham Myers (no relation to the quartermaster general) and W. W. Peirce, were accused of serious breaches of conduct. The North Carolina Myers was a former Salisbury merchant who received large authority to engage in contracting and manufacturing.[129] On behalf of the state of North Carolina, Myers contracted with numerous local merchants, including his own firm of A. and W. Myers.[130] Under the terms of one contract with his own firm, Myers agreed for $12,700 to manufacture 1,000 tents from materials that "belonged to the State." In another contract, he agreed to furnish tents from his own materials for $25 each. In pursuit of these projects, Myers and his brother, Solomon, established themselves at Richmond and "contracted with the cotton mills here, to deliver to them a certain quantity of cloth, as fast as it could be manufactured." Myers then employed the services of Henry C. Jenks, formerly a clerk in "an old established mercantile house" in Richmond, "to cut 1000 tents from the State of North Carolina cloth."[131] The scam was to switch North Carolina duck canvas for ordinary osnaburg made at Richmond, but it did not work.

According to Jenks's testimony to the North Carolina adjutant general, "instead of using your cloth in whole to work the tents he bought common cloth at 10 cts pr yd and used your cloth in making his tents, which he sold at twenty five dollars a piece." The brothers, Abraham and Solomon, also had "some ten or fifteen women employed by the day for the State of North Carolina and the women made some two hundred tents and flies for Myers's individual account." When the state contract "for the thousand was finished, there was left between seven & eight thousand yards of duck which S. A. Myers kept and made tents of and sold at twenty five dollars each."[132] In rebuttal, Solomon Myers admitted to substituting cloths but insisted that no harm was done to the interests of the state. North Carolina quartermaster Lawrence O'Bryan Branch found no wrongdoing and recommended no punishment.[133] Within a year, Myers was again under attack. Nathan R. Mendenhall, a member of an important manufacturing family at Greensboro, North Carolina, and T. W. Allison swore in the Rowan County Quarter Sessions Court that they witnessed Myers receive from Richmond $100,000 but deposit only $80,000 in the local bank.[134] Some of the missing funds were later found in the quartermaster's office, but the rest disappeared.[135] Although Myers's shortages were an embarrassment, his career was unaffected.

Charges against W. W. Peirce, a Charlotte quartermaster principally responsible for contracts with the Rock Island factory, were equally unavailing. Colonel Peter Mallett, son of a Fayetteville manufacturer, charged Peirce and his son, a clerk, with "neglect of duty, and unbecoming conduct, etc."[136] Nothing came of the charges until an inquiry was ordered by the War Department. An investigating quartermaster from Richmond "was greatly embarrassed & his report delayed, by the disinclination of this officer [Peirce] to submit his affairs to inspection; by his habits, which render it impossible to transact business with him with any degree of satisfaction; and, by the confusion and want of system that pervade his affairs." Peirce held agreements with 106 contractors, mostly "able-bodied men," and yet "no copies of his contracts have ever been forwarded to this department, and no list of names or numbers of contractors were kept in the office."[137]

Peirce's son, the clerk, was "but 21 yrs of age, without business experience, capacity, training or habits." In expenditures that were "unauthorized and extravagant," the younger Peirce built a storehouse "that was unnecessary, as he had already, more room, for storage, in the large building—formerly a hotel—than was necessary."[138] He erected "a guard house at a cost of $2,680" for which there were no guards, but it was occupied by a brigadier general without authority. Young Peirce also purchased Charlotte's Lawlin Excelsior Gas Works for $102,459. He employed numerous clerks and ninety-one of his own slaves on public payroll. The inspector recommended that father and son "be immediately relieved," but under war conditions no action was taken.[139]

The recurring charges of fraud received full and graphic depiction on the floor of the Confederate Congress and in the press. In fact, congressional investigating committees were often overwhelmed by the flood of unsubstantiated accusations against the War Department and its contractors. On April 17, 1863, Congressman Henry Foote, a political gadfly from Tennessee, initiated an investigation into the case of Quartermaster Wood, who was described as "formerly a horse trader, and so poor that he could not get credit for a beefsteak," but "since his connection with the Government, accumulated an immense fortune."[140] An Atlanta quartermaster whom Foote professed to know was "estimated to be worth five millions of dollars, though before the war he could not count more than twenty thousand to save his life." Quartermasters were "surfeited with money," Foote continued: "Pass your eye around and you will see these quartermasters and commissaries living in palatial wealth, with their fine houses, driving their fine horses, (and some of them with body servants) dressing in the finest style, and many of them possessing the most magnificent landed estates." Many of these men who reckoned "their wealth by the hundred thousand and some of them by the million—were before the war, poor men, living in their humble cottages and surrounded by scarcely a scant support."[141] Although Foote was given to hyperbole and emotional outbursts, no champion for quartermasters rose on the floor of Congress to challenge him. The outrage created by constant charges of quartermaster criminality did much to undermine Myers's position as the controlling agent of Southern manufacturing. They only strengthened the hand of his critics and speeded his subsequent fall from the Confederate hierarchy.[142]

Despite Myers's control of factories, the erratic flow of supplies to the troops raised criticism, and his efforts fell short of the full mobilization demanded by some Southern army officers. Deprivation among the troops was a strong indication of his bureau's ineffectiveness. Basil Washington Duke, an officer in Morgan's Tennessee cavalry, testified that "it was hard to maintain discipline, when men are required to perform the most arduous and harassing duties without being clothed, shod, paid, or fed" (Duke 373). These were all Myers's responsibilities. He faulted Myers's bureau for saying "these articles cannot be procured," when every Federal raid disclosed filled warehouses "unknown to all but the officials and employees, that hoarded and stored them away" (374). Commands would often file the requisite papers only to have the Richmond office respond that the "regiment was unknown." "There were certain officers at Richmond," wrote the exasperated Duke, "who, if their souls had been tied up with red tape, indorsed in accordance with the latest orders, and stuffed into pigeon holes, would have preferred it to a guarantee of salvation" (320).

Understandably, Myers developed bitter altercations with a succession of military field commanders over his policies. He fought with Thomas R. R. Cobb over military firewood; Alexander R. Lawton incurred his wrath by seizing and distributing the cargo of the blockade-runner *Bermuda*; and General Henry A. Wise was denied supplies for threadbare troops after the debacle on Roanoke Island.[143] Wise, a former Virginia governor and an owner of the vituperative *Richmond Enquirer*, proved to be one of Myers's most untiring critics.

In the summer of 1862, following the death of a son and the loss of most of his command by the Union seizure of Roanoke Island, General Wise attempted to refit his exchanged men at Richmond.[144] Abraham Myers ruled that under military regulations the troops were financially responsible for their loss of clothing, blankets, and accouterments. This was acknowledged policy. To an Alabama regiment that lost its baggage in an engagement at Dranesville, Myers explained, "I do not feel at liberty to authorize even under the peculiar circumstances of this case, an issue of clothing & the payment in full of commutation money to the same troops."[145] The only form of relief lay in a special act of the Confederate Congress. As an added irritant, then Secretary of War Judah P. Benjamin simultaneously threatened to disband Wise's famous legion, a military unit recruited and trained by him early in the war.[146]

As a fire-eating secessionist who had ordered the hanging of John Brown, Wise was not to be put off by bureaucratic humbug. The staff officers in the War Department were a special object of his wrath. On July 14, 1862, he went to General Lee with another complaint against Myers "that though the proper estimates have been made, sent in, his troops have not been paid neither within the last eight months." This was Myers's responsibility, but he responded that there were "no estimates for the pay of Genl Wise's command remaining over in this office."[147] Confederate troops frequently went without pay for months, but being stationed in Richmond and on friendly terms with the political leadership, Wise aggressively pressed the plaint of his legion. In response, Myers lodged a vigorous protest against officers coming to see him personally.[148]

Wise's controversy took a new turn in November 1862, when a contingent of Confederate soldiers "marched through the city without shoes, *in the snow*" (John Jones 1: 186). The *Richmond Whig*, a persistent critic of the military supply system, printed an article by "Bedford," who described the troops as naked and the Quartermaster Bureau as "inadequate to the task" of clothing them (*Richmond Whig*, October 21, 1862). A few days later a "private" cited "incontrovertible proof" that the armies of the South were "huddled around a scanty fire . . . with no tent to shelter them from the inclemency of the season, with no clothing to protect them from the piercing cold, with no blankets to wrap them in the few hours of sleep, and no shoes to cover their feet in the rugged marches" (*Richmond Whig*, November 1, 1862). In contrast, most Federal forces were well provisioned with tents, overcoats, blankets, uniforms, and food. Contrary to Myers's explicit advice, the *Whig* editorially called for county courts and voluntary associations to raise aid (*Richmond Whig*, November 4, 1862). Then on November 10, several regiments paraded down 9th Street in front of the War Department, and residents observed "numbers of soldiers marching barefoot through the melting snow." While the ragged procession was taking place, explained the *Whig*, "the Quartermaster General and some thousands of able bodied young clerks, were sitting by rousing fires, toasting their well-shod feet, and thinking of anything but the soldiers" (*Richmond Whig*, November 10, 1862). Myers's department "was wanting in the forethought, the comprehension, and the energy demanded by a proper regard for the well-being of the army and the vigorous prosecution of the war" (*Richmond Whig*, November 13, 1862). In a word, Myers's bureau had not developed the methodology of system and planning that characterized the Ordnance Bureau.

From his brigade headquarters near Chaffin's Farm, General Henry Wise now again seized the cudgel. In a signed article to the *Whig*, he repeated an earlier conversation with Myers: "My men are suffering for shoes—requisitions were made, the reply of the Quartermaster General, Col Myers, was 'Let them suffer' " (*Richmond Whig*, November 19, 1862). Wise denied Myers's "assurances" that the Virginia troops were getting regulation issues (*Richmond Whig*, November 12, 1862). As the winter snows deepened, the Richmond press heatedly debated the growing deprivation of the army.

On November 19, the *Whig* cited a major general to the effect that "one-third of the men of his Division are without shoes" (*Richmond Whig*, November 19, 1862). A staff officer in Hays's Louisiana Brigade found that "among 1500 men reported for duty there are 400 totally without covering of any kind for their feet"; some had neither blankets nor underclothing while "overcoats, from their rarity, are objects of curiosity" (Alexander 318).[149] One quartermaster found that "sixteen hundred men of his Division are barefoot" (*Richmond Whig*, November 19, 1862). The press found that a requisition for 19,000 brogans for General Jackson's army was unfilled (*Richmond Enquirer*, November 14, 1862). Death by exposure and disease exceeded by a large ratio all battle casualties.

The editors of the *Richmond Enquirer* gave Myers an opportunity to present his views. He rebutted that the battles of the summer forced the abandonment of large quantities of supplies, while the blockade and the limited capacity of Southern mills made replacement difficult. The soldiers, too, he could not omit saying, were improvident, for "many a blanket is thrown aside in the weary march on a warm day" (*Richmond Enquirer*, November 12, 1862). At least one officer was charged with selling clothing drawn for his company.[150] After this display, the *Enquirer* exonerated Myers of malfeasance: "a man may be an honest man and a worthy officer, and yet not be an angel." As for supply, the *Enquirer* rejoined, "there has been a good deal of exaggeration and misapprehension as to the deficiencies of our army" (*Richmond Enquirer*, November 12, 1862).

The *Richmond Whig* responded by citing a reporter for the *Rockingham Register* who "noted yesterday many of the men of the 10th Regiment wading through the snow without the sign of a shoe upon their feet." Many soldiers, "with their blankets wrapped around them, sat by the comfortless camp fires, trying to shield their feet, and shivering bodies from the cold snow and piercing winds." A correspondent of the *Petersburg Express* traveling with the army agreed that "many of our boys are suffering very much for the want of shoes and other articles of clothing" (*Richmond Whig*, November 19, 1862). The *Whig* insisted that "the army is suffering terribly, and if the Quartermaster General does not know this, then the sooner some one takes his place, who will keep himself advised of the condition of the army, the better" (*Richmond Whig*, November 13, 1862).

In apparent contrast to the government, relief associations, ladies' societies, state agencies, friends, and families responded in an overwhelming manner. The Richmond Young Men's Christian Association collected over 6,000 pairs of shoes. South Carolina authorities sent 7,000 coats and 6,000 blankets to McGowan's brigade (*Charleston Mercury*, October 28, 1862). War clerk Jones recorded on November 10 that "a committee of citizens to-day obtained an order from the War Department, for the impressment of all the boots, shoes, blankets, and overcoats in the shops" (John Jones 1: 186). Myers deprecated such self-help; as Jones noted, "they are now sending two thousand pairs of shoes to Lee's army in opposition to the will of the Jew Myers, Quartermaster General, who says every thing must be contracted and paid for by his agents, according to red-tape rule and regulation" (1: 186).

In the meantime, General Wise's formal charges against Myers were submitted to the Adjutant General Samuel Cooper for consideration. Cooper refused to decide whether his old friend had uttered the offending words, "let them suffer," and so sent Wise's "letter to the Quartermaster-General before either the Secretary of War or the President saw it" (1: 203). Officers in the line sometimes resorted to duels, but Myers used the interlude to prepare a "charge and specifications against Brig Genl. Henry A. Wise P.A.C.S.," which he in turn submitted to the secretary of war.[151] In the document, he formally denied uttering "with indifference, 'let them suffer.' "[152] Myers then formally requested a court martial since Wise's accusation "in regard to my official conduct, has been made the subject of much newspaper comment, affecting both my personal and official character." Since he was "prevented by the regulations of the service from vindicating myself through the public print," he called upon Secretary James Seddon to endorse a formal, public judicial investigation.[153]

In the wake of the debate, Myers invited reporters from both the *Whig* and *Enquirer* to inspect the Clothing Bureau, under the supervision of Major Richard Waller. Reporters interviewed James B. Ferguson and his brother, William. James Ferguson promised a larger effort with the introduction of foreign supplies into the Confederacy. William Ferguson challenged the accusations of Wise and the *Whig* that "the Quartermaster

THE REIGN OF QUARTERMASTERS 81

General and his subordinates are not using sufficient energy in obtaining supplies for the army." He reported that the department held "contracts for more than a million pairs of shoes, and as many blankets." Uniforms had been plentifully supplied, and "cloth for a million men has been contracted for—all the resources of the South are employed in furnishing supplies for the army." In the preceding year, the Richmond depot alone, with 60 cutters and 2,000 women constantly employed, issued 153,347 blankets, 320,000 pairs of shoes, "and a proportionate amount of other clothing." Each day the Clothing Bureau manufactured 2,500 additional garments. The young Ferguson concluded that Myers "feels the deepest interest in the comfort of the army and is using his utmost energy to supply them."[154] There was merit in this rebuttal, for troops were frequently improvident. Others sold military clothing to secure money for their families.

The whole imbroglio stirred up by General Wise disappeared in the flurry of military activity surrounding the campaign at Fredericksburg in November and December 1862. The *Whig*, for its part, surrendered the battle with a lame editorial on "the lack of manufacturing machinery in the confederate States" (*Richmond Whig*, November 22, 1862).

Alexander H. H. Stuart, a prewar Whig representative from Staunton, attempted to launch a Confederate Congressional investigation into the quality of Myers's tenure in office, but the effort failed. Stuart submitted to the War Department a paper on "the alleged mal-administration of the Quarter Master's Department at Staunton by Col. Michael G. Harman."[155] Harman operated the Staunton depot, which served as the base for Confederate offensive operations in the Valley and Maryland, and he enjoyed the confidence of General Thomas J. "Stonewall" Jackson, under whose command his brother served. Stuart was apparently solicitous toward the Staunton woolen factory and other small Valley factories which were under Harman's direct control. While Myers was willing to audit the accounts of the Staunton officer, he found Stuart's charges "were professedly but a reiteration of rumors that were in circulation in regard to the general administration of these departments, upon which he based the suggestion that they should be investigated by a committee of Congress."[156] To Myers's satisfaction, Major Harman's accounts revealed no discredit to his administration, and the general investigation was quashed.[157]

As the winter campaigns of 1862 ended, Myers found a political threat on a new front. The Georgia legislature passed a resolution requesting that William Porcher Miles's Military Affairs Committee investigate "the misconduct of Quartermasters, Commissaries, Surgeons, &c." The hopes of the Georgians were dashed when Edward Sparrow of Louisiana, a committee member, suggested that "investigations into the misfeasance and malfeasance of the officers named in the resolutions was the proper duty of the Secretary of War" (*Richmond Examiner*, February 6, 1863). "Most of the charges . . . had been discovered to be unfounded," Sparrow continued, but nevertheless with Myers and his colleagues "it was a labor of love to inquire into all cases of malfeasance occurring in their respective departments."[158] On February 14, 1863, Secretary James Seddon formally requested Myers to ascertain "if the alleged abuses exist."[159] Myers subsequently dispatched Colonel Aurelius F. Cone of the Clothing Depot to inspect "the administration of the Quarter Master Department at Columbus and Dalton."[160]

The Cone tour was quickly completed. As in previous investigations, no criminality was uncovered. The Columbus depot had shipped 1,800 inferior uniforms to Knoxville and fifty-one cases of clothing, which were later condemned by a Board of Survey, to Charleston.[161] Francis W. Dillard, the depot quartermaster, was an officer of proven ability. In June 1862, his "monthly production of 240 wooden boxes of uniforms, which filled fourteen railroad cars, were shipped to the Quartermaster Depot at Richmond for distribution in the field" (Standard 37). At Dalton, Georgia, Cone ordered the dismissal of nine clerks, the only result of his investigation.[162]

The public pressure on the Quartermaster Department did produce several limited reform measures. In December 1862, the control of railroad transportation was transferred from Myers by General Order No. 98.[163] The Confederate Congress prescribed criminal penalties for those quartermasters misusing either public funds or transportation.[164] And supernumeraries attached to the depots as clerks were brought under the force of the Conscription Act.[165] Under prodding by Secretary James Seddon and Jefferson Davis, Myers helped draft General Order No. 13 "to restrain competition between quartermasters in the purchase of army supplies."[166] Each state became a special purchasing district with a designated quartermaster holding exclusive control "of all purchases of supplies needed by this Department."[167] The quartermaster manufacturing depots were removed from the authority of district commanding generals.[168] Operations at the Richmond Clothing Depot were also systematized into departments devoted respectively to clothing, shoes, and contracts.[169] The reforms did little to placate irate manufacturers and yet fell short of the full mobilization demanded by the army. Myers was increasingly caught between the upper and nether millstones.

The winter of 1862–63 created renewed strains upon the supply system. Increasingly, General Lee's letters made references to destitute and barefoot troops. Davis forwarded General Lee's January report to Myers, in which the Virginia commander noted the "strong representations of the scarcity of provisions in his command, and of great delay in the transportation of stores of every description which were essential to the Army of Northern Virginia, menaced, as it was, with the advance of the enemy."[170] Examples of delays abounded. Thirty carloads of uniform cloth and stores lay on the sidetracks at Charlotte, and trains took two weeks to move thirteen boxes of clothing and shoes from Florida to Dalton, Georgia (*Richmond Enquirer*, November 28, 1862). An unguarded train was looted at Meridian, Mississippi.[171] In the face of these criticisms, Myers took refuge in the ageless practice of bureaucrats: he invited James L. Corley, Lee's quartermaster, to make continued requisitions for supplies that were not yet purchased.

Myers's official correspondence became increasingly acerbic. In March, he lectured General Lee, whose army was already on short rations, on "the absolute importance of economy" in the use of forage, suggesting that "the men should be required to make troughs of some kind, so as to save the waste."[172] As Lee positioned his army along the Rappahannock River in preparation for General Joseph Hooker's initiation of spring hostilities, Myers sent Corley, army quartermaster, 6,000 blankets, the first available in several months. But field jackets he refused to issue. As he explained to the incredulous Corley, "I have on hand some 30,000 of these garments which I desire to hold on to, as far as possible, for the cold weather."[173] While previous battlefields were gleaned principally for the benefit of invalids and noncombatants, after the battle of Chancellorsville Myers pleaded with Corley "that all the blankets and overcoats captured from, or abandoned by the enemy, in the recent battles, should be promptly secured, and sent to this City, that they may be cleaned and otherwise prepared for issue to our troops."[174] In a further indication of his reduced circumstances, Myers proposed the collection of all Confederate military blankets for reissue in the fall season.

While the Army of Northern Virginia faced growing deprivations, the troops around Richmond and in the Lower South were relatively better provisioned and clothed than others. North Carolina maintained a Richmond warehouse stocked with 10,000 uniforms, while other state depots contained thousands more. An officer in Lee's army voiced concern over this, writing that "we made requisitions for uniforms and never get them" and that "the best clothing provided for our army is distributed to the soldiers and second class militia about Richmond, whilst the inferior and refuse clothing is sent to the army" (*Richmond Enquirer*, November 3, 1863). The supply situation became more desperate with Lee's invasion of Pennsylvania in June 1863. The Confederate offensive drew supplies from the depot at Staunton, connected by railroad with Richmond. Several thousand wagons hauled stores along the army's invasion route.

As the Gettysburg campaign unfolded, Myers saw an opportunity to replenish Confederate stores from the occupied territory. For this purpose a representative of the Quartermaster Department, George F. Maynard, was detailed to accompany Lee's headquarters "to Winchester and thence as occasion may require, into Maryland and Pennsylvania." Maynard's responsibility was "to gather such army supplies as most needed by this Department, especially horses, harnesses, & shoes, and to send all such as can be spared from the immediate wants of the troops to interior points within this State for safety."[175] Regimental quartermasters were supplied with barrels of Confederate currency in anticipation of buying essential goods. As the invasion progressed, Myers curtailed shipments to Staunton. When James L. Corley requisitioned a lot of shoes for the Army of Northern Virginia in July, the quartermaster general responded, "I have been in anticipation of receiving stores from you and not to supply you."[176]

The pressing need for supplies contributed to Lee's difficulties at Gettysburg. Barefooted men were sent to the rear. When the Army of Northern Virginia dispersed across southern Pennsylvania to better provision itself, the Federal forces under General George G. Meade concentrated for battle. The battle at Gettysburg was precipitated by a Confederate attempt to secure supplies. According to Major General Henry Heth of A. P. Hill's Corps, on June 29, 1863, upon "hearing that a supply of shoes was to be obtained in Gettysburg, eight miles distant from Cashtown, and greatly needing shoes for my men, I directed General Pettigrew to go to Gettysburg and get these supplies."[177] Edward P. Alexander, Lee's artillery commander at Gettysburg, recalled that "Heth heard that shoes could be purchased in Gettysburg and, with Hill's permission, authorized Pettigrew's brigade to go there next day and get them" (Alexander 380).[178] As the Confederates drove into Gettysburg, the memorable first day of battle was precipitated on Seminary Ridge.

On the second day of the engagement, James L. Corley sent Myers an urgent request for "twenty thousand pairs of shoes as quickly as possible." Myers forwarded half the order from Richmond to Staunton but decided to withhold "the other ten thousand pairs until I hear from you."[179] In fact, there were no shoes in the Richmond depot. A frantic appeal to Hutson Lee uncovered "a few thousand pairs in Columbia" and others on board a blockade-runner at Wilmington.[180] As these were rounded up, the spent Confederate army retired to the banks of the Potomac River. Federal cavalry commander General Judson Kilpatrick created more problems for Myers by pitching into the Confederate rear guard and seizing "the wagons of Ewell's entire corps," a train several miles long.[181] Lee moved back into Virginia with his army "a little footsore, and much in need of shoes for man and horse."[182] When Myers could not provide the necessary refit for the army, he lost any remaining confidence in his leadership among the line officers.

After consultation with Lee, Davis elected to replace Myers with "an officer of greater ability and one better qualified to meet the pressing emergencies of the service."[183] But his removal of the quartermaster general proved to be one of the most tortuous ordeals of his administration. Unlike Cabinet secretaries who were dismissed with alacrity, Myers had a strong coterie of friends and admirers within the Confederate Congress, as did his wife, Marion Twiggs Myers. While Myers carefully cultivated political leaders impressed by his vast patronage and control over the larger share of the Confederate budget, his wife bedazzled them.

According to Edward A. Pollard, who missed little capital gossip, after Gettysburg there was the Battle of Richmond in which Jefferson Davis ousted "the most important officer in his government—his Quartermaster-General—because a female member of the family of the latter has presumed to criticize Mrs. Davis figure" (Pollard 157). Other witnesses in the War Department attested that society politics, not the lack of organization or threadbare condition of the army, hastened Myers's decline. The women's war, while real, was but a diversion from the central issue: deficient system and planning within the Quartermaster Bureau. Upon learning of the clothier general's political difficulties, James Barron Hope, a naval officer on service within the bureau, wrote his wife that "I've no doubt some of the female statesmen of Richmond are at the bottom of it."[184] Robert Kean, chief of the Bureau of War, thought the quarrel originated in a report "to Mrs. President by a gentleman who himself told me of it, that Mrs. Myers had called her [Mrs. Davis] a SQUAW, Mrs. Davis being of very dark complexion" (Kean 90). Both Marion Twiggs Myers and Varina Howell Davis were active in Richmond's parlor society and had powerful allies made previously in Washington and among the military elite. Mrs. Myers's purported insult sent Varina Davis into high dudgeon, whereupon "the lady President sought her out and charged her with it, Mrs. Myers denied it, burst into tears, and a high scene ensued" (90). Pollard, no admirer of Davis, ungraciously found Varina Davis to be a "brawny, able-bodied woman, who had much more of masculine mettle than of feminine grace." To the point of the controversy Pollard acidly wrote, "her complexion was tawny, even to the point of mulattoism; a woman loud and coarse in her manner." He added that Mrs. Davis, whom most acquaintances considered a model Southern lady, "was excessively coarse and physical in her person, and in whom the defects of nature had been repaired neither by the grace of manners nor the charms of conversation" (Pollard 154). Rumors of the controversy quickly spread, undoubtedly fed by angry line officers. While aboard a Southern train, Mary Chesnut described a conversation about Colonel Myers of "the tribe of Levi." Marion Myers, the colonel's wife, Chesnut concluded, was "of the 'lost tribe,' unless she is awfully slandered" (Chesnut 459). One of Marion Myers's admirers, Willie Munford, wrote "for private circulation (strictly private) a burlesque poem satirically dealing with Mrs. Myers quarrel with Mrs. Davis," but upon finding herself disparaged, Varina Davis confronted the embarrassed poet (Chesnut 532). According to Secretary of the Navy Stephen

Mallory, Varina Davis was herself an accomplished mimic who gave devastating renditions of social adversaries in the popular pantomimes of wartime Richmond.[185] The women's war was further enriched with the arrival of Rachael E. Myers on the truce boat at Norfolk.

A late resident of South Carolina but recently domiciled in New York, in 1862 Rachael E. Myers secured permission at Washington to return to Charleston to dispose of her family estate.[186] She was a "free colored person of Indian descent," a mulatto, and grew up in Charleston's St. Michael's Church as "a remarkably pretty and more remarkably clever girl." There in her youth she was "kept by the head of the Quarter Master department, Myers, by whom she had some two or three children." From Myers and other patrons, she "acquired property to the value of some $15 or $10,000." Rachael Myers entered the Confederacy, via Norfolk, with the understanding that after disposing of her property in Charleston, she would "take her family over to Europe, or to Canada." But Rachael Myers encountered some difficulties in securing an exit visa from the Confederate government.[187] Apparently the intervention of both John Jones, the diarist who was then serving as clerk of the passport office, and Jefferson Davis was required to send her safely north.[188] Throughout the ordeal, Abraham Myers relied on the discretion of Congressman William Porcher Miles and other supporters to smooth the way for Rachael's exit. This was more grist for Richmond's gossip mills.

The women's contretemps was only a skirmish before the real battle. As the debate moved into the Confederate legislature, Myers's friends attempted a preemptive maneuver. William Porcher Miles, powerful chair of the House Military Affairs Committee, and Senator Louis T. Wigfall of Texas, who together had demanded the surrender of Fort Sumter in April 1861, now allied themselves with Myers against Jefferson Davis. They led a campaign on two occasions to secure Myers's promotion to brigadier general, an act deemed sufficient to silence his critics within the administration and protect his status as quartermaster general. The original legislation creating Myers's bureau authorized the appointment of a colonel as quartermaster general, if the president so chose. Myers, a lieutenant colonel, served in the office as acting assistant quartermaster general until February 15, 1862, when he was promoted and made quartermaster general.[189] In October 1862, Myers's congressional friends passed a bill stipulating that he should receive "the rank, pay, and allowances of a brigadier general"; however, Davis vetoed this measure.[190] The bill was passed again by an overwhelming vote in March 1863.[191] Again Davis resisted. On April 28, 1863, seventy-six representatives and senators petitioned the Confederate president to make Myers a brigadier general because he had "shown himself able, honest, and diligent in the discharge of his responsible & laborious duties."[192]

Despite the congressional pressure, Davis was determined to replace Myers or place a brigadier general over him, preferably one with field experience. He considered two officers. According to John Jones, Howell Cobb was approached but declined because "his wife is ill, and he prefers to remain with her; besides, he doubts his qualifications—he who was Secretary of the Treasury of the United States" (John Jones 1: 329). The other officer may have been James Chesnut Jr. of South Carolina who, like Cobb, was deeply involved in efforts to bolster the defenses of his home state. When Davis's efforts became known, there was a flood of indignation from Myers's Greek chorus in Congress, a group derisively referred to by the press as "Moses men." As Jones wrote, "it has got out that the President intends to dispense with the services of Mr. Myers, the Jew Quartermaster-General, and Mr. Miles, member of the Congress from South Carolina, who happens to be his friend, is characteristically doing the part of a friend for his retention" (1: 354). Robert M. T. Hunter of Virginia, generally a supporter of Davis, warned Secretary of War James Seddon "to let the Quartermaster-General alone, that he is popular with Congress, and that his friends are active" (1: 364). Nevertheless, a month after the battle of Gettysburg, on July 28, 1863, Secretary James Seddon recommended one of Myers's old antagonists, Brigadier General Alexander R. Lawton of Georgia, as quartermaster general, and on August 7 Davis made the interim appointment and forwarded the nomination to Congress.[193] Officially, Myers was not removed, but as a colonel he was outranked by General Lawton.

Lawton, a Georgian who had been trained at West Point, class of 1839, and Harvard, was a successful Savannah lawyer and planter before the war. He served as president of the Augusta and Savannah Railroad from 1849 to 1854 and counted himself a political opponent of Governor Joseph E. Brown.[194] Although Lawton had limited experience with logistics problems, he was an experienced administrator and held a commendable record as a field officer. Early in the war he commanded the Georgia volunteers who seized Fort Pulaski. Later, after making Lee's acquaintance on the Georgia coast, he brought his brigade to Virginia and served with distinction under Jackson in the battles of the Seven Days, Second Manassas, and Antietam, where he was wounded.[195] Fully recuperated, on August 10, 1863, Lawton arrived at the quartermaster general's office and was introduced to the staff by Myers. Kean, in the Bureau of War, noted that "the event which has put the gossips agog in the last two days is the taking off of the Quartermaster General's head" (Kean 89). The view among the staff officers was that Myers "has long been the object of the President's dislike," but that the colonel had "a good deal of popularity in Congress and this will make his friends furious" (89). James Hope, a Norfolk naval officer, was present as the officers exchanged civilities around the bureau. Like many others, he thought the departing Myers was "a capital officer & full of urbanity" who was "a victim to Mr. Davis's personal animosity."[196] General Lawton was a "gentleman" and "a very handsome, pleasant looking man." The Georgian immediately put the men at ease by announcing that he did " 'not desire, nor intend' to make any changes in the Staff" and that he had " 'no friends' to advance."[197]

The seemingly tranquil transfer of power was deceptive. The *Richmond Enquirer* immediately editorialized that "Col. Myers did his duty, or used his best endeavors to do it as well as the difficulties of his position admitted" (*Richmond Enquirer*, August 21, 1863).[198] A few days later an anonymous "X" from Demopolis, Alabama, used the pages of the *Enquirer* to excoriate Jefferson Davis over the issue. Myers, "X" wrote, was the architect of the Confederate supply system, where "there is not a single department but what has its depots well filled, manufactories of every description increasing daily" (*Richmond Enquirer*, August 29, 1863). But if the army were profligate and if the impressment and conscription acts bore heavily on individuals or companies, Myers was the scapegoat.

On September 1, 1863, a new contribution to the controversy appeared in the *Richmond Examiner* as a "long and ironical letter signed 'Orient' " (Kean 103). The satirist depicted Jefferson Davis as a "humble-minded, but infallible" oriental despot ruling with the aid of "Yahoos." Alluding to the battle of the wives, "Orient" wrote, "sir, you may write till your face is yellow as a Comanche squaw's, and until your hair is kinky as a Guinea negro's, before you put Myers back into his place, or make any mortal entertain a single doubt as to the causes of his expulsion." He continued, "when Congress first began to interfere about Myers, our President swore (it was before he got religion), that he would be d——d if Myers should ever be a Brigadier General." Yet Myers was "a quiet, elderly, meritorious Left-tenant Colonel" who suffered great financial losses because of the war. Union General Benjamin Butler had lately seized the Colonel's New Orleans property, and the writer had "seen an auctioneer's catalogue of the sale, under the confiscation act, of all the real and personal property of the said Myers." Nevertheless, the Confederate oriental despot was unlikely to "restore Myers, though the salvation of the human race depended upon it" (*Richmond Examiner*, September 1, 1863).

The press attacks upon Davis were echoed within the Confederate Congress. James and Mary Chesnut were in the center of this storm. As Mary Chesnut aptly wrote, "the Confederate Congress devoted the winter of 1863 to a hand-to-hand fight with Mr. Davis on account of Mr. Quartermaster General Myers." The battle was arranged, she believed, not by Colonel Myers, but rather by "the friends of Mrs. Myers, led by Mr. Miles, and the enemies of Mr. Davis formed a brigade of great strength, formidable indeed for perfect equipment and drill" (Chesnut 438).

The fourth session of the first Confederate Congress, which met from December 7, 1863, to February 18, 1864, frequently departed from recriminations over defeats at Vicksburg, Gettysburg, and Chattanooga, for which some blamed Davis, and from debates over impressment, substitutes, and corruption in the quartermaster and commissary corps, to weigh the fate of Myers. On December 10, 1863, Senator Edward Sparrow of Louisiana introduced a resolution inquiring whether "the Quartermaster General is discharging the duties of that office, and if not, who is; whether that person has given bond; whether he has been confirmed by the Senate; and whether he is an officer of the Confederate States army" (Kean 126; *Journal of the Congress of the Confederate States of America* 3: 456). Agreed to unanimously, the "curious" resolution forced Davis to respond on December 23 with a lengthy and legalistic defense of his interim appointment.[199]

Senator Louis T. Wigfall of Texas, still chafing over military defeats in the West, claimed that Davis's motives were personal and that "Colonel

Myers was still the quartermaster-general."[200] The Senate had never given its consent to Lawton's appointment and had been cheated out of the right by the chief executive. On January 21, 1864, the Senate Committee on Military Affairs concurred, and in a report that encompassed "forty-one pages of foolscap" stated that the ousted colonel was the legal quartermaster general and was "by law authorized and required to discharge the duties thereof."[201] The report faulted Davis, for Lawton had not been confirmed as a brigadier by the Senate, had not given bond, and was exercising duties "to which he has never been appointed by the consent of either the provisional Congress or the Senate." Reporting for the Senate Committee on Military Affairs, Edward Sparrow of Louisiana declared, "The committee believe that A. R. Lawton is not Quartermaster General, nor legally exercising the office, and that every dollar which has been drawn from the Treasury, for the use of the Quartermaster General's Department, since the 10th day of August last, has been issued without authority and in violation of law."[202] Almost half of the War Department's annual budget of $400 million was in dispute. The full Senate endorsed the report by a vote of fifteen to six. On February 12, Senator Wigfall, who was prepared to strip Davis of all his appointive powers, again prodded Davis to reply. Fortunately for the president, the House, after considerable verbal thrashing, refused to concur in this assault.[203]

When the Confederate chief executive finally sent General Alexander Lawton's name forward for confirmation in January 1864, another vicious debate ensued, much of it in secret legislative sessions. Senator Sparrow refused to permit Lawton's name to be presented for a vote. Myers then deepened and prolonged the agony by lodging a suit in the Richmond district court to receive his pay "as quartermaster general" (Kean 126).[204] In frustration, on March 4 Lawton requested to be relieved from "this responsible & thankless office."[205] Only in February 1864 did the affair finally came to an end, when the Confederate attorney general ruled that Lawton's appointment had "been duly and legally made."[206] Faced with the removal of either Davis or of Myers, the Congress finally acquiesced.

The office General Lawton assumed was beset with critical financial and logistic problems. John Jones noted that "an expose of funds in the hands of disbursing agents shows there are nearly seventy millions of dollars not accounted for" (John Jones 1: 182). The Virginia troops were unpaid for six months because the Treasury Department would not honor the quartermaster general's requisitions.[207] Unpaid bills to Southern manufacturers amounted to $47.6 million and were increasing rapidly.[208] The *Richmond Enquirer* lamented, "with gin- houses and warehouses stored with cotton, we are scarce of the plainest cotton goods," and further, "our farmers are wearing out their implements, our factories their machinery, our railroads their rails and rolling-stock—not only do we suffer for want of a sufficiency of these articles, but the small supply is held at the most cruel rates" (*Richmond Enquirer*, November 14, 1862). Nevertheless, under these adverse conditions Lawton charted a course toward the full mobilization of Confederate resources.

3

Confederate Mobilization

In late August 1863, following the battle of Gettysburg, a correspondent of the *Augusta Constitutionalist* surveyed the condition of the Army of Northern Virginia at Culpepper and lamented the "sad waste and destruction." General Dick Ewell's Second Corps lost most of its baggage train in the retreat to Falling Waters, and his troops were deficient in "clothing and shoes." One colonel forwarded a requisition to Georgia quartermaster general Ira Foster "in which he reported his command as destitute of everything" (*Charleston Mercury*, August 26, 1863). Some men had worn out two pairs of shoes on the Northern march, and all faced the prospect of frostbite, pleurisy, or pneumonia in the coming winter.

Refitting these men was the immediate challenge that faced General Alexander Lawton upon becoming quartermaster general of the Confederacy. Lawton inherited a bureau still steeped in the bureaucratic style of the old army. Within the War Department, Lawton found little cooperation. Josiah Gorgas and Lucius Northrop ran independent agencies. The Navy Department freely ignored army regulations. Within the armies, either in northern Virginia or Tennessee, there was little sympathy over his plight and little understanding of the reasons for the lack of supplies. Both armies frequently resorted to self-help. Outside of Richmond, state authorities carved out large fields of activity for themselves, laying special claim on the limited manufacturing capacity of the South. Everywhere manufacturers stoutly resisted regulation and cagily played departments and governments against each other. In the Confederate Congress and the press, Lawton found his most bitter and persistent critics, who often fabricated facts from rumors.

Moreover, the continued deterioration of Confederate finance under

Secretary of the Treasury Christopher Memminger placed the government several hundred million dollars in arrears with payments to troops and factories alike.[1] Foreign quartermaster stores arrived only at irregular intervals. At home, the scarcity of raw materials, wool, leather, and finally even cotton and corn grew with each passing month. Railroad transportation, due to the draft, excessive usage, and the vicissitudes of war, continually declined in performance. Although General Lawton had little prior experience in dealing with manufacturers, he possessed considerable common sense, the business habits of a trained lawyer, and the boldness of a field trooper. With forthrightness and vigor, he pressed for a uniform standard of procurement and production, and in this he distanced himself from the traditionalism of his predecessor.

A Georgia reporter in residence with the Second Corps on the Rapidan acutely described the organizational dilemma. "Now is the time," he wrote, "for the State Bureaus, and the Associations, and the Ladies' Societies, and the friends and families of the soldiers at home to be engaged, heart and soul, in supplying the present destitutions, and preparing for the coming winter." The state quartermasters and the relief associations should "supplement the Confederate Government by doing what the Government may not be able, or what it does not undertake to do, but which we think ought to be done" (*Charleston Mercury*, August 26, 1863). Failure to do so would fill the hospitals and cemeteries come the first frosts.

Richmond's centralized supply system did not allow troops in the field to be supplied without proper requisitions from the home office. As an example, the reporter cited the Georgia legislature's appropriation of $1.9 million for state troops. The "red tape formula" would make these soldiers suffer "without proper clothing and shoes, while these articles, in great abundance, are packed away in the store rooms of Quartermasters at Augusta or Atlanta." To be supplied, troops needed "a requisition, drawn up and signed by the proper officer according to the conditions of some unbending and inflexible law" (*Charleston Mercury*, August 26, 1863). Centralized acquisition and a dispersed distribution system seemed to offer the best hope.

Lawton was quickly challenged over whether he could fully mobilize Confederate resources, supply armies maneuvering in the field, secure favorable foreign contracts, master the bureaucracy, and garner the resources of the states previously monopolized by the governors. On September 7, 1863, he began to make fall clothing issues to the Army of Northern Virginia. He wrote General Robert E. Lee optimistically that he would "commence with the troops at Fredericksburg tomorrow."[2]

While supplying the two great armies, east and west, Lawton was invited to participate in a series of high-level strategy sessions at the War Department. The bureau heads were often consulted in strategic planning. According to Colonel Gilbert Moxley Sorrel, one of General James Longstreet's staff officers, "the important movement now impending was the subject of deep and secret discussion by the President, Generals Lee and Longstreet, and General Lawton, Quartermaster-General, whose part in it would be of the first consideration" (Sorrel 188). The plan was to maneuver General Longstreet's corps from the Virginia front to north Georgia, unite it with General Braxton Bragg's Army of Tennessee, and drive General William Rosecrans from his hold on the Tennessee River at Chattanooga. Longstreet had long wanted to go west, and troop transfers from General George G. Meade's forces presented an opportunity. General Lawton, in his inexperience and perhaps out of concern for his native state, gave his full assent to this important military maneuver, believing that Longstreet in the South could draw supplies from the Georgia depots and thereby relieve the pressure on the resources of Virginia.

The quartermaster general, newly ensconced, therefore embraced a strategic plan fraught with considerable logistic risks. A portion of Longstreet's corps of 16,000 men quickly moved south through Atlanta and fought brilliantly in the battle of Chickamauga on September 19–21, 1863. But then, instead of aiding Bragg in guarding Chattanooga, with the commanding general's concurrence, Longstreet impetuously elected to march upon General Ambrose Burnside at Knoxville, whom he besieged on November 16, 1863. Although Lawton, Longstreet, and the entire War Department anticipated that a sufficiency of supplies could be found in Quartermaster James Glover's department of east Tennessee, that region was barren, having been stripped by both contending armies. As a harsh winter set in, Burnside stubbornly held Knoxville and deprived Longstreet of the area's limited resources. The Confederate Quartermaster Bureau was forced into a logistics quagmire. In addition to supporting two major armies in the field, Lawton had to supply Longstreet's command by shipping corn and clothing from the Lower South to Lynchburg, then sending the stores south to Knoxville via the damaged Virginia and East Tennessee Railroad. A major Confederate army of almost 20,000 men dangled at the end of a supply line almost 1,000 miles long.

Within a month of laying his siege, Longstreet's supply situation at Knoxville became precarious. In a battle report of December 13, the Confederate commander ominously wrote, "we shall be obliged to suspend active operations for want of shoes and clothing."[3] Colonel Moxley Sorrel remembered that "the men were happy and cheerful, but awfully in want of clothing and shoes" (Sorrel 219). Many of the soldiers' shoes were handmade by army cobblers whose primary task was to make repairs, and Sorrel recalled a pathetic movement against Union lines held by General Gordon Granger at Dandridge. The east Tennessee winter was especially bitter, the ground was iced over, "and not less than 2,000 of our little army were without shoes" (219). With little success, impressment squads scoured the mountains and valleys. General Edward Porter Alexander, artillery officer, also found this campaign "one of much hardship." He wrote, "I have seen bloody stains left on frozen ground where our infantry had passed." In the artillery battalions, General Alexander "took the shoes from the feet of the drivers to give to the cannoneers who had to march" (Alexander 491). Frequently, rations were only raw corn, normally used as animal fodder. By regulation, Northrop's Commissary Bureau was responsible for feeding the troops; however, in emergencies such as this, men took corn fodder provided for their animals by the Quartermaster Bureau and made meal.

Alexander's command was "so deficient in horseshoes that on the advance to Knoxville we stripped the shoes and saved the nails from all dead horses, killing for the purpose all wounded and broken-down animals" (491). Instead of emulating the swift movements of Jackson at Second Manassas, Longstreet risked imitating Napoleon before Moscow. In Richmond, Secretary of War James Seddon called Lawton's attention "to the alleged want of shoes and clothing, which it is hoped it may be in his power to supply."[4]

In light of Lawton's original endorsement of Longstreet's strategy, the bureau was forced to make heroic attempts to relieve the desperate situation. Lawton reasserted control of the Railroad Bureau, which had been transferred from the Quartermaster Bureau to Adjutant and Inspector

General Samuel Cooper. Fifteen locomotives and 200 cars were added to a special routing from Augusta, Georgia, to Richmond. Lawton arranged uniform schedules for through trains to speed supplies from the Lower South; with fifty locomotives inoperative for want of wheels, he pressed the War Department to detail more skilled workers to keep the trains moving, and he urged the completion of the Danville-to-Greensboro railroad link between Virginia and the Lower South.[5]

By December 1863, after four months in office, Lawton was doubtful that he could continue to resupply Lee's troops and also provide for Longstreet at Knoxville. Lee's army drew twice the quantity of goods and cereals from the Lower South as in the previous year, and in east Tennessee Longstreet's correspondence grew more desperate. Lawton found Longstreet's requisition for 10,000 blankets too large "in proportion to the command" and sent forward only 3,500 received from recent imports.[6] Longstreet also requested 5,000 uniforms, 20,000 pairs of socks, 10,000 pairs of drawers, and 10,000 pairs of shoes, hardly an extravagant request for a maneuvering army. Although several thousand uniforms were sent, Lawton's response was meager.

On January 2, following two months of unusually severe weather and with continued separation from military railroad transportation, the reports from east Tennessee became bleaker. Longstreet wrote that his command was "in great distress for want of shoes and clothing, and in that way so much reduced that we cannot make other details and remain so near the enemy and live by foraging."[7] The beleaguered Tennessee commander soon forwarded a second requisition to outfit his cavalry arm of 6,000 men.

Jefferson Davis called on Lawton for a full report regarding the situation. The chief quartermaster denied any deficiencies in his department, explaining that the main problem in supplying Longstreet's corps was "due to the fact that I had looked some little time back to supplying it from the depots in the State of Georgia."[8] The Richmond depot was emptied by the fall requisitions of Lee's army, especially in Ewell's corps and those of General Samuel Jones in southwest Virginia. Also, he told Davis, there were major failures in foreign supply, for "the loss of one hundred thousand prs. of shoes & as many blankets off Wilmington since Sept. has left us in a sad condition in reference to these all important articles."[9]

Lawton characterized Longstreet's second requisition as being "of a more extravagant character, and [one that] demands blankets, overcoats, shoes, and entire suit of clothing for every man and officer in the corps." He argued, based upon an interview with an officer from east Tennessee, that one-third of the requisition would "relieve the wants of the troops."[10] With empty warehouses, Lawton scaled the cavalry request down by two-thirds and found enough English brogans and double blankets in quarantine at Wilmington to satisfy this minimal demand.

At this critical moment, North Carolina's Governor Zebulon Vance provided help in saving Longstreet's command by making a timely advance from state stores, a move that Lawton may have anticipated. As Vance wrote, "In the winter succeeding the battle of Chickamauga I sent to General Longstreet's corps 14,000 suits of clothing complete" (Dowd 490). Many of these were made in Salem by Francis Fries. This was the principal supply that Longstreet received during the trying east Tennessee campaign, although on December 12, 1863, Lawton ordered Aurelius F. Cone, of the Clothing Depot, to forward to Knoxville 4,000 trousers, 3,000 field jackets, 4,000 pairs of shoes, and other supplies to refit an additional two regiments.[11]

With the troops making "the bread of the army" from corn provided as animal fodder, even these supplies quickly diminished. To move fodder for this army, since local forage was scarce, with 10,000 horses needing 160,000 pounds a day, Lawton calculated, required "*all* the rolling stock of all the roads between this [city, Richmond] & Georgia without allowing for the frequent disturbances caused by the movement of troops, & raids of the enemy."[12] Under the circumstances, General Lee strongly recommended terminating the campaign and bringing Longstreet back to Virginia. However, this was not accomplished until April. Lawton's failure to sustain the Confederate army in east Tennessee fortified his political opponents and provided a powerful object lesson in the limits of Confederate logistics. In the coming months, he more carefully fitted promises to possible performance. To this end, he determined to survey the extent of available Confederate resources and reform the entire production operations of the bureau.

Lawton's previous tenure as president of the Augusta and Savannah Railroad gave him some experience in administering large-scale operations involving the coordination of personnel and machines. Railroads utilized modern precision tooling, interchangeable parts, and systematic assembly. The successful administration of such a technology required careful organization, planning, the timely and efficient coordination of skilled workers, and the creation of quality control or inspections. Much like Vernon K. Stevenson, another former railroad president who served successfully as chief quartermaster in the Army of Tennessee, Lawton's ambition was to reduce the work of the Quartermaster Department to a system with uniform procurement, manufacture, and distribution.

In December 1863, in the midst of the Longstreet difficulty, Lawton determined to maximize production by establishing control over the process of fabrication of regional quartermasters and to mobilize the remaining manufacturing resources of the Confederacy.[13] He intended that clothing, camp, and garrison equipage should be produced following strict guidelines. With consolidation and standardization, all bureau manufacturing of shoes and uniforms would be made from standardized patterns for the different sizes. Efficient cutting procedures could reduce wastage of cloth and leather to a minimum, while mechanized devices such as steam-powered sewing machines increased the speed of production. A system of periodic inspections would reveal weaknesses within the production process. Above all, Lawton needed accurate data. To accomplish this, he first appointed roving inspectors to compile a census of Confederate factories and their productivity; then he ordered surveys of activities at regional military depots; and finally, he mandated a uniform and universal contracting system. Since the bureau was falling increasingly in arrears in payments to vendors, his roving inspectors going to the field often faced hostile quartermasters and mill owners.

On December 19, Lawton began with a survey of the Atlanta depot, then under the vigorous management of George W. Cunningham, a former Nashville merchant and quartermaster for the Army of Tennessee. Atlanta, a convenient railroad junction, was in the throes of transformation into a depot and manufacturing center in service to the Tennessee forces: barracks, warehouses, iron works, machine shops, and quartermaster operations constantly increased.[14] In a long missive, Lawton solicited Cunningham's advice on how to increase production and economize in "the expenditure of all raw material used in connection therewith."[15] This meant cutting cloth efficiently from bolts for standard-sized uniforms using set patterns. The Atlanta clothing depot was a model of activity, with twenty-seven male cutters and 3,000 seamstresses constantly at work. In the half year ending in April 1863, Cunningham manufactured over 37,000 uniforms, 90,000 cotton shirts, and comparable quantities of undergarments and other apparel. Each seamstress produced a garment a day, for a total of 90,000 a month. With three dozen workers, Cunningham operated a subsidiary shoe factory that produced 500 pairs a day.[16] Across the Lower South, at twenty-five other depots quartermasters engaged in similar activities. In 1863, the depots at three factory sites in Mississippi produced 2,000 uniforms a week, while those at Tuscaloosa, Selma, Columbus, and Augusta were comparatively larger.[17] Lawton determined to start at Atlanta and implement an efficient manufacturing process across the whole Confederacy.

After having satisfied himself with the activity at Atlanta, Lawton ordered Cunningham "to proceed, without delay, to make a thorough inspection within the States of South Carolina, Georgia, Alabama, Florida, Mississippi, and to the extent that circumstances permit, Tennessee, of all matters in any way incident to the production of the supplies referred to." While maintaining his base at Atlanta, Cunningham was to move "from point to point, as occasion may require," and inspect all depots and the operations of all purchasing officers and "ascertain how far the resources of the country have been made productive." Particularly, he was instructed to specify "how far the different factories within the states maintained [mentioned], have been heretofore employed on Government account."[18] Before the war, the region contained about a hundred mills, but Richmond had no precise information on how these resources had been exploited.

In each location, Cunningham was ordered to identify "what particular officers of this Department possess peculiar fitness as manufacturers of this description of supplies."[19] He was authorized to appoint sub-agents. Lawton assigned other inspectors to visit sites in Virginia, North Carolina, and the Trans-Mississippi on similar missions. The collective reports formed the foundation of his grand mobilization plan.

Cunningham's reports graphically revealed the unplanned, even chaotic, conditions that prevailed in departments across the Lower South. By visit and telegram, Cunningham surveyed only thirty-one large mills, mostly in Georgia, ignoring dozens of mills that were small, remote, or in contested territory. His report on January 29 indicated that Lucius

Northrop's Commissary Bureau had exclusive "control of Eight (8) Cot. Factories."[20] These large mills were generally used to produce grain sacks and sandbags for the army. The Navy Department maintained a bakery at Albany, Georgia, where hardtack was produced and boxed, while the army Commissary collected corn in sacks for grinding by the troops on portable grist mills. Solely to manufacture these sacks, Northrop controlled the product of Enoch Steadman's Gwinette factory, the Princeton factory at Athens, the Scull Shoals and Covington factories, and several mills established during the war. Commissary officers from the Army of Tennessee, appointed by General Joseph E. Johnston, maintained exclusive contracts with two Georgia mills, the Grant and Troup factories, the latter well known for making excellent cotton duck.[21]

Georgia governor Joseph E. Brown, in response to an appeal by the state legislature to care for state troops and their families, had control of five other mills. These included two large establishments, the Milledgeville and Flint River factories, and three smaller mills, Ocmulgee, Franklin, and Waynmanville.[22] Cunningham believed that "this latter business can be broken up I think if the Conscript Bureau will only act vigorously and rigidly in the matter."[23] Only a threat to draft workers would coerce Brown and the manufacturers into diverting their supplies to the Confederate army. To Cunningham's great distress, he soon discovered that several other governors exercised similar controls. In Alabama, Governor Thomas H. Watts claimed the products of the Prattville factory, while in North Carolina the irrepressible Zebulon Vance held exclusive control of several mills and allowed only the state quartermasters to contract with the others.[24]

The Cunningham investigation revealed that the Navy Department had "control of one very important Factory in So. Ca. which is engaged *solely* in the manufacture of *Osnaburgs* and which would yield to the Gov't about *50,000 yds per month* if working under the same rules as others now under contract with this dept."[25] In this instance, James Gregg's improved mill at Vaucluse delivered "to the navy Dept. about 1/10 of its production only, but in consideration thereof procures all the details it requires."[26] Secretary of the Navy Stephen Mallory's requirement for osnaburgs was only 5,000 yards a quarter, leaving James Gregg free to sell the remainder of his production on the open market at a considerable profit. The navy also maintained contracts with other factories, but mostly to secure goods for barter.

As an addendum to his survey, Cunningham agreed with Lawton on the need for the bureau to exercise exclusive control over all large mills remaining in the South and for the creation of a uniform system of purchase and manufacture. Particularly, he recommended that "some arrangement be made with that Department [Navy] by which they would be content to receive a certain proportion of the cotton goods collected by the QM Dep't."[27] General Lawton lauded these recommendations and used them within the War Department to justify a program to rationalize procurement.

The Cunningham reports revealed that many factories had no government contracts at all, having carefully worked themselves free of all military claim. The use of the Confederate substitute law had almost ceased, and mills discovered that they could free themselves to sell all of their goods on the open market by simply dismissing their detailed soldiers and avoiding the impressment officer. Their profits were then not subject to control by the Quartermaster Bureau. Counting only thirty-one of the larger mills in the Lower South, the Confederate government lost over 150,000 yards of cloth each month. This was equivalent to 30,000 cotton uniforms. There were numerous large mills operating outside of bureau controls.[28] William Gregg at Graniteville produced 3.7 million yards in 1863 but sold the bureau only 38,000 yards. Enoch Steadman's Gwinette factory, nominally under state control, provided the Confederacy with 110,000 sacks, but James G. Gibbes's large Saluda mill at Columbia sold the Confederate government nothing out of a production of 22,700 pounds of yarn and an unspecified amount of cloth. He gave Cunningham a report "almost blank" on the mill's future capacity. The Macon mill provided 123,235 yards of cloth and freely "furnished bacon" amounting to 200,000 pounds to Joseph E. Johnston's army in north Georgia before selling all remaining production on the open market.[29] While the bacon was a welcome donation to military rations, the gift only underscored the factory's independent condition.

Cunningham compiled detailed statistics on looms, spindles, and cards; the production of cotton and woolen goods; and the number of workers exempted from the military. His study included only a portion of Lower South mills, twenty-three in Georgia, five in Alabama, and three in South Carolina. Dozens of factories, many with fewer than 1,000 spindles, were excluded. Based on the data, by May 1864 the surveyed mills admitted to a production of more than 20 million yards of goods a year. More important for military purposes, the woolen production of the surveyed mills was 1.5 million yards a year, equivalent to over 250,000 uniforms, and of this output the Confederate government received less than two-thirds.[30]

Of 20 million yards of cotton cloth produced annually, the Confederate government obtained 8 million yards. Cotton yarns, precious as a bartering tool, were produced at a rate of 4 million pounds a year, equal to 12 million yards of cloth, but less than 1 percent of this, 36,000 pounds, went to the Confederate depots.[31] In Cunningham's summation, from these larger factories, during the winter months of 1863–64, the army secured 69 percent of the woolens, 43 percent of the cotton goods, and 1 percent of the yarns manufactured. The reports showed conclusively that large mills in the full flush of operation sold most of their production on the open market, while army corps, such as that of Longstreet, endured severe distress.

While the Cunningham survey was under way in Georgia, Lawton dispatched Colonel Eugene E. McLean, a highly respected bureau officer, to inspect quartermaster activities in Alabama. McLean, a native of Maryland, received high praise within the War Department for efficiently clothing and equipping his troops in the Army of Tennessee. McLean arrived in Montgomery in March 1864 and reported, "so far as I have observed there is no organization at all, in consequence of which things exceedingly useful to the government go into the hands of speculators, and must finally be purchased from the first buyers at an enormous advance." Captain A. P. Calhoun, who commanded the depot, manufactured over 22,000 outfits of pants, shirts, drawers, and caps in 1863. Nevertheless, McLean found him to be "a young officer not possessing the necessary experience or knowledge of business." Inspecting the Selma depot, McLean gave Captain William M. Gillaspie, the commanding quartermaster, a good report, finding him to be "a very capable officer in that line of duty," and recommended that "the establishments at Marion Ala. and Columbus Miss. be merged into that at Selma." But the Selma shoe factory was languishing, while another at Montgomery was "nearly ready to go into operation, with nearly all of the machinery."

McLean recommended that these also be consolidated under Gillaspie's control, turning Selma, like Atlanta, into a major manufacturing center. The quartermaster noted that the cloth "for pants and jackets is principally obtained from the Tallassee factory, and is very substantial."[32] From these materials Gillaspie was able to supply up to 2,000 uniforms a week for General Dabney Maury's forces at Mobile and other commands.[33] In Mississippi, James Wesson's extensive factory complex at Bankston represented the main source of supply of troops in that district. Three Mississippi factories, Woodville, Jackson, and Chactaw, provided goods for about 1,000 uniforms a week.

To conduct a census of Virginia mills, on March 11, 1864, Lawton ordered Colonel Aurelius Cone of the Richmond depot to assemble information on "the Factories under contract with you to furnish supplies, stating the number of detailed men engaged in each, the monthly production of each Factory, & the proportion thereof secured to the Govt. with the terms of the contract, as to price &c."[34] The Union military offensive in May 1864 quickly brought the war front to the James River and made Cone's task difficult. In June, William B. B. Cross, senior quartermaster in the Richmond Clothing Depot, reported that "the exact yield of the Factories in Virginia cannot now be stated."[35] After military affairs in Virginia settled into a constant siege in August 1864, the bureau again prodded Cone into revealing the basis upon which the Richmond, Manchester, and Petersburg factories were "engaged in delivering cotton & woolen goods to this Dept."[36] The Richmond and Petersburg mills were constantly hindered in their operations by shortages of raw cotton and the calls upon their militia companies for front-line service.

Some indications of the scope of operations in Virginia were rendered by the periodic abstracts prepared by Richard Waller, supervisor of the Richmond Clothing Bureau. For five weeks in early 1863, the bureau received 0.5 million yards of cotton goods from local mills.[37] Between June and December 1863, the depot drew 1.3 million yards from Petersburg's three largest factories, Battersea, Ettrick, and Matoaca.[38] When in full operation, these factories monthly consumed nearly 600 bales of cotton and fabricated over 0.75 million yards of cloth.

The increasing military control of railroads often left companies in the lurch. In February 1864, Lynch and Callender, agents for the Petersburg mills, complained that "our three mills are nearly out of cotton and unless we obtain some soon will have to stop."[39] William Ferguson intervened with the transportation office and effected an agreement that "600 bales a month would be transported by the Dept. at the cost of the parties interested for the factories in this vicinity."[40] By such methods production was maintained at the mills until the siege of Petersburg forced many workers into the trenches. Between January and July 12, 1864, the Richmond depot procured only 1.5 million yards of cotton goods from local mills.[41]

Lawton's census provided evidence that the Confederate share of Southern production could be dramatically increased, as many newspapers and political leaders asserted. Further, he could impress additional supplies from smaller mills, although this would only increase the plight of the civil population. Without waiting for a report from North Carolina, Lawton consulted with Secretary James Seddon and embarked on the next major step of his planned mobilization. On April 9, 1864, "after a careful consideration of the whole matter," he ordered Cunningham to assume control of all the factories in the Lower South. Factories would be controlled through use of exemptions, impressment of goods, or rationing of raw materials. To simplify supply, the Atlanta quartermaster was given a monopoly over "the collection of the wool crop in the same region of country." Lawton desired to implement a "uniform system in connection with the Factories." He designated the Atlanta depot "the sole power to contract with the same & will regulate the price, proportion of product to be delivered on govt account & other matters connected with these establishments." He further empowered Cunningham "to exchange cotton for wool; & if you can use it to advantage tobacco may be sent you, for the same use, from this region." In turn, Lawton charged the Georgia agent to respond "to the requisitions of the various officers of this Dept. in charge of Manufacturing Depots for materials."[42] On April 23, the department issued a circular notifying all twenty-five quartermasters in Cunningham's Lower South district of the new system.[43]

Meanwhile in Richmond, with the approval of the War Department, Lawton consolidated all Confederate purchases of cloth under his bureau's control, with the intention of supplying materials to other departments within the government. William B. B. Cross, assistant quartermaster, explained the new policy to his chagrined naval counterpart,

John de Bree: "this department proposes to take exclusive control of the factories and regulate them under some uniform system so as to increase their production on Government account."[44] With affairs in the cotton states regularized, the quartermaster would "come under an obligation to the other Bureaux to respond to their calls."[45] General Lawton assumed that the other agencies of the War Department would require only their necessities, not goods for barter, an erroneous conclusion as events proved.

Based on Lawton's recommendations, Secretary Seddon "gave orders to the Quartermaster Department to furnish all the bureaus of the War Department with cotton goods sufficient to supply their wants."[46] John de Bree, who headed the navy's Office of Provision and Clothing, quickly responded, "this bureau is upon the eve of making very advantageous contracts for cloth, etc., but will cheerfully yield them and offer no obstacles to the arrangements proposed, provided it is put on equal footing with similar bureaus of the Army."[47] De Bree submitted a quarterly estimate of 60,000 yards of cloth, which was almost equal to the navy's annual requirements previously. The navy needed cloth and yarn for barter purposes. As de Bree explained to Secretary of the Navy Mallory, "in all the interior districts the people have a little more provisions than they absolutely need, but are short of tea, coffee, sugar, molasses, and especially of osnaburgs, yarns, and shirtings." Like manufacturers seeking wool, de Bree discovered that "in many districts where not a pound of bacon or wheat can be bought at any price, for money[,] the sight of a pound of yarn, or a yard of cloth will produce an effect almost magical."[48]

Other Confederate agencies soon arrived at the same insight. Lucius Northrop's Commissary Bureau, which annually drew 1 million yards of cloth out of Georgia, submitted inflated estimates based on the assumption that Confederate currency would buy very little but that wheat and corn could be had for cloth and yarn. The commissary officers in Virginia alone requested almost 400,000 yards of cloth and 200,000 pounds of yarn. The North Carolina mills remained firmly under Governor Vance's authority and were not even considered in these estimations, but in South Carolina the Charleston commissary agent sought over 1 million yards of cloth and 71,000 bunches of yarn. In Georgia, the subsistence bureau required 600,000 yards of cloth and 750,000 pounds of yarn, while the Mississippi office wanted 1 million yards and the Florida agent requested 70,000 yards.[49] The Commissary Bureau demanded a grand total of 3 million yards of cloth, a threefold increase over previous acquisitions. In addition to these items, Northrop wanted 95,000 grain sacks a month, or over 1 million a year. The commissary chief divided the needs of his Richmond office into 488,750 pounds of yarn to secure grain, 651,000 yards of cotton cloth to barter for meat, and another 850,000 yards to manufacture grain sacks.[50] Even if Lawton impressed all 20 million yards of production in the Lower South, filling such quotas would be difficult.

These heavy requisitions were unanticipated. In Atlanta, Cunningham lamented, "in every case their demands are greater than they have ever been able to collect by previous arrangements." The Atlanta quartermaster urged the revocation of the departmental agreements: "with all the disadvantages of the present organization in regard to Factories I should prefer having it as it is rather than engage to meet such demands from the other Bureaux as are here made."[51]

Estimates from other branches of the War Department were also staggering. The surgeon general called for 1.5 million yards of cloth for hospital uses, while the requests from the Ordnance Department, Engineering, and the state governments of Alabama and Georgia were also substantial. Josiah Gorgas, with a growing leather scarcity, wanted oil cloth for gun coverings and canvas for horse gear. Canvas was increasingly used as a substitute for leather in shoes. For the Ordnance Bureau, Gorgas requested almost 1 million yards of material to manufacture 300,000 knapsacks, haversacks, shoulder belts, and gun strings.[52] But no request exceeded that of Oscar T. Weisiger of the Richmond Clothing Bureau. Based on an army of 400,000 men and three issues of uniforms a year, Weisiger demanded 8 million yards of woolens and 8.5 million yards of cotton goods.[53] Lawton reduced this request to more manageable proportions but still granted Weisiger an annual cloth budget of over 10 million yards.[54]

Faced with such enormous requisitions, totaling over 20 million yards of cloth, Cunningham and Lawton decided to apportion out the total collection among the various agencies. They adopted a formula that gave the Quartermaster Department 85 percent of the total production; the Commissary, Ordnance, and state agencies about 5 percent each; and the

Medical and Engineering Departments together 1 percent of the total.[55] But even this plan was not easy to realize. Paper agreements made in Richmond were easily breached in the field. John de Bree of the navy, among others, lacked confidence in Lawton's new arrangement and wrote the bureau "that our contracts with Vaucluse factory must go on for the present, but that they will be waived at any time he can make definite pledge of issues to us."[56] Despairing officers in the medical bureau complained that "as yet not a yard has been furnished, and there seems to be no probability of obtaining a supply from the source."[57] This agency then proceeded to abandon the plan and made arrangements "with a company in South Carolina to sell to the Medical Department . . . the entire product of their factory."[58]

Despite the lack of cooperation by the navy and the other bureaus of the War Department, Lawton remained optimistic, writing Cunningham on July 9, 1864, "I still hope to effect such a reduction of these calls as will enable one to complete the proposed arrangement, & so exclude from your field of operation all competition." As to de Bree and the navy, he believed "so soon as he can be seen the irregularity connected with the Vaucluse Factory will be corrected."[59] Cunningham found even the revised request from the Commissary Bureau to be daunting. Although Lucius Northrop agreed to reduce his estimate by one-third, still it was "far more than every branch of the service had ever received in the past from all the factories." With the control of 100,000 spindles at stake in the Lower South alone, representing slightly less than 20 percent of the South's prewar capacity, the Richmond office advised Cunningham that "caution has to be practiced in this matter."[60] To meet these revised departmental demands, Cunningham calculated on receiving from his selected Lower South mills 2,300 bales of cloth or one million yards each month.[61] Supplemented by Upper South mills, this would have approximated Lawton's cloth budget.

Having finishing his census of Southern mills, Lawton determined next to establish a system of uniform contracts with factories. In April 1864, he accepted a proposition by factory agents in Petersburg and Richmond to sell "to the Govt *two thirds* (2/3) of their product at twenty five per cent (25) profit on the cost of production; the *other third* to be disposed of by them as they deem proper, to outside parties."[62] To sell two-thirds of their production to the government at fixed prices in order to sell one-third at open market value had some appeal. By such a policy manufacturers could evade the 75 percent limit upon profits established and enforced under Abraham Myers's regime. Because of the elevated market prices, such a policy placed manufacturers' profits beyond the statutory limit of 75 percent on the goods sold to the public; however, the agreement gave the government lower prices. Although no Confederate law sanctioned the practice, Lawton accepted the proposition. His chief subordinate, Quartermaster William B. B. Cross, endorsed the Virginia proposal on condition that "care should be taken to see that the cost of production is estimated in a proper way, as abuses, in this particular, have prevailed throughout the country."[63] With one modification, this method was adopted in the Lower South: there profits on government account were raised to 33.3 percent.[64]

General Lawton's attempt to enlarge and standardize Confederate control of manufacturing and to rationalize the methods of production met great success in Virginia and Georgia; however, strong opposition developed in North Carolina, where notions of states' rights were rigidly held. The Old North State represented the largest reserve of untapped resources in the Confederacy, and as the spring campaigns of 1864 unfolded in central Virginia and north Georgia, Lawton, like Myers before him, cast his gaze upon these factories. The Confederate chief quartermaster quickly found an able opponent in Governor Vance, while local manufacturers obviously preferred Vance's suzerainty to that of Richmond.

The North Carolina practice of exercising exclusive control over mills had its origin in the early days of the war, when the state equipped and armed local regiments under the commutation system.[65] In that period, the desperate Confederate War Department warmly welcomed such initiatives. The near-emergency conditions that prevailed after First Bull Run moved the North Carolina legislature to action, and the "State clothing department was got up under a resolution of the Gen[era]l A[ssembly] ratified 20 Sept. 1861, entitled 'Resolution to Provide Winter clothing for the Troops.'"[66] State authorities agreed "to receive the commutation clothing money of the troops, and clothe and shoe them herself." Upon North Carolina's agreement "to sell the Confederate authorities all the surplus supplies that could be procured in the State, they agreed to withdraw their agents from our markets and leave the

State agents the whole field without competition."[67] Effectively, Confederate quartermasters abandoned the state.

Periodic attempts on the part of Richmond to readjust the situation failed. In March 1862, Abraham Myers wrote Vance, "I find that the manufacture of Army Clothing in the State of North Carolina, is still carried on through state agents." The quartermaster general thought "it very desirable, with a view to systematizing & extending this branch of the service, that there should be a complete transfer to the Confederate authorities, of all the contracts & facilities held by North Carolina for the manufacture of Army Clothing."[68] He proposed to transfer immediately the North Carolina main quartermasters, James Sloan at Greensboro and Charles Garrett at Raleigh, to the Confederate service. Vance did not deign to answer himself but directed a secretary "to say in reply he is unwilling to make such transfer without consulting the General Assembly."[69] Neither the governor nor the North Carolina General Assembly approved the transfer. In June 1862, James B. Ferguson, of the Richmond office, "visited most of the woolen mills in North Carolina" and reported that "they are under contracts with that state."[70]

The factory owners refused to contract with Richmond, and Ferguson was "decidedly of the opinion, that [the] State ought to turn over the entire department now under its management to the Confederate States."[71] In response to this report, Myers tried again. He requested James G. Martin, North Carolina's adjutant general, to place the state's troops on the same footing as the rest of the army with regard to issues, reminding him of "the suggestion made in my previous letter, that the arrangement existing between North Carolina and the Confederate States should be abandoned, that all the supplies of clothing & your stores now here on hand be turned over to this Department."[72] In one instance, Myers noted, three North Carolina regiments "refused to secure clothing from the state and made requisitions upon this Department."[73] State officers proved remarkably uncommunicative about the issue.

In October 1862, the Confederate War Department abolished the commutation system, and Myers lost no time in writing Vance that "the State of No. Carolina cannot be reimbursed for such clothing as it may supply to its troops, nor can any arrangement between the State and the C.S. Government similar to the heretofore existing [one] be continued."[74]

Undaunted by even this threat, Vance quickly built up a debt of over $4 million against the Confederate government.[75] A compromise was finally reached whereby William W. Peirce, the chief North Carolina quartermaster at Raleigh, filed regular reports on his clothing issues with the Confederate authorities, but otherwise Peirce received requisitions directly from captains of North Carolina companies. On occasion, Peirce aided the Richmond depot in securing supplies within the state, one time providing an innovative canvas shoe for army use.[76]

This compromise worked reasonably well. In the year ending October 1862, North Carolina made 49,000 jackets and 68,000 pairs of pants (Webb 124). By March 1863, Peter A. Wilson of the state Clothing Bureau relied on the annual purchase of "four hundred thousand yards, wool cloth, and seven hundred thousand yards, sheeting and osnaburgs" to manufacture 75,000 uniforms.[77] In May 1863, Myers made a final attempt to secure control of state production. He dispatched Samuel R. Chisman, a trusted adviser, to Greensboro to establish a quartermaster's office for the Confederate government. This was done without consulting Governor Vance.

Chisman, a young professional quartermaster with many contacts in the military, arrived in Greensboro to find that James Sloan, an old merchant and the North Carolina agent, held exclusive agreements with local mills. When called upon "to turn over his contracts" to the Confederacy, Sloan responded that "he would have to see Gov. Vance before doing so."[78] Wasting no time, the North Carolina quartermaster at Raleigh, William Peirce, informed the Richmond interloper that "the Governor holds on to his contracts & insists on Sloan's acting in the two fold capacity of State Q Master & Confederate States chief Commissary for dist. of N.C."[79] Chisman declined to report to Myers on the true state of Vance's intransigence. The Richmond officer was placated by being permitted to purchase "hats, shoes, domestic jeans, cotton, and other quartermaster stores" on the open market.[80] With ambiguous authority and an undefined position, Chisman satisfied himself by procuring a few "wagons, harness, collar, heavy horse shoes, trace chains, leather & shoes."[81]

Upon becoming quartermaster general, Lawton resumed Myers's controversy with the North Carolina governor. The governor and the bureau chief quickly sparred over the control of the *A. D. Vance*, or the *Advance*, as it was popularly known. The state of North Carolina purchased the "long-legged steamer" in England and used it to make "eleven round trips from Bermuda into the port of Wilmington, carrying out cotton and bringing back supplies of those things which could not be procured at home" (Dowd 454–55). During this phase of the ship's long career, it was especially active in bringing in "grain scythes, card clothing for the factories, hand cards for our old-fashioned looms, and medicines, with large quantities of shoes, blankets and army cloths" (455). To finance these imports, Vance purchased 11,000 bales of cotton and 100,000 barrels of rosin (490).

After a successful voyage of his little ship in June 1863, Vance received a telegraphic inquiry from the quartermaster general asking "whether you are willing to turn over the articles mentioned to the Government of the Confederate States, upon payment of costs and charges."[82] Getting no favorable response, William B. B. Cross made another attempt a few months later, at the time of Longstreet's desperate straits at Knoxville. Having heard that the *Advance* brought in 40,000 pairs of shoes, Cross inquired about "the resources at the command of the authorities of the State of North Carolina, especially those enjoyed abroad for supplying clothing to the troops."[83] Without exaggeration, Vance's prospects of getting stores were excellent. He responded, "I have now at Bermuda and on the way there eight or ten cargoes of supplies of the very first importance to the Army and the people, consisting chiefly of some 40,000 blankets, 40,000 pair of shoes, large quantities of army cloth and leather, 112,000 pair of cotton cards, machinery and findings to refit twenty-six of our principal cotton and woolen factories, dye stuffs, lubricating oils, &c."[84] Large quantities of bacon were also aboard. North Carolina owned a warehouse in Richmond filled with supplies, and the state had additional bulging depots. State quartermaster Peirce reported that he was "constantly receiving a large amount of clothing sufficient to keep all the NCarolina [sic] troops well clad for the year 1864." There was even enough surplus to refit Longstreet's forces with 14,000 uniforms.[85]

Lawton's importunities to Vance were no more successful than those of his predecessor. On January 21, 1864, the quartermaster general wrote, "I am informed that the authorities of the State of North Carolina hold a large quantity of woolen goods, partly imported, beyond what can passably be needed for some time to come to meet the wants of the troops from that State." The Richmond Clothing Depot was "greatly in want of woolen goods and cloth (heavy) of any description and blankets; shoes, too, would be acceptable."[86] Vance refused to budge, even after a searching and bitter exchange with Jefferson Davis that touched on all the outstanding controversies between the two governments: control of the clothing factories, salt purchases, conscription, and impressments.[87] But despite polemics as to who was the greater traitor to the Confederate cause, Vance held on firmly to his clothing contracts.

The guerrilla war between General Lawton and Governor Vance escalated during the spring of 1864. In April 1864, General William H. Whiting, Confederate commander at Wilmington, requested additional supplies from the Confederate government, and Lawton, in response, elaborated upon his conflict with Vance: "the whole management is attended with injustice to troops from other states and I am now endeavoring to effect a change."[88] In addition to Whiting, Lawton sought the support of William Peirce. In February, Lawton wrote him, "you seem to have abandoned the field entirely to the State authorities; still there is no obligation resting on this Department to do so."[89] A month later, Lawton ordered Peirce "to bring this matter to the attention of the Governor."[90]

Wisely, Peirce wrote the state adjutant general, Richard C. Gatlin, instead. Gatlin offered little support for the Richmond schemes: "the heavy importations of woolen goods, refered [sic] to in your letter, does not more than meet one half the demands upon us, and the recent restrictions placed upon blockade running warns [sic] us of the danger of placing too much reliance in future upon that source of supply, hence we cannot share with the Confederate States in the products of our woolen factories." But with respect to the cotton mills, few of which "furnish us with more than one third of their productions," Vance was willing to make some concessions, and he agreed to allow Confederate authorities to contract for surplus goods.[91] This was still unsatisfactory to Lawton.

In June 1864, with Richmond under siege by Grant's Union forces, Lawton renewed the issue. He enlisted Peirce's support to get Vance to relinquish "the quartermaster Stores of the State to the Confederacy for general issue with the understanding that the necessities of the troops from North Carolina should always be first met." Lawton's arguments, delicately forwarded by Peirce, dwelt on the pathetic condition of the troops and were most convincing: "the incroachments [sic] and incursions of the enemy of late bold and extensive have paralised [sic] and destroyed most of the factories in the Confederate States." Of necessity, North Carolina needed to merge its operations with those of the Richmond depot because "almost all of Virginia[,] the whole of Tennessee[,] the manufacturing districts of Georgia[,] Alabama[,] Mississippi[,] and Louisiana are virtually occupied by the enemy." South Carolina, although virtually untouched by war, had fewer factories, and "Florida furnishes but little." In the Trans-Mississippi, "the Manufactories of Texas and Arkansas very limited in extent before the war have been lessened by the presence and inroads of the enemy." But North Carolina, "one of the principal manufacturing States of the Confederacy[,] has lost but one cotton factory, and in other respects has suffered very little in her products of the factory."[92] Governor Vance was moved by the plea to release 10,000 more uniforms and 2,000 pairs of shoes for Confederate issue, but no further would he go.[93]

Reports within the Confederate War Department that North Carolina troops usually fared better than average Confederate soldiers had some factual basis. In General Henry Heth's division of the Army of Northern Virginia, three of the eight brigades were mostly composed of North Carolina soldiers. These men received most of the supplies going to the division between October 1863 and March 1864, getting 2,000 of the 3,233 blankets issued.[94] There were complaints of favoritism in other divisions as well.

Vance's intransigence threatened to unravel Lawton's supply arrangements, as other states sought to emulate North Carolina's example. The Georgians were careful students of Vance's tactics. In November 1863, Ira B. Foster, the state quartermaster for Georgia, petitioned General Lawton to allow his state "to enter into arrangement[s] similar to those referred to, and lend the aid of its energy and credit to the important and difficult task of clothing our army."[95] Like Vance, Georgia's Governor Joseph E. Brown freely interfered with Confederate factory contracts. Under legislative authority to clothe Georgia troops, he controlled five Georgia factories, imported foreign cloth on state account, and, on one occasion, arrested a large lot of warps at Stone Mountain that Enoch Steadman at Lawrenceville was "supplying some woolen factories in Virginia."[96] At another time, on the grounds of states' rights, Governor Brown nullified a contract between Isaac Brown of the Macon factory and Burnes and Monnon, knapsack manufacturers at Mobile, "to make and ship to them 30,000 yards of cotton duck."[97] In the winter of 1863–64, Georgia quartermasters manufactured and distributed to state troops "about 15,000 suits of clothing and about 30,000 pair of shoes."[98] As in the case of North Carolina, Lawton sought valiantly to combat these restrictive tendencies.[99]

In February 1864, A. M. West, the state quartermaster of Mississippi, in an action endorsed by his legislature, proposed to General Lawton that the state "clothe its soldiers in the service of the confederacy" and requested "that the control of all the tanneries & shoe shops in the state . . . be transferred to him." Lawton refused and lamented that "a partial arrangement somewhat similar to that now proposed, was entered into with the State of North Carolina & its evil effects have been felt."[100]

In June 1864, Governor John Milton sought to exclude Florida's Monticello factory from the quartermaster general's snare. In response to a request from the owner, William Bailey, Milton wrote Cunningham that "the State has a contract with that Factory for all the woolen goods it can make, the goods being needed for clothing for the troops from Florida in the service of the Confederate States." Milton particularly objected "to the Factory being interfered with and thereby prevented from filling the contract with the State."[101] Bailey encouraged the governor to write the War Department that he had "used the factory almost entirely for soldiers' families and for the poorer class of persons" and had sold all his woolen goods and much osnaburg and thread to the government "at less than half what they would have had to pay elsewhere" and at a loss to himself of over $300,000.[102] Lawton, probably under orders from Jefferson Davis, finally acquiesced in this rank insubordination, "satisfied the Factory in its present operations is accomplishing much good."[103]

In July 1864, Governor Thomas H. Watts of Alabama raised a dispute with the War Department over control of mills in his state. Watts particularly wanted to share the product of the Prattville mill. Again, Lawton retreated from his high ground, writing the governor, "I certainly had no desire to interfere unnecessarily with the operations of State authorities, whose aim it was to clothe the army." Yet the quartermaster general insisted "that this Dept. could in the end accomplish more were the Home resources of the Country left to its management."[104] After negotiations,

Lawton agreed to take only half of Prattville's product for the Confederacy, believing that "the State of Ala would be able to supply its demands out of the remainder."[105]

Lawton's attempt to secure total control of Confederate manufacturing also met a challenge in the Old Dominion. In 1863, Virginia's state quartermaster, L. R. Smoot, scoured the state for goods to clothe state troops, the indigent, and the families of soldiers. He returned with a bleak report: "It will suffice that I found the manufacturing interest of this commonwealth under contribution to the Confederate States government, and that the supplies required could not be secured in great part within the state." Smoot was "compelled to look elsewhere for many articles," and he "visited in person, the cities of Wilmington, Charleston, Columbia, Augusta, Atlanta, Macon and other cities, in vain."[106] On March 9, 1864, with an evident sense of desperation, the Virginia General Assembly appropriated half a million dollars and authorized the governor "to make requisitions upon the factories under your control, for the manufacture of raw cotton into cotton yarns, from numbers four to twelve, inclusive, or into cotton cloth, plain and unbleached." However, Samuel French Bassett, the Virginia commercial agent, was enjoined to avoid making "requisitions" that impeded factory operations for the Confederacy.[107]

Bassett immediately discovered that in Virginia "the universal response has been that the whole working capacity of every mill is entirely absorbed by the Confederate Government." Over two dozen remaining factories in Virginia operated strictly under the authority of General Lawton and were required to account for their production and sales only to the Confederate government. In both North and South Carolina, Bassett "was assured that the Confederate Government had contracts for the entire produce after their respective states were supplied." As a result, he could not "obtain from a single factory a single pound of yarns or yard of cloth, nor even a promise of any in a remote future."[108] Only Petersburg's Matoaca factory was willing to aid the state, and this required a special permit from the secretary of war. With Secretary Seddon's approval, French returned to the Lower South and purchased half a million yards of cloth and 88,000 pounds of yarn for state use.[109] Some of this bounty clothed wards in the penitentiary.

The Virginia demand for the Matoaca mill put Lawton in a subdued rage. He wrote Secretary Seddon that although Virginia had freely shared resources with the Quartermaster Department, "this appeal is not without its difficulty, especially as the factory referred to is by large measure the most productive establishment within the State." But the issue was obviously much larger: "I have aimed for some time, as you are aware, to increase the yield of the cotton and woolen factories to a point which would enable this bureau to respond to the demands of the other branches of the service." In the previous month, however, Sherman's army burned at least six factories around Atlanta, and Grant besieged six others within Petersburg. Nevertheless, "the Governor of Florida controls the only factory within that State, and the Governor of Georgia monopolizes the production of four within that State through details controlled by him." Nor were these solitary examples, for "Governor Watts, of Alabama, has just made an appeal for a similar favor, while now, as all along from North Carolina, owing to the peculiar policy, pursued by that State, we drew not a single yard of any kind of material." Lawton pleaded with Secretary Seddon to exclude the states from taking factory production, arguing that "the necessities of the people and the objects of charity must be postponed to the wants of the Army."[110] Lawton's letter convinced Seddon and Jefferson Davis to grant him "the countenance of the Confederate administration" for full military control of mills.[111] Within the week, Lawton ordered Samuel Chisman at Greensboro to conduct a factory census in anticipation of Confederate seizure of all North Carolina factories.

After years of bureaucratic struggle, the urgency of the battlefield convinced Davis and Seddon to martial the government's full power to win the battle of the mills. Chisman's instructions, sent on August 2, 1864, ordered him to compile "a list of the Factories in the State[,] their capacity & what portion of the production of each can be secured on Govt account."[112] Chisman immediately responded that four paper mills and several iron foundries in his area were available for Confederate supervision, and in his "judgement, tents & tent flies may be produced in large numbers by obtaining, if practicable[,] control, in whole or in part, of some of the large cotton factories in this region."[113] The Greensboro quartermaster then called on the Fries and Rock Island factories to remit information on their production.[114] After interviews with John M. Morehead and Edwin M. Holt, "two large manufacturers" who expressed a willingness to do business with Richmond, Chisman was "confirmed in my opinion that the most speedy & desirable plan is to send in a competent agent to obtain the desired information, report thereon, & make contracts for the Dept."[115]

In response, Lawton dispatched William A. Miller, a former North Carolina merchant and bonded quartermaster, to visit "as the Agent & representative of this Dept all the cotton & woolen Factories in the state of N Carolina." Miller's instructions, like those of George Cunningham, were to compile a factory census with information on costs, production, number of details, and "the terms upon which contracts can be made."[116]

Lawton's investigations revealed for the first time the extensive manufacturing activity within the state. Through Quartermaster James Sloan, Governor Vance procured one-third of the cotton production of thirty-seven factories for which, in return, he "imported through the blockade a lot of card clothing and other necessary articles for factory purposes which are being sold to the factories and by this means they are able to run for the next few months."[117] This yielded the governor monthly over 100,000 yards of cotton goods and 44,300 yards of woolens, enough for 10,000 uniforms. The survey by William Miller revealed that forty-six factories operated within the state, some outside of Vance's control, and produced annually 3,945,432 yards of cotton goods, 531,600 yards of woolens, and 3,086,100 pounds of yarn, which was itself equivalent to 9 million yards of cloth.[118] This output of 13 million yards was slightly less than the 20 million yards of Cunningham's thirty-one mills in the Lower South, which taken together represented about one-third of the antebellum capacity of the slave states.

North Carolina state quartermaster Abraham Myers controlled the product of six mills—Eagle, Buck Shoals, Turner's, Laurel Falls, Swift Island, and Elkins—from which he collected 500 bales of yarn monthly for exchange by the North Carolina Commissary Department. Governor Vance kept four mills under his personal direction, including the Orange and Saxapahaw factories. Eleven factories sold one-third of their cotton product to the state government, four sold more, and several small yarn mills did a meager government business. Another eleven factories furnished either nothing or only token quantities to the state quartermaster.[119] The prospects for increasing Confederate purchases in the state seemed considerable.

On behalf of the Confederacy, Miller went to work with great energy. He immediately visited Fayetteville, location of seven factories, and "saw all the Presidents or agents and addressed to all of them the questions that we wished answered." The manufacturers, long accustomed to working with state authorities, were not happy about the prospect of greater government control. Miller wrote Lawton that "the two largest factories in Fayetteville refuse as you see from their answer to furnish any of their products to the QMD C.S. [Quartermaster Department, Confederate States] viz Rockfish Co. and Beaver Creek Co." The others were marginally more accommodating but alleged that "they have to use a large portion in purchasing raw material provisions." Miller next rode over to Charlotte, site of several woolen mills, and visited "two of the largest in the state."[120] These meetings were a splendid success, for he found "the factories in this part of the state much more disposed to furnish their production to the Confederate States than those I first visited about Fayetteville."[121] John M. McDonald and Sons was willing to sell the Richmond depot 11,000 yards of tent cloth a month, while Phifer and Neisler offered him two-thirds of their monthly production of 7,500 pounds of yarn. This rich harvest delighted Lawton, who offered McDonald the standard profit of "33 1/3 pr cent on cost of production; that to be estimated in accordance with the rules established for the Georgia Factories."[122] The Richmond noose was tightening on North Carolina.

Chisman's plan "to call a meeting of the presidents or agents of all the factories at some convenient place and make the arrangements" was unnecessary, since most "manifested a willingness to let the C.S. have a portion of their products but not many of them as much as 1/3."[123] Miller calculated that his North Carolina contracts would produce an increase of 75,000 yards of cloth and 40,000 pounds of yarn monthly for Richmond.[124]

To strengthen the Confederate posture in North Carolina further, Lawton appointed Chisman to control all troops detailed to the factories as workers. The quartermaster general impressed the Danville and Greensboro Railroad and gave control to Chisman. Simultaneously, several regiments engaged in the Petersburg siege were detached to sweep through select North Carolina counties, including Randolph, seeking deserters, while the Confederate Conscript Bureau ordered into camp many of Governor Vance's state officers, including six men in State Quartermaster Dowd's office. William A. Miller reported on the resulting confusion in the mills, "as I am making my visit obtaining propositions the enrolling officers are just calling for some of the detailed men." "This looks," Miller wrote, "as if every thing was arranged in Richmond with special reference to forcing them into measures and they so express themselves."[125] Vance warned, "I am not willing that General Lawton should break down the State of North Carolina in this way and deprive her of the power to clothe her armies in the field," but the governor could do little.[126]

Jasper Stowe, a crusty manufacturer in Gaston County, was supremely irritated by the proceedings. Having previously avoided all contact with the Richmond government, Stowe unburdened himself to Edwin M. Holt on the new regime being imposed, or what he called "my observations and history of my dealing with the Confederate Quarter Master Chisman at Greensboro." The manufacturer's ire fell principally upon Captain Miller. Stowe lamented, "Capt Miller who visited this section, after much duplicity contracted with me for 2/3 of all our product." The Confederate quartermaster employed naked force in claiming to control the factory because "a small percent of the labour employed is male, within the conscript age." The manufacturer believed "the whole proceedings to be corrupt & said so to him." At issue was Miller's apparent insistence that the contracting terms be kept secret, but Stowe quickly learned that while he received $28 for each five-pound bunch of yarn, the nearby Linebarger company received but $20.[127]

In the days following Miller's visit, Stowe continued to rage. He finally took the train to Greensboro to complain personally to Major Chisman that "there is a decided preference given to Georgia & South Carolina manufacturers and I feel that [it] is due to North Carolina manufacturers to know why such distinction is made & who authorized it." Since General Lawton was a Georgian, Stowe suspected that he harbored "a partiality for his native state." Lawton, Stowe explained, permitted the Georgia factories to generously calculate the costs upon which their 33 1/3 percent profit was allowed. The Georgia spinners took the recent price of cotton in the vicinity of the mill and the actual cost of labor and supplies and then depreciated $5 for each spindle each month and $25 for each loom.[128] But according to Major Chisman, North Carolina mills had to figure their costs solely on the original outlay in pre-inflation currency. As Francis Fries explained to Waller at the Richmond depot, "this view seemed to us so manifestly absurd that we can not think that the expounder of the law would construe it in this way."[129] Card clothing, worth $1 in specie for each foot in 1861, cost $10 to $12 in specie in 1864. Machinery could not be replaced at the costs allowed by Chisman.

Nevertheless, General Lawton ruled that the Georgia rate could be conceded only to such mills as "will yield up 2/3 of their production on Confederate account." Since the North Carolina mills sold Richmond only their surplus, never two-thirds of production, Lawton ruled that "the contract with Mr. Stowe can stand, for the present."[130] In November, Lawton sent still another appeal to Governor Vance "to abandon the entire field to this Dept."[131]

Vance responded with a "splenetic" letter to Secretary Seddon outlining the state's position on the factories (John Jones 2: 290). Lawton, the governor wrote, had "conceived the idea that the whole business of this State supplying her own troops must be broken up, no doubt for the reason that it is done better and cheaper than it could be done by him." At half the prices paid by the Confederate Quartermaster Department, North Carolina clothed half of the troops defending Richmond. In return, within North Carolina detailed hands were being ordered to the field, and Vance was "in receipt of a letter announcing the suspension of an extensive factory this morning for that cause." The governor did not propose "to surrender everything now to Mr. Lawton and allow him to seize our mills by force."[132]

Lawton responded in kind. North Carolina depots were filled with over 92,000 uniforms (Dowd 490). One large lot of clothing, amounting to "several thousand suits," was stored in a Richmond warehouse, and "on inquiry it proved to be as was supposed—North Carolina clothing that had been there for over a year." Finally, Lawton professed no knowledge of an "agreement by which the resources of the State of North Carolina were dedicated to the exclusive benefit of the troops therefrom."[133]

Although Vance did not concede defeat, with the war rolling upon North Carolina from both the north and south, he acquiesced to Lawton's taking one-third of his mills' product, leaving one-third for himself, with mills selling the remainder on the open market. The Confederate government hastily appropriated $400,000 to buy North Carolina cloth for sandbags at Charleston, tents for the Richmond depot, and yarns for the use of the Commissary Bureau.[134]

With the Confederacy in extremis, General Lawton finally achieved a full mobilization of sorts. In May 1864, Cunningham began to impose Richmond's new contractual terms upon his mills in the Lower South. He demanded "2/3 of all mills making only cotton goods," but "those making desirable woolen goods delivd. from 1/2 to 3/5 of their cotton goods & all or 9/10 of their woolens."[135] With Lawton's approval, he modified the standard contract by decreeing that "where Factories produce woolen goods in sufficient quantities I demand only one-half their cot. goods conditioned that all their woolen machinery shall be employed on Gov't account."[136]

The governors, as well as the Commissary and Ordnance Departments, agreed to these provisions. The most dramatic result was to increase the government yield of yarns from 1,000 pounds a month in 1863 to 78,174 pounds a month in May 1864. Yarn was the new national currency and literally worth many times its weight in bacon, leather, wool, and grains. Mary Chesnut ably described the result: "Yarn is our circulating medium. It is the current coin of the realm. At a factory here, Mrs. Glover traded off a negro woman for yarn. The woman wanted to go there as a factory hand, so it suited all round." "That's nothing," her friend responded, "yesterday a negro man was sold for a keg of nails" (Chestnut 747). Nails would outlast slavery.

In Atlanta, Cunningham quickly extended his controls. Using the threats of impressment of goods or conscription of workers, in May 1864 he contracted for future deliveries with numerous new mills—the Estatahatchee, Eatonton, Hopewell, McDonough, Newton, and Potters factories—which provided him with two-thirds of their products.[137] He wrote Lawton that "with some few exceptions these terms are acquiesced in by the Factories." Also for the first time, the Elwood factory in Alabama and the Buena Vista, Bivingsville, Cedar Hill, Crawfordville, and Valley Falls mills in South Carolina fell under his control.[138] The Grady, Hawthorn, and Perry mill at Greenville, previously under contract with Beauregard's quartermaster at Charleston, was placed under the new regulations. Still Cunningham found that several factories were defiant. The Amiss factory of Georgia contracted only with the Commissary Bureau, and

Vaucluse clung tenaciously to the protection of the navy.[139] And numerous factories made no contracts with any government agency, including Macon, Bainbridge, and Thomaston in Georgia; Autaugaville, Oakfusky, and Planters in Alabama; and Saluda and Batesville in South Carolina. On his official returns, Cunningham listed these companies as ones "with which Maj. C. hopes to contract."[140] Collectively, under the regulations, the derelict mills owed him each month 130,000 yards of osnaburgs and shirtings, 20,000 yards of woolens, and 17,000 pounds of yarns, enough to clothe and maintain a small army.

By mid-1864, Lawton approached the pinnacle of Confederate mobilization. With his enlarged list of factories and increased demands, Cunningham reported to Lawton that the amount of goods expected for July included 695,000 yards of sheeting, shirting, and drills; 271,000 yards of osnaburgs; 100,000 yards of duck and tent cloth; and 248,500 pounds of yarn.[141] Cunningham's contracts with forty-four mills, representing about half the factories in the affected states, yielded the bureau 1,066,000 yards of goods for the month. In addition, his woolens averaged about 100,000 yards a month, equivalent to 20,000 uniforms. While a few mills successfully defied Lawton's regulations, many regulations were simply ignored.

In late summer, with the approval of Governor Vance, Quartermaster Samuel R. Chisman began to apply the new regulations across North Carolina. Vance remained in control of the six mills producing woolens, although he allowed Chisman to share the production of Rock Island and Mountain Island and take half the production of the James Town factory—some 2,000 yards a month—on condition of furnishing the raw wool.[142] State quartermaster Abraham Myers continued to draw 28,500 pounds of yarn monthly, along with 10,000 yards of shirting and 4,000 yards of osnaburgs, from the Swift Island, Eagle Mills, Buck Shoals, Turner's, and Laurel Falls mills. The yarns were exchanged for corn, and the osnaburg was made into produce sacks. The Wood Lawn mill continued to supply yarns to the John Judge sock factory at Columbia, South Carolina.

Commencing on September 1, 1864, Chisman demanded one-third of all the production at twenty-one of the state's forty-six factories. Eight other mills were signed to individual contracts. Major Chisman's share was one-third of the monthly production of 328,786 yards of cotton goods and 257,175 pounds of yarns. Several mills, such as Stowe's, Hamburg, and Ivy Shoals, held no state contracts but were now forced to sell Chisman one-third of their product at $4 a pound for yarns and $2 a yard for cotton goods.[143] At least seven mills made no contracts with either the Confederacy or the state, and in November the Concord factory turned its fifty-two looms and 2,200 spindles solely for the private market. Nevertheless, General Lawton's mobilization of North Carolina factories afforded the Richmond bureau a measure of satisfaction in the final months of the war.

With much of Southern manufacturing consolidated in the hands of Cunningham in the Lower South, Chisman in North Carolina, and Ferguson in Virginia, Lawton finally achieved in large measure the supply system he envisioned. Between June and December 1863, Lawton purchased from mills in the Lower South 3.6 million yards of cotton goods, 545,059 yards of woolens, and 20,000 pounds of yarns.[144] Within the same months, the factories at Petersburg yielded the Richmond bureau an additional 1,290,583 yards of cotton goods, with the Battersea mill alone providing 776,013 yards.[145] Substantial quantities of woolens were also drawn from Virginia mills through William Ferguson's contracts with such factories as the Manchester Cotton and Woolen Company, Crenshaw's, Danville, Bonsack's, Scottsville, and the Fredericksburg émigré company, Kelly, Tackett, and Ford.[146] In June 1863, Richmond's Manchester factory manufactured 18,886 yards of woolens for the Clothing Bureau.[147] In Mississippi, Livingston Mims, head of the Confederate clothing depot at Enterprise, drew 4,000 yards of osnaburgs a week from local mills for fabricating into shirts and underclothing, while George Jones in north Alabama processed 6,000 yards of osnaburgs a week secured from two factories.[148]

In the spring of 1864, Lawton's efforts were redoubled. Between January and July 12, the Richmond depot drew 1,497,012 yards of cotton goods from three Petersburg mills alone.[149] In the first six months of 1864, Lawton continued to take one-third of the cotton production of mills of the Lower South, claiming 4,213,311 yards compared to 3,671,519 taken in the fall.[150] Cotton goods production at thirty-one contracting mills fell from an annual rate of 21,447,600 yards in 1863 to 19,940,400 yards in 1864, while woolen production remained nearly stable, rising slightly from 1,578,600 yards in 1863 to 1,652,532 in 1864. With full mobilization in May

1864, two-thirds of all cotton production and nearly all of the woolens were taken by the Confederacy. In soldiers' terms, with full mobilization Lawton was finally able to supply the Confederate army its regulation gray uniform and other clothing two or three times a year.

By the end of 1864, Lawton's reputation as a supplier stood high. More than Myers, he recognized the South's large capacity for self-sufficiency. He wrote Lee in February 1864 that "our main reliance must be our home resources," and at a time when the army often had no more than a few days' rations in reserve, Lawton provided the troops with an abundance of cotton goods and a sufficiency of woolens and leather.[151]

Nevertheless, pressing shortages continued within the Clothing Bureau. Blankets were an especially difficult item to procure. Although several companies manufactured light blankets, heavy woolens had to be imported. Lawton found that there was "not a solitary establishment within the limits of the Confederacy where they are made, nor is there one since the destruction of Crenshaws, at this place, by fire that possesses the appliance for making them."[152] When troops such as those of General Joseph Kershaw at Rapidan Station complained of no footwear in September 1864, Lawton was able to demonstrate that supplies were adequate and issues ample.[153] On November 19, 1864, and again on December 10, army quartermasters reported that supplies were plentiful but distributions were tardy. Lawton explained in December that "of shoes the department for four months past has had an ample supply, and of blankets a fair supply, at this point, and large numbers stored elsewhere."[154]

Although Lee's quartermaster, James Corley, continued to report "great deficiency of clothing," Lawton demonstrated that supplies were flowing to the army in excess of regulation requirements. Of course, regulation requirements were inadequate to a maneuvering army in combat, but within the trenches at Richmond-Petersburg, the troops were reasonably well clothed. Lawton wrote in December 1864, "there has not been a time within the two months prior to your call when, upon short notice, the army could not have been fairly supplied with every article except overcoats which are not made up."[155] Between October 26 and December 20, 1864, the Clothing Bureau received 546,000 pairs of shoes and 316,000 blankets (*Frank Leslie's Illustrated Newspaper*, April 8, 1865). Lawton forwarded 10,000 blankets to Corley and invited him to call upon the department "for whatever you may need in the way of either shoes or blankets . . . to make the Army comfortable."[156] To meet the threatened deficiency, he ordered production at the Richmond depot increased to 1,000 uniforms a day, a task requiring the constant efforts of 3,000 to 5,000 seamstresses and trimmers.

Despite a widespread belief to the contrary, the armies of the east and the west received comparable supplies during Lawton's tenure. In February 1864, Joseph E. Johnston, upon inspecting the formerly well provisioned Army of Tennessee, complained that "the want of shoes is painful to see even in this mild weather." "Although the chief quartermaster promised when I arrived to supply the deficiency very soon," Johnston continued, "it is increasing fast."[157] Lawton responded that though the Tennessee army was not well shod, "a full share of the supply at command has been sent to General Johnston."[158] Losses to the blockade off Wilmington were considerable, but Lawton optimistically anticipated enough hides would be received from army beeves "in two months' time to manufacture 600,000 pairs of shoes."[159]

In April 1864, Eugene McLean, the roving Richmond quartermaster, visited General Thomas Hindman's division at Dalton, Georgia, and found the men "badly supplied with blankets and shoes." Many soldiers in General William Quarles's brigade were "barefooted in consequence of the shoes obtained in Mobile (heretofore reported on by me) being very inferior, purchased in Charleston by order of Genl Maury."[160] The situation was better in General Patrick Cleburne's division. There the divisional quartermaster was Major Absalom L. Landis, formerly a cotton manufacturer from Bedford County, Tennessee.[161] By Landis's accounting, the division of 4,000 men was well supplied, in the last three months of 1863 receiving 7,500 jackets, over 13,000 pairs of pants, almost 6,000 pairs of shoes, 11,000 shirts, and 22,000 pairs of socks. In the first three months of 1864, clothing supplies fell to about half the previous levels, except for the issue of shoes, which rose to 7,000. During the final stages of the Atlanta campaign in the summer of 1864, the division received 2,000 jackets and 3,000 pairs of shoes. But for the entire year of 1864, the troopers received 2,000 blankets and almost 28,000 pairs of shoes.[162] If the entire Army of Tennessee received supplies on a proportionate basis, General Johnston's issues exceeded the Confederate standard.

In contrast to meager supplies rendered to General Longstreet at Knoxville, Lawton was later able to keep the Army of Tennessee shod all the way to Nashville. Following the battles about Atlanta in July and August 1864, General John B. Hood, the Confederate commanding general, maneuvered the Tennessee army across Sherman's supply line at Allatoona and then entered Tennessee by way of Tuscumbia, Alabama. Sherman's subsequent movements through central Georgia isolated Columbus and forced the resupply of Confederate forces from Augusta. Hood's quartermaster, Major William F. Ayer, with an ambition hardly inferior to that of his superior, submitted a quarterly requisition in November 1864 that called for 100,000 pairs of shoes, 75,000 pairs of pants, 50,000 jackets, 30,000 overcoats, and "other articles in proportion."[163] Lawton pared this request into "20,000 suits of clothing, & like number of shoes," enough to outfit half the Confederate force.[164] But he lectured Ayer that "it cannot certainly be expected, in the present limited resources of the Country, in way of leather, wool &c that this Dept. should supply a command of the strength of Genl Hood's upon such an estimate."[165] Following this, on November 8 Lawton sent Hood's command at Tuscumbia another supply consisting of "28,408 *Jackets*; 38,305 *Pants*; 36,856 pairs of *shoes*; 21,561 *drawers*; 17,910 *shirts*; 40,800 prs. *socks*, and 141 bales of *blankets*."[166] An additional 6,500 pairs of shoes and 2,900 blankets were subsequently dispatched. The Confederate Army of Tennessee that fought the battles of Franklin on November 30 and Nashville on December 15 was dashingly outfitted.

Although Sherman's military operations in Georgia disrupted the operations of George Cunningham's depot at Atlanta, for the last two quarters of 1864, from June to December, the Army of Tennessee received 102,558 pairs of shoes compared to 167,862 pairs distributed to General Lee's larger force in Virginia.[167] Other clothing was distributed in the same proportion. But the Virginia forces, being in a more northern climate, received more blankets by a ratio of three to one. General Dabney Maury's command on the Gulf Coast and Hardee's troops on the Atlantic seaboard were allocated 60,718 pairs of brogans and other articles in like proportion. As Lawton explained to Congressman Samuel A. Miller, "more clothing has been issued to our armies in the field, the item of overcoats excepted, than either their comfort or efficiency demanded."[168] In response to published reports in Virginia that the soldiers were undersupplied, Lawton pointed out retailers in Petersburg and Richmond whose stores were filled with clothing of Confederate issue. He deemed it "impossible with the amplest supply to keep the army clad unless this abuse is stopped."[169] A congressional committee found that although some clothing in stores was gleaned from the battlefield, sales by soldiers were common, and "a walk through the business streets of Richmond will satisfy anyone of this fact." The committee noted that "large quantities of government clothing are possessed by persons in civil life, and by dealers in such articles."[170] Soldiers, deficient in pay, were bartering their clothing to civilian merchants, and civilians, as well as slaves, were often adorned in Confederate gray (*Journal of the Congress of the Confederate States of America* 7: 568).

As General Grant's armies closed upon Richmond, Lawton's issues were the subject of a special report to the Confederate Congress. He wrote that "with the exception of overcoats, which have not been made up, owing to the great consumption of woolen material for jackets and pants, and the item of flannel undershirts but partially supplied, the armies have been fully supplied."[171] Between January and June 1864, he distributed 397,594 pairs of shoes, of which 37,657 came from the state government of Georgia and 9,263 were supplied by North Carolina. During the same period, the Quartermaster Bureau issued 242,337 field jackets. Of these, Georgia provided 26,745 and North Carolina 21,301.[172] The army received 353,433 pairs of pants, almost 60,000 a month, with 28,808 of the total coming from Georgia and 32,104 from North Carolina.[173]

Between July and December 1864, even with the addition of the state issues of Georgia and North Carolina, Lawton's figures showed a slight decline over the previous spring. Shoe issues fell to 347,257 from 397,594, field jackets to 215,793 from 242,337, and pairs of pants to 342,399 from 353,433.[174] Still, 36,000 jackets and 57,000 pairs of pants were issued each month of the fall. A greater abundance of cotton goods, drawers, and shirts was available. The development of two sock factories made the Confederacy practically self-sufficient in this product and allowed Lawton to issue 271,285 pairs between June and December 1864, while still retaining a reserve of 100,000 pairs in Richmond. The issues for 1864 amounted to 744,851 pairs of shoes, 458,130 field jackets, 695,832 pairs of pants, and an abundance of cotton shirts and underclothing.

As Lawton explained to the last Confederate Congress, meeting within sound of the enemy artillery, "all the factories are under contract to deliver at fair rates two-thirds of their production." He had finally perfected a "uniform system, one built up with care and labor, and with a result perfectly satisfactory."[175] However, with factories under siege, Lawton's imports through Wilmington played an increasingly significant role in keeping the Confederate armies in the field.

4

Factories under Siege

Confederate military authorities were more successful in controlling factories than in succoring them. The Confederate system of controls through impressment, details, profit limitations, supply of raw materials, and management of railroads and blockade-running created challenging operating conditions for manufacturers. Bereft of parts and machinery and threatened by marauding armies, manufacturers were often imperiled by a hostile local press that offered considerable sympathy for economic independence but decried rising prices as pure extortion.

The problems of factory operation were numerous, and one of them was Confederate policy. In an early address to the Manufacturing Association of the Confederate States, William Gregg explained that "if the war continues, it will be absolutely essential that machinery, and tools to make it, shall in large quantities be imported." He invited an assembly at Augusta to bring "an influence to bear on our Government that would be irresistible in obtaining permission to take out cotton and bring in supplies—and if necessary, steamships might be purchased for the purpose."[1] An essay in the *Charleston Mercury* on June 5, 1863, inspired if not written by Gregg, challenged that "if this war is to continue, then we will need new factories." The writer charged that Confederate government policies hindered the drive for economic independence, for "to import machinery now costs from twelve to fifteen prices, and we feel quite well assured that no large establishment in our country has earned money enough in two years past to pay for the importation of machinery that would add twenty percent to their production, and they will remain as they are, to the great detriment of the country" (*Charleston Mercury*, June 5, 1863). In North Carolina, Francis Fries mused that "this country will

never be *independent* until men of intelligence & capital pay more attention to manufacturing of all kinds."[2]

In Arkansas, manufacturer Henry Merrell critically wrote that "had
encouragement been given to mechanics, & certain conditional exemption, then no man's son would have been above learning a useful trade,
and the blockade would have enriched the South by raising up a class of
Southern mechanics and manufacturers that would have rendered the
Southern people practically independent" (Merrell 296).[3] However, circumstances proved otherwise: "planting was to be the privileged order in
the Confederacy, our remedy lay in becoming planters ourselves" (296).

The isolation of the Confederacy by blockade initially created considerable optimism that industrial expansion would quickly follow Southern independence. Even the *New York Herald*, which carefully followed
events in the South, argued that the "the states of the Southern confederacy are bestirring themselves in the manufacturing line, with a view to
provide for their own wants in those articles for which they were heretofore dependent upon New England." The editor perceived that Lowell
and Lynn, Massachusetts, faced new competition, for "cotton mills, shoe
factories, yarn and twine manufactories are being put extensively into
operation in Georgia and other states" (*New York Herald* March 17, 1861).
While such reports were exaggerated, the knowledgeable editor of the
Augusta Daily Constitutionalist believed that Southern manufacturers, in
their quest for commercial self-sufficiency, would quickly improvise "a
variety of findings, such as shuttles, temples, pickers, reeds, harnesses,
spindles, flyers, roller leather, roller cloth, card clothing, lace leather,
rings, and travelers." He believed that Georgia's Roswell factory could
manufacture the wire combs to card wool and cotton, while "some of
your Augusta machine shops would find the manufacture of rings and
travelers, flyers, and spindles, and supplies of shuttle findings, a profitable business" (*Augusta Daily Constitutionalist*, July 10, 1861). James
DeBow optimistically predicted that "nearly all the articles wanted by
our mills, are now or soon will be supplied by our own people."[4] In actu-
ality, the war and government policy inhibited the realization of these
national goals.

The Confederate government took little cognizance of industrial
problems until late in the war. Factories, along with railroads, foundries,
and mines, lost workers to the military and suffered the imposition of

stringent regulations. Governors were more sensitive to the plight of manufacturers, but in the first instance, the growth and survival of Confederate industry were due to the efforts of enterprising local manufacturers such as Fries, Merrell, and Gregg. Simply replacing essential parts and materials became difficult. Wise spinners like Henry Merrell of Arkansas, George Camp of Georgia, and Edwin Holt of North Carolina secured quantities of oil and spare parts before secession.[5] Merrell noted, "In anticipation of the War, I had in the fall of 1860 laid in at least three years supply of 'findings' necessary to keep our works in order" (Merrell 307). However, others, like James Watson, of Virginia's Millville factory, were immediately short of reeds, dyes, shuttles, and the extensive and miscellaneous paraphernalia connected with producing cloth.[6]

While initially seen as a bounty, the blockade proved to be a blight. Manufacturers were forced to improvise endlessly. In the fall of 1862, Francis Fries, generally a wise manager, found his supply of pickers depleted. Pickers, originally made of dressed leather and then of metal, rested on the shuttles and absorbed the impact of forceful motions across the loom. Fries queried a mill agent in Petersburg, Virginia, where considerable metal work was done, and then he approached George Makepeace, the New England–born manager at the Cedar Falls factory who had an encyclopedic knowledge of such things.[7] Still unsuccessful, he wrote a Hawkinsville, North Carolina, mechanic, explaining that "we now need some pickers for our looms, & shall need tubes for our Danforth frames." Proprietary spinning frames, such as those manufactured by Charles Danforth, needed individually designed "findings." Fries found himself "somewhat short" of card clothing. These were mounted on drums to prepare the raw cotton for spinning. He was "advised by a friend of ours in Columbia that there is an establishment there, that will probably be in operation in a week or two that will make that & this will ease off manufacturers on that score."[8]

Fries traded bolts of cloth to James G. Gibbes, of the Saluda factory, for a quantity of blue vitriol, or copper sulfate, his favorite dyeing agent to fix blue colors.[9] He filled a warehouse with rosin, which was boiled to provide fuel for the factory's gaslights. He bought 200 barrels but wanted more, thinking that "we ought to have about 1000 bbls. so as to have some for the next year or two."[10] While other manufacturers stocked linseed or cottonseed oil, used to lubricate wool before carding, Fries laid in barrels of peanut oil.[11] At the nearby Alamance factory, Thomas Holt preferred plain lard to peanut oil. The lack of a substitute lubricating fluid, to replace sperm oil previously secured from New England whalers, especially threatened the production of woolens. Some substitutes, such as coal oil, evaporated "50 per ct faster than sperm."[12] In general, by the fall of 1862 Fries believed "we can make out for some time with our other findings."[13]

In the search for supplies, the larger mills of Petersburg commissioned Hugh Bone, a resourceful English-born mechanic, to tour the South from Virginia to Georgia.[14] Bone bought whatever items he could find, and he found 500 old flyer spindles at Roswell, but mostly the market was bare.[15] Southern merchants long accustomed to supplying the manufacturing trade quickly emptied their shelves of leather belting, indigo dyes, and "bleached winter elephant oil suitable for burning."[16] The scarcity was reflected in some contracts between the factories and the Quartermaster Department. In June 1862, J. Rhodes Browne, of Georgia's Eagle factory, engaged to sell the Confederacy all his enameled cloth, popular for gun carriages, knapsacks, and raincoats, "so long as we may be able to procure the articles needed in the manufacture." When faced with vanishing stocks of varnish and lamp black, Browne despaired, "we do not know, & cannot possibly calculate upon the length of terms we shall be able to furnish the supply."[17]

For factory products made of wood, the Confederacy possessed an abundance of raw materials and an adequacy of milling machinery. Manufacturers who needed boxes, barrels, and spindles often improvised. In North Carolina, George Makepeace, a skilled cotton spinner and bucket manufacturer, kept his fellow millers stocked with spools.[18] Georgia machinists, many trained by Samuel Griswold at his gin factory and manufacturing complex near Macon, leapt into the market. In Augusta, Georgia, H. T. Nelson advertised in the *Daily Constitutionalist* that he had "been engaged in the manufacture of bobbins and spools, at this place, for several years." Nelson's shop employed thirteen lathes, with more under construction by a local machinist. His production, which had commenced on a small scale, quickly mounted to 30,000 bobbins a month, even though he was "several hands short of a full complement, they having gone to the war." From Petersburg mills alone, in two months Nelson received orders "for nearly twenty thousand and orders from this and adjoining States exceeding forty thousand more." He declined sales to "parties that could not wait 'their turn,' to the aggregate of over fifty thousand." The machinist was optimistic that "there is little needed South that cannot be made South," and he warned that "if we would be free we must also be a mechanical people."[19]

Not all of Nelson's early customers were satisfied. George Camp purchased 20,000 of his bobbins, since Roswell factory was filling "an order for warps from Virginia and have not spools enough to run more than one mill."[20] He found some of Nelson's work made of unseasoned wood, which easily broke.

E. J. McCall's Athens Bobbin Works was patronized by the Savannah River factories. This entrepreneur solicited business by circular and was chosen by James Montgomery to supply the Graniteville factory.[21] In Alabama, Daniel Pratt, who ran a foundry in connection with his cotton mill, established a large bobbin factory. Pratt began in January 1863 by purchasing some "mill machinery, tools, & effects" from Ephraim S. Morgan for $10,860.[22] This he added to his inventory of woodworking tools. By 1864, Pratt's order book was filled, and he shipped that year 93,000 spools, bobbins, cones, and quills for wrapping yarns. The Gigger and Gunn factory, established at Benton in Lowndes County, Alabama, ordered in two months 4,000 bobbins and 6,000 filling quills. The Planter's factory in Alabama purchased 5,000 warp bobbins, and the Eagle mill at Columbus purchased 16,000 mule quills and 10,000 bobbins. Pratt himself ordered 32,000 spindles. Alabama's Chockolocco cotton mills, recently converted from a foundry, secured 500 warp bobbins, and Georgia's Grant factory took 8,000 quills and bobbins. The Mississippi Manufacturing Company at Bankston, Kirkman and Hays at Tuscaloosa, and Simpson and Moore at Bradford, Alabama, along with numerous factory agents, were among Pratt's largest customers.[23]

Shuttles and other mill findings were successfully manufactured at Columbus by A. D. Brown. A writer for *DeBow's Review* found Brown's factory on the first floor of the Carter Variety building, surrounded by active shops making canteens, scabbards, swords, and shoes (*Augusta Daily Constitutionalist*, September 24, 1861). According to *DeBow's*, Brown fabricated "the machinery required to make shuttles" and then supplied both the Roswell factory and the Green and Scott mill in Fredericksburg.[24] The *Augusta Daily Constitutionalist* rated his shuttles "smooth, even, and run better we learn, than those purchased in the United States" (September 24, 1861). However, George Camp at Roswell was no more satisfied with Brown's shuttles than with Nelson's bobbins; he complained that "they are narrower than the sample and cannot be used in our looms, and would be entirely worthless if we had not 14 looms with moveable box."[25]

Nevertheless, manufacturers of pickers, shuttles, and other incidentals of spinning rapidly multiplied across the wartime South. The Union Manufacturing Company in Virginia, a reputable company that made sewing machines, secured a lively business in producing factory parts, as did J. and J. C. Denham at Eatonton, Georgia.[26] The Union company manufactured rings, tubes, and other metal components for looms that were especially popular among the mills of North Carolina.[27] At the Salem factory, Francis Fries trained a local worker to make ring travelers, a wire guide for spinning frames much in demand by Petersburg manufacturers.[28]

Manufacturers who operated machine shops with their factories did a heavy casting and tooling business. Both Daniel Pratt and George Camp kept highly skilled workers engaged in this activity.[29] William E. Jackson, president of the Augusta factory and an owner of a local foundry, masterfully improvised. In a report to his stockholders on June 30, 1864, he explained, "our entire machinery & premises are in good condition." Within the mill "the whole number of looms having been at work constantly & the average daily production of each (43 yds) is evidence of their skillful management, as also the carding & spinning which have kept them supplied with yarn." Like many other companies, he reported, "we have made & are still making portions of machinery and improving what we have." Although expensive, Jackson believed "it is the most economical time we could do it." Such machinery as he manufactured for the company's three mills was "already more than paid for by the increased production."[30]

Many Southern companies fabricated looms. John Scott, apparently associated with a Fredericksburg woolen mill, advertised locally made twill looms for $100 each. George Camp of Roswell purchased forty of them, enough to equip a building adjacent to the company's three other factories.[31] Another company, J. and R. Winship of Atlanta, made looms based on the popular Jenks pattern, which Camp also ordered.[32] The

Crenshaw Woolen Mill at Richmond had an attached machine shop that constructed broad looms, including fifteen for the factory's own use (*Richmond Enquirer*, October 17, 1861). When ably handled, these could fabricate blanket pairs. In the Trans-Mississippi region, machinists Anderson and Richards of Montgomery County, Texas, manufactured spinning jennies that produced thread "equal to that of the State penitentiary."[33]

An especially difficult item to procure was card clothing. Hand cards were also in great demand as planters revived the use of old loom rooms for the duration of the war. In September 1862, Francis Fries noted with pleasure that the brother of a prominent Columbia hardware merchant, an old friend, had "gone into the manufacture of cards & has fair prospects of success." He was delighted because "this Confederacy has been woefully deficient in men that are willing to invest their means in enterprises of this kind & we now see the evil of it." Fries was willing to buy any card clothing, even that which was used, and upon learning of another manufacturer of such, he immediately inquired "if there be anything in this country that you would like in payment, I think I could get it for you."[34] Production was limited because cards could be manufactured only on special machinery and required large quantities of wire and leather.

Amos Wittemore invented a card-making machine in the Federal period. The sophisticated device was guided by cams, perforated leather, and inserted wire staples; however, most Confederate models came from Europe, where the original device was imported and considerably refined before the war. Apparently, J. C. Plant of Macon, Georgia, and Bankston, Mississippi, operated such a machine in his factory in 1863. Barrington King of Atlanta visited him, sanguine about "having some card clothing made for our mills."[35] However, Plant's operations depended upon scarce raw materials: wire and leather. Wire-pulling machinery was scarce, and wire was difficult to acquire in the Confederacy. As an owner of the Mississippi Manufacturing Company at Bankston, an important supplier of the western forces, Plant had high priority in getting supplies from Mexico. In May 1864, Plant and his partner, James Wesson, ordered 700 pounds of fine wire to manufacture hand cards and card clothing. From their supplies they regularly furnished the state of Mississippi "with some five hundred to one thousand pair of hand cards pr month at five dollars a pair." These cards were conveyed in turn to "the wives and widows of the soldiers" for plantation use. More important was the mill card clothing manufactured by the company, for "the amt furnished the factories enables them to make 40,000 yards of goods per day that they otherwise could not have made."[36]

The issue of securing machinery to make hand cards and card clothing was one that racked the Confederacy. The problem, lamented a western manufacturer, was lack of government patronage. Everywhere, he wrote, there was wool and cotton, "but it remained in the condition of raw material for want simply of hand cards, which any enterprising merchant would have found means to procure at his private risk, could he have been sure that he would not be denounced as a 'speculator' and the whole taken from him, or put into a tariff of prices [for impressment] so low as to deprive him of his profits & fair reward for his trouble & risks" (Merrell 309). In fact, nearly all of the Confederate state governments entered into the manufacture and distribution of hand cards. Skillful manufacturers could make serviceable carding strips for factories with the same machinery. In June 1863, Governor John G. Shorter of Alabama purchased on behalf of the state a half interest in the Alabama State Card Manufacturing Company at Selma for $12,000 (John Jones 1: 358). The six machines used "for the manufacture of wire and cards" were fabricated by James M. Keep, "without a pattern."[37] The company employed ten hands, operated a tannery, and maintained a steam engine for power. Production amounted to over 500 pairs of hand cards each week; these resources were available for Alabama factories.[38]

In December 1862, Governor Joseph E. Brown secured an appropriation to purchase half interest in the Pioneer Card Manufacturing Company for $60,000. This company at Cartersville, Georgia, possessed "one machine for setting the teeth of *cotton cards* for factories." Brown's card company had a steam engine, a stock of leather, and other materials. Wire enough to manufacture 12,000 cards "had been brought in from the United States, at considerable expense." The governor placed the machinery in the armory building at Milledgeville, behind the walls of the penitentiary, and made ten duplicate machines, each of which was capable of turning out twenty-four sets of hand cards a day.[39]

At the request of Governor Vance, a North Carolina agent was permitted to disassemble the Georgia machinery and make drawings in order to fabricate similar devices.[40] But the resourceful war governor was unwilling to rely on this expediency alone. In the summer of 1863, Vance commissioned John White, a Warrenton merchant, to go abroad with an order "to purchase a lot of cotton & wool cards and a machine for making them with a good supply of wire."[41] Vance considered the needs of the factories. When White forwarded 112,000 pairs of cotton cards to the West Indies in January 1864, large amounts of factory card clothing were included in the shipment.[42]

Manufacturers enjoyed considerable success in replenishing their card clothing, and they did not neglect other opportunities to secure supplies. When the *Tropic Wind* breached the blockade with a cargo of logwood dye salvaged from a wreck on the Cuban coast, the Crenshaw company "was enabled to furnish their less fortunate manufacturing friends throughout the South with as much logwood as can be needed for months to come" (*Richmond Enquirer*, October 17, 1861). In the midst of General Ambrose Burnside's sudden seaborne invasion of New Bern, North Carolina, in March 1862, the machinery of the local cotton mill was evacuated to Kinston.[43] Francis Fries sensed a bargain in the offing. Upon finding that John C. Washington held possession of the machinery, Fries promptly inquired as to "what there is, & whether for sale, [and] whether the cards (which we understand were saved) have good clothing."[44] Fries sought all of the machinery and bought at the public sale in August 1862 "some cylinders & doffers [a studded roller to remove rolls from cards] with the clothing on them."[45] The card clothing cost $7 a foot, a bargain. The shafting and gearing were offered to Caleb Phifer's Charlotte mill at 35 cents a pound.[46]

Ralph C. Brinkley's Wolfe Creek factory at Memphis was exposed to Federal incursion in early 1862. When Milner and Wood of Florence discovered that Brinkley was "anxious to sell the factory and land," they undertook steps to purchase the machinery.[47] Brinkley declared that the "machinery is not for sale" and exiled himself within the Confederacy upon the fall of Memphis.[48] In 1863, another factory within easy reach of Federal raiding parties was put on the block. James Webb's cotton and woolen mill at Hillsboro, North Carolina, was advertised, and several who inquired proposed dismantling the factory for the machinery.[49] One potential purchaser demanded detailed information on the capacity, age, and condition of all machines but finally declined to buy, appar-

ently because of the military hazards involved.⁵⁰ A naval agent participated in the final bidding. In January, the Navy Department authorized
Captain T. A. Jackson "to purchase Cotton Factory machinery for its
mills and rope walks; now being located in Petersburg for the purpose of
spinning warps to make cotton rope."⁵¹ The discovery by the navy that
tarred cotton cordage could serve many of the purposes of hempen rope
spurred such efforts. Archibald McIlwaine leased the navy a facility for
manufacturing rope near his Ettrick mill.⁵² After negotiations, the navy
declined to purchase Webb's machines but evacuated similar machinery
from the Scott factory in Isle of Wight County, Virginia.⁵³

Factories destroyed by conflagration were another source of machinery and spare parts. The Crenshaw company's mill in Richmond burned
on May 14, 1863, and the remains were immediately salvaged to replace
worn and dilapidated machinery in the nearby factories (John Jones
[May 15, 1863] 1: 324). George Schley, owner of the Belleville factory in
Georgia, found that after its second devastation by fire in February 1862,
"a good many manufacturers came to purchase what was saved from the
burning." Choice items among the debris included "a large lot of scrap
iron, boiler iron, steam boilers, shaftings, couplings, & hangers, leather
belting, gas pipes, spindle steel, and three large copper kettles." Among
the bidders again was the Confederate military, and Colonel William G.
Gill, of the Augusta Arsenal, "insisted on purchasing what we had
saved."⁵⁴ Another hoard of parts was salvaged from the remains of the
Dog River factory, which burned at Mobile. For $41,990 Garland Goode,
its agent, sold the Confederate government a boiler, two engines, a sawmill, and assorted tools, all "situated in an exposed position and liable
to be taken by the enemy."⁵⁵ The remainder of the machinery was probably taken by Alabama factories.

Idle machinery was also much in demand. James B. Pace of Danville
aggressively sought out such machinery and put it into operation. After
securing control of the old Danville mill, Pace ingratiated himself with
the War Department by offering military goods "at comparatively low
rates."⁵⁶ In June 1864, Pace discovered that David Bill and Dexter Snow
of Pulaski County, Virginia, a Unionist stronghold, "now hold at their
property in said county a portion of the machinery of a woolen factory,
purchased by them several years ago in Boston Mass." The mountain
mill remained inactive because an important component "still remains

in the enemy's country & cannot now be obtained." With ten or twelve looms and spinning machinery to match, the mill offered to double Pace's output to 10,000 yards a week, enough woolens to clothe two regiments. However, Bill and Snow refused "to sell & will entertain no proposition to this effect." Thus Pace wrote General Alexander Lawton requesting the impressment of this property for his personal use on the grounds that his own mill was "supplying large quantities of woolen cloth for the use of the Government."[57] General Lawton endorsed the impressment and removal of the machinery to Danville.

Salvaged and discarded machinery were both sometimes used to erect new factories.[58] William Amis of Carroll County, Georgia, wrote the secretary of war that he "procured and put in operation all the idle cotton machinery he could obtain, consisting of seven hundred and twelve spindles, which if well managed, will spin about three hundred and fifty pounds of cotton per day."[59] The Amis factory wove yarns exclusively for the Confederate Commissary Department. In a similar way, several new Georgia factories such as Alcova and Alquandon were created from spare and surplus machinery. One source was the extensive equipment of the Greensboro factory, made at Matteawan Machine Company in New York, which the proprietors sold off just before the war (Merrell 242–42, 323).

The pressing demand for machinery encouraged a keen competition for that which was available. In 1862, when the old Salem Manufacturing Company, originally erected by the Moravians in 1836, was placed on the market, Francis Fries made an eager bid for the property. It was adjacent to his two thriving factories, and he knew the machinery intimately, having made the original purchases himself. But the bidding became quite intense when former governor John M. Morehead formed a group of stockholders to purchase the establishment. Chagrined, Fries wrote, "the machinery of the old cotton mill in this place has lately been put into operation, & we do not suppose it could be bought now."[60] Rather, he turned to the Richmond factory in Georgia, writing the company "to ascertain whether you have any spinning frames for sale." His Salem mill, Fries explained, had "just machinery enough for the work we have been doing, but I would like to spin finer numbers of yarn if I had more machinery."[61] Unsuccessful, the resourceful Fries tried another tactic. He wrote Pace's Danville factory, offering to exchange card clothing, probably purchased from the New Bern mill, in return for any of his surplus acquisitions.[62]

Maintaining the factory's motive power required the service of large forging facilities. Iron mills at Richmond and Manchester, Virginia, did much of this work in the Upper South. Robert Baird of Manchester produced the popular Bodine-Jonval turbine water wheel, in common use along the fall line. The Bodine-Jonval, a downward flow turbine constructed of a single piece of iron or brass, generated power as water circulated through curved blades revolving around a stationary axis (*Appletons' Cyclopaedia of Applied Mechanics* 2: 918–19; *Appleton's* [*sic*] *Dictionary* 2: 894–902). A twenty-one-inch wheel could generate over five horsepower. In 1864, Thomas M. Holt, then owner of the Granite factory, sent Baird an order for a wheel "to drive 8 Danforth cap spinning frames, 12 cards, 2 drawing frames, 2 speeder, 12 cards, & 2 lappers."[63] After calculating the head of water and the depth of fall, Baird made the usual drawings of the necessary gearing and fabricated the parts out of Virginia wrought iron.[64] The demand for Baird's skills was considerable.[65]

In December 1862, Henry Merrell scoured the lower Mississippi, from Memphis to New Orleans, searching for a small steam engine to supplement the water power at his Arkansas mill. Not finding a machine, he "concluded we must try & build the Steam Engine in Arkansas, at the Camden furnace" (Merrell 303–4). Motivated by a desire to run at night, he achieved a measure of success: "The steam Engine, a very good one we got up in Arkansas, by a little here and there, at considerable cost" (304).

Despite improvisations, large quantities of Confederate machinery stood idle for want of parts or raw materials. General Lawton's census of Southern factories in 1864 revealed that thirty-one Lower South mills had 255 looms and 10,789 spindles inactive, almost 10 percent of the total machinery surveyed, while in North Carolina 145 looms and 1,332 spindles were inoperative. Such a volume of machinery normally had the capacity to fabricate 300,000 yards of cloth a month, so the loss was considerable.

Following William Gregg's advice to bring machinery through the blockade, many Southern manufacturers turned to import companies like John Fraser of Charleston. Fraser maintained a Liverpool office, branches in the British West Indies, and an excellent fleet of blockade-runners. His firm was practically an adjunct of the Confederate government, serving as official depository for government funds in Europe; however, doing business through the blockade was complicated. As George Camp explained to one of his stockholders, "we have written to England about looms, but if the blockade continues, [it looks] rather bad for our works."[66] Securing foreign funds, inspecting goods, and running the blockade were great hazards. William Gregg also patronized Fraser's company. Theodore D. Wagner, Fraser's Charleston agent, was a Graniteville stockholder, which facilitated matters.[67] In fact, perhaps reflective of larger expectations, Wagner and James Montgomery of Graniteville were among the stockholders of a newly proposed manufacturing company chartered by South Carolina for $350,000.[68]

Francis Fries also looked to England "for supplies which heretofore we have obtained from our unnatural & tyrannical 'brethren.' " He was gratified that merchants were prepared "at the earliest practicable moment to engage in the direct trade with Europe."[69] Fries's initial order for Fraser consisted of ninety-three sheets of card clothing, numerous sheepskins for rollers and reeds to separate warps and beat up filling, bichromate of potash, and a ton of dyeing compounds.[70] Such shipments often required a year for delivery, if they passed the blockade.[71] After months of waiting, Fries despaired of getting his supplies because "they load vessels with something that they think pays better, although we would pay any price for freight & run the risk of capture."[72] Sets of machinery, designed to work together, needed to be delivered intact, but blockade-runners often broke lots into small parcels to lessen the risk of capture. Barrington King complained in August 1863 that "the machinery for making card clothing [was] sent on 3 different steamers to run the blockade [and has] not yet arrived, & may turn out a bad speculation."[73] Some of this lot of machinery apparently arrived and was placed in J. C. Plant's card clothing factory in Macon.

However, the Charlotte woolen factory of Young, Wriston, and Orr was successfully enlarged through the importation of machinery. The factory originally ran four sets of cards, with sufficient looms and spindles to weave the product. During the secession crisis, John A. Young "procured from the Northern machine manufacturers two sets more, besides a considerable amount of cotton machinery."[74] This was housed in a separate factory building. For further expansion, Young called at John

Fraser's Charleston offices. Fraser explained the difficulties of the blockade and required at least eighteen months for delivery. Fries, learning of Young's visit, wrote Fraser to please "consider us in any arrangement you may make with him relative to manufacturers' goods of any kind."[75] Not until February 1863 could Young report that his machinery "had arrived in Charleston, [and] this will enable us to add 50% to the production of our mill and will necessarily consume a corresponding amount of cotton."[76] Because of this success, Young and Fries were capable of supplying a large portion of the woolen uniforms used by North Carolina troops.

Upon learning that George Schley of Augusta intended "going to Europe to buy some machinery," Fries wrote him an appeal to secure card clothing and small articles "that cannot be bought in the Confederacy."[77] Like many others, Schley sought a Confederate passport to purchase machinery abroad. In May 1863, Governor John Gill Shorter interceded with the secretary of war on behalf of Joseph Tannenbaum and Isias C. Meyer, "respectable and loyal citizens of the Confederacy," who carried foreign purchase orders "from one of our Alabama factories for machinery & materials." The Tallassee mill "had and still has large contracts with the government."[78] Tallassee, "from which the State has received the greatest quantity of the material for clothing her troops in the field," provided Governor Shorter with all of its duck cloth, which was "manufactured into tents at the State penitentiary."[79]

Still another foreign mission was undertaken by Nathan R. Mendenhall, a North Carolina Quaker. In August 1863, Mendenhall appeared before General John H. Winder, the stern administrator of martial law in the Richmond military district, and swore that he was "a loyal citizen of the Confederate States." Mendenhall prayed "to visit Europe for the purpose of procuring machinery to increase the opperations [sic] of his woolen factory."[80] The crusty Maryland-born provost general, who also administered local prisoner-of-war camps, was unmoved by the pleas of a young Quaker of obvious military age. Winder immediately ordered Mendenhall conscripted and placed in one of the Richmond camps of military instruction.[81] The manufacturer secured a lawyer and apparently found a way to continue his journey, for a year later North Carolina quartermaster Samuel R. Chisman found Mendenhall's new factory in Jamestown to be one of "considerable power." Chisman reported that "the factory in question was originally a gun shop: It is now, however, fully equipped, with excellent machinery as a cotton mill."[82] William Miller, General Lawton's special investigator in North Carolina, visited Mendenhall's mill in November 1864 and concurred: "this is a new factory just being established; it will be a very large one; cotton & woolen and will work almost altogether for Q.M. Department."[83]

Other manufacturers sought to emulate Mendenhall's example. In November 1863, F. W. Lineback, an employee of Fries's factory, appeared before Secretary of State Judah P. Benjamin requesting an exit visa.[84] That same fall, M. Baum, a South Carolinian, prayed the secretary to let him depart from Wilmington because he wished "to establish a Card factory and desires to go to Nassau to procure machinery."[85] John H. Chisolm, a Georgian, wanted to visit Europe "to buy Factory machinery." Still another Georgian, Gustavus H. Bates, desired passage rights to Nassau "for the purpose of purchasing machinery, wire & to manufacture cotton cards."[86] However, blockaders interfered with some of these ventures. Armed with over $6,000, partly in specie, L. Ohlmans was captured by the Union bark *Roebuck* en route to Nassau via the Gulf Coast. His letters indicated that "he was going abroad to purchase machinery with the intention of starting a woolen factory in the South."[87]

Major manufacturers in the Lower South worked tirelessly to secure machinery imports. In January 1864, Daniel Pratt intervened with General Lawton to secure a passport for W. W. Fay, an Alabama mill agent, pleading, "it will be to the interest of all parties to extend to him facilities for going abroad to purchase the articles needed." General Lawton approved the passport because "it is of importance to keep up the productions of this factory." However, Lawton refused to provide Pratt with foreign funds from the sale of Confederate cotton. Rather, after some negotiation, he ordered Thomas L. Bayne, who handled foreign cotton sales for the bureau, "to ship from Mobile, in the space allotted to this Department, at that port, cotton enough to procure at Nassau or Bermuda, or in England, as the company may wish it placed, a credit to the extent of . . . fifteen thousand dollars."[88] Pratt agreed to provide sixty bales of cotton and pay the transportation charges.

As Pratt's agent prepared to sail to the islands, another application was submitted by Enoch Steadman, the well-known manager of Georgia's Gwinette factory. Endorsed by a member of the House Committee on

Military Affairs, Steadman petitioned "to visit Europe with the view of purchasing machinery to bring to the Confederacy for the manufacture of cotton goods." He was recommended as one "thoroughly acquainted with the business and has been already by his public spirit, energy and patriotism of great benefit to his branch of industry." Ignoring the fact that Steadman's factory was controlled by Governor Brown, his congressional patron argued that "the cause of the Southern States would be enhanced by the introduction into them of machinery under the supervision of such a finished machinist and manufacturer."[89]

Like Steadman, Henry Merrell was an experienced manufacturer in service to the Confederacy. With the advance of the Union army upon his Pikesville, Arkansas, factory in February 1863, Merrell first sold the mill to a local merchant; then, under orders from the Confederate government, which secured the factory in November 1863, he removed the machinery by wagon train to Mound Prairie, East Texas (Merrell 100–101, 230–32, 379–83). There General Edmund Kirby Smith and the Trans-Mississippi Clothing Bureau established a military manufacturing center. At Mound Prairie in the winter of 1863, Merrell found that "machinery had been collected by purchase & by impressment from all quarters too near the Enemy for safety," that "our old factory in Pike County was there," and that "six steam engines in all were on the ground & a mass of building material lying about, besides several buildings already in a forward stage of erection" (383). The western command intended "that this manufacturing town should be projected on a scale so extensive as not only to furnish Clothing & Blankets, ordnance, fabrics, shoes, & hats for the army but a surplus to be bartered with the Country for Commissary stores when Confederate money would no longer purchase supplies" (379). Although suspected as a Unionist because of his New England origins, Merrell was drafted and assigned to serve as an engineer on the staff of Lieutenant General Theophilus Holmes.[90] When General Kirby Smith learned of Merrell's special skills, he ordered him to confer with quartermasters at Houston and Matamoras and to go abroad for more cotton mill machinery. If possible, he was enjoined to stop in Cuba and confer with Charles Helm, Confederate agent in Havana. Merrell's mission, funded with $100,000 from the Clothing Bureau, was to purchase "machinery, that will manufacture material ample in quantity for providing clothing, camp & garrison equipage for the Trans-Miss.

Army." While in Europe, he was ordered to inspect "the work shops and manufactories of army goods in England & France, adopting and purchasing such machinery and appliances as in your judgement are best suited to our wants."[91] The Confederate Treasury agent in Liverpool, Colin J. McRae, was to establish a special account for him, "specifically for the purchase of cotton and woollen machinery."[92] With his private secretary, Merrell crossed into Mexico and sailed for England. Since McRae had received no funds, Merrell "made no purchases or contracts at all under his instructions."[93] While Merrell's mission was not productive, others were.

Governor Zebulon Vance sent at least four agents to England to procure "in foreign markets" materials such as shoes, blankets, machines, and findings.[94] John White, a Warrenton merchant, and Thomas M. Crossan, a former ship's captain, were the most effective.[95] In return for North Carolina clothing its own troops, Secretary of the Treasury Christopher Memminger provided Vance with bonds that were transferred to North Carolina agents in Liverpool.[96] Some $2.5 million was dispatched to John White by July 1863.[97] Sales of state cotton and rosin through the blockade supplemented these funds. To bring the supplies into Wilmington, Vance purchased at Crossan's insistence the "long-legged steamer"; the *Advance* made eleven round trips from Bermuda to Wilmington, bringing in "supplies of those things which could not be procured at home, especially grain scythes, card clothing for factories, hand cards for our old-fashioned looms, and medicines." With an eye to North Carolina factories, Vance instructed White to bring in findings, or spare parts, and "to purchase a lot of [50,000] cotton & wool cards and a machine for making them with a good supply of wire" (Dowd 454–55).[98] An abstract of four cargoes brought in by the *Advance* in 1863 showed large quantities of factory materials: wire, belting, leather, and oils.[99] Before the end of the year, Vance had at Bermuda or en route there some eight or ten cargoes, including "machinery and findings to refit twenty-six of our principal cotton and woolen factories, dyestuff, lubricating oils, etc."[100] Due to this success, Vance advised his agents in July 1863 to buy no more English clothing, for "the resources of our State and the Confederacy have developed in such a degree that we have every assurance of being able to clothe our troops with our own goods."[101] This outfitting was accomplished despite the opposition of James M. Mason, Confederate commissioner in London, who prohibited the sale of North Carolina's cotton bonds.[102]

The supplies from the *Advance* were sold to North Carolina factories by state quartermaster Henry A. Dowd. Henry Fries at Salem requested his share of the cargoes, writing, "I have also been patiently but anxiously waiting for advice of the arrival of 'that card clothing.' " Without the materials, he threatened, "I must stop part of the machinery."[103] The Randolph Manufacturing Company received "a small order at the suggestion of Gov. Vance."[104] Dennis Curtis, at the Deep River factory, wrote that "he (the Gov.) had now on hand a lot of card clothing and that he (Mr. Makepeace) would visit Raleigh in the course of a few days to see you in regard to purchasing clothing."[105] The purchases were substantial. In December 1864, the Union Manufacturing Company bought 160 sheets of card clothing and findings worth $32,000.[106] Thomas Holt secured 20 sheets for his Granite factory.[107] Fries at Salem expended $75,000 between December 31, 1863, and February 3, 1865, for card clothing, leather, hand cards, oils, wood, copperas, logwood, and other incidentals.[108]

The state of Texas rivaled North Carolina in its patronage of manufacturers. The isolated position of the Trans-Mississippi military district strongly encouraged self-sufficiency. Francis Lubbock, war governor until 1863, and General Kirby Smith, military commander of the district, vigorously endorsed proposals to promote manufacturing. Under Lubbock's patronage, on December 10, 1863, a complicated measure to raise $2 million for foreign purchases of machinery became law.[109] By this act the governor was authorized to create a military board to receive lint cotton from parties in Texas needing to make foreign purchases. The board exported the cotton to Europe through Matamoras and then provided foreign credits to the companies needing tools and machinery. The factory equipage was brought back through Mexico. As cases demanded, Lubbock made state loans to worthy projects. He wrote, "it was . . . a part of our policy to make advances in cash and cotton to private individuals, in order that they might be enabled to establish needed industries" (Lubbock 369). The export board was constantly in session ruling on new proposals.

The Texas legislature also undertook to augment "the Erection of Certain Machinery" by distributing public lands to newly formed companies. Any group erecting machinery to make cotton cloth or other needed military stores was entitled to one section of 320 acres for every thousand dollars of investment in improvements.[110] The legislature was overwhelmed with petitions to incorporate cotton mills, lead mines, flour mills, and foundries. Austin's *Texas State Gazette* filled its columns with the names of those receiving the new charters. In 1863, numerous new cotton mill companies were chartered including the Brazos, Chappell Hill, Hempstead, Trinity, and Waco factories. Ten more companies were organized in 1864, including the Bastrop, Cairo, Comal Springs, Dallas, Falls of Brazos, Holly Springs, Houston City Mill, San Marcos, Fort Bend, and Guadalupe manufacturing companies (Finlay and Simmons 106–46; *Texas State Gazette*, December 14, 1864; Lubbock 370, 478). James K. Metcalfe of Washington County, Texas, assisted by an expert weaver and machinist, erected a new cotton "factory on his plantation at his own expense."[111]

With a need to supply 50,000 troops, including many of those in Arkansas and the Indian Nation, General Kirby Smith created a Clothing Bureau for the Trans-Mississippi military district that rivaled Confederate operations in Richmond and Atlanta. Texas was divided into subdistricts, with headquarters at Tyler, San Antonio, and Houston. These were staffed with quartermasters empowered to secure and export cotton, buy machinery, erect mills, and manufacture clothing and equipage. Under state and Confederate patronage, by January 1864 plans were completed to build a woolen mill at Tyler and other factories at Waco, New Braunfels, and Bastrop.[112] Quartermaster William H. Haynes, chief of the Clothing Bureau in the Trans-Mississippi district, expected the Tyler woolen factory to substantially increase his supplies. Along with 10,000 pairs of shoes a month, he received 1.2 million yards of woolens, mostly from the Huntsville prison factory, but Haynes reported "the machinery sent to Tyler, Tex., when put in operation, will turn out in the same length of time at least 200,000 yards of woolen jeans."[113] In addition to the Tyler factory, Haynes reported that contracts for cloth were signed "by my predecessor (the Waco manufactory) and by myself (the Ward manufactory), but neither of them have been put in operation in consequence of delays attending the introduction through the Mexican Republic and Rio Grande frontier of machinery from Europe." He was confident that the Waco factory, incorporated in 1863, "will be in operation within the year, the machinery being in Texas and their products sold to the Government."[114] The machinery for this mill, capable of turning out 300 yards of cloth and 500 pounds of warps a day, "was purchased in England, and brought in . . . through Mexico" (*Texas Almanac for 1867* 138; *Texas Almanac for 1865* 19). The company soon commenced operations with five planing mills, an iron foundry, and brick houses for operatives. The Ward and Munger company was in Bastrop. Initially the company owned "buildings, lots, engine, spinning, and all the factory machinery" of the partners, but in 1864 the company was reorganized as the Bastrop Cotton and Wool Manufacturing Company with a view to supplying the Confederacy (Texas, Legislature, *General Laws* 4–5). Sylvester S. Munger, a Houston business leader, and A. J. Ward were the leaders of the concern.

The Comal Manufacturing Company at New Braunfels was chartered on March 2, 1863, with a capital of $500,000 by Henry and Herman Runge and John Torrey. The German-born Runge brothers were merchants at Indianola before embarking upon cotton manufacturing. In the spring of 1863, Herman Runge went abroad to make contracts "for the introduction for a Cotton Factory."[115] Runge purchased and shipped back to Matamoras machinery to run a factory of twenty-one looms and 800 spindles. John A. Wilcox, a congressman and one of the owners, obtained the sanction of the Confederate government to admit "free of duty, the machinery of the Comal Manufacturing Company into the State of Texas."[116] In November 1864, a correspondent for the *Texas Almanac* reported that "the Messrs. Runge and others have the works for an extensive cotton and woolen factory, to be located at New Braunfels, now on the way from Europe—that the machinery has even reached Brownsville or Matamoras—and is only waiting transportation to be brought up . . . better late than never" (*Texas Almanac for 1864* 39–41). The machinery was placed in a stone building on the Comal River and powered by two iron turbine water wheels.[117]

Quartermaster William H. Haynes contemplated that "another manufacturing establishment of large capacity (the Brazos manufactory) will be in operation before the spring of 1865." This mill, built at Houston by Sylvester S. Munger, was also fostered by Governor Lubbock's cotton export board. Haynes expected that the Brazos factory and another, "under the directory of Major Busby, quartermaster, will furnish resources within the department for supplying the troops without recourse to importations."[118] The other establishment was the Bastrop factory, "the oldest in the State," which was built for 1,100 spindles and sixteen looms. Real estate was acquired in 1864, and the new company was probably associated with the old Bastrop Steam Mill Company.[119] When finished, the factory turned out 800 yards daily (*Texas Almanac for 1867* 236). Still another mill was fostered at San Antonio by Major Thornton A. Washington, a Confederate quartermaster sent out by Abraham Myers from Virginia in 1862. After receiving a donation of land from the city and making detailed drawings for wool and leather-working establishments, Washington contracted with an agent "for machinery, labor, & c."[120] Washington then purchased 600 bales of cotton, transported them to Mexico by way of Eagle Pass, and exported them to Europe through Matamoras. When the war ended, a considerable amount of new machinery, perhaps some for this factory, was waiting in Mexican ports for Texas mills.

As elsewhere in the Confederacy, Texas developed home resources. An enterprising quartermaster, Major E. C. Wharton, ordered thirty spinning frames and a wool-carding machine from Anderson and Richards, machinists at Danville, which he proposed to place in a converted foundry at Hempstead, "so as to use the steam power to drive the spindles and looms."[121] Such activities, supplemented by Mexican imports, made Texas largely self-sufficient in military supplies.

In addition to spinning and weaving machinery, Confederates imported other sets of equipment vital to clothing the army. Several sock factories were established in 1863. John Lee ran the Coal Spring Mill Sock factory at Fayetteville, John Judge's mill at Columbia was the largest in the Confederacy, and Bridges and Ausley did large contracting with the army at Augusta.[122] By June 1864, when General Lawton embarked upon a policy of full mobilization, Judge and Company had machinery to turn out 3,000 pairs of socks daily and contracted with Hutson Lee of the Charleston depot to deliver 1 million pairs a year. The arrangement was mostly by barter. Lee exchanged five pounds of Georgia lint cotton with the Wood Lawn factory in North Carolina for each pound of yarn. The yarn was then traded with Judge and Company, one pound for 4 pairs of socks. Bridges and Ausley were located at Augusta; the quartermaster at that post did contracting with them to the amount of 240,000 pairs a year.[123] By the summer of 1864, General Lawton's bureau calculated that about 90 percent of all field issues of socks were supplied by these new knitting mills.

Within the factories, the war brought gradual changes to the work floor. Henry Merrell noted in midwar that "it had become necessary that our works should run by night as well as day, and that the speeds should be increased" (Merrell 303). Saturday, a traditional half day, generally became a full day. By judicious use of lights the workday was lengthened. At night the machinery was serviced and the carding room was staffed. Mills that possessed indoor lighting, usually gaslights fueled by rosin, had more flexibility than those that did not. The mill routine called for the machinery to commence turning at daybreak. Bells summoned the workers to begin a workday that averaged at least eleven hours, maybe more. With lunch and dinner breaks, the labor lasted into the evening hours as workers took cotton or wool through the complex machine rituals of carding, spinning, and weaving. The exact nature of mill routine depended upon the managers who were hard-pressed to maintain high production levels with a constant flux of personnel.

The gradual loss of white male workers forced mills to turn increasingly to women, children, and slaves for labor. In January 1862, Francis Fries noted in his Memorabilia Book that "the volunteering of so many young men out of our employment left us very short of hands, but it was not until brother & Joe Hine spoke of entering the army that I undertook to remonstrate against being left alone."[124] The absence of managers or skilled workers made the training of new workers more difficult. The growing absence of males was notable at North Carolina's Cedar Falls factory, which normally operated 50 looms and 2,400 spindles. This mill, which at the beginning of the war "stopped to call for volunteers," had only 6 men left out of 85 workers by May 1864.[125] The new employees were women who brought 48 dependents into the mill with them.[126] Some other mills maintained a more balanced workforce. A survey of ten Savannah River factories in June 1864 found 833 men and 1,046 female workers. With the loss of military-age white males, factories turned increasingly to slave workers. All ten Savannah River mills employed slaves, and the Hopewell factory used a mixed force of 37 whites and 83 blacks.[127] Frank Fries at Salem, with a considerable wool trade, employed the services of as many as 40 slaves, half of them leased. They ran his sawmill and did farm work and general hauling for the company and by July 1862 were handling wool in the mills.[128] Some became skilled spinners. Henry Merrell used black workers at his mill, writing, "I never failed to make a good workman of a smart Negro, first having a care to select my man . . . [for] Negroes have the manipulation for anything the most difficult" (Merrell 169). Nonetheless, he had one racial caveat, "They barberize & they fiddle better than white people with the same opportunity, but they are, the smartest of them, puzzle-headed, & must have their orders given to them one at a time" (169). However, Confederate policy toward slave laborers could be as capricious as toward white males of military age. In August 1863, Fries lost the services of John King, Giles, and George, who were impressed by state authorities to work on coastal fortifications.[129] These skilled men were not returned until the next November. The chagrined Fries wrote, "everything has been made to yield to the wants of the military."[130]

The wartime operations at the Cedar Falls factory probably reflected the conditions at many mills. In December 1861, the hands got Christmas off but worked full days on December 24 and 26; in the spring of 1862, five young women "ran away," perhaps in pursuit of men in the army; in May 1862, Lucy Precenal "got mad and left the mill"; in the following summer there were three marriages among mill workers; in November 1862, Elizabeth Pugh set a mill production record of 365 cuts (either loom cuts of cloth forty-five yards long or bunches of yarn) in one month; the mill stopped for one week in October 1863 to put in "a New Penstock" wheel; on Christmas 1863, the mill "stoped [sic] two days to frollick"; on January 10, 1865, the mill closed down for four days because "the river this day is higher than was ever known even by the oldest inhabitants"; and on April 26, 1865, the mill closed "to take up some horse thieves."[131] Otherwise, the mill operated continually and regularly. By barter through the company store, the company secured provisions of meal, milk, eggs, and bacon, which were used to reimburse and provision workers.

The working days were long, arduous, and monotonous. The Cedar Falls mill workers averaged ten and a half hours each day in November 1860 and twelve and a half hours by May 1861. Winter, summer, and Saturday hours were extended as a concession to the war until workers were at their machines nearly seventy-seven hours each week.[132] The factory measured productivity in cuts each month, and the peak period of activity rose in the early war period from 1,127 to 1,605 cuts. After a slight decline, during the summer of 1863 the factory still manufactured between 1,173 and 1,363 cuts monthly, but after Gettysburg production rarely exceeded 1,000 cuts. Overall productivity at Cedar Falls declined 28 percent through the war. This loss was slightly greater than the general decline evidenced in Confederate manufacturing. In the month of November 1864, however, the mill still produced 30,000 yards of cotton cloth and 5,000 pounds of yarns.

The successful importation of machinery and mobilization of domestic resources stirred the Confederate press to high praise. In 1863, the *Winston-Salem People's Press* printed a long list of new enterprises and explained to a public increasingly aware of the value of industry that "the machinery for new mills is partly manufactured at home, and partly obtained by running through the blockade" (March 13, 1863). The *Charleston Mercury* drew hope from reports in *DeBow's Review* that the war had turned villages into workshops. The press could cite numerous establishments that fabricated swords, canteens, boots and shoes, matches, and oilcloth. Across the South, once-small villages could boast of new arsenals, powder mills, bread factories, laboratories, iron mills, machine shops, and shipyards. From Selma to Columbus and Augusta, across northern South Carolina, and from Fayetteville to Petersburg, new thriving manufacturing centers emerged. Hundreds of towns claimed tanneries and government workshops. There were new manufacturers of peanut, linseed, and cottonseed oils (*Charleston Mercury*, April 29, 1861). In virtually every village, women gathered to sew and knit. At the peak of mobilization perhaps 50,000 civilian workers, mostly women, labored at quartermaster and ordnance depots fabricating military clothing and equipage. Practically every factory and major railroad depot acquired workshops and warehouses. However, despite the growth of manufacturing, full mobilization brought the painful realization that there was a great dearth of machinery within the South and that such machinery as operated also constantly depreciated from wear. In the Confederate Quartermaster Department, there was a reluctance to acknowledge these problems, and, in stark contrast to the activities of William H. Haynes and the Trans-Mississippi Clothing Bureau, Richmond authorities proved remarkably negligent of the very mills upon which they drew for succor. Rather, Confederate quartermasters turned increasingly to the importations of military supplies, an activity that presented at least some opportunity for manufacturers to secure materials vital for their continued operations.

5

The Bureau of Foreign Supplies and the Crenshaw Line

Until the end of the war, most garments and goods provided to the Confederate army came from domestic resources through Alexander Lawton's mobilization of manufacturing. However, to supplement these goods, the Confederate War Department turned increasingly to imports; in this endeavor, James B. Ferguson Jr., a former dry goods import merchant, and William G. Crenshaw, a Richmond woolen manufacturer, played important roles.[1] In doing so, Ferguson and Crenshaw rendered Upper South mills modest but vital support by procuring essential items from abroad. Otherwise, the War Department displayed little concern about the needs of private manufacturers and mostly devoted official energies to building large-scale military industries such as the Augusta Powder Works and the Macon Arsenal. Yet quantities of machinery, oils, and chemical dyes did enter the Confederacy on government account.

This official neglect was lamented by Henry Merrell, an Arkansas manufacturer, who believed the Confederacy needlessly "undertook to clothe the Army, leaving the poor people to clothe themselves" (Merrell 306). As he saw the situation, a generous importation of machinery and cards would have made the cotton-rich South industrially independent; however, another policy prevailed. General Alexander Lawton's bureau "undertook to take the place of merchants, & import goods from beyond the Mississippi River [in the East] by running the blockade for the benefit of the people, exchanging the same for their labor, & for the little surplus of provisions that some had concealed, & would not bring forth from their hiding places except to exchange for clothing" (306). In fact, most supplies for barter were produced by eastern mills, but the War Department did effectively establish a near monopoly of blockade-running that gave it control over all machinery imports.

As early as June 1863, a correspondent for the *Charleston Mercury* derided the "unfriendly spirit" directed "against manufacturers" and evidenced by the Confederate Congress and some state legislatures, which discouraged "many who have accumulated money from investing it in English machinery to run the blockade." The author believed, as did Henry Merrell, that 15,000 hand cards would produce "as much cloth as a factory of eight thousand spindles and three hundred looms," but there was little government encouragement to secure them (*Charleston Mercury*, June 5, 1863). Richmond officials, schooled in the ways of the plantation and the military, were not responsive to the needs of manufacturers.

This was the substance of a letter from Thomas E. McNeill, a Lynchburg manufacturer of spinning and weaving machines, to Jefferson Davis. McNeill wrote that the war demonstrated a direct relationship between the mechanical and martial arts, that if the conflict were to be won, "more machinery must be put in operation, under some well-regulated system, so that the whole country may become one great manufactory." He enjoined Davis to promote "the establishment of more factories by stimulating the manufacture of more machinery."[2] A Richmond editor endorsed this idea: "we are not learning the lessons of the war as fast as we should" until "we shall have prepared ourselves for independent life, by establishing among us all the necessary branches of productive industry" (*Richmond Enquirer*, November 14, 1862). William Gregg and Francis Fries constantly elaborated on such themes before professional societies of manufacturers, but the basic tenets of King Cotton diplomacy were deeply embedded in the thinking of the Richmond War Department: that Europe should serve as the Confederate armory in return for cotton.

General Alexander Lawton, like Abraham Myers before him, saw great advantages in securing as many foreign goods as possible. He found in Josiah Gorgas, from the Ordnance Bureau, a valuable model of what might be done by placing purchasing agents abroad. As its first foreign agent, the Quartermaster Bureau posted James Ferguson to England in December 1862. The sixty-year-old "bred merchant" of impeccable habits ran a successful import firm in Richmond and Petersburg.[3] Once he made it through the blockade, Ferguson's orders were to purchase speedily large quantities of woolens, blankets, and shoes for the Confederate depots, and for this purpose he carried a bureau draft for $533,333 in British sterling and $1 million in Confederate bonds.[4]

Ferguson was well acquainted with many Upper South manufacturers and carried some private commissions from them to purchase machinery and parts, although his official orders were silent on this. Francis Fries of Salem urged him to forward orders already placed with John Fraser and Company: "we heard of the safe arrival of the funds, but have never heard whether the goods were shipped."[5] By his orders, once in England Ferguson was able to gain "the confidence of all the first class manufacturers" and place his military contracts.[6] To supplement his efforts, the bureau shortly sent Richard P. Waller, supervisor of the Richmond clothing and shoe shops, to Nassau, where he could help forward supplies purchased by Ferguson.[7]

The simplicity of the scheme appealed to General Lawton. Cotton was constantly increasing in value because of the blockade, and English merchants willingly accepted large military orders. This system worked for Josiah Gorgas and the Ordnance Bureau. On October 1, 1863, in the midst of the Longstreet supply debacle at Knoxville, Lawton wrote Secretary of War James Seddon that the requisitions of the three field armies were "being pressed with impatience," and in his view, they could not be met. The armies needed great coats, blankets, and tents more than rations or ammunition. Although troops from North Carolina and the Trans-Mississippi were essentially self-sufficient, Lawton was doubtful about the other commands. Not yet having surveyed Southern mill capacity and with Northern armies mounting increasingly serious threats in Tennessee and northern Virginia, he argued that the "home market cannot of course be looked to" and that no major "portion of what is needed can be furnished by it."[8]

A few days later Lawton unburdened himself to Colin J. McRae, who represented the Confederate Treasury Department in England: "I have but recently assumed the control of affairs, and the condition in which I find our supplies is the occasion of great anxiety." The chief quartermaster believed that "the domestic resources—in many particulars limited at best—[were] nearly exhausted." He felt "constrained then to look abroad."[9] Lawton cited unnamed Richmond merchants, including probably William Ferguson, who may have helped compose the message, to the effect that "the resources of the Southern States cannot supply the necessities of the Army of the Confederate States with the essential articles of cloth for uniform clothing, blankets, shoes, stockings, and flannels."[10] Since Confederate forces were in fact being supplied from these very domestic resources, Lawton may well have anticipated an enlarged scope of future military activities that would endanger mills. He also couched an argument that would bring him the greatest amount of scarce Confederate foreign exchange. Lawton continued, "the Government would save largely by purchasing abroad, even if one of every three cargoes were lost."[11]

Since Gorgas's Ordnance Bureau expended the largest measure of funds within the War Department, Lawton's language suggested a need for a more even distribution. The general, who was to demand over twenty million yards annually from Southern mills within a few months, in this letter argued that the Confederate army could be better clothed and fed through Liverpool and Manchester. While it is likely that Lawton did not yet fully realize the extent of Southern resources, he viewed importation as a vital supplemental, short-term strategy.

His bureau, Lawton wrote, "for all its need has not enjoyed facilities possessed by others for drawing from abroad; and now there is hardly time to provide them."[12] Indeed, Gorgas was more dependent on foreign supplies and more vigorous in securing them than any other officer in the government. Early in the war he dispatched three young War Department agents abroad: Major Caleb Huse was thirty-one years old, a native of Massachusetts, and a West Point graduate from the class of 1851; Henry Hotze was a native of Switzerland and a journalist for the *Mobile Register*; and Thomas De Leon was twenty-two and a brother to Confederate Surgeon General David C. De Leon. Hotze soon dedicated himself to propaganda with the editorship of the *Index*, a Confederate newspaper in London. Huse and Thomas De Leon worked almost exclusively for the Ordnance Bureau. The men were young, naive, and sometimes reckless in their actions, but their ardor for the Confederate cause endeared them to their superiors, especially Gorgas, whose bureau desperately needed their purchases. To bring ordnance through the blockade, Huse purchased four 300-ton steamers and established a shipping line.[13]

Although Lawton occasionally placed quartermaster stores on ordnance ships, his facilities for importing were decidedly inferior to those of Gorgas. In order to redress this, in August 1863 Lawton endorsed a critical appointment, that of Major Thomas L. Bayne to head the new Bureau of Foreign Supplies. Bayne, a brother-in-law of Josiah Gorgas, immediately took up his station in Wilmington.

As Seddon explained the situation to Jefferson Davis, the importing business "became so large and important that it was found necessary to devote officers of the Department and special agents at Wilmington to its management."[14] Although Bayne's agency was designated a "separate branch" under the secretary of war and was given a budget of $20 million a year, the agent effectively worked for Lawton.[15] The prospect of increasing foreign purchases through the new agency encouraged the chief quartermaster to assign more personnel abroad. Major Smith Stansbury sailed to Bermuda to aid the Confederate commercial agents, John T. Bourne and Norman S. Walker (Vandiver xxxii). Officers Thomas Rhett, L. Andrew, and F. F. Minter went to England, and other agents were posted to France and Canada.[16]

Lawton's men quickly found themselves in buying competition with Huse, Hotze, De Leon, and scores of other agents from the Navy Department, state governments, Trans-Mississippi district, and private associations. In desperation, John T. Bourne at Bermuda advised Lawton that "the fewer Agents sent from the Confederacy to the Island and Europe the better; this would insure secrecy with men of business & the wants of the Confederacy supplied without the knowledge of the Enemy & their friends" (cited in Vandiver, ed. 55). The vigorous competition of Union agents further confused the situation.

Ferguson, the importer, and Crenshaw, the woolen manufacturer, were Lawton's most effective agents. Ferguson originally established his operations at Liverpool, where James Bullock carefully orchestrated the construction of a Confederate navy under the watchful eyes of Federal agents. To be closer to pertinent manufacturers, he moved north to Manchester. The first order sent to Ferguson, in the fall of 1863, reflected Lawton's desperate supply problems incident to Longstreet's campaign. Ferguson was authorized to secure 1.2 million yards of woolens, 22 ounces per yard, with half in blue for trousers and 500,000 yards for great coats, 300,000 blankets, an equal number of shoes, 150,000 wool hats, and 600,000 pairs of socks.[17] By comparison, in Richmond the Crenshaw Woolen Mill produced 260,000 yards of woolen fabric a year, the Eagle mill at Columbus 660,000 yards, and the North Carolina mills about 531,600 yards. Southern mills were spinning over 1.2 million pairs of socks annually. Lawton's order probably reflected his expectation of substantial losses in running the blockade, an anticipation quickly borne out as events transpired.

Ferguson found English woolen manufacturers overwhelmed with business. He competed directly with Union agents in securing the product of sixteen Yorkshire woolen mills.[18] The Lancashire cotton famine jeopardized their source of warps, and their chief advocate in Parliament, William E. Forster, spoke out strongly for the Union. Nevertheless, Ferguson reported to Lawton that he "proceeded to the manufacturing districts" and made the acquaintance of numerous Yorkshire woolen mill owners, who cordially received him. A few mill men delayed Yankee orders to help the Richmond government, and Ferguson was gratified by the results, writing later from his office in Manchester that "having been an importer for several years, I was not unfamiliar with the various kinds of the goods ordered and well acquainted with the proper locality where they could be procured on the best terms."[19]

Ferguson shortly reported the purchase of one million yards of cloth and one million pairs of shoes, placing his "orders directly with the best manufacturers."[20] In these transactions, the former Virginia merchant believed his trade experience allowed him "to purchase from dealers on much more favorable terms than other agents who have not the benefit of such knowledge and experience."[21] In addition to the annoyance of Union bidders, Ferguson quickly found himself in competition with his colleague, Major Caleb Huse, of Gorgas's bureau.

Huse was a favorite with Gorgas, and he enjoyed practically a carte blanche to make purchases in Europe since he was the principal source of Confederate arms (Huse 14, 25). As Huse's debts mounted, Gorgas secured an order from the War Department directing Ferguson "to turn over to Major Huse of the Ordnance Dept. all the funds in my hands and to stop purchasing until his [Huse's] debts were paid."[22] Many of Huse's purchases were of doubtful merit. In one celebrated purchase, Huse negotiated "a contract for 100,000 rifles of the latest Austrian pattern, and ten batteries, of six pieces each, of field artillery, with harness complete"

(Huse 26). These stores came directly from the Austrian arsenal. Within the Confederacy, there was criticism of such expensive purchases.[23] The ramrods were made of wood, which became swollen when wet and would not fit the rifle bore. Many of these controversial weapons proved useless.

Nevertheless, at the insistence of Gorgas, Huse also "volunteered to do service for the Quartermaster Department to which he was induced by his sense of the nakedness of our Army."[24] Huse's quartermaster purchases quickly stirred up problems with Ferguson. Unexpectedly, the Virginia quartermaster found numerous irregularities in the ordnance officer's affairs and on April 18, 1863, filed a long complaint to Richmond. Major Benjamin F. Fickling, a Treasury agent in England on a mission to purchase engraving supplies and recruit engravers, had previously written home on January 3, 1863, that Huse was "robbing" the government. Ferguson elaborated on the theme (Vandiver, ed. xxiii).

Huse customarily purchased quartermaster stores from commission houses, not directly from the manufacturers, thus incurring large service charges. He especially patronized Saul Isaac, Campbell and Company, a large British merchant firm with a questionable reputation from dealings in the Crimean War. This company added extravagant surcharges to the Confederate accounts. Further, the ordnance major added his own commission of 2.5 percent to the total price of goods. None of Huse's goods were inspected before being shipped. Under protest, Ferguson delivered his remaining funds up to Huse but filed a personal disclaimer that the young officer had "caused me more annoyance than all others combined on this side, and has defeated my plans in a great measure for keeping up the supplies of our department."[25]

Huse admitted no wrongdoing. He acknowledged receiving a large commission from Saul Isaac but explained that "he intended to use a part of the money to pay his traveling expenses" and that the balance, amounting to 100,000 British pounds, was to purchase a military library, which he intended to present to the Ordnance Department.[26] Other Confederate agents faced similar temptations. James H. North, a Virginia naval officer in London, testified that "Mr. Isaac did in the course of a conversation make an offer to divide with me a commission of 5 per cent. on a business transaction for the Confederate Government, and that I did regard that offer as an attempt to induce me to enter into a transaction to defraud the Confederate Government."[27]

Upon inspecting Huse's most recent purchases, Ferguson discovered that 12,000 yards of cloth purchased at $1.50 a yard were worth only 90 cents and that upon the "extortionate prices . . . a commission of 2 1/2 per cent. for purchasing is charged on the face of said invoice."[28] William G. Crenshaw, the Richmond woolen manufacturer then in London, wrote the War Department that Huse had contracts requiring the delivery of $5 million of goods in two weeks and these would "be carried out to the loss of many millions of dollars to our people and Government."[29] Crenshaw's letters, according to John Jones, the rebel clerk, finally set the War Department ablaze.

When the old Austrian muskets arrived without accouterments and with wooden ramrods, Jones wrote, "it appears that Major H. has contracted for 50,000 muskets at $4 above the current price, leaving $200,000 commission for whom?" (John Jones 2: 14–15). Even James Seddon believed Huse's "conduct in regard to the Austrian rifles was certainly extraordinary remissness, to say the least."[30] Within the War Department, the charges precipitated a debate upon the character of Huse that lasted after the guns fell silent at Appomattox. Huse had a staunch defender in Judah P. Benjamin, who applauded his vigor and initiative.[31] Gorgas also vindicated his protégé, explaining to Seddon that "I have no doubt Major Huse was frequently compelled to pay quite 50 pr. cent. over the actual market value of his purchases." Should Huse have submitted the extraordinary expenditures to Gorgas for approval, "authority to that effect would have been given to him without a moment's hesitation."[32]

In London, Colin McRae called for a public accounting of the business ledgers of Saul Isaac, Campbell and Company, with whom Huse had accumulated over $2 million in debts.[33] Secretary Seddon harbored "strong suspicions that the practices of that firm were more sharp than honest, and that Major Huse, through overconfidence or some other motive, was allowing the interests of the Department to suffer in his transactions with them." Although Seddon had often warned the ordnance major "to bring all dealings with that firm to as early a close and settlement as possible . . . Major Huse has seemed more inclined to thwart than carry out the wishes of the Department."[34] A Confederate audit revealed deceptive accounts and false invoices, resulting in a loss of more than $250,000 to the War Department. Saul Isaac, who had routinely charged the Confederacy "from 50 to 20 per cent more" than the market value of the goods, died in the midst of the revelations, leaving many questions unanswered.[35]

After Ferguson's charges, Huse's usefulness to the Quartermaster Department was at an end, and Seddon resolved, "I should have recalled him."[36] But through Gorgas's influence, Huse was not removed, only credited with bad judgment. He continued to serve as an ordnance officer until the end of the war, expending $12.4 million, more than any other Confederate officer abroad.[37]

Burdened by Huse's debts, Ferguson attempted to implement a systematic program of British purchases. In June 1863, when he received additional orders from the War Department for supplies costing £600,000, Ferguson anticipated paying for them with $5 million taken from the Erlanger loan.[38] Much of the £3 million of Confederate cotton bonds was claimed by the issuer, the Paris banking house of Emile Erlanger and Company. The limited success of this loan raised new difficulties. To be certain of covering his debts, Ferguson advised the Quartermaster Bureau, "if you cannot send money, send cotton to Major Walker at Bermuda, with instructions to write me at once on its arrival and I can make arrangements with Messrs. John K. Gilliat & Co. of London to advance on the cotton." Gilliat was "well known to all the merchants & bank presidents of our city" and held over 1 million pounds sterling which belonged to the tobacco interests of Virginia and North Carolina, a sum upon which Ferguson could draw.[39]

The success of Ferguson's plans depended upon establishing a line of blockade-running steamers solely under the control of the Quartermaster Bureau. Richard Waller at Nassau or Norman Walker at Bermuda could receive cotton brought through the blockade and credit it to the account of John Fraser, J. K. Gilliat, or some other merchant house. Lawton estimated that 37,200 bales of cotton, a quantity almost impossible to export, was required to pay for the June 1863 supply order alone. But Ferguson was confident of success: cotton could come out by the same steamers that brought goods in. He wrote Richmond, "you have control of the rail roads & if you can get control of two or more of the government steamers for the use of our department, I can't but think that the above arrangement would result in such good to the service."[40] As Confederate funds in Europe dwindled, the exports of cotton became more critical. Since Gorgas was loath to surrender use of his steamers, the issue of a joint venture between the Quartermaster Department and private capitalists was raised.

The Crenshaw brothers offered to help. Three woolen manufacturers from Richmond, William G., James R., and Lewis D. Crenshaw proposed a partnership whereby they and the bureau would establish a steamship line to carry quartermaster and commissary stores to the Confederacy. The Crenshaw brothers held solid Confederate credentials. Their Crenshaw Woolen Mill at the Rocketts, near the Tredegar Iron Works on the James River, worked almost exclusively for the military. William Crenshaw had organized a battery of artillery, while brother James served as a staff officer in the Commissary Bureau (*National Cyclopedia of American Biography* 36: 203). The Crenshaw brothers were also proprietors of a large Richmond flouring mill, one in which Frank Ruffin, Lucius Northrop's assistant commissary general, held a financial interest.[41] In fact, War Department contracts with the flour company were the subject of a fruitless congressional investigation led by the ineffable Henry S. Foote, a Tennessee senator, in January 1862 (John Jones 1: 237–38).[42] The Crenshaw woolen factory, with over 3,000 spindles, was a valuable asset for the Clothing Depot, and early in the war the brothers imported and set in motion the best set of blanket machinery within the Confederacy and produced 23,400 heavy blankets a year (*Richmond Enquirer*, October 17, 1861).

The origins of the shipping company scheme lay with Secretary of the Navy Stephen Mallory, who invited William Crenshaw "to go to Europe on some business for the Navy Department" in November 1862.[43] Learning of this, Frank Ruffin urged Seddon to commission William Crenshaw to purchase for other bureaus in the War Department. Ruffin then unveiled a "scheme" that was "an association of individual enterprise with Government Capital."[44] He proposed that the War Department enter into a partnership with the Crenshaw company to bring supplies into the Confederacy. When informed that the army faced a deficit of twenty-two million rations for the coming year, Seddon quickly assented to the unusual joint arrangement. The War Department secretary wrote that he was "satisfied of the character and energy of Mr. Crenshaw" and was "only solicitous that the faith of the Department be observed with him."[45]

The joint venture between a profit-motivated business and the bureaus of the War Department was fraught with great danger. By the terms of the agreement, the War Department secured cotton for export in the name of the Crenshaw brothers, while Crenshaw contracted for the European ships. Isaac Winnemore, quartermaster at Augusta, agreed to purchase the necessary cotton for transport, and Thomas Bayne's deputy at Wilmington, Quartermaster James M. Seixas, received the bales and loaded them aboard ship. James Crenshaw was authorized to establish an office for the firm in either Charleston or Wilmington to receive the military stores that William Crenshaw forwarded on the ships from England. Secretary Seddon advised the men, "I expect the business to be conducted by you and your associates on the basis of a separate mercantile business."[46] The agreement permitted the brothers to take commissions on all military merchandise shipped, as Caleb Huse had done.

Arriving in England in January 1863, William Crenshaw called upon James Mason, the resident Confederate commissioner, and explained his agreement with Ruffin, that in the construction of twelve blockade-runners the Crenshaw brothers "were to have 1/4 interest; the Government the balance."[47] But Mason, short of funds, was influenced by the opposition of Colin McRae and Caleb Huse and decided to reduce the government's liability from three-quarters to one-half interest.[48] As a result, Seddon in Richmond changed his mind and declined to accept more than half ownership in the projected line, explaining to William Crenshaw, "I prefer you should continue to give your experience, energy, and judgment to the conduct of a business in which, I hope, with reasonable profits to yourself and your associates, you will be enabled to render valuable service to the cause of your country."[49]

As a fellow Virginian and an accomplished manufacturer, William Crenshaw readily won the support of James Ferguson for his venture. Upon meeting Crenshaw, Ferguson found him to be a blunt, frank man, an honest contractor, and "a very business man who means to do what is right."[50] The two shared a common hostility toward Huse and a sympathy for the cotton and woolen manufacturers within the Confederacy who needed essential supplies.[51] General Lawton approved a division of labor whereby Crenshaw was employed "in purchasing and bringing over subsistence stores and such Quarter Master stores as Major Ferguson has orders for."[52]

Crenshaw then made his way to Alexander Collie, an exporting merchant at Manchester and Liverpool and, according to the *Richmond Examiner*, a "pawky Scotchman." The negotiations were complicated by the fact that Crenshaw no longer held an official position within the Confederate government; he was a private contractor operating under instructions from Lawton, Seddon, and Ruffin. The Virginia manufacturer proposed an equal partnership with Collie in the construction of a steamship line, reserving half ownership for the War Department. The proposed company was offered a monopoly on carrying all quartermaster and commissary stores through the blockade and a commission on all cargo transported either way. A single successful trip offered the prospect of paying the entire cost of a steamer. Collie was agreeable and advanced funds to build the first vessel.[53]

The ship was built by Dudgeon and Brother of London, who constructed at least seven double-wheeled blockade-runners, five for the Crenshaw partnership and two separately for the Collie company.[54] In the summer of 1863, the *Havana* came off the stays, or supports, and was readied for its voyage. According to Lewis Crenshaw, "the Government failed to comply with its obligations with respect to payments and not furnishing its portion of funds in time one of the steamers [the *Havana*] when ready and tendered by the builder, was taken by A. Collie & Co. who had issued their obligations to pay for the steamers." Although failing in this, James Seddon and James Bullock, the ranking Confederate naval agent in England, advanced enough funds to meet the government's share of the next two steamers, the *Hebe* and the *Venus*.[64] The Crenshaw line was finally afloat.

To secure payment for the succeeding vessels, which eventually amounted to a dozen ships, Crenshaw was forced to borrow funds and sell the cotton brought out through the blockade. In the midst of these negotiations, on May 14, 1863, the Crenshaw company's mill in Richmond burned, representing a loss of over $200,000. This made the family largely financially dependent upon the European joint venture (John Jones 1: 324; *Charleston Mercury*, May 19, 1863).

Apparently appealing to neutral British investors, War Department officials argued that a legal distinction might be maintained under international law between Gorgas's ordnance stores, which were contraband of war, and Lawton's quartermaster stores imported by Crenshaw, which might be neutral or free goods. While Gorgas obviously intended to ship ordnance stores on government-owned steamers, supplies from Ferguson and Crenshaw might be designated as noncontraband if placed on private ships.[56] The Union navy, of course, never accepted this argument, but friendly English investment might have been encouraged.

In July 1863, Crenshaw reported to Seddon that "there will be no difficulty in sending forward as rapidly as need be all of the supplies that are wanted under the contract with Collie and myself at a commission of 2 1/2 per cent."[57] During the summer of 1863, the *Havana*, *Venus*, and *Hebe*, laden with stores that apparently included dyes and parts for Virginia mills, were dispatched to the Confederacy via the West Indies. Within the War Department, plans were expedited to aid this new mission. Rails were laid to the North Carolina coal pits in order to stockpile fuel for the blockade-runners. Observant to Lawton's orders, Isaac Winnemore, depot officer at Augusta, procured one million pounds of lint cotton and commenced forwarding it over the deteriorating rail system to Wilmington.[58]

The first Crenshaw steamer made a successful run into Wilmington. Afterward, when James Ferguson and John White, the foreign commissioner for the state of North Carolina, called on Alexander Collie, Collie was jubilant. Having just loaded a second steamer, the *Hebe*, with most of the spring purchases, Ferguson and Collie were filled with optimism about the venture. According to Ferguson, "when the information was received in London that the said Havana had arrived with their cargo in the Confederate States and returned to the islands with cotton aboard, the house of Collie & Co of Manchester offered to extend to me a credit of £20,000 which I accepted and at once placed orders for Blankets, materials for Overcoats and Shoes." Ferguson obtained his stores in Manchester and had them "inspected & packed under my eye, & forwarded to London for shipment."[59] Two new vessels, *Ceres* and *Dee*, were selected to convey the cargo to Wilmington.

Upon calling for the bills of lading at Alexander Collie's London office, Ferguson was chagrined to learn that William Crenshaw had seized them and upon their face value demanded a contractor's commission. The flustered quartermaster could "find no article or no regulation to fit his case" and complained to General Lawton that Crenshaw wanted "his commission on all goods shipped by the steamers under his control."[60] For his part, Crenshaw was desperately short of funds at a time when he was accumulating a large quantity of beef and pork in Nassau and Bermuda for Ruffin's Commissary Bureau.

Colin McRae lacked confidence in the arrangement, writing Seddon, "I respectfully suggest that these partnership contracts be annulled; or, rather, that the Government buy out the interest of the other parties in the steamers and run them on its own account."[61] James Bullock, Confederate naval agent in Britain and a man well acquainted with Georgia manufacturing, also disputed the value of such private contracting, writing: "Their transactions are based on and dependent upon the cotton belonging to the Government, and, with authority to pledge the cotton, any officer could perform all that any contractor is doing, thereby saving to the country the enormous profits accruing to the private and irresponsible speculator."[62]

The issue of private versus government steamers went to Secretary Seddon and Jefferson Davis. On behalf of the government, Seddon firmly defended the contracts and wrote James Crenshaw that the War Department deprecated the squabble because it entailed "serious embarrassments in the importation, through your brother's agency, of some of the most important freight of the Government."[63] Only Colin McRae, the Confederate disbursing agent, resolved the dispute by remitting funds to Crenshaw.

Far greater problems awaited the Crenshaw scheme in American waters. Ferguson's first cargo of winter stores "was shipped to Nassau with instructions to an agent [Richard Waller] at that point to forward them with all possible dispatch." On August 18, in the dark of the new moon, the Collie-Crenshaw steamer *Hebe*, loaded "with the greater part of them," encountered the Federal blockading squadron near Fort Fisher at Wilmington.[64] After a brief chase, the *Hebe* was beached nine miles north of the Fort, where its cargo of coffee, drugs, clothing, and "a few bales of silks" was burned.[65]

On September 5, 1863, the 700-ton steamer *Venus* successfully evaded the blockade and entered Wilmington, a feat accomplished in fifty of seventy-five attempts by vessels during the first nine months of 1863.[66] This steamer carried a cargo of Crenshaw's meat and Ferguson's dry goods and shoes. The contractors loaded an outward cargo of 600 bales of cotton and 200 barrels of tobacco. In order to fill Crenshaw's tobacco quota, General Lawton was forced to buy the commodity from farmers in central Virginia.[67] But on the next voyage into Wilmington, the *Venus* was hulled by a shot from a Federal warship and driven ashore near the hulk of the *Hebe*.[68] The ship, 264 feet long, carried a select cargo of Ferguson's dry goods and Crenshaw's bacon.[69] The loss of the second ship cast a pall over the whole arrangement with Crenshaw.

General William Whiting, the Confederate commander at Wilmington, blamed the *Venus* disaster on the removal from Fort Fisher of some Whitworth three-inch rifles, "a gun that in the hands of the indefatigable [Colonel William] Lamb has saved dozens of vessels and millions of money to the Confederate States."[70] On this basis, the Crenshaw brothers complained to the War Department that "two of these vessels were lost during the summer of 1863 on the coast of North Carolina in consequence of the removal of some Whitworth guns which had been kept on the beach for the purpose of keeping the Yankee blockaders a distance from shore."[71] Frank Ruffin testified in support of this view to a congressional investigating committee.[72]

With considerable understatement, General Whiting's report of August 1863 added, "the efforts of the enemy to stop our steamers are increasing."[73] During the fall season of 1863, the Federal navy destroyed twenty-two steamers attempting to enter Wilmington.[74] U.S. consul Charles M. Allen's summation of blockade-running activities at Bermuda between January 1862 and May 30, 1864, was that eighty-six different steamers were involved; there were 165 safe arrivals of such ships at the islands, and sixty-five returned after successful trips to the Confederacy, carrying out 40,000 bales of cotton worth perhaps £1.6 million, or $16 million in Confederacy currency. Twenty-two blockade-runners were captured or destroyed on the first voyage, and nineteen more were captured or lost after making one trip or more. The hazards, like the rewards, were rising.[75]

A tragic fate awaited other vessels loaded by Ferguson and Crenshaw. The Crenshaw company lost three additional ships, "two of them on their first attempt to come in to Wilmington, the other after making 3 round trips and attempting to come in the fourth time."[76] The *Ceres* and the *Vesta*, 300 tons each, were among these. The *Ceres*, carrying one of

Ferguson's large cargoes of shoes and blankets, was captured on December 3, 1863, and the *Vesta* was taken on January 11, 1864.[77] Under these conditions, the quartermaster general wrote to General Lee of his straitened circumstances in January 1864, "passing over minor losses, which on the aggregate are very heavy—less than two months ago the 'Ceres,' a fine steamer from England, was destroyed at Wilmington with 26,000 blankets, 16,000 prs of shoes and 15,000 yds of heavy woolen goods for over coats: all on account of the QM Department." Then a few days later "came the intelligence of the destruction of another, the 'Vesta' freighted with a cargo duplicate of the above."[78] A month later the U.S. consul in Bermuda jubilantly wrote, "the *Nutfield* and cargo reported totally destroyed, cost more than one million of dollars and was the most valuable cargo they have ever sent from here to attempt to run the blockade."[79] Crenshaw's beef and pork were among the captures.

Nevertheless, between August and December 1863 the Quartermaster Department succeeded in exporting 2,175 bales of cotton on its own account. About half of these, 1,035 bales, went to the Crenshaw brothers, and the rest were credited to Richard Waller's account in Nassau.[80] Waller also received 2,203 bales in the spring of 1864, compared to 2,074 sent to Crenshaw and Ferguson, and 9,081 bales were retained for general department use.[81] Waller usually received a single allotment of 245 bales each month.[82] The major's individual expenditures on behalf of the Bureau of Foreign Supplies in the Nassau market amounted to about £75,000.[83] Through the spring of 1864, the Commissary Bureau expended over £200,000 on supplies, equivalent to 5,000 bales of cotton.[84] Of this, Crenshaw's company received 1,787 bales worth £45,625.

With the proceeds from cotton sales, Crenshaw filled warehouses in Bermuda and Nassau with beef and bacon, while Ferguson and Waller bought large quantities of quartermaster stores. During the summer of 1864, Charles Allen, the U.S. consul at Bermuda, found the Confederates occupying nearly all of the available warehouses in the islands.[85] Waller, who managed local shipping, refused to allow private vessels to carry commissary stores but rather required "all of the steamers of the Crenshaw line to put the meat on at a rate of freight much less than the rate allowed in the contract." This created some friction, for with the blockade tightening, the result was that millions of pounds of meat spoiled after standing in a tropical climate, and much of the meat that arrived in Wilmington was deemed "in a very bad condition."[86]

A second group of Crenshaw steamers, chartered in 1864, fared little better than the first. A Crenshaw ship, costing £24,500 and rated by Lewis Crenshaw at twenty-four miles an hour, was lost on the Irish coast. Another, the 300-ton *Caledonia*, made a single round-trip to Wilmington, carrying out 300 bales of Major Bayne's cotton. But capable of making only six knots an hour, it was captured on the next voyage on May 30, 1864.[87] Two additional vessels, the *Mary Celestia* and the *Atalanta*, "were sent over & paid for by large advances made by W. G. Cr[enshaw] Co."[88] The former was a 250-ton ship. On one trip the *Atalanta* brought in 400 barrels of goods weighing 32,000 pounds, marked "onions" (Vandiver, ed. 131). This ship was finally impressed by the Confederate Navy Department for its own use.

Not all steamers that arrived in Wilmington were well served by Bayne's Bureau of Foreign Supplies. Lewis Crenshaw wrote that "there was difficulty in obtaining Cotton from the Govt. to load them and Crenshaw Bros. had to use their own Cotton for that purpose."[89] Rail transportation from Augusta was hazardous and slow. For this reason, the Crenshaw brothers invited the presidents of the major railroad companies to join in organizing a new line of twelve steamers. This proposal gave birth to Richmond's "Supply Importing Company, composed of various railroad companies and others interested in railroads at the South."[90] The Manchester Cotton and Woolen Company and the Augusta factory were heavy investors in such stocks at a time when they could have been expanding their own mills. The new vessels "were built and paid for by the credit of the private parties," and by the fall of 1864 three-quarters of all Confederate subsistence stores were carried to Wilmington by such ships.[91]

Often at Bermuda as many as ten steamers were in port loading for the Confederacy, while at Wilmington an equal number were stranded, waiting to be unloaded or for a cargo of cotton and favorable weather. With the dark of the moon they raced to sea. Securing and transporting cotton to Wilmington increasingly became a problem. In March 1864, Lawton relieved Major Seixas, Bayne's agent responsible for all loading at Wilmington. Seixas, initially an appointee of Myers, failed to get 700 bales of cotton on the correct ship.[92] The cotton dearth became more serious through the summer of 1864, and Secretary Seddon complained that there were only 14,000 bales of government cotton "east of Alabama, and this quantity is scattered about over the face of the whole country."[93] With the eastern railroads subject to military impressment and almost totally committed to supplying armies in Virginia, moving trainloads of cotton in the direction of the front was difficult.[94]

The commercial relationship between William Crenshaw and the Confederate government emboldened Lawton's critics within the Congress. In October 1863, J. Marshall McCue of Augusta County, Virginia, wrote Jefferson Davis regarding the recent burning of the *Hebe*. McCue then read his letter before the Virginia House: "you will be surprised when I inform you that we are now destitute of a supply of blankets and overcoats for our troops this winter, and that there are no factories in the South engaged in the manufacture of blankets" (McCue 5). Because of the risks of importing, McCue deprecated being dependent upon a supply of woolens from England. He told the assembly, "I am informed we had 350,000 yards of English cloth burned at Charleston a few weeks since" (5).[95] In fact, the loss was even greater, amounting to a cargo valued at $350,000. The *Venus*, sunk a few days later, represented a comparable expense.

In the summer of 1864, the *Richmond Examiner* broached the debate over foreign supply with an analysis of the strange fates of the Crenshaw steamers, "the whole seven being lost in the first or second voyage, though commanded by experienced captains" (cited in the *New York Times*, September 4, 1864). Alexander Collie's own line of steamers running the blockade enjoyed far greater successes: "The *Hansa* has made nine round voyages, paying for herself twenty times over; the *Edith* and the *Annie* have made each three round voyages, and are now prosperously running; the *Falcon* has made two voyages, and the *Flamingo* has come in successfully on her first trip" (*New York Times*, August 21, 1864). The *Don* made six successful trips before being run down at sea, the *Fanny* and *Alice* made seven round-trips each, and one captain negotiated the blockade for twenty-nine trips. The *Examiner* wondered whether Collie had purposely endangered the ships of a competing line and questioned the motives of his Wilmington agent, "one Andrea, a Hebrew" (cited in the *New York Times*, August 21, 1864). Hearing this, Alexander Collie wrote an indignant letter to James Mason, complaining of those who "*supposed* that my people in Bermuda & Wilmington do what they can to injure the Crenshaw steamers—as if *my own* clerks would have any interest in injuring my own property."[96] Indisputably, Collie's private vessels were eminently profitable while the Crenshaw losses cost the Quartermaster Bureau a heavy investment and cost the army most of the quartermaster supplies purchased in Europe. Other government steamers, those owned by the Ordnance Bureau and the state of North Carolina, fared much better.[97]

Governor Zebulon B. Vance of North Carolina was much impressed by Collie's record. The intrepid governor sold the *Advance*; purchased one-quarter interest in four Collie steamers, including the *Hansa* and the *Don*; and successfully ran into Wilmington large quantities of stores, including machinery and findings for North Carolina mills.[98]

Despite the ship losses in the Crenshaw line, William Crenshaw indefatigably built new vessels and continued in business. In July 1864, he had three steamers running and two more under contract with John K. Gilliat. Altogether, McRae wrote from London, provision was made "for fourteen steamers, four of which will leave here during the month of August, eight in December, and two (the last of the Fraser, Trenholm & Co. line) in April, 1865."[99] By October 1864, Crenshaw was the agent for eight of the blockade-runners tarrying at Bermuda.[100]

Many of the Crenshaw and Collie ships running into Wilmington carried crates of tools, hardware, machinery, and findings. The cargo of the *Lynx* at Bermuda in May 1864 included "431 packages machinery and hardware" (Vandiver, ed. 131). Crenshaw and Ferguson loaded vessels with large quantities of dyeing materials as well as with other manufacturing necessities. In July 1864, the *Boston* carried 24 barrels of copperas, and the *Advance* in the same month brought in 100 barrels of logwood, 10 barrels of copperas, and 20 kegs of blue stone. Logwood was purple-black dye; copperas, or ferrous sulfate heptahydrate, was a green dye; and blue stone was a blue sulfate. In August, the *Ella* and the *Wando* carried cases of calfskins for factory rollers, and the *Emma Henry*'s cargo in November included 24 packages of undescribed machinery. The *Harkaway* bore 32 more cases of machinery and 40 cases of cotton cards as well. The *Susan Burne* had 100 barrels of copperas, and the *Lady Milne*, in January 1865, sailed with 6 casks of blue stone (136–46). Other vessels brought barrels of soda ash, acids, linseed oil, or painting materials, all valuable to Southern manufacturers.

The loss of Crenshaw's early steamers encouraged General Lawton to seek supplies in "the island," the West Indies and Bermuda. In September 1863, he wrote Richard Waller in Nassau that he was "constrained to resort for the present to the nearest point of supply to save time" and requested 25,000 blankets with an equal number of shoes.[101] In Nassau, Waller found that local merchants carried large stores of useful goods, but the prices were high, costing 30 percent more than in England.[102] Nevertheless, Lawton's orders to Nassau were designed "to replace more than double the cargo of the 'Hebe.' "[103] Waller paid with cotton brought out to the island aboard private steamers since the Crenshaw line controlled its own cargo and the Ordnance Department maintained authority over all government steamers.

Despite the inability of the Bureau of Foreign Supplies to deliver all the promised cotton, Waller made considerable progress in Nassau. Between August and December 1863, he forwarded at least twenty-one small shipments of supplies aboard private steamers, mostly bound for Wilmington.[104] Altogether he sent in 39,100 pairs of shoes, 6,250 blankets, and 45,400 yards of cloth.[105] While the larger cargoes shipped by Crenshaw and Ferguson were perishing at sea, at least three-quarters of Waller's goods arrived safely ashore.

In London, following the destruction of William Crenshaw's first fleet of steamers, James Ferguson won Lawton's approval to strike an agreement with British merchants whereby they would haul their own goods to Wilmington in British bottoms in return for payment in Confederate cotton. In a rather large speculation, Ferguson promised to deliver cotton bales on the Wilmington docks at 6 pence—or 12 cents—a pound, one quarter of the Liverpool price; merchants braving the blockade were promised from 50 to 100 percent profit on their goods, with the War Department paying freightage almost to the value of their ships.[106] Bayne at the Bureau of Foreign Supplies anticipated fulfilling Ferguson's contracts by either buying the lint cotton or receiving it through the tax-in-kind. Several British companies evinced interest in this venture.

On October 2, 1863, Ferguson reached an agreement with the British firm of Davis and Fitzhugh. Among the speculators were "certain English merchants of large means; & they all went to work with promptness &

fidelity."[107] Much of this contract was then purchased by the prominent provisioner Power, Lowe, and Company, who agreed to deliver a "large lot of shoes, to be paid for in cotton."[108] General Lawton secured 700 bales of cotton in Augusta for this delivery, but the cargo was inadvertently placed aboard a Crenshaw vessel and exported.[109] Nevertheless, Power and Lowe continued to ship large quantities of both commissary and quartermaster supplies into the Confederacy through the summer of 1864. Some of their contacts required no prior inspection of goods, and James Ferguson discovered that many items rejected by him in England were purchased by this firm and delivered to Wilmington.[110]

In January 1864, Ferguson struck an agreement with Rosenberg, Haiman, and Brother that was similar to the Power and Lowe contract. This German company agreed to deliver 100,000 suits of clothing and an equal number of blankets and shoes, "in quality like that furnished by the Prussian govt."[111] Having no vessels of their own and only six months to make deliveries, Rosenberg called on Henry Lafone, the Liverpool partner of Gazaway Bugg Lamar in the Importing and Exporting Company of Georgia. The Germans found that Lamar's blockade-running company had "4 steamers & will have 9 & . . . agreed to carry in these goods at £20 a ton."[112] Lafone managed several *Owl*-class steamers, newly built by James D. Bullock especially for blockade-running. Cloud-gray, long and sleek, with rakish smoke stacks, the vessels represented the evolutionary pinnacle of development in blockade-runners; they were the fastest ships afloat.

Despite the enormous profits for private investors, the War Department contracts with William Crenshaw, Collie, Power and Lowe, and Rosenberg provided the Confederate army with important supplies in 1864. Frank Ruffin calculated that "from Aug. 26th to Sept. 19th only five vessels, out of seventeen, had brought in any subsistence for our armies, of which Messrs. Power, Lowe & Co owned three, the fourth being Messrs. Crenshaw's and the fifth, as it has turned out, running from Halifax."[113] In some months, more cotton was exported on behalf of William Crenshaw's line than on the Confederate government account. That was the rub. Treasury Secretary George Trenholm, a partner in John Fraser's competing trading company, pointed out that while Crenshaw required 30,000 bales of cotton to fulfill his contract, a mere 5,000 bales in England were worth £200,000 or the entire value of the agreement. The remainder represented profits to Crenshaw's company.[114]

Over the protests of Frank Ruffin, Seddon and Lawton canceled all agreements with private contractors in the fall of 1864. Criticism in the press and Congress made the contracts untenable. As a replacement for private contracts, the option of space impressment was endorsed.

A series of Confederate acts and administrative regulations beginning in March 1864 gave Lawton and Seddon almost complete control over foreign trade. Thomas L. Bayne was promoted to lieutenant colonel, and the Bureau of Foreign Supplies was given a larger responsibility in loading ships. A statute of February 6, 1864, prohibited the export on private account of cotton, tobacco, or other critical staples and limited the importation of luxuries. In April 1864, Lawton ordered that space previously used to ship cotton to Crenshaw, Collie, and Rosenberg be taken by the bureau to send cotton to Richard Waller for purchases in the islands. In addition, the Confederate Congress resolved that, with the exception of state-owned vessels, half of all cargo space on blockade-runners be reserved for the use of the War Department (*Journal of the Congress of the Confederate States* 7: 368–71).

Even as Lawton mobilized factories within the Confederacy, he sought increased supplies from abroad. His initial estimates for foreign purchases in 1864 were designed to clothe 150,000 men, about one-third of the Confederate force. For this he requested 525,900 yards of cloth, 300,000 hats, 200,000 blankets, and uniform cloth for 20,000 officers.[115] In contrast, William Haynes of the Trans-Mississippi district alone ordered 108,000 hats, 40,000 uniforms, and 120,000 pairs of shoes.[116] Later, Lawton doubled his requirements, writing Secretary Seddon that "the great scarcity of wool compels me to rely upon drawing from abroad fully over half of the cloth required for army purposes."[117] Although the Confederacy had mills to produce about 3 million yards of woolen cloth a year, the scarcity of wool, inadequate transportation, and problems of finance made imports more attractive. One million yards of English woolens, with linings made of domestic cotton cloth, were sufficient to make 250,000 uniforms.

Upon receiving the order, Ferguson complained that "it is no light matter to get up 100,000 blankets, 100,000 yards of cloth & 100,000 pairs of shoes in a month's notice & do it all as it should be done." Ferguson's shipments in January 1864 were hastily accomplished and some of the goods water-damaged upon arrival in Nassau, but the lots amounted to 40,000 blankets and 15,000 to 20,000 pairs of shoes.[118] Lawton's foreign contracts were valued at £390,000 in 1864, but the bureau received less than half of the purchases.[119] In Nassau, Richard Waller steadily accumulated stocks, holding 51,456 pairs of shoes by June.[120] The *City of Petersburg* ran the blockade in May 1864 with 178 cases, or 7,476 pairs, of Waller's shoes aboard.[121]

The most glaring deficiency in domestic production was blankets, and Lawton turned his attention to this in the summer of 1864, a year after the broadlooms in Crenshaw's factory were destroyed by fire. He wrote James Ferguson to purchase several sets of "machinery required for the manufacture of blankets."[122] At the same time he dispatched Thomas Sharp, a bureau mechanic, to find "appliances" to manufacture shoes.[123] Specifically, Sharp was instructed to "proceed without delay to Nassau and thence to Nova Scotia" for the purpose of purchasing three complete sets of leather-working machines. Lawton wrote Waller to meet these expenses from his cotton sales, for "your experience will tell you that this will in time form a far better investment of a portion of the means of the command of this Dept. than even shoes or blankets."[124] In England, Ferguson and Sharp looked for bargains, since funds were scarce.

The two men finally purchased three sets of machinery that would "make 2700 prs pegged shoes [with soles fasted by wooden pegs] & 900 prs of sword shoes daily." After adding two steam engines, they "got more machinery & at a lower price than was calculated."[125] Next Ferguson and Sharp recommended, and Lawton approved, the acquisition of four sets of blanket-making machinery at £2,300 each.[126] These devices were designed to produce blankets from cotton warps and shoddy wool, or wool made from shredded rags. This manufacturing technique was the scourge of the Union army and the brunt of many jokes between the armies about "shoddy." There were fabled Union soldiers whose shoddy uniforms disintegrated in the Southern rains.

Nevertheless, in 1864 Southern wool lay mostly in the west. Each set of blanket machinery required seventy-five hands to manufacture "250 to 300 prs daily." Ferguson anticipated that three skilled hands with a workforce of "negro labor & disabled soldiers" could produce 37,500 nine-pound army blankets a year on each machine.[127] The anticipated quality was equal to items purchased by Richard Waller in Nassau.

Lawton applauded the purchases, believing them "an excellent investment and they will serve to make the Confederacy independent of the foreign market & of the contingencies of the blockade."[128] He advised sorting the machinery into different sets and placing them aboard the fastest steamers at Bermuda. The first set was loaded on the *Bat*, one of Bullock's fast new side-wheel steamers, which sailed from Liverpool on its first voyage in September 1864.[129] In attempting to enter the Cape Fear River, the ship was hulled and captured by a Union vessel, whose captain reported its principal cargo to be "machinery for manufacturing shoes."[130] A second set of machinery arrived through the blockade in December, probably aboard the *Owl*. This set was dispatched to Augusta to be worked by Union prisoners if necessary.[131] On January 6, 1865, the *Stag* arrived at Wilmington from England with forty-four cases of machinery aboard, but the Federal seizure of Fort Fisher on January 15, 1865, precluded any further importations.[132]

In August 1864, Treasury agent Colin McRae calculated the expenditures to date of Confederate supply officers in Europe. Chiefly on behalf of the Ordnance Bureau, Caleb Huse purchased armaments worth $12.4 million; the expenditures of William Crenshaw were incurred principally for commissary stores and amounted to $2.4 million; James Ferguson expended $1.9 million, to which Richard Waller added another $575,958, for quartermaster stores.[133] This scale of expenditures revealed the European priorities of the War Department: first arms, then beef, then clothing.

Although Thomas Bayne's reports showed some discrepancies, they indicated that eighty-two steamers on Quartermaster Bureau accounts entered Wilmington and Charleston between early April and late December 1864.[134] These vessels carried 311,521 pairs of shoes, 169,868 blankets, and 803,761 yards of uniform cloth.[135] In his official report for 1864, Secretary Seddon increased that quantity, probably adding other foreign sources, to 545,000 pairs of shoes and 316,000 blankets.[136] In the final months of the war, the Confederate army received substantial supplies from imports, but these figures should not obscure the considerable domestic production raised by Lawton's mobilization. For 1864, Lawton issued 744,851 pairs of shoes, of which 545,000 pairs were imported; the bureau manufactured 199,851 pairs. Since the Confederacy was almost bereft of blanket machinery, probably most of the blanket issues in 1864 were from the 316,000 items imported. Ninety percent of all military socks were made in the South.

The scant million yards of woolens brought through the blockade would have provided no more than 200,000 uniforms, while Lawton issued 458,131 field jackets and 744,851 pairs of pants. That left two-thirds of Confederate issues, or 258,131 field jackets and 544,851 pairs of pants, that were made of domestic goods. Imports contributed significantly to the war effort, but the Confederate army depended upon millions of sandbags, grain sacks, undergarments, shirts, cotton uniforms, waterproof coverings, bunches of thread, coils of rope, and tents that came solely from Southern production.

Josiah Gorgas's Richmond arsenal alone issued over one million knapsacks, haversacks, gun and canteen straps, and saddle blankets. Such uniform cloth that came through the blockade was fabricated in military depots by Southern seamstresses and lined with domestic cottons. Although Lawton permitted the importation of some dyestuffs, oils, and machinery parts, a greater emphasis on the needs of domestic manufacturing would have benefited the Confederacy. With more machinery in the wool-producing regions, the Confederacy could have achieved a still greater degree of self-sufficiency.

While foreign products, especially weapons and beef, were critically important to the maintenance of the Confederate army in the last months of the war, General Lawton's successful mobilization of Southern manufacturing more fully explains the enormous outpouring of supplies in the winter of 1864 than the vigorous exertions of Crenshaw, Ferguson, and Waller. However, with more emphasis on importing machinery, the domestic contribution might have been far greater.

6

The Coming of Total War

As the Union blockade wreaked destruction upon Confederate sea-borne commerce, planned devastations by both armies laid waste the home front.[1] Early in the war the governments of both the North and the South made disclaimers that the fighting would be on a civilized plane, with solicitude for noncombatants, protection of private property, and an honorable treatment of enemy captives, but long before the battles of Gettysburg and Vicksburg both governments settled into a system of planned economic destruction. Jefferson Davis endorsed a scorched-earth policy of burning cotton, subsistence stores, transportation facilities, and buildings liable to be of benefit to the enemy, while General Ulysses S. Grant and General Henry Halleck, with the sanction of President Abraham Lincoln, subsisted their armies off the enemy's country and undertook the systematic destruction of Confederate manufacturing and the deportation of skilled workers. Factories that lay near the paths of contending armies faced additional hazards from marauders, discontented workers, and a severely deprived civilian population.

Early in the war, Confederate officers in the field faced a dilemma about the preservation or destruction of manufacturing properties within their lines. In 1862, in north Arkansas, General Sterling Price was forced to decide the fate of John H. Herman's factory. Herman, a practicing physician, owned large carding and flouring mills. Politically, he was an outspoken follower of Carl Schurz, the Missouri Free Soil Republican. In 1861, Herman implored "every man in his employ to go to the polls & vote against secession." Although within Confederate territory, "Herman's mill became a center of Unionist activities, serving as a hide-out for runaway Negroes and for refugees fleeing North." Against the express orders of General Price, Herman befriended the Unionist Cherokees. As a result, he was forced to flee Arkansas, and "his mill [worth] between $15,000 and $20,000 including residence and carding machine was burned by the rebels." The advancing Federal army found his extensive properties "returned to a state of nature" (Klingberg 101–2).

For their part, advancing Federal commanders quickly discovered the close relationship between Southern manufacturers and the Confederate government. Most mills were beehives of activity, manufacturing uniforms and other military equipage on site; nearby were often other facilities leased to Confederate contractors. Ten mills on the Savannah River had over 550 persons on average in each community. Some older factories were leased for Confederate use as arsenals or prisoner-of-war camps. For Federal commanders, this was prima facie evidence of manufacturers' complicity in the rebellion.

Since Southern mills were commonly enclosed by walls, abandoned facilities were useful as military prisons. The tobacco warehouses at Richmond served the same purpose. Early in the war, the old North Port factory in Tuscaloosa was leased to the Confederate Quartermaster Department for this purpose and immediately received a large consignment of political prisoners from east Tennessee. The Madison Steam Factory Cotton Mill in central Georgia was surrounded by "substantial plank fence with gates and lock attached."[2] After its machinery was removed, this mill with three rooms, "130 feet by 55 feet together with three out buildings and lot," was employed "for the safe keeping of Federal prisoners, spies, bridge burners, &c."[3] In addition, a frame building containing three rooms was used as an office and for the storage of commissary and medical supplies. In North Carolina, the owners of a factory in Alamance County refused a Confederate lease, but the governor secured "a very large and commodious building" at Salisbury.[4] The military prison established within the stone walls of the Salisbury factory became one of the most controversial of the war; designed for no more than 2,000 men, it ultimately housed 10,000 Union captives, some of whom were forced to work for the Quartermaster Bureau.

Josiah Gorgas established a Confederate arsenal in one of the several factory buildings at Barnett and Micou at Tallassee, Alabama. The Ordnance Bureau officer who inspected the site in 1864 found large mills, one old and another new, "the former full of machinery, in active operation, the latter about one half filled with machinery, also in active operation."[5] Gorgas leased the old mill, a two-story building, eighty by forty feet, with good water power. Since the town of Tallassee consisted "entirely of the cottages of the factory operatives, all which were fully occupied," he erected twenty-five double tenements for the arsenal workers, giving each family a quarter acre for a garden.[6] Tallassee possessed skilled mechanics, grist and lumber mills, and access to local railroad transportation.[7] Additional workers and armory machinery from Richmond soon arrived at the burgeoning factory community. Such arrangements posed considerable danger to private property.

The Union military offensive in the spring of 1862—with drives to seize both the Mississippi and Tennessee Rivers—and upon Virginia's peninsula and the Outer Banks opened the possibility of destroying Confederate military depots and factories located at all points along the front. Individual commanders exercised wide discretion in this regard. As commander of the Union forces in Missouri and Tennessee, General Henry W. Halleck energetically sought to disable Confederate manufacturing. Before leaving the West to become general-in-chief of all Union forces in July 1862, Halleck ordered his river gunboat flotillas to raid wharves and warehouses at Florence, Alabama, and adjacent areas to seize Confederate stores of small arms and clothing.[8] A typical raid was carried out on March 27, 1863, by the energetic LeRoy Fitch, who commanded the river gunboat *Lexington*, then cruising on the Tennessee River. After seizing twenty-five bales of cotton at Florence, Fitch stopped at Boyd's Landing in Hardin County, Tennessee, "having learned that back about 3 miles from the river was a cotton factory doing work in a indirect way, so as to aid the rebel soldiers." Fifty armed sailors from the *Lexington*, along with two companies of infantry from Fort Heiman, Kentucky, conducted a quick reconnaissance. Fitch's "expedition moved out to the factory with caution, as Colonel [Nicholas N.] Cox's rebel cavalry regiment was encamped but a mile or two beyond."[9] Arriving at the mill, Fitch threw up a breastwork of cord wood across the road and began an investigation of the manufacturing operation.

The company apparently held no Confederate contracts. The lieutenant found that "the books were all clear, and contained nothing to condemn the factory." Some companies, such as Graniteville, carefully kept a double set of books for such emergencies. From what the Federal troops learned, "the mill was run on shares with the country people; the material went, in an indirect way, to the aid of the rebel soldiers through their friends at home." The Yankee officer then carefully disabled the property: "knowing that the mill did, in an indirect way, aid the rebels, it was thought proper not to destroy it, but to effectually prevent its doing more work." Almost within earshot of the Confederate cavalry, Fitch removed "the running gear, pistons, cylinder heads, brasses, and all like portable portions" and placed them aboard the *Lexington*. Two mules and a wagon were impressed to "haul the machinery down to the boat."[10] Other factories on the Tennessee River were handled in a similar fashion. On April 2, 1863, General Granville Dodge reported that "the gunboats *Lexington*, *Silver Lake*, and *Robb* shelled rebels out of Florence Tuesday." After silencing the Confederate batteries, the crews "destroyed all the cotton factories this side of Florence."[11] On May 24, the gunboat *Covington*, at Savannah, Tennessee, "crossed and covered a small force which proceeded a few miles back and destroyed a cotton and woolen factory and a mill used by the rebels."[12]

The defensive maneuvering of Confederate military commanders sometimes drew Federal attention to factory sites. In skirmishing across northern Mississippi following the battle of Shiloh, the Confederate forces established a defensive line near Bay Springs factory, thirty miles south of Corinth. On August 9, 1862, Union general Robert B. Mitchell conducted a successful attack against this position and disabled "the cotton factory at that place in such a way as to require a communication between this country and New England in order to effect repairs."[13] In the fall of 1862, following the battles of Iuka and Corinth, Confederate general Sterling Price converted some of the Bay Springs factory buildings into a Confederate prison. Chickasaw, one of General Ulysses S. Grant's prized Mississippi scouts, spent a night there but escaped.[14]

General Ambrose Burnside on the Virginia front, in contrast to his later policy, also adopted a policy of disabling rather than destroying manufacturing properties early in the war. In November 1862, following the battle of Antietam, Federal forces occupied Duff Green's Falmouth mill on the Rappahannock River north of Fredericksburg. At the same time, the Union forces seized a second mill partly owned by Montgomery Slaughter, the Confederate mayor of Fredericksburg. General Edwin V. Sumner, who commanded Burnside's right wing, was offended that local "mills and manufactories are furnishing provisions and the material for clothing for armed bodies in rebellion against the government of the United States."[15] Nevertheless, the mills were spared upon Slaughter's promise that they would "not furnish any further supplies of provisions or material for clothing for the Confederate troops."[16] Despite that promise, David Tillson, an escaped mill operative and native of Maine, soon testified to the Federals that "a large portion of the machinery of a woolen mill was carried out of Fredericksburg after the arrival of the Federal army."[17] Practically under the eyes of the Union commanders, the Falmouth Cotton and Woolen Mill was dismantled and hauled by wagon and railroad to Manchester, Virginia, where it was worked for the remainder of the war almost exclusively for the Confederate War Department.[18]

Of far greater embarrassment to the North was the conduct of manufacturers at Florence, Alabama. Following the Federal occupation of the area in 1862, Robert Patton, a local manufacturer, wrote Governor John Gill Shorter of Alabama that "the cotton and woolen factorys [sic] of Lauderdale County have entered into [an agreement] not to sell the goods made by them to the Confederate Government." This arrangement "was required by the Yankees since they occupied the Country."[19] Cotton spinners like Richard B. Baugh, owner of a Lauderdale County mill, gave "bond to the U.S. Forces not to sell directly or indirectly to the Conf. States."[20] Obviously, Union military commanders had some hope of winning political support by observing a lenient policy toward alien property owners. Robert Patton observed that "as these large cotton mills and woolen factory have not been able the last four or five months to send their goods south (while they have been working full time) I have no doubt the stocks of osnaburgs & woolen goods for soldiers have greatly increased, perhaps to thousands of bales." He proposed a Confederate military offensive to retrieve these goods, writing that "as soon as the enemy are driven north, and the Southern market is open to their goods, they will be sold indirectly, or through second hands to the Confederacy or to the state at exorbitant and speculative prices."[21] General Braxton Bragg's offensive into Kentucky in September 1862 opened the prospect of securing these goods.

Soon after the Federals evacuated Alabama in a race to reach the Ohio River before General Bragg and his Confederate army, Major George W.

Jones, a Confederate quartermaster and "a plausible shrewd man," arrived in Huntsville on a sick leave.[22] The major, a former congressman from Tennessee with many political connections, quickly discovered the large warehouses filled with goods. These he immediately impressed. As Robert Baugh explained, the factories and their goods "were pressed by order of Maj. G. W. Jones, C.S.A. in the fall of 1862, and most of the goods manufactured were taken by Maj. Jones (under a protest of the Company) at prices very greatly below the market price."[23] Nevertheless, the bond of the Lauderdale factory with the Federal army was broken, and Jones obtained for the Confederate Quartermaster Bureau "over 500,000 pounds of leather" (*Richmond Whig*, December 19, 1862). According to the same report, Jones also "secured woolen cloth, enough, (30,000 yards,) to make 5,000 coats and pants for our soldiers, and also 1,000 bales of osnaburgs, about 550,000 yards." The enterprising major also impressed 1,000 bales of cotton. From his depot at Marion, Alabama, he soon presented the astonished officers of the Richmond Clothing Bureau with over 30,000 drawers and shirts made from his booty.[24]

With the Confederate press cheering over such incidents, the Union command moved cautiously to punish the north Alabama millers. The Federals soon returned to north Alabama, and one officer was so bold as to occupy the Bell factory at Huntsville and free fifty of Robert Patton's slaves. But when elements of an Indiana regiment happened by in October 1863, the mill was again busy. An artillery gunner was astonished to find that the "large woolen mill" was "owned by a Yankee from Connecticut named Faber [William B. Taber] and was a very substantial brick building four stories high" (Rowell, *Yankee Artillerymen* 138–39). Taber's junior partnership in the mill apparently convinced the Union commanders to relinquish control.

The Federal War Department changed its policy regarding alien properties with the full realization of the extent of Confederate mobilization. General Henry Halleck arrived in Washington in July 1862, demanding a sterner conduct of the war against the property of noncombatants. Civilian confiscation laws were of little value to military commanders in the field. The experience of the Federal army in the occupation of Tennessee and northern Virginia was undoubtedly a factor in shaping the new code of military conduct. Grant and his subaltern, William T. Sherman, especially urged upon Halleck and the War Department the notion that "when one nation is at war with another, all the people of the one are the enemies of the other: then the rules are plain and simple of understanding" (Sherman 1: 294). These views were incorporated in General Order No. 100, issued on April 24, 1863, by which Halleck adopted a Federal military code for the destruction of "Public and Private Property of the Enemy."[25] Many of the provisions of the military order reflect the philosophy of Karl von Clausewitz, the Prussian military strategist, as interpreted by Francis Lieber, an academician at Columbia College.[26] The precept of "total war" had a special appeal to many Radical Republicans. The new military code attempted to distinguish between civilized European warfare and a state of savagery. Civilians in a hostile country, who might be either friend or foe as was the case in occupied Tennessee, were to be treated henceforth as "an enemy."[27] As an act of war, enemy noncombatants were to be allowed to starve, and their property could be forfeited or sequestered for military purposes, exempting only churches, schools, libraries, and art works. With or without warning, places of habitation could be bombarded. If necessary, a policy of military retaliation was sanctioned, although "civilized nations acknowledge retaliation as the sternest feature of war."[28]

The military order allowed the "destruction of all property, and obstruction of the ways and channels of traffic, travel, or communication, and of all withholding of sustenance or means of life from the enemy; of the appropriation of whatever an enemy's country affords necessary for the subsistence and safety of the Army."[29] Halleck was vigorous in recommending the application of these new orders to his commanding generals. In November 1863, he reported to Federal Secretary of War Edwin Stanton that "instructions have been given to the generals in hostile territory to subsist their armies, so far as possible, upon the country."[30] He further approved the shelling of fortified towns and the forcible removal of noncombatants from the war front. Halleck wrote Sherman, who questioned him on these matters, "I would destroy every mill and factory within reach which I did not want for my own use." This, he argued, the Confederates had done in Pennsylvania and elsewhere in Union territory within their reach, and "in many sections of the country they have not left a mill to grind grain for their own suffering families, lest we might use them to supply our armies."[31]

Implementation of the stern new policy was quickly evident. On April

16, 1863, General Burnside through James Garfield ordered General David S. Stanley to raid the territory between the Stone and Cumberland Rivers in Tennessee. Moving toward McMinnville, Stanley was enjoined to "destroy the cotton-mills there, and all depots of supplies for the rebel army." Burnside particularly desired him "to make thorough work this time, so there will be no need of another expedition."[32]

In April 1863, Colonel Abel D. Streight of the Federal Army of the Cumberland, preparing for a raid from Tuscumbia, Alabama, to Rome, Georgia, was ordered "to destroy all depots of supplies of the rebel army, all manufactories of guns, ammunition, equipment, and clothing for their use."[33] Streight immediately understood his role in implementing the new policy, responding that "the destruction of manufacturing establishments engaged in manufacturing directly for the rebel army I consider a duty which I have no right to leave undone, when in my power, even in absence of instructions."[34]

The report of Florence M. Cornyn of the Tenth Missouri Cavalry, riding along the Tennessee River near the Alabama border in June 1863, revealed the dimensions of the new strategy. Cornyn wrote, "we reached Rawhide [Hardin County, Tennessee] at about 9 o'clock, and from this point I sent out to the north and left off the main road two squadrons of the seventh Kansas . . . to destroy the grist-mills and cotton and woolen factories in that neighborhood, which, I am happy to say was effectually executed." At daybreak on May 29, the column destroyed "a large cotton factory about 20 miles from Hamburg, and known as Valentine's Factory."[35] J. B. Valentine's mills, toll bridge, and shops at Herbertsville were a valuable private property rendering little aid to the Confederacy.[36] Shortly after, Federal troops visited Asa Butterworth, an enterprising manufacturer of English extraction at Winchester, in Franklin County, Tennessee, and "his Buildings were all Burned."[37]

Cornyn was especially anxious to call again on the mills at Florence, Alabama. For several months after the Union evacuation of the area in the fall of 1862, these factories and those in the surrounding countryside were turned on behalf of the Confederate Quartermaster Department. Samuel D. Weakley, who with James Martin owned three mills on Cypress Creek, was chair of the local defense committee and a "Special A D C to General Pillow."[38] These were not credentials to impress a Federal cavalry commander riding under the authority of General Order No.

100.[39] On May 28, 1863, Cornyn burned the three Martin and Weakley factories, as well as a flour mill, storehouses, other structures, and 400 bales of cotton.[40] He also rode over other mill sites. Richard B. Baugh, whose previous bond had been violated, wrote that his "factory was burned by Gen. Dodge in Nov. 1863."[41] Cornyn's military report reflected the consequences of the new military order: "we destroyed seven cotton factories, not one of which cost less than $200,000, and the raw material and finished goods in them were worth infinitely more than the cost of the factories and machinery." One mill "contained 300 looms, and employed not less than 2,000 persons." The loss was estimated at "several millions of dollars."[42]

In Lauderdale County, Alabama, at least six factories were destroyed.[43] Charles Willis, an Illinois soldier, passed Cypress Creek shortly thereafter and found that "something like 50 or 60 girls, some of them rather good looking, had congregated and they seemed much pleased to see us." All of the workers "avowed themselves Unionists" (Willis 199). The soldier found that "there had been a large cotton mill at this crossing, Comyn [Cornyn] burned it last summer, which had furnished employment for these women and some 200 more" (109). A village disappeared.

On a subsequent raid along Shoal Creek in the same district, General Edward Hatch of the Second Iowa Cavalry ordered the destruction "by fire [of] a flouring mill, which was located above a factory." Unable to cross the creek at Baugh's Ford because of high water and Confederate skirmishers, Hatch's troops resorted to shelling Baugh's mill without much success (Surby 209).[44]

Other raids along the Tennessee River were conducted by Brigadier General Alfred W. Ellet, commander of a brigade of marines aboard the Union army's ram fleet. In April 1863, the local naval commander reported that "General Ellet is now in the river with his brigade and will doubtless attend to cotton mills, etc., out of my reach and doing work for the rebels."[45] After landing at Eastport, Mississippi, and Savannah, Tennessee, among other towns, Ellet organized mounted raids against factories and mills in the contested zone. He wrote his friend Secretary Edwin Stanton shortly thereafter that he "made several raids into the country and destroyed a number of important mills and considerable amount of subsistence supplies belonging to the enemy."[46] After being transferred to the Mississippi River in May 1863, Ellet captured "two men,

Messrs. Barker and Keefe, cotton manufacturers, with a cotton machine, recently bought at Macon, Ga., at a cost of eight thousand dollars" (Crandall and Newell 329–30). These Confederates "had crossed the river with their machine just a little while before their capture, and were en route to Camden, Ark., where the machine was to be used in making cloth for the Confederate army" (330). Later, Ellet gained considerable notoriety by burning Austin, Mississippi, the Tunica County seat, in retaliation for the local citizenry's supplying military information to the Confederate authorities.

The Northern press slowly warmed to the new military policy regarding Southern property. On April 25, 1863, the *New York Herald* took favorable note of General Joseph J. Reynolds's seizure of McMinnville, Tennessee, while his division was en route from Murfreesboro to Chattanooga. The Union troops took 300 prisoners; destroyed bridges, 600 blankets, and 30,000 pounds of bacon; and left in ashes "two hundred bales of cotton, one large cotton factory," and several grist mills (*New York Herald*, April 25, 1863).

The Confederate authorities responded in kind. On March 17, 1862, the Confederate Congress made statutory provision for the systematic destruction of all cotton, tobacco, and military stores likely to fall into the hands of the enemy. The Confederate burning of cotton began almost immediately in middle Tennessee. Following the Battle of Shiloh, General Pierre Beauregard commenced burning cotton throughout the Tennessee Valley (Duke 158–59). "Hundreds of thousands of bales were put to the torch during the spring and summer of 1862," with perhaps 100,000 bales destroyed at Memphis alone (Owsley 47–48).

The pace of destruction accelerated thereafter. As the Vicksburg campaign unfolded in late 1862 and early 1863, much of the pattern of devastation developed in the Tennessee Valley was transferred to Mississippi and Louisiana. With great effectiveness, retreating Confederate armies burned cotton and other supplies between Memphis and Vicksburg.[47] The practice of burning all cotton within five miles of the river cost one planter over 1,000 bales (Dennett 101). At the same time, the advancing Federals laid waste to the factories, business shops, foundries, hotels, and public buildings in Mississippi towns like Austin, Oxford, Corinth, and Grand Gulf. Stock, provisions, and fodder were systematically impressed for use by the Union forces or destroyed.

As Grant recalled, soon after Halleck arrived in Washington, he received orders "to live upon the country, on the resources of citizens hostile to the government, so far as practicable" (Grant 397). He was also directed to "handle rebels within our lines without gloves" (397–98). Subsequently, he burned bridges, destroyed railroads, and sent secessionist families south, and his seizure of forage and food in Mississippi was so successful that he could subsist his army for twenty days on five days of military rations. This demonstrated that Federal armies could operate detached from supply bases. Among Union commanders, William T. Sherman was especially conscious of the strategic value of desolation. In opening the Vicksburg campaigns, he wrote his brother, Congressman John Sherman, that "the South abounds in corn, cattle and provisions and the progress in manufacturing shoes and cloth for the soldiers is wonderful." The Confederate soldiers, "though coarsely, are well clad" and were "as well supplied as we and they have an abundance of the best cannon, arms and ammunition."[48] Such views encouraged the vigorous application of extreme measures.

In May 1863, three Wisconsin infantry regiments, located at Port Hudson, Louisiana, and led by the redoubtable Colonel Benjamin Henry Grierson, mounted a raid upon Clinton, in East Feliciana Parish. After fighting all day, the Confederates finally relinquished the town to the Federals, whereupon "an extensive cotton factory was destroyed" (Surby 139).[49] Afterward, the colonel noted that "some of the inhabitants seemed altogether despondent."[50] Within a few months, residents in the neighborhood of the factory represented to their Confederate congressman that the "manufactories of coarse and woolen and cotton cloths have all been destroyed by the enemy, and they are without clothing." For want of cards, the inhabitants were "unable to weave homespun cloths or to hide and protect their nakedness."[51]

In the spring of 1863, a Federal cavalry troop from Natchez, Mississippi, rode all night to raid the Woodville factory of Edward McGehee. Arriving at noon, the Federal major and his 300 troopers detained John McGehee, who served as the factory manager, and demanded that he show his hospitality by providing lunch.[52] In the midst of these proceedings, Edward McGehee arrived. An eminent member of the Natchez aristocracy who had twice declined positions in prewar Cabinets, McGehee greeted the major with the declaration, "I believe I am a better Union man to-day than you are." The manufacturer protested that "I have spent my time and money for the preservation of the Union but when my State seceded I was obliged to go with it."[53] As the owner of 1,000 slaves, a cotton mill, and a railroad, McGehee spoke with the confidence and authority of a self-made aristocrat.

The Federal major was unconvinced and continued his conversation until nightfall. "From the way the Major talked and his long delay in firing," John McGehee later wrote, "I thought he wanted some money and told father that $5000.00 put would probably save the factory." "Not a cent," Edward McGehee replied, for if he paid "it would become a common practice to raid him."[54] The Federal officer may have been evaluating the situation. Edward McGehee had been a Unionist, but he was also regularly selling to the Confederate quartermaster in Jackson dyed jeans for uniforms and osnaburgs for feed sacks. He even sold two brass cannons to the local Confederate commander.[55] Most of his numerous sons and grandsons were in the Confederate service.

Some of Edward McGehee's goods also supplied local Confederate contractors. One was Betty Bentley Beaumont, an English-born seamstress who "hired girls" and established a factory to make army hats (Beaumont 178). For her sewing group, she wrote, "Judge McGehee's factory, about a mile from town, furnished a large amount of cotton cloth for under garments" (170). Grant's and Sherman's standing orders to Federal officers were to pay cash to the loyal for forage supplies, give conditional receipts to anyone of doubtful loyalty, and give nothing to rebels. The Yankee major finally made up his mind about "nine or ten o'clock, and then fired the factory and rode away by the light."[56]

Nor were Edward McGehee's woes ended yet. Woodville lay in a contested zone between the Confederate cavalry, which patrolled the eastern side of the river, and the Federal enclaves at Baton Rouge and Natchez. In a successful cavalry raid against Woodville in 1864, the Third United States Colored Cavalry pursued a company of Confederate soldiers through the McGehee plantation. Edward McGehee recognized some of the black soldiers, who adroitly took family stores of food and silver, then burned the plantation house, gin house, and 350 bales of cotton worth $300 in gold each.[57] Mary Burruss McGehee, the manufacturer's wife, subsequently wrote an articulate and pathos-laden account of this incident for the Confederate *Army & Navy Herald*, which was widely copied by newspapers across the Confederacy.

As Grant's army moved on Vicksburg in May 1863, it marched down the west bank of the Mississippi River, crossed to the east bank at Grand Gulf, and flanked the river fortress after seizing Jackson from the south. The Confederate evacuation of Jackson was especially destructive and an indication of Jefferson Davis's scorched-earth policy. Following orders, General Joseph E. Johnston burned all Confederate cotton at the capital along with the rolling stock of the Mississippi Central Railroad worth $5 million.[58]

Then it was the Federals' turn. Grant was greeted upon his arrival by Judge William L. Sharkey, a prominent Whig from a manufacturing family. Sharkey offered his home to General James B. McPherson for a military headquarters, thereby establishing his Union credentials and saving his property.[59] Having refused to do business with the Confederate authorities, Sharkey was in an admirable position to know those who did.

General Sherman assumed responsibility for wrecking Confederate property in Jackson. He first burned "the arsenal buildings, the Government foundry, the gun-carriage establishment." The resulting conflagration consumed a variety of private foundries, machine shops, and cotton warehouses. The Mississippi penitentiary, which operated a large cotton factory, was also destroyed. Sherman insisted that this work was accomplished "by some convicts who had been set free by the Confederate authorities."[60] Nevertheless, there remained of that factory "with all its machinery but little save the rubbish of the walls." Mississippi's Governor John Pettus observed upon his later return that "one steam engine and a lot of iron and copper is all that can be recovered from the ruins."[61]

The cotton factory of the Greene brothers also attracted attention. Grant and Sherman jointly toured the mill, "which had not ceased work on account of the battle nor for the entrance of Yankee troops." At first the presence of the Union officers "did not seem to attract the attention of either the manager or the operatives, most of whom were girls" (Grant 1: 507). Quantities of tent cloth, with "C.S.A." neatly emblazed on each bolt, were coming from the looms. Outside the factory were immense stacks of baled cotton. At last Grant told Sherman, "I thought they had done work enough." Then, "[t]he operatives were told they could leave and take with them what cloth they could carry" (507).

The Greene brothers frantically appealed to the generals to spare the mill "based on the fact that it gave employment to very many females and poor families, and that, although it had woven cloth for the enemy, its principal use was in weaving cloth for the people."[62] But Sherman countered that "machinery of that kind could so easily be converted into hostile uses that the United States could better afford to compensate the Messrs. Greene for their property, and feed the poor families thus thrown out of employment than to spare the property."[63] After assuring the workers that if they came to the riverbank they would be fed or transported to a loyal region, Sherman and Grant followed the literal instructions of General Order No. 100. In a few minutes "a very valuable cotton factory" with its contingent of raw materials was ablaze.[64]

Considerable pillaging by soldiers, camp followers, and migratory slaves followed in the wake of this destruction. In the Confederate War Department, such losses were fully appreciated; the quartermaster general viewed the occupation of Jackson as "most serious," believing it would result materially in "the interruptions of the arrangements made to furnish supplies to the troops."[65] The burning of Jackson was Grant's repayment in kind for General Earl Van Doren's brilliant cavalry raid against the Union base at Holly Springs in December 1862 (*Charleston Mercury*, January 12, 1863).[66] Other factory towns that lay along the invasion routes of the Union armies were equally at risk.

Sherman's raiders destroyed thousands of bales of cotton and millions of bushels of corn at Jackson. A Union cavalry command under General Benjamin H. Grierson conducted an equally effective action along the Mobile and Ohio Railroad through the center of Mississippi. Several months later, one company of this group, the Fourth Iowa Cavalry, was guided by a scout to James Wesson's large factory and army manufacturing depot at Bankston. Arriving at midnight, "they found the place quiet—the inhabitants having had no intimation of the Yankees being in their vicinity" (Surby 379).[67] The raiders found "at this place a large manufacturing establishment, which was turning out one thousand yards of cloth and two thousand pairs of shoes per day" (379). The mill workforce consisted of 500 hands, but the manufacturing village of Enterprise was much larger. James Wesson managed the factory. As the Federal troopers set fire to the buildings, "the superintendent of the factory made his appearance, in his night clothes, swearing, threatening to arrest the guard and night watchers, and wanting to know what in h——l they were about that they did not extinguish the fire." Captain Warren Beckwith of the Fourth Iowa "told him that the night was so very cold that he had concluded to have a fire" (379). The superintendent would indulge no such humor and retorted, "h——l and d——nation, would you burn up the manufactory to make a fire to warm by?" (380).

As the factory burned, a large flouring mill "underwent the same fate." Products precious to the Confederate army were then consigned to the flames: "a large supply of cloth, shoes, cotton, wool and commissary and quartermaster's stores were also destroyed" (380). Grierson's custom on such occasions was to invite poor families from the neighborhood to share in the spoils, and such became a standard feature of Sherman's marches (386).[68]

One discriminating western manufacturer, Henry Merrell, who observed such a raid, took careful note of the Federals' attire: "as to the clothing of Federal soldiers generally, it was of course more uniform in appearance, but the shoddy material of which it was made soon went to rags," while "the Confederate Gray, of domestic make, presented a less shabby appearance" (Merrell 365–66). After a few weeks' wear, both armies looked very much alike.

General Order No. 100 was also vigorously implemented on the Atlantic coast. In imitation of General Ellet's work on the Tennessee River, a Union naval brigade was created to operate on Chesapeake Bay. On June 3, 1863, this brigade and four companies of supporting infantry, accompanied by the gunboat *Smith Briggs*, raided Ayletts, on the Mattapony River north of Richmond. General Edward D. Keyes, who planned the excursion, expected to find "several factories, warehouses, and other public buildings at the place which it is desirable to destroy." The brigade consigned to flames a foundry, "an immense amount of machinery of all kinds, and also a very large quantity of flour and grain, which was in a large flouring mill belonging to the rebel government."[69] A few months later the *Smith Briggs* was ordered down to the Nansemond River to accompany another force striking at Smithfield, Virginia. Anticipating the attack, the Confederates struck first, capturing 100 prisoners and the gunboat. In the Richmond War Department, John Jones was exuberant, writing, "we learn that this Yankee force was commissioned to destroy a large factory at Smithfield in Isle of Wight County" (John Jones 2: 142).[70]

The military objective, the machinery of the cotton factory at Scott's Mills, was laboriously evacuated to Petersburg and given to the navy before Federal troops could mount another attack.[71]

In July 1863, Colonel John G. Foster led a Federal raid out of New Bern with Rocky Mount as the objective. There he burned a bridge, a train of railroad cars, an ironclad under construction, and William Battle's "cotton-mill employing 150 white girls, built of stone and six stories high . . . and immense quantities of hard-tack [biscuits] (already manufactured staple cotton, and manufactured goods filled the store rooms of the cotton factory), a machine shop filled with war munitions, several separate storehouses."[72]

The intensification of the war with the prospect of an almost assured destruction of mill property gave manufacturers a considerable impetus to form home guard units. An act of the Confederate Congress on October 13, 1862, authorized the creation of local defense forces whereby factory workers were enlisted in military units. The additional dimension of aiding factory discipline encouraged most factories to comply. Mill managers or injured soldiers were often used for company officers, while detailed men, men over forty-five years of age, and youths were placed in the ranks. Daniel Pratt organized the Prattville Grays early in the war and maintained a military company thereafter, apparently at his own expense. This company was composed "of our mechanicks, clerks, overseers and a few planters in the neighborhood." When the Federal armies moved into north Alabama, Pratt added a mounted force of twenty-five men but declined to move his company out of the county because, with so many workers absent, no portion of the mill "would have an overseer or many hands."[73] The New Hampshire native anticipated short shrift at the hands of the Federal army. He wrote Governor Thomas Watts in July 1864, "I feel that we all ought to be prepared to meet the enemy at an hour's notice." His foundry and machine shops were capable of refurbishing old weapons from the state arsenal, and Pratt requested Governor Watts to "make arrangements to furnish the Prattville Co with rifles and cartridge boxes [and], if so we will have them all put in order and kept together in a safe room." In concession, Pratt volunteered to send "sixty or seventy" armed men from the factory company to Montgomery, if necessary, to defend the state capital.[74]

As the war front came nearer, Benjamin Micou, of the Tallassee mill in central Alabama, wrote Judah P. Benjamin of his growing concerns. Tallassee's three factories were most vulnerable. Having heard "some poor men talk that the war is killing up their sons & brothers for the protection of the slaveholder," Micou advocated the arming of slaves in self-defense. He believed that President Davis was "empowered to impress any property of citizens deemed necessary for public defence." The use of slave labor on the coastal defenses or to grow cotton was a waste of labor; rather, he thought that "the people are clamoring too for the slaves to be brought into service for defence of our rights & liberties & on this last point I agree with them fully & have thought for eighteen months that the government would be forced to use that great element in our Social compact for defence."[75] He found his slaves loyal and believed that, when organized in battalions, they would defend his mill property. Many Alabama leaders advocated such extreme measures, which eventually won the endorsement of Davis, Lee, and the Confederate government.

Georgia manufacturers armed themselves as well. Men detailed by the army at the larger mills in Columbus and Augusta formed military companies. In December 1863, J. Rhodes Browne, president of the Eagle factory at Columbus, explained his state of preparedness to Secretary James Seddon. At the factory, "the arms bearing employees of all ages were formed into a military organization under the call of the War Dept. for 6 mos. troops for local service." The cotton mill boasted "two complete companies, comprising one hundred & twenty-three men (123) which were received and commissioned by His Excellency the Gov. of this State." These companies were "completely equipped for service, well drilled, armed, &c ready to serve, in case of need, at a moment's notice."[76] The custom at some establishments was for workers to gather on Sunday mornings for drill.[77] Browne warmly endorsed his military formations, for they served "both as a measure of precaution for the safety of these mills & the other valuable Govt. interests and property at this point & also for the better control and discipline of the men, while engaged in regular employment."[78]

Other mills at Columbus, including Howard's factory, organized militia groups. A survey of the city's defense forces in May 1864 revealed that there was "one battalion regularly and legally organized numbering 245 men, composed of factory and railroad hands." In addition, there were at the "naval iron-works 138 men; at the arsenal and workshops under its control 175 men; in the quartermaster's office 200 men; and at the Government transportation works 37 men, making an aggregate of 795 men."[79] At least one Columbus weaver and cotton carder, who had previously worked at mills across the South, refused to join his assigned home guard unit. Being a "small, pale man, of very unobtrusive manners," he wore old clothes, grew a beard, and pretended to be ill and aged. He remained on "a small farm two or three miles out in the country" and convinced Confederate authorities that he was decrepit (Dennett 298).

Other Georgia mill communities armed themselves. James W. Atwood commanded the Manufactory Guards at Thomaston, "a company formed of the operatives of the Flint River & Waynmanville Cotton Factorys." The Connecticut-born manufacturer wrote Governor Joseph E. Brown that his group of 50 men was "pretty well drilled, & have been prompt to dutys [sic] & believe they would do invaluable service, in case of raid in this country, or in arresting deserters, &c."[80] Thomas M. Turner, proprietor of a Sparta factory, organized a Hancock State Guards unit composed of "about 55 men capable of doing pretty good service." Turner's company included a dozen denizens who were "entirely too old to do much." Like other Georgia guards, they preferred "not to be sent off any distance."[81] David A. Jewell, of the Rock factory at Mayfield, raised a force "of about twenty-five men which is organized at this place for home defence."[82] The proprietors of the Trion factory, Spencer Marsh and A. P. Allgood, had a guard consisting of several hundred men from Chattooga and Walker Counties divided into eight companies.[83] At the New Manchester mill in Marietta, Arnoldus V. Brumby, a graduate of West Point, "organized a company of State Guards, composed mainly of our employees."[84] Other factories, such as the Eatonton, Troup, and Augusta, had military units, although many were poorly armed and drilled.[85] George Schley led the Beauregard rifles at the Richmond factory, a company of "Silver Grays," as the older men styled themselves.[86]

In South Carolina, William Gregg sought arms from the War Department to equip his own militia company.[87] He obtained permission to purchase 150 rifles manufactured by Cook and Brother at Athens.[88] In Virginia, two guard units were formed from factory workers at Petersburg, one becoming Company 6 in the Twenty-third Virginia regiment and the other Company 8 in the Thirty-ninth Virginia. At least twenty-five men were enrolled from the Matoaca mill, twenty-two from Ettrick, and thirteen from Battersea.[89] Hugh Bone, an expatriate Englishman, was one of the captains.[90] Larger forces were available in the woolen and iron mills about Richmond.

While home guard units afforded some minimal protection against raiders and marauders, they could do little to control the threat of incendiarism. During the early years of the war, the number of factories destroyed by fire was considerable: for example, Dog River at Mobile, Belleville and Lawrenceville in Georgia, Lincolnton and Yadkin in North Carolina, and Crenshaw in Richmond. Suspects were fatigued workers on night shifts, malicious slaves, and hired arsonists.

Workers, mostly women and children, had reason to be exhausted. At the Cedar Falls factory in North Carolina during May 1861, for each of twenty-three days of the month workers labored 13 hours, and for three days, usually Saturdays, they labored 10 hours.[91] This represented an increase over peacetime hours and was probably designed to offset the loss of skilled personnel to the army. By contrast, in November 1860 workers logged 262 hours, or an average of 10 hours a day, while in May 1861 they worked 329 hours. For this last month the mill compiled its best production record of the entire war.

By the summer of 1864, at ten Georgia factories on the Savannah River, five ran eleven hours a day and the remainder twelve or more hours.[92] These were lengthened summer hours. The principal method of extending the work week was to add hours on Saturdays, formerly a half day, and by providing mill lighting, especially at night. However, rosin-fed gaslights or torches for night work created a constant threat of conflagration caused by careless or tired workers. As a defense against accident and arson, some mills increased the size and vigilance of the night watch.

On May 14, 1862, at Roswell, Georgia, where four different factories were in operation, the "cotton house & picker room [of] mill no 2 was fired, damaged from 10 to $15 M [thousand dollars]." The workers were called out and promptly responded to the fire alarm. Men, women, and children brought "water &c, and saved the factory only 30 feet off, which was not the least injured." Barrington King, the proprietor, wrote soon afterward that "we have now a guard of eight men every night."[93] Nor did doubling the night watch provide any certainty that such acts would not be duplicated.[94] The loss of the flour mill, three cotton mills, and a woolen mill, he noted, "would be more serious at this time to our Confederacy, than to our stockholders," for "money will do no good, should the vandals conquer us."[95]

While the damage at Roswell was repaired, a search was conducted for the perpetrator of the crime. King wrote, "we suspected a man that has been working in the willow room, came here about 8 weeks since—he did not work that day, *saying he was sick*, but was seen in the mill about stopping time." With a little coercion the suspect confessed that "2 men from Tennessee offered him $500 to burn the mills, that we went with them to within 20 steps of the cotton house, & one of the men threw in a box of matches." Although "it was hard to keep the people from hanging him," the culprit was eventually lodged in the Marietta jail.[96] Those guilty of such offenses were usually sentenced to Confederate military prisons.

In December 1862, a factory was burned in Petersburg. John Jones wrote in his diary, "this is bad; they are calling for a guard at Petersburg against incendiaries" (John Jones 1: 210, 324). Also in December 1862, L. D. Childs's mill at Lincolnton, in the foothills of North Carolina, burned to the ground.[97] The New England–born manufacturer quickly recouped his loss, buying a vacant factory and its machinery at Columbia, South Carolina.[98] In March 1862, a large public building in Richmond burned, and the quartermaster general immediately issued a warning for officers to adopt "every precaution to prevent the occurrence of such a calamity in the Clothing Depot."[99] The depot warehouse was located nearby, and many goods were stored in private houses scattered around Richmond, all highly vulnerable to fire.

On February 27, 1863, the Yadkins factory in North Carolina burned. A proprietor, M. D. Holmes, wrote a North Carolina quartermaster that the mill was "all an entire loss as to machinery and stock in the house; but few pieces of cloth taken out, and but little on hand." This calamity made "many a family suffer in this section of country, thrown out of employment about 100 hands and them mostly women whose only chance for support was from the factory."[100]

After the burning of Henry Merrell's "dry house" at Royston, Arkansas, he created a home guard and "forted the Factory at our own expense & prepared an armory" (Merrell 321–22). The situation was conducive to raids because the mill stored considerable supplies of livestock, food, and clothing; fugitives and displaced persons abounded in the community; and the proprietor was suspected of speculation and harboring Northern sympathies. Merrell finally sold the factory and fled to Camden, with the sound of gunfire echoing over his head.

A very destructive fire occurred in Richmond on the evening of May 15, 1863. Originating in the picker room on the second floor of the Crenshaw Woolen Mill, the conflagration consumed the five-story building and portions of the nearby Tredegar Iron Works. Despite the best efforts of night watchmen and firemen, the losses included forty bales of manufactured cloth valued at $25,000 and 30,000 pounds of wool, enough to clothe two of Lee's divisions (*Charleston Mercury*, May 19, 1863).

Exhausted workers, the presence of night lights, and warming fires among the factory's combustibles were perpetual hazards of factory life, and arson was a constant threat. In a single night, before home guard units were posted, three fires were started by arsonists at Tredegar Iron Works (Dew 94). Clandestine agents, deserters, Heroes of America (a Unionist secret society), slaves, and "bush whackers" were usually implicated in such acts.

Indeed, the mill communities attracted a diverse population: women seeking work, speculators, deserters, and malingerers. Samuel Graham, of Tennessee's Pinewood factory, was so sorely troubled by "Jay Hawks" or "Bush Whackers" that he prayed to "never see another man in arms as a soldier."[101] The Confederate provost marshal for Athens, Tennessee, arrested some conscripts near Dixon's factory. He had "no doubt that old Dixon and all he has connected with him are doing all they can for Lincoln," but the Unionist boss was unmolested because "the factory was spinning gun-cotton for the Government so they said and it could not run if he was taken away."[102] John Ashmore, an up-country South Carolinian, found in August 1863 that in his community "the number of deserters are increasing daily." He wrote that one house in Spartanburg was burned, "as it is alleged, by deserters," and "another rendezvous, near Lester's factory, about twelve miles south of east from this place, has been established, and Mr. Lester informs me to-day that they have threatened to burn him up."[103] In March 1864, a battalion of General Nathan Bedford Forrest's cavalry raided an enclave of malingerers near the Bankston factory in Choctaw County, Mississippi, destroying all private distilleries en route. The command was specifically ordered "to move to Bankston (ten miles south of Greensborough), and report to J. M. Wesson, president of the manufacturing company, for the purpose of arresting some detailed men (as shoemakers) that have been disturbing the citizens and producing dis-organization."[104]

In October 1864, reports of a similar nature brought a Confederate detective to a factory at Fincastle, Virginia. He discovered that "about 1,000 deserters had passed through the country." In southwest Virginia, east Tennessee, and western North Carolina, the influence of the Heroes of America was pervasive. The detective learned that Amons, "the owner of the factory nearly opposite his house was a member of the order."[105] Apparently Amons sought to protect his valuable wool mill from the Union army by membership in the clandestine society. Another stronghold was found at Bonsack's factory on the East Tennessee and Virginia Railroad. Nearby at Marion, Virginia, A. Thomas, a mill owner, accepted a Confederate commission as captain and organized a company to protect "his factory & furnace from the deserters & outlaws who infested the mountains in this section of the country."[106]

The sources of dangers to the mills were not always clear. In June 1864, Enoch Steadman's Lawrenceville factory in Georgia inexplicably burned.[107] This company worked exclusively for Governor Joseph E. Brown, but Georgia quartermaster Ira Foster was forced to keep it under surveillance to ensure that the state received its goods. One of Steadman's employees learned that Quartermaster Foster had "parties watching your concern and that he has expressed the belief that you are sneaking and that he says he will have goods or blood."[108] However, no culprit was found.

Adding to the domestic danger for factories was the widespread destitution of the civilian population. At Graniteville, William Gregg contended with unending pressures from the public for goods. As he explained to his stockholders, "sometimes as many as two hundred letters were received in a day, and I had to answer the Government requisitions and all the beggars that came in person or by letter." Those soliciting him included "soldier's aid societies, sewing societies, stocking knitters, soldier's wives, indeed, every class of applicant had to be answered and conciliated."[109] People who often traveled long distances to the factory towns in search of small allotments of yarn or cloth were frequently disappointed.

Henry Merrell graphically described the chaotic scene accompanying sales: "The woods round about our village was an encampment of people anxiously waiting [for] their turn," and "every particular tree, or stump, or post seemed to have a horse or a mule tied to it & often without provender, horse and rider both" (Merrell 297). Detachments came afoot and by horse from the Native America nations, from neighboring states, and from the military. There were "planters whose Negroes were in rags, asking for nothing for themselves, but a little for their poor servants"; there were "war-widows and mothers anxious for their sons in the War, often in the rain and sleet, fifty [or] a hundred miles from home alone and in parties poorly clad themselves, & draggled in the wet & mud, crying, railing, begging for a only a little, or even a promise of a little if they would come again" (297). Then there were mobs and committees, petitions and resolutions, threatening letters and official military requisitions, all of which demanded a polite response.

Occasionally, violence ensued. In the fall of 1863, an armed group, including women, seized the loaded wagons of the New Manchester factory as they were conveyed from Marietta to Atlanta. Arnoldus Brumby, the company's president who headed a local home guard unit, explained his impotence in the matter to Governor Brown: "we could protect the mill with our operatives; but with them, we cannot protect our waggons [sic] on their way to Market." Some of the vigilantes were arrested, and "we have sued in damages & have prosecuted all the parties we could find who robbed our wagons some time back, but this seems to have no good effect." Like many other manufacturers, Brumby sought a solution in more Confederate rifles to arm his workers, because the threatening parties "which have robbed us of our property . . . are now assembling in such force as to render it impossible to carry on our work with any security even of life." Governor Brown deprecated the "mobs [that] attack the N.[New] Man[chester] Fac[tory]," but there was little to be done.[110] Across the state, "twenty-eight armed women took a wagonload of cloth en route from the Seven Islands Factory to Forsyth" (Coulter 423). In May 1864, Florida deserters captured "10,000 blankets and 6,000 pairs of shoes intended for State troops" (Lonn 70). One objective of the women's riots in Richmond and Petersburg in April 1863 was the seizure of cloth and clothing. An observer, Sallie Putnam, found that the looters "carried immense loads of cotton cloth, woolen goods, and other articles, and but few were seen to attack the stores where flour, groceries, and other provisions were kept" (Putnam 209).

The threats from a deprived domestic populace were overshadowed by the Federal military offensives that developed through the summer and fall of 1863, following the Union victories at Gettysburg and Vicksburg. Like other manufacturers, William Gregg was concerned that "if the Yankees reach Augusta they will be apt to make a raid to this place and to burn our factory." On this premise, he requested that Theodore Wagner of John Fraser's importing company "transfer stock to English house & claim British protection for the property."[111] Barrington King at Roswell anticipated enemy raids because "the defeat of our army at Chattanooga makes our situation more dangerous." He also expected that "our mills may be destroyed by the Yankeys, should the army fall back to Atlanta" and took the precaution of manufacturing some British flags to fly over the establishment.[112]

Such destructive actions were in fact contemplated.[113] After replacing Grant as commander in the West, Sherman planned a giant wheeling move through Georgia and South Carolina that would carry his army on to the siege at Richmond. General Halleck specifically instructed him, "I would destroy every mill and factory within reach which I did not want for my own use." With regard to the principles of General Order No. 100, Halleck wrote Sherman, "you are almost the only one who has properly applied them."[114] In a military conference before launching his campaign in the spring of 1864, Sherman instructed his generals to "burn all the mills, factories, etc. etc., that could be useful to the enemy, should he undertake to pursue us, or resume military possession of the country" (Sherman 2: 169). Special Field Order No. 120 spelled out the conditions: the Confederate civilian population was also the enemy.

Moving out of Chattanooga with three large columns on May 7, 1864, Sherman began a four-month march upon Atlanta. After the battle of Kennesaw Mountain on June 27, the Union army occupied Marietta, where Brumby's New Manchester factory was quickly burned. Barrington King at Roswell was greatly apprehensive, anticipating "a visit from the Vandals." He determined that it was "impossible to remove machinery & concluded to keep the factory in motion to the last hour sending off yarn &c as fast as produced." Despite the panic in the village, all of the hands were kept "at work, having divided 2 months provisions with them, it being safer with the people than our store, in case of a raid."[115] After hoisting British and French flags over the mills, King took the company books and departed south. His brother, William King, by reputation "a strong Union man," and the New England–born manager George H. Camp, were left behind to negotiate with General Sherman.[116]

An Illinois soldier arriving on the scene on June 17, 1864, recorded his impressions for the home folks: the whortleberries were abundant, a member of the Forty-eighth Illinois was drowned in the Chattahoochie while bathing, and "of several hundred factory girls, I have seen hardly one who is passably handsome." But like General Sherman, he noted, "these Roswell factories have been turning out 35,000 yards per day of jeans, etc. for the Confederate Army" (Willis 280). An Indiana volunteer had a different impression, writing on July 13 that the "Roswell Cotton factory was taken by our forces the other day and with it 700 girls who were working in it." The operatives he believed "likely arrived from England" while the mills were "worth over $1,000,000." The Georgia women "were somewhat alarmed at first, but were soon pacified and seemed pleased at being transferred from the Confeder'cy to Uncle Samuel." Some at least "said they believed they liked the Yankees the best anyhow, as they wore the best clothes and were the best looking men." The women proposed a dance and cleaned out a large hall, while the soldiers found some army fiddlers. The festivities commenced, and all "was merrie as a marriage ball" until General Sherman detached "a squad with a pocket full of matches and soon the buildings were no more."[117]

Sherman's decision to destroy the mills was made after an investigation by General Kenner Gerrard.[118] The status of the Roswell factory under Halleck's orders was quite clear, as the mill had ably supplied the Confederate manufacturing depot at Atlanta for years. Sherman's report to the general was brutally to the point. At Roswell, he found "several valuable cotton and woolen factories in full operation, also paper-mills," and "the main cotton factory was valued at a million of United States dollars." He confiscated the cloth and "ordered Gen. Garrard to arrest for treason all owners and employes [sic], foreign and native, and send them under guard to Marietta, whence I will send them North." Finally, he declared, "the whole region was devoted to manufactories, but I will destroy every one of them."[119]

Before ordering the properties burned, Sherman dismantled some buildings for lumber to bridge the Chattahoochee River for the crossing of his left wing upon Atlanta. William King's efforts to save Roswell failed, and on July 9 he learned from informants that "the factories had been destroyed & they & all the operatives men & women, had been arrested & were in Marietta on their way to the North." The arrested workers "all spoke in very bitter terms of my Brother (B) & of some other officer [Camp] there."[120] Throughout Roswell, every house, except that of the Presbyterian minister, was plundered of all valuables, and this was accomplished "almost entirely by *the operatives*," since the "the soldiers had committed but few depredations."[121] Barrington King was especially bitter: "our own people have done us more injury than the Yankee, for it appears that old Satan broke loose, & they could not stand the temptation to plunder."[122]

After a brief consideration, General Sherman decided to deport the civilian population of Roswell to the free states. On July 12, the first train left Marietta for Chattanooga, "sixteen car loads of them and one guard to each car" (Upson 118–19). One Federal soldier thought the operatives were "glad their fighting is over for a while at least" (119). Some of the young women he found "tough," and hard work was required "to keep them straight and to keep the men away" (119). Four hundred young women were detained in the seminary at Marietta, and General Sherman was reported to say that "he would rather try to guard the whole Confederate Army, and I guess he is right about it" (119). Few tried to escape. With the fall of Atlanta on September 1, 1864, Sherman enlarged his deportation order and gave the populace the choice of following the workers north or going into exile within the Confederacy.[123] The 2,000 female workers at George Cunningham's manufacturing depot in Atlanta were forced to evacuate the city.

General Henry Halleck applauded Sherman's fidelity to his orders: "we have tried three years of conciliation and kindness without any reciprocation." Specifically, the transportation orders met with his approval, for "not only are you justified by the laws and usages of war in removing these people, but I think it was your duty to your own army to do so."[124]

The intense fighting around Atlanta took a heavy toll of foundries, factories, machine shops, laboratories, and railroad facilities. Twenty acres of the inner city were burned, including buildings used by Major Cunningham and the Quartermaster Bureau that were scattered throughout the city but especially concentrated near the railroad depots (*New York Herald*, December 22, 1864). The human costs were also considerable. A phenomenon that manifested itself first in Sherman's Meridian raid now reappeared: thousands of freedmen, old and young, mothers with sucklings, unaccompanied youths, some almost nude and almost starved, trudged along after the Union troops. An accompanying reporter for the *New York Herald* wrote that "a very large majority of them were women and children, who, mounted on mules, sometimes five on an animal, in ox wagons, buggies and vehicles of every description, blocked the roads and materially delayed the movement of the columns" (*New York Herald* December 22, 1864). Sherman's guards held the self-emancipated assembly at the riverbanks until the army could pass.

Many Georgia factory home guard units were part of the state militia that fought in the Atlanta trenches as Governor Brown attempted to raise a levy en masse. In the environs of the city, Sherman also burned the Alcova factory, refurbished during the war with machinery evacuated from other mills. On November 11, Federal troops destroyed the factories and bridges at Rome, Georgia. The Confederate losses in factories and depots were staggering. The Ivy Woolen mill at Roswell, before being burned, supplied the Confederate Army of Tennessee with 15,000 yards of goods a month, from which about half of George Cunningham's military uniforms were made. When added to the loss of the Lawrenceville factory, Sherman's swath of destruction through north Georgia deprived the Confederate army of "900 bales of yarn, sheeting, & osnaburgs per mo[nth]."[125] The general's intentions were to visit a similar devastation upon central Georgia.

Sherman's movement into central Georgia created major problems for Confederate quartermaster Cunningham, who evacuated his operations to Augusta. Many mills stopped delivering on Confederate government contracts. Two Alabama mills, Simpson and Moore of Coosa County and the Tallassee factory at Tallapoosa County, ceased all deliveries. The first cited as a reason "the old one about exposure to raids."[126] Under threat of impressment, the proprietors finally agreed to sell the Confederate quartermaster half of their product at 70 percent advance on costs. Tallassee simply "refused to furnish him with cotton goods, drillings, &c., although under contract to do so."[127] William Gillaspie, the Confederate quartermaster at Montgomery, impressed the Simpson and Moore mill and threatened to seize the Tallassee factory as well. When both sides appealed to political authorities at Richmond, a compromise was effected that the goods, not the mills, could be taken for public use.

In August 1864, the Augusta factory, the largest Georgia supplier of cotton goods to the Richmond Clothing Bureau, "declined to furnish any more goods to the Government through Major Cunningham, in consequence of their (the Govt) non-compliance with a contract."[128] Graniteville was also in difficult straits, for by the end of July 1864 Quartermaster Cunningham's debt amounted to $800,000. That company also declined "to deliver any more goods to the Government Agents until arrears be paid" and conditioned all future deliveries on cash. Cunningham, who received $3.7 million in Confederate currency in August, was unable to pay either in cash or bonds more than one-quarter of his debts. For the remainder, he was ordered to give the mills "certificates of indebtedness," interest-bearing papers that would be exchanged for Confederate bonds whenever the Treasury might issue them.[129] Following a meeting with Cunningham, the Augusta factory board "declined" the new proposition, which left Cunningham with the option of impressing his two-thirds quota or doing without cloth.

After September 1864, Gregg at Graniteville received no payment from Cunningham through the rest of the year, and his board of directors consequently resolved that "it is impossible to continue to supply the Confederate Government with two-thirds of our production unless prompt Cash payments be made." The Graniteville treasurer was "directed to sell the two-thirds product of the mill laid aside for the Government in December, and continue to do so until all arrears be paid."[130] In North Carolina, Jonathan Worth advised his manager at Cedar Falls to take only cotton as barter from the Quartermaster Department, for Confederate currency was worthless; otherwise, "in my opinion the factory should deliver no more goods to the State or Con. Govt."[131]

Without adequate currency or bonds, Quartermaster Cunningham found himself in "great anxiety on the subject of payment of the amounts due the Factories with which I have contracts in the States of

S. Carolina, Alabama, Florida, Georgia, and Mississippi."[132] As Sherman maneuvered through the Confederate heartland, General Alexander Lawton's debts rose from $41 million in March 1864 to $56 million in November, with $2 million alone due Governor Vance of North Carolina on his factory account.[133] Confederate fiscal policy did nothing to stiffen resistance to the intrepid Yankee invaders.

Only on November 15, 1864, after General John Hood had maneuvered his army far to Sherman's rear, marched into Alabama, seized Florence again, and threatened Franklin, Tennessee, did Sherman embark upon his long-planned Savannah campaign, the march to the sea. Sherman divided his army. The right wing moved down the Macon Railroad and the left wing toward Augusta. They united after a week at Milledgeville, the state capital. Factories and mills as well as railroads and bridges that lay along the Ocmulgee, the Oconee, and the Ogeechee Rivers were systematically destroyed. On the right, General Oliver O. Howard burned 2,000 bales of cotton, much of it at Planter's factory, which was partially dismantled to bridge the Ocmulgee above Macon.

Arriving at the Planter's mill with the vanguard, a trooper with the Eighty-first Ohio found "quite a village here, mostly women who were employed in the Factory." While impressing mounts for the army, he tarried long enough to "view the 'Ocmulgee Mills' and Factory this afternoon—both were very large and fine, especially the mill which is the finest I ever saw."[134] Near the flour mill was a warehouse containing 560 bales of cotton. General Oliver O. Howard ruled that the factory with 1,500 spindles and 150 employees should be destroyed because it "had been used for military purposes by the rebel Government."[135]

Five days from Atlanta and twenty-three miles from Milledgeville, Major Henry Hitchcock encountered the Eatonton factory, the property of Stephen Marshall, an officer in the local militia, on the Oconee River. Hitchcock wrote, "Twas a quite a good factory, say 500 spindles, and employed thirty to forty operatives, girls and women" (Hitchcock 79–80). There were also slave workers. Confederate snipers contested the passage of Federal troops into town, and this may have hardened General Henry W. Slocum's decision to burn the mill and 100 bales of cotton. Major Hitchcock observed that the operatives "begged to spare it, but it came within the policy and order to destroy whatever is of use to an adverse army" (80). Moving with a parallel Federal column down the

Oconee River, General John W. Geary encountered and burned three factories.

Geary also burned a "large tannery and shoe factory and store owned by James Denham, one of the most extensive establishments of the kind in the South." These shops at Warrenton normally supplied shoe lasts, the upper leather, for Dillard's shoe factory in Columbus. The Federal army found that most of the stock had been evacuated, but "a few boxes of shoes and leather were found hidden in a barn and were turned over to the quartermaster's department for issue."[136] The destruction of Denham's shoe shops "greatly impaired" the operations of the Richmond Clothing Depot.[137] On November 25, a detachment of Pennsylvania cavalry riding with Sherman's left wing reached "Ogeechee Shoals and destroyed a woolen mill and a grist mill."[138]

Milledgeville was taken without resistance. Sherman, accompanied by a marching band, led the army into town. As the different parts of the Federal army concentrated upon the state capital, the owners of the Milledgeville cotton mill frantically attempted to save their property. In a panic, the Georgia stockholders quickly deeded 80 percent of the factory's stock to two German-born merchants, Ezekiel and Michael Waitzfelder.[139] While one hundred officers of the Twentieth Corps, joined by General Hugh J. Kilpatrick, held a mock session of the state legislature, rescinded the ordinance of secession, and debated reconstruction policy for Georgia, Sherman was waited upon by the Waitzfelders. Major Hitchcock recorded the interview: "Old Jew (E. Waitzfelder) says all want peace, but want slaves." The general "told him *too late*" (Hitchcock 86). But all was not too late for the Waitzfelders. Having done an embarrassingly large business with the Confederacy, they now presented themselves as owners of the Milledgeville mill.[140] Ezekiel and Michael Waitzfelder pleaded that peace was at hand, that Alexander Stephens as well as they were Unionists at heart, and that the state legislature, in session the week before, might yet endorse a separate peace pact. In fact, Alexander Stephens was making reconstruction proposals in Richmond and working for an armistice between the governments.

Sherman was already convinced through negotiations with William King, his emissary to the governor, and several others that Brown and Vice President Stephens wanted to separate from the Confederacy and establish peace. Constantine G. Baylor, a commercial representative of the state of Georgia, had carried the same message to Federal authorities at Bermuda and Washington.[141] In the summer of 1864, Baylor quietly slipped through the blockade, probably sailing on the *Little Ada*.[142] A short while thereafter he presented himself to Charles M. Allen, U.S. consul at Bermuda, as a peace commissioner from the state of Georgia. In the belief that Baylor represented a peace overture from Georgia, Allen permitted him to pass on to Washington. After meeting with political leaders there, he went on to the Niagara Falls Peace Conference, and later he addressed the Cooper Union Institute on the subject of an immediate political compromise to end the war based on the principle of states' rights (*New York Times*, October 18, 1864).[143] The episode undoubtedly encouraged caution in Sherman, who was then cut off from all communications with the North.

The Union commander was besieged by the leading citizens of Milledgeville, who assured him that the Confederacy was "played out" (Hitchcock 86). Finally, Sherman surrendered. The fact that the Milledgeville factory worked exclusively under the control of Governor Brown, with whom Sherman was negotiating possible terms of peace, may have contributed to its success in escaping the torch. By Sherman's account, "General Slocum, with my approval, spared several mills, and many thousands of bales of cotton, taking what he knew to be worthless bonds, that the cotton should not be used for the Confederacy" (Sherman 2: 190). Major Hitchcock drew up bonds for 1,800 bales of cotton (Hitchcock 86).[144] The destroyer of Jackson, Meridian, and Atlanta had shown mercy. The Milledgeville prison was burned but little else.

The *New York Herald* reported that the mill owners "bonded this property for half a million dollars, pleading that the stock and machinery should never benefit the rebel government, and that all efforts would be made to get the cotton into loyal states" (*New York Herald*, December 28, 1864). Sherman remarked that "he was aware that his [Waitzfelders'] bond would not be worth the paper it was written on after his troops crossed the Oconee; but he knew it would be advertised far and near that 'Sherman was not destroying cotton to punish individuals, but to damage the resources of the confederacy' " (*New York Herald*, December 28, 1864). As the Federal army moved on, the Waitzfelders evidenced little inclination to relinquish control of their new possession to the old stockholders, and one unexpected legacy of Sherman's visit was a lengthy litigation over ownership in the Georgia courts. A reporter for the *Herald* confessed, "It is only a matter of surprise that General Sherman, in evacuating the city, did not lay the buildings in ashes" (*New York Herald*, December 22, 1864).

Like a spent hurricane, Sherman's corps arrived at Savannah on December 10, 1864, leaving in their wake burned factories, grist mills, gin houses, depots, and bridges. The left wing alone burned 17,000 bales of cotton. One million rations and 5 million pounds of grain were also consumed.[145] More than a quarter of Georgia's railroad mileage was laid waste; for a distance of 117 miles the Georgia Central Railroad was systematically destroyed in the peculiar method developed by Grant and Sherman of heating rails and twisting them around trees. General Joseph Wheeler, who provided the only obstacle to Sherman's passage, expected Augusta, with its arsenal and factories, to be the Union general's next objective. For this reason, he pressed hard upon Sherman's flanks, "being mindful of the great damage that could be done by the enemy's burning the valuable mills and property which were not protected by fortifications, including factories in the vicinity."[146] Under these conditions, the factories along the Savannah River were hesitant to invest their Confederate bonds in cotton. What cotton the Confederates did not destroy, the Federals would. What the Federals missed, the Confederates would destroy. William Jackson of the Augusta factory wrote, "it was considered by me, and acquiesced in by the Directors, that it was imprudent, in the then state of affairs, to increase our stock of cotton, as no assurance could be given us, it would not be burned by the [Confederate] authorities."[147]

Sherman rested his army at Savannah until February 1, 1865, and then moved his corps north into South Carolina, bypassing Augusta. His movement created panic at the Augusta factories. The local Confederate commander "stopped all the factories, and sent the men, with the rest of the home guards, down on Briar Creek, twenty miles from Augusta, to defend the city at that place."[148] If necessary, the city was to be surrendered peacefully like Milledgeville. On February 5, the indefatigable William Gregg "commenced moving goods off" from Graniteville. He secured thirteen teams to carry his cotton and goods to Columbia and Ninety-six, South Carolina. After this, "every available team was employed in hauling dividend goods from 4 to 8 miles off."[149] He kept careful records of each storage location. Across the region, many other manufacturers were doing the same. After a week of hauling, only eighty bales and about 25,000 yards of cloth still remained at Graniteville.

On February 10, 1865, with Sherman's forces passing within twenty miles, Commissioner W. Leman of the Soldiers' Board of Relief arrived at Graniteville demanding 50,000 yards of cloth as payment for the South Carolina state tax. Leman found bedlam prevailing, "all the hands in great commotion." The mill's superintendent was "engaged in dividing out gratis, to the people of the town the provisions of the Company."[150] The company store was "dispensing flour bacon etc. at half price to the operatives taking a memo of the same."[151] Angry wagoners were rushing about to escape, goods were scattered all about "promiscuously," and no one paid the state commissioner any heed.[152] In the confusion, much of the evacuated cotton and cloth was hauled directly into Sherman's path.

During this chaotic scene, elements of General Wheeler's cavalry drove in. Having fought a rear-guard action with Sherman, the troopers now selected the Graniteville company store as their objective. Gregg reported that the shop was "sacked by Wheelers stragglers and the rabble white and black," and the subsequent loss "of merchandise and produce will not fall short of $125,000." The resulting riot soon spread to the granite-walled factory building. After the milling crowd was dispensed by a show of arms, Gregg "found but 33 bales remaining, and the cloth room entirely cleared, and all the cloth taken from the 3 weaving rooms, together with the cloth cut out of 52 looms." He calculated the mill's loss at "from $250 to $350,000."[153] After a standoff with some of Wheeler's troopers, the home guard company finally restored peace and secured the remaining property.[154] Such goods as were saved were promptly claimed by state commissioner Leman.

Sherman's campaign completed the disruption of Cunningham's operations in Georgia. Writing in November, General Lawton explained to William Porcher Miles of the Confederate Congress that "it is a mistake to suppose that much material has been worked up of late, in the State of Geo. . . . within the past six months no work of any description has been done at Savannah." In middle Georgia, "military operations compelled the suspension of work at Atlanta in June last; while at Columbus & Augusta, the only other points within that State at which clothing was manufactured, very little cotton goods has been consumed for garments, owing to the fact that [there was] the heavy accumulation of both shirts & drawers in all the Depots."[155]

Several months later, on March 17, 1865, with Sherman in transit across the Carolinas, George Cunningham attempted to rebuild his depot. He wrote Lawton hopefully that "the woolen goods from Columbia will be sent forward as soon as transportation can be had from this point." In his refugee depot at Augusta, his "stock of cotton goods for clothing material is extremely limited and I see nothing but suffering ahead unless I am enabled to pay up the contracts with the mills." Factories like Graniteville and Augusta that "make materials for shirt and drawers are the loudest in their complaints." Few goods were coming in, for in "the last two months my receipts of this class of material have been less than *Fifty Bales* when it should have been about *Four Hundred*."[156] With the loss of Fort Fisher and all imports cut off, Lawton sent Cunningham $3 million in Confederate currency to facilitate purchases, especially of wool, but apparently Sherman captured the currency. On March 20, at Gregg's insistence, the Graniteville directors agreed "to deliver the Government (at an equivalent for such details as may be necessary to carry on the business), one-fourth of the product of the mill gratis."[157] The Graniteville president wrote Cunningham that "it is idle to talk about taking Government credits for our goods, nothing but cash will support our population and keep our wheels going, and I think all things considered, a gift of 1/4 of our product ought to satisfy our Government, as they can purchase all the balance if needed at current rates."[158] At the Augusta factory, where Cunningham continued to demand two-thirds of the production, from January through June 1865 the earnings were $2.2 million, much of this in nonnegotiable certificates of indebtedness.[159] From its public sales, Graniteville's profits for 1864 were $3.2 million.[160]

Having threatened Augusta and Charleston, Sherman elected to seize Columbia, South Carolina, while marching to Grant. After passing the Savannah River, General James S. Robinson reported from Ninety-Six that "my foragers on this day captured a considerable number of fine houses and mules and burned one cotton-mill."[161] Approaching Columbia, Sherman's plan was "to cross the Saluda [River] at the factory" and fall upon the city from the north.[162] On February 15, 1865, the Federal army was at the old Saluda mill. Major George Nichols noted, "when I visited the factory our skirmishers occupied the windows facing the river, and were exchanging shots with the Rebels, who lay concealed among the bushes and timber on the other side." The sniping from the home guard "did not hinder the operatives, all of whom were women, from hurrying through the building, tearing the cloth from the looms, and filling bags with bales of yarn, to be 'toted' home, as they called it" (Nichols 157).

As a backdrop for his sketch of the crossing of the Saluda, James E. Taylor, an artist traveling with Sherman's command, prepared a drawing of the old mill for *Frank Leslie's Illustrated Newspaper* (April 8, 1865). The factory "was a large stone building, filled with machinery for the manufacture of yarns and the variety of coarse cotton cloth known as Osnaburgs" (Nichols 159). Three stories high with large double windows, the structure was "situated a few hundred yards above the pontoon bridge" and was "considered of sufficient note to be laid out on all the maps, old and new." A road "winds along the bank of the stream, which is prettily bordered with trees" (157).

Major Nichols interpreted the general deterioration of the factory and the debility of the workers as a product of the slave oligarchical system. Much in the vein of William Cullen Bryant and Frederick Law Olmsted a decade earlier, he wrote, "it must not be imagined that these Southern factory operatives are of the same class with the lively and intelligent workers of New England" (157–58). He noted in his diary, "I remember that while reading descriptions of Saluda factory and discussing the probability of finding it on our line of march through South Carolina, many of our officers drew fanciful sketches of pretty, bright-eyed damsels, neatly clad, with a wealth of flowing ringlets, and engaging manners." Indeed, he recalled, "such factory-girls were visible in the great mills of Lowell, and the enthusiastic Northerners doomed to fight on southern soil were excusable for drawing mental pictures of them" (158).

The Saluda women, having heard of the fate of Roswell's workers, obviously were in no romantic mood. Major Nichols found "when we came to see the reality at Saluda Factory, sensations of disgust and mirthfulness struggled for the mastery—disgust at the repulsive figures whom we encountered, and amusement at the chopfallen air of the gallant young staff-officers who were eager to pay their court to beauty and virtue." He felt that "it would be difficult to find elsewhere than at this place a collection of two hundred and fifty women so unkempt, frowzy, ragged, dirty, and altogether ignorant and wretched." Rosy ideals were put to flight by women "chewing tobacco," while others "more elegant in their tastes, smoked," and still another "set indulged in the practice of 'dipping' " (158).

Indeed, after four years of deprivation and eighty-hour work weeks, many Southern workers were in a poor physical state. An investigation by William Gregg in August 1864 showed that the operative wages at Graniteville were only three-quarters of the 1860 levels after accounting for inflation.[163] At the Richmond factory in North Carolina, workers earned still less. William Barton, a detailed worker, made $152 in August 1864, a tenfold increase over 1860, but this wage represented an increment rising at half the rate of inflation and was hardly enough to buy a barrel of good Virginia flour.[164] In December 1864, Mrs. Thomas Barton, an operative at the same mill, was paid solely in bartered goods, which consisted of two loads of wood, two gallons of syrup, twenty-four pounds of flour, one bushel of peas, and some salt for the month. A month later she received three bunches of yarn, one-quarter bushel of peas, nineteen and a half pounds of bacon, two plugs of tobacco, and miscellaneous items.[165] With legitimacy, a group of workers at the Richmond Clothing Bureau needing money for rent, fuel, and food petitioned for a raise of wages, "at least to enable us to live for that is the only object and end we have in view."[166] Women working at the Confederate government depots earned only "four dollars for each jacket, three for a pair of pants, two for a shirt and one for a pair of drawers," a wage, reported a Confederate congressman, insufficient to provide them with bread.[167]

At Saluda, Major Nichols found that workers' residences "accorded with their personal appearance" (Nichols 158). He inspected the "dirty wooden shanties, built on the riverbank a few hundred feet above the factory, where the places called homes—homes where doors hung shabbily by a single hinge, or were destitute of panels; where rotten steps led to foul pots and pans, and other accumulations of rubbish; where stagnant pools of water bred disease; where half a dozen persons occupied the same bed-chamber; where old women and ragged children lolled lazily in the sunshine; where even the gaunt fowls that went disconsolately about the premises partook of the prevailing character of misery and dirt" (158–59). These, he believed, "were the operatives, and these the homes produced by the boasted civilization of the South" (159).[168]

The mortality rate among such operatives was quite high. At ten mills along the Savannah River, communities containing 5,417 persons in 1864, 18 of the 450 children employed there died. The children were from ten to fifteen years of age. Along with slaves, children were much needed to replace drafted soldiers. Working in the mills were 621 youths between fifteen and twenty years of age, of whom 16 died within the year.[169] The Augusta factory kept a special storeroom filled with "coffins for the operatives [sic] most of which are small."[170] Life on the home front was often as exacting as that in the lines.

Nor did Nichols have a high regard for the old Saluda mill: "the looms were dirty and rusty; the spindles were worn out by misuse; the spools appeared conscious that they had fulfilled their mission; the engine was out of joint and dirty." Convinced that "filth and ignorance reigned over the entire business," Sherman's Yankee major left Saluda, "passing a group of the degraded and unfortunate women already described toiling up the hill with back loads of plunder." Some of the Union soldiers "were helping them to carry their cloth and yarns" (159).

Such partisan views steeled the Federal soldiers to their task, to make war hell. Two days later James G. Gibbes, the owner of Saluda, witnessed from Columbia large columns of smoke rising in the east about three o'clock in the afternoon, "two to five miles off, which turned out to be . . . the cotton and card mill" (Gibbes 7). A reporter for the *New York Herald* stoically noted that "this place contained the Columbia Mills, the largest manufactory in the South, and gave employment to about four hundred hands, chiefly females" (*New York Herald*, March 20, 1865). He confused Saluda with Columbia Mills, a second factory located within the city and owned by L. D. Childs. The journalist found it "sad to see in Saluda groups of female operatives weeping and wringing their hands in agony as they saw the factory—their only means of support—in flames" (*New York Herald*, March 20, 1865). Properties including the residences of Wade Hampton, George Trenholm, and others soon followed. In Columbia, retreating Confederates, fugitive blacks, Federal prisoners of war, refugees, and vengeful Union soldiers pillaged and burned cotton bales and hundreds of private homes.

After moving slowly across the state of South Carolina, on March 12, without contest, Sherman took Fayetteville, North Carolina. Troops of the Third Cavalry added the Rockingham cotton mill to the 170 sawmills, 70 gristmills, and 20,000 bales of cotton burned by the troops since leaving Savannah.[171] General Howard's Seventeenth Corps occupied Rockfish community and quickly "burned a factory, throwing about 150 women out of employment" (Willis 360). Melinda Ray, a mill worker, recorded the event in her diary. By her account General Sherman, "when besought to spare the factories for the sake of the women and children, replied they were the very ones he desire to make feel the war; had it not been for them, this rebellion would have been crushed long since."[172] Fayetteville was soon surrounded by pillars of smoke as Sherman, after due consideration, ordered the burning of the Phoenix, Blount Creek, Union Mills, Cross Creek, Beaver Creek, Little River, and other mill properties.[173] In Fayetteville, E. J. Hale Jr. wrote that "it would be impossible to give . . . an adequate idea of the destruction of property in this good old town." His father's cotton mill, bank, and railroad properties were worthless. Young Hale noted that his family's property was consigned with a certain flourish, for "[General Henry W.] Slocum, who executed the order, with a number of other Generals, sat on the veranda of a hotel opposite watching the progress of the flames, while they hobnobbed over wines stolen from our cellar."[174] Sherman posted officers to prevent the burning and pillaging of private dwellings in the desolated town; then he pointed his Federal columns northward toward Goldsboro and Raleigh, where their momentum was temporarily arrested by the troops assembled by General Joseph E. Johnston at Bentonville.

On the Virginia front, Federal cavalry generals also taught manufacturers the lessons of total war. A Federal raid against Salem, Virginia, in 1862 found "shoe, harness, clothing, blacksmith, & wheelwright shops in operation." When informed of the approach of Federal cavalry under General William W. Averell, the local Confederate quartermaster hauled six flatcars of salt and quantities of other goods to Lynchburg. But General Averell still consigned to the flames 60 tons of bacon, 100 barrels of flour, and 5,700 pounds of leather, clothing, and other supplies.[175] In their haste, the Federal soldiers did not discover the Bonsack factory nearby. When Union General David Hunter returned to Salem in June 1864, General Alfred N. Duffie "caused the depot to be burned and an extensive woolen factory which was engaged in the manufacture of clothing for the Confederate Government."[176] Jacob Bonsack laconically wrote Quartermaster General Lawton, "the forces of the enemy . . . fired and burned my factory situated at Bonsack's Depot, Roanoke County."[177] Commissary stores of "immense value" were put to the torch, including "the burning of 2 iron and 1 woolen factory; the capture of some 400 horses; the destruction of Arrington, Bonsack's, and Big Lick Depots."[178] The large Washington woolen factory at Staunton, another mainstay of General Lawton's Clothing Bureau, was also a victim of Hunter's raid.[179]

In Lunenburg County, the Union cavalry rode into a tannery defended by a home guard company. The owner explained to William Ferguson of the Richmond Clothing Bureau that "the yankees got within a few hundred yards of the yard & was met by our men & drove them off." The hands subsequently "ran off from the tan yard & it was broken open & robbed."[180] At another tannery near Ford's Depot, "as soon as the report of the enemy being in our vicinity reached us, all hands were set to work to carry [the leather] . . . to the woods & bushes fearing that the buildings would be burnt." The Federal scouting party arrived, seized some leather, and announced that they were going to return, "secure the rest and then burn the buildings," but their regiment rode on.[181]

As General Grant advanced from the Rappahannock River line to Petersburg in the final stages of the war, Union cavalry commanders raided deeply into the Confederate interior, leaving a wake of destruction. The elevation of General Philip Sheridan to Federal command in the Shenandoah Valley intensified the war against property in that theater, a tactic that Confederate General Jubal Early's depleted forces were helpless to prevent. On September 29, 1864, at Port Royal, the Ninth New York "burned the iron works in Brown's Gap belonging to a Mr. Lewis who was a non-combatant and had refused to join the secessionists."[182] Nevertheless, the owner's sixteen-year-old son joined Sheridan "to avoid conscription by the Confederates" (Cheney 225). In Loudoun County, Virginia, alone, General Wesley Merritt reported the destruction of 10,000 head of cattle, 435,802 bushels of wheat, 71 flour mills, 1 woolen mill, 8 sawmills, 1 powder mill, 4 tanneries, 7 furnaces, and 1,200 barns.[183] At Martinsburg, Daniel S. Rentch, who ran "a store and factory" which sold "gray cloth to rebels," merited a visit by Union forces.[184]

After Early's defeat at the battle of Cedar Creek on October 19, 1864, Sheridan moved unopposed from the Shenandoah Valley to join Grant before Richmond, sending columns down the Rivanna River and the James River Canal to destroy "all large flour mills, woolen factories, and manufacturing establishments."[185] On March 6, at Scottsville, his Michigan and Massachusetts cavalry "totally destroyed and burned, together with a large cloth mill, and tobacco warehouse," numerous buildings "crammed with the products of its manufacture to a surprising extent."[186] At Palmyra, Colonel George R. Maxwell, First Michigan Cavalry, burned "one cotton mill, one flouring mill, and immense amounts of wheat, flour, cotton, and wool."[187] Sheridan's final report credited the destruction of cotton and woolen mills to the commands of Colonel Peter Skagg, First Brigade, First Division; Brigadier General Alfred Gibbs, Reserve Brigade; Captain Edward H. Leib, Fifth U.S. Cavalry; and Colonel Alexander C. M. Pennington, First Brigade, Third Division.[188]

At Petersburg, Federal forces took a heavy toll of factories, some of which were practically within the range of siege artillery. The Federals particularly kept a careful eye on "Whitehead's Factory," located on the north side of the Appomattox and guarded by a battery of Confederate artillery. In an effort to block Grant's flanking move across the railroads south of Petersburg, several companies of operatives from the Ettrick, Matoaca, and Battersea mills "were called into the field" under the command of General Henry Wise.[189] On July 12, William Ferguson, of the Richmond Quartermaster Bureau, explained that "the mills are stopped by withdrawal of hands, and the cards for the most part of May and June."[190] Female operatives could do little spinning without the carding of cotton and the maintenance of the machinery by the men. After two months of stoppage, the Quartermaster Department petitioned General Pierre Beauregard, Confederate commander of the Petersburg district, for the release of the units. William Ferguson bravely endorsed the petition: "the factories mentioned within have been furnishing me with nearly all the cotton goods used in the clothing bureau, besides warps & cotton yarns which are much needed at present." Ferguson's summer product consisted "of tent cloths for which there is at this time a pressing demand to furnish shelter for the sick and wounded of the army." He added, "I am nearly out of cotton goods at present & find it almost impossible to get woolen goods for want of transportation to keep the poor women who are employed in the dept with work."[191] After conferring with General Lawton, Beauregard approved the release of the workers, but Grant's renewed assaults forced him to detain them in the defensive line along with thousands of other clerks and laborers from Richmond.

In the intense Union assault on the Shand House on June 16, 1864, Grant's first major attempt to seize Petersburg, "a large number of the operatives were captured by the enemy."[192] The losses further curtailed factory operations. Although some of the mechanics were retrieved through an exchange effected in October, the decline of cotton stores caused by the degradation of Southern rail lines, the constant alarums, and the weariness of living under siege threatened to paralyze General Lawton's last remaining source of material.[193] In March 1865, a Union scout within Confederate lines reported to Meade that "the machinery has been removed from the four cotton mills on the Appomattox above Petersburg."[194]

As Sheridan marched up the valley and Sherman completed his fiery trek through the Carolinas, a Union cavalry pincer movement mounted in Tennessee by General George H. Thomas's Army of the Cumberland prepared a coup de grace for Southern mills. These cavalry maneuvers were intended to provide a diversion to Sherman's march north. Commanding Generals James H. Wilson and George Stoneman were ordered to destroy all facilities aiding the Confederate war effort. Wilson commanded a column of three cavalry divisions, numbering almost 15,000 men. On March 22, this formation rode out of Eastport, Mississippi, in the direction of Montgomery and Selma, with orders to fall upon Columbus and Macon. In east Tennessee, a parallel raid led by General George Stoneman with 4,000 cavalry marched from Jonesboro on March 20 with orders to raid up the Virginia and Tennessee Railroad to Salem, Virginia, then turn south along the North Carolina Central Railroad, from Greensboro to Charlotte, wreaking havoc upon all within reach.

Wilson's raiders moved out on March 22, 1865, pressing General Forrest before them, and found in their path a rich harvest of mills producing iron, flour, and cotton goods. On April 4, General John T. Croxton entered Tuscaloosa almost uncontested and burned the university buildings, in use as a military school, along with "the cotton thread and cloth mill of Baugh, Kennedy & Co., . . . the foundry and hat factory of Leach and Avery," a brick hotel, tannery, several cotton warehouses, and other property (Maxwell 283). One warehouse contained 700 bales of cotton owned by the Tuscaloosa factory (Owen 3: 987–88). In addition to the

Tuscaloosa factory, the Warrior and Scottsville cotton mills were put to the torch.[195] At Scottsville, General Edward McCook found a niter works attached to the factory, which he also burned (James Jones 68). The advancing Union cavalry "burned a large cotton factory" at Daviston, as well as mills at Jackson, Oxford, and elsewhere.[196] In Talladega County, General Croxton's men uncovered the large Choccolocco factory complex. Jacob B. and Benjamin Knight operated a gin factory, a foundry, and "a large cotton factory for the spinning of yarn" (Armes 89). Their iron work was popular in the state. Major Francis L. Cramer, First Alabama Cavalry Union, moved into Tallapoosa and "burned a steam cotton factory."[197]

As General Wilson's forces coalesced upon Selma, the Eighth Iowa encountered the Gunn factory in Dallas County. Gunn, the owner, had "two plantations besides, and an interest in a tanyard" (Trowbridge 221).[198] The troopers quickly put everything to the torch, including 800 bales of prize cotton. Gunn remonstrated, "I was making Osnaburgs for the government for a dollar a yard, when citizens would have paid me four dollars; and do you imagine I'd have done that except under compulsion." But the Federals were relentless, "because I happened to be running my mill for the Confederate Government" (221). Nevertheless, Gunn had some good fortune. An old black woman hid his gold and silver, a black carpenter buried three barrels of fine china, and "an old Negro saved the tannery by pleading with the vandals, and lying to 'em a little bit" (221). The destruction was still considerable, and Gunn calculated that "three hundred and fifty thousand dollars wouldn't cover my losses" (222).

After fighting a decisive battle with Forrest at Selma, Wilson's mounted army found a small manufacturing city producing large quantities of naval iron, horseshoes, shovels, clothing, powder, wagons, and nearly all types of military accouterments.[199] Moving from Selma through Montgomery to Columbus, in twenty-eight days the cavalry captured and destroyed seven iron works, seven foundries, seven machine shops, and thirteen factories.[200]

In Georgia, George Swift, owner of the Waynmanville factory in Upson County near Columbus, watched the storm rising in the west with mounting concern. On April 11, he wrote Louis Hamburger, his manager, "I fear the enemy will have possession of Montgomery soon and if so, Columbus and Macon will go next, so I think you had better make your arrangements accordingly." Like other manufacturers, Swift dispersed his cotton and goods; some mill owners hauled lots to distant points in south Georgia, trusting that portions there would survive the invasion. The Northern-born Swift gathered his family at Macon, since he could not "tell how long or soon before the enemy may have possession of the [factory]."[201]

On April 16, 1865, Wilson swept into Columbus, brushing aside the local reserves, which included the factory guards. Twenty thousand pieces of military cloth and 8,000 pairs of shoes were taken at Dillard's manufacturing depot, which were then "issued to the troops and negroes or destroyed."[202] Among the casualties of the Federals' frantic dash across the Chattahoochee River was William H. Young, president and principal owner of the Eagle factory. He wrote, "during the night attack I with the rest of the old men of the city was upon police duty & being hard of hearing was fired upon by the Union forces & received six serious wounds upon my body."[203] While Young survived the attack, his mill did not.

A Union surgeon accompanying Wilson's force noted that "the women and children who had been employed in the factories and arsenals turned out with one accord to pillage the stores and Government warehouses."[204] Desperation rested at every doorstep. General Edward F. Winslow found "thousands of almost pauper citizens and negroes, whose rapacity under the circumstances of our occupation, and in consequence of such extensive destruction of property, was seemingly insatiable," and these "citizens and negroes formed one vast mob, which seized upon and carried off almost everything moveable."[205] With considerable dispatch the Yankee commander ordered four cotton factories destroyed.[206] Consigned to the flames was Eagle factory, which provided the Confederate quartermaster with large quantities of woolen goods. Two adjacent mills manufactured oiled and lacquered cloth. A sock factory and a shoe factory were nearby. Also burned were Howard's and Grant's cotton mills.[207] The Columbus navy yards, the Naval Iron Works, paper mills, the Haiman sword factory, a rope walk, a tannery, and the Columbus cotton factory were casualties of Federal wrath.[208] One Federal officer correctly estimated that along the city's canal 10,000 spindles were destroyed and 5,000 employees were "thrown upon the community." In the campaign, the cavalry corps destroyed at least 200,000 bales of cotton.

Moving on toward Macon on April 18, General Wilson's advance guard captured the Flint River bridge and thirteen wagons of machinery.[209] The following day Colonel Robert H. G. Minty, commander of the Fourth Michigan, camped near Thomaston and "destroyed three large cotton factories."[210] Here, as elsewhere, the factory floors were covered with lint cotton, kerosene was poured on, and the mixture was ignited. Burned was the large Flint River factory at Thomaston.[211] As the Federals prepared to fall upon Macon with the intention of burning its mills, General Lee surrendered in Virginia. This event and the prolonged negotiations of Macon city authorities spared the mills.[212] Griswoldville, with machine shops, soap and candle factories, and foundries, had been burned early by Sherman's men.

The second cavalry raid by the Army of the Cumberland was commanded by General George Stoneman and designed as a Northern counterpart to that of Wilson. Stoneman rendezvoused near the Mossy Creek factory, outside Knoxville, on March 20, 1865. Burnside's forces had originally seized this area in November 1863 and commissioned Colonel Orville E. Babcock to "run the cotton-mill and spin the cotton" in order to manufacture large quantities of rope for the army.[213] The owners probably cooperated and secured "protection" papers, which saved their mill from destruction. Stoneman's orders were to ride through southwest Virginia, then follow the railroads though western North Carolina as far south as Columbia, South Carolina.

Reports filtering across the mountains described considerable manufacturing activity on behalf of the Confederacy along this route. In fact, the Confederates had long anticipated such a move as Stoneman contemplated. A year before, Gabriel Cannon, a mill owner and former South Carolina lieutenant governor living at Spartanburg, requested Confederate authorities to station a repelling force near the mountain passes. He wrote Treasury secretary Christopher Memminger, "it may be that the war department does not fully comprehend the importance of the upper part of S.C. & the western part of N.C." Enemy sympathizers in the mountains harbored deserters and carried information to the Federals. At risk in Spartanburg District alone were "six cotton mills, several small woolen mills & many valuable flouring mills." In the adjoining county were "four or five cotton mills, the gun factory at Greenville C.H. & many flouring mills, also all the iron & rails made in the state is made in Spartanburg, Union, & York." Cannon concluded, then "add the cotton, woolen, & iron mills in the adjoining counties of N.C. and you will perceive at once the [region's] vital importance."[214] These were the rich enticements that brought Stoneman across the mountains in March 1865.

The first detachments of Stoneman's Union cavalry to enter Virginia enjoyed considerable success. They destroyed railroad facilities "nearly to Lynchburg, seven thousand bales of cotton and two large factories, and captured four hundred prisoners" (Van Horne 342). After devastating the Confederate salt-works at Saltville, the Federal soldiers fell upon Marion and discovered the woolen mill owned by A. Thomas. By Thomas's account, after Stoneman destroyed his iron furnace, fixtures, and house, "a portion of his army passed very near his factory but owing to the fact that he was not manufacturing for the Government but weaving entirely on private account his factory was spared." Although the furnace used detailed labor and worked on Confederate account, Thomas believed that if Stoneman "had known all the facts in relation to his furnace he could not have ordered the destruction of that."[215]

On March 29, 1865, with Sherman approaching Goldsboro, Stoneman opened his campaign in western North Carolina. The Union Thirteenth Tennessee Cavalry rode out of Boone and "reached Patterson's factory in the afternoon, got rations and food, burned the factory and destroyed everything in the way of subsistence and resumed our march in the rain and kept it up until after dark, when we went into camp."[216] The product of the Patterson mill was under contract both to Major Samuel Chisman, Confederate quartermaster at Greensboro, and to Governor Zebulon Vance, who drew half of the output of cloth and yarn. Jefferson Davis himself noted the loss of this mill and wrote Lee that "you will be able to judge better than myself the probability of this report, and of the proper directions to be given in view of it."[217]

On April 1, Stoneman's Fifteenth Pennsylvania Cavalry, maneuvering north of Winston-Salem, found another mill. As one Union cavalier wrote, "about 4 P.M. we reached the village of Elkin, where we found a large cotton factory, in which sixty girls are employed" (Colton and Colton 279–80). The mill did little contracting with Confederate authorities, and the young women in the old German community were apparently a delightful diversion for the weary soldiers, for "all of them welcomed the Yankees" (280). Clark, the superintendent, boldly invited the troopers to tour the facilities. As a result, one soldier wrote, "we did not molest the mill, which was a fine one, but connected with it was a storehouse filled with supplies of flour, meat, butter, honey, molasses, tobacco and chestnuts, all of which was a perfect Godsend to us" (280).

After tarrying at Germantown briefly, Colonel William Palmer of the Fifteenth was "instructed to proceed to Salem and destroy the large factories engaged in making cloth for the rebel army."[218] As the Federal troops approached, Henry Fries distributed commissary stores to the residents to store in their homes.[219] Upon the arrival of the soldiers, Colonel Palmer instructed the workers to take whatever remaining cloth and stores that they needed.[220] Henry Fries dutifully kept a ledger list of 149 persons who took cloth, thread, wax, tools, brooms, bobbins, and other items.[221] The saintly mood of the Fifteenth continued during this visit. Contrary to the regiment's expressed orders, the mill was spared, although Confederate warehouses may have been burned (Van Horne 340). Many of the Pennsylvania troopers came from Pennsylvania's Moravian communities that historically maintained close ties with the "Unitas Fratum" Brethren in North Carolina. After the Pennsylvania cavalry moved on south, ninety-two Salem residents returned their booty to Henry Fries.

Departing Salem, Stoneman's men raced on toward Statesville. The Turner factory, which lay directly in their path, may have been saved by the home guard. The owner was a Unionist, and the mill did little Confederate contracting. According to a Confederate account, the Federals "stopped at Eagle Mills and burned that,—then started towards Turnersburg to burn our factory."[222] When Turner discovered the soldiers' intentions, he "sent to Statesville and got the militia headed by Col S. A. Sharp, and stationed them on a hill above the factory, and built breast works out of cotton bales, with space to see between."[223] The Southern version was that the two armed groups confronted each other across Rocky Creek for a day, then the Federal troops rode on; however, Colonel Palmer, the Union officer, acknowledged burning "two large factories and 7,000 bales of cotton" but made no mention of an incident at Turnersburg.[224] The Union cavalry may have passed without ever discovering either the Confederate militia or the Turner factory.

Riding farther south, Stoneman's men fell upon the mill at Lincolnton with a vengeance, perhaps knowing that Confederate General Robert F. Hoke was an original owner. A Union cavalry officer, William L. Bratton, "found that they had made and were making a great deal of cloth for the Confederate army at Factoryville [near Lincolnton], and I told everybody that we were going to destroy the factory." He instructed the workers that the cavalry "would burn all the cotton in a short time, and we did not want them to suffer by it, but we would not allow any more cloth to be made there." Thereupon he ordered the operatives "to get pillow cases, mattresses and bags of all kinds and fill them with cotton and take them to their homes." In a short time, "bags of all kinds, filled with cotton, were being carried by the people" (Coulter and Coulter 292). Then the factory was fired.

On April 12, with Sherman approaching Raleigh, Stoneman's men stormed Salisbury, where 10,000 Federal prisoners were kept in the abandoned cotton factory. Some prisoners worked along with slaves and detailed Confederates in Confederate enterprises supervised by W. W. Peirce, quartermaster for North Carolina. After a small battle the Yankee horsemen burned a treasure-lode of government stores. General Stoneman's report on the property "captured mostly at Salisbury and destroyed by us" was almost as lengthy as General Wilson's captures at Selma and Columbus: "four large cotton factories and 7,000 bales of cotton, four large magazines containing 10,000 stand of small-arms and accouterments, 1,000,000 rounds of small arms ammunition, 10,000 rounds of fixed artillery ammunition, and 70,000 pounds of powder, 85,000 bushels of corn and wheat, 160,000 pounds of bacon, 100,000 suits of gray uniform clothing, and 250,000 blankets."[225] For miles around the air was filled with the smoke of burning debris. The Yankee major to whom the destruction was entrusted reported burning $15 million in Confederate currency and "medical supplies valued by the rebel medical director at $100,000 in gold" (Van Horne 341).[226] Only Lee's surrender and the truce between Generals Johnston and Sherman saved Raleigh, Charlotte, and upper South Carolina from a similar devastation.[227] Stoneman's cavalry rode on to Athens, Georgia, in pursuit of Jefferson Davis, who was in flight with his staff.

Under the combined onslaught of Sherman and the cavalry commands of Sheridan, Wilson, and Stoneman, General Alexander Lawton's last remaining supplies in Richmond quickly dwindled away. On January 12, 1865, with the fall of Wilmington, all hope of foreign supply ended; in desperation, Lawton sent Generals Lee and Beauregard a copy of Special Order No. 310, designed to secure the release of detailed "mechanics employed on Govt. contracts in wool & cotton factories in your department from the performance of military duty." He complained that "the interruptions of late have been so frequent & protracted that the interests of this Department & of the service at large demand that the full benefit of the protection afforded by this order should be extended to the factories referred to." With Confederate forces under severe duress, Lawton's argument that mechanics "render more service to the cause employed in the factories, than they possibly can in the field" was disregarded.[228] However, without these workers and raw materials from the south, the Richmond and Petersburg factories could operate only sporadically in the final months of the war.

When Lee surrendered at Appomattox on April 9 and Johnston at Durham's Station on April 26, Confederate quartermaster and commissary stores were mostly depleted. Except for a few regional warehouses, General Lawton's system of supply was in shambles. In large measure, General Henry Halleck's total war against Confederate manufacturing successfully destroyed the mechanical improvements of a generation and effectively paralyzed Confederate supply. Those factories not destroyed by the Union military were dilapidated and worn down by four years of constant use. Southern manufacturers, reluctant Confederates in the first place, now received a full measure of the consequences of defeat.

7

The Tortuous Course Toward Economic Reconstruction

After Appomattox, a "New South" emerged that was characterized by the rapid rebuilding of factories, railroads, mines, stores, and homesteads. Manufacturers, railroaders, former Confederate officers, educators, and editors, deeply shocked by the wartime scarcity and deprivation, asserted leadership in this endeavor and widely called for the adoption of modern science and technology as tools to rebuild the conquered South. From the pulpit and the podium, the press and the statehouse, there was a renewal of the great antebellum campaign to introduce a system of technology to the South, to bring the factories to the fields. At hand were the successful examples of the Confederate War Department in discovering and utilizing iron and coal resources, building and integrating railroad systems, and mobilizing factories. The lenient reconstruction policies of President Andrew Johnson fostered this process of rejuvenation by bringing mill leaders to the forefront of Southern leadership.

Johnson, a former senator and military governor from Tennessee who assumed the presidency following Abraham Lincoln's assassination on April 14, 1865, adopted a policy of economic reconstruction. This policy was attractive to many in the Northern business community who sought renewed commerce with the South and to the South, desperately in need of Northern investments and goods. The ultimate success of such a program hinged on Johnson's ability to lead the victorious commercial North into the acceptance of a policy of sectional reconciliation while permitting the loyal business interests of the South to guide the former Confederacy toward national integration.

The policy of economic reconstruction was fraught with grave dangers. Wartime Republican legislation placed the North squarely on the path to becoming a major industrial power, while the much vaunted antebellum King Cotton economy of the South lay in shreds. However, the greatest difficulty lay in readjusting the master-slave relationship to give freedmen civil rights protection under state and federal law. As the Southern phoenix bestirred itself to rise, a bitter national political struggle emerged over racial equality—the acceptance of blacks as free voters and as free laborers. The Radical Republicans wanted reconstruction based on the Wade-Davis Bill of 1864, which demanded political equality for freedmen but political proscription for former Confederates. This conflict over racial politics led ultimately to Johnson's impeachment, the onset of Radical Reconstruction, and a hiatus in the Southern economic boom culminating in the Panic of 1873.

For two years Andrew Johnson's role in Southern reconstruction was paramount, as he appointed generals, governors, and federal officers; restored postal services; collected revenues; and ended blockades. Johnson's political career began inauspiciously in east Tennessee, where he rose from the Greenville city council to the Senate. He cast himself as a Jeffersonian-Jacksonian, harbored suspicions of corporations and monopolies, and once opposed the expansion of railroads into east Tennessee. In campaigning for office as a defender of yeoman farmer democracy, his political style was often partisan, invective, and personal. A staunch Unionist in the secession crisis, Johnson returned South with Federal troops upon the fall of Nashville in 1862 and served almost three years as military governor of Tennessee. Much like Benjamin Butler in occupied New Orleans, he confronted intransigent Confederate opposition and, especially in Memphis, corruption from the illegal trade across the lines (Hall 210–23; Robert Winston, 217–43; *The Papers of Andrew Johnson* 4: 205–6, 687).[1] Amid a chaotic military situation in which Confederate generals Nathan Bedford Forrest, John Hunt Morgan, and Braxton Bragg contested for the state with periodic and prolonged invasions, Johnson vigorously disfranchised former Confederates, expelled the disloyal, taxed others to support the indigent, took hostages, proscribed the disloyal from doing business in the state, and nurtured a grassroots Unionist movement based on his east Tennessee constituency. His policies undermined both the Peace Democrats and the secessionists and received the cordial approval of President Lincoln and Secretary of War Edwin Stanton. After assenting to the recruitment of large numbers of black troops around Memphis, Johnson named himself the "Moses" of the black community, secured black emancipation since Tennessee was excluded from the provisions of the Emancipation Proclamation, and allied his political fortunes with state radicals who wanted to enfranchise black soldiers and give all freedmen equal legal rights in the courts.[2]

While he was military governor, Johnson cultivated manufacturers, an important element of the old Whig constituency. Several large Tennessee manufacturers devotedly served the Confederacy. Samuel D. Morgan of Nashville, founder of the Lebanon factory and a brother of the Confederate general John Hunt Morgan, worked with Archer Cheatham, owner of Nashville's Eagle Cotton Mill, to arm and secure powder for the Confederate western forces.[3] Ralph C. Brinkley, owner of Memphis's Wolfe Creek factory, fled south in the war with his friend Sam Tate, president of the Memphis and Charleston Railroad.[4] A few others, such as Absalom L. Landis, of the Sylvan Mills, entered the Confederate army.[5] However, most of the several dozen manufacturers in the state, men such as William Lenoir at Knoxville, William Parks at Lawrenceville, Pitzer Miller of Bolivar, and William Montgomery of Gallatin, welcomed the success of Federal arms.

Johnson worked with these self-made men. They had resisted secession, chafed under Confederate military occupation, and employed free laborers. Although some were slaveholders, they offered excellent leadership for economic rebuilding. As defenders of Hamiltonian economic principles, they were the traditional opponents of Johnson's nemesis, the Black Belt planter aristocracy. While military governor, Johnson made strenuous efforts to win the confidence of loyal manufacturers and merchants as he established a Board of Trade at Nashville to regulate commerce with the North and completed the important Nashville and Northwestern Railroad link. As military campaigns allowed, Johnson encouraged the rebuilding of mills. He permitted only those manufacturers and merchants within his lines who in good faith were willing to swear an oath of future loyalty to the Union and who ardently desired "the suppression of the present rebellion" to reopen their businesses and freely trade. To maintain the economic blockade of the Confederacy, Johnson and his agents adopted the policy that "it is eminently proper that no one should be permitted to manufacture and sell who is an improper person to be trusted as a trader."[6]

In January 1863, Pitzer Miller, a mill owner at Bolivar, wrote Johnson that "4/5 of my county are and have been opposed to the breaking up of the Union . . . but because of violence have been afraid to oppose the rebel faction."[7] Two months later, with advancing Federal troops burning properties near Holly Spring, Miller wrote the governor again, "I am deprived of my necessities by both armies . . . the Secesh. taking 3/4," and he complained that "the Rules for Importing our necessities if we had the money are very stringent."[8] Johnson's strictures on relaxing trade required both sworn personal affidavits of allegiance to the Union and supporting testimony from reliable witnesses. Then, trade in noncontraband goods was permitted. Based on these rules, Miller's partner, William Montgomery of Gallatin, sought the governor's help in getting mill machinery past the blockade.[9]

Other manufacturers did the same. In February 1864, after the decisive battles around Chattanooga, William Parks, an English-born manufacturer boldly trusting in the continued Union occupation of his region, sought to rebuild his Lawrenceburg factory, which was located on the lower reaches of the Tennessee River near the Alabama border. Parks petitioned the military government for permission to import Northern machinery. The Federal Treasury agent at Franklin, Tennessee, responded that "he had no blanks to fill that would suit the case of getting the 14 boxes of Factory findings that are permitted by the Board of Nashville to be shipped from Paducah to be forwarded home to Lawrence Co."[10] After qualifying, perhaps through Johnson's intervention, Parks secured his machinery and began rebuilding his mill in the summer of 1864. Apparently neither General Forrest nor General Hood burned these properties on subsequent incursions back into the state.

William Parks, however, like many other Southern manufacturers, soon disputed ownership of cotton with Federal Treasury agents who were permitted to seize any bales abandoned or owned by the Confederacy. All cotton south of the Cumberland River was in danger of seizure or destruction. In Tennessee alone over 100,000 bales were burned by the retreating Confederates. Any mill moving the staple in the war zone was constrained to carefully secure official sanction from Nashville. In September 1864, Parks, with his mill back in operation, petitioned to move thirty bales previously purchased under proper authority "to their mill, there to be manufactured into cotton yarns which they wish to take to some place in a loyal State for sale."[11] As Hood swept around Lawrenceville en route to Nashville, the matter became more deeply involved in red tape, but, conditioned on Parks's continued loyalty, Johnson's military government permitted him to manufacture and sell in the North. Johnson's carefully regulated restoration of commercial ties was a means of achieving his larger political goal of reunion.

Exactly when Andrew Johnson began personally investing in cotton mills is uncertain and may date to the antebellum period. In the postwar era, he acquired a large interest in Prather and Snapp, a cotton factory at Union on the Holston River in east Tennessee.[12] Two of his children subsequently became mill proprietors. Such interests may explain in some measure his greater emphasis on economic reconstruction than on social change while he was president.

Johnson's assumption of the presidency brought him into a far more complicated economic arena than that of Tennessee. Wartime Republican legislation offered much to Southern leaders interested in economic development: over 1,000 national banks, a freely circulating paper greenback currency, a protective tariff with 25 percent duties on cloth, land grant colleges, and preemption of western lands.[13] Only the last, based on the Homestead Act, received Johnson's hearty approval as a senator, and with few exceptions, the Southern planter aristocracy favored none of these measures. However, political reunion of the war-weary South with the triumphant North promised enduring economic benefits of trade and revenues to a nation increasingly bound by steel rails and telegraph wires. The vast devastation of the South, the rampant and lawless corruption in Southern port cities over seized cotton, and the apparent contrite demeanor of Southern business leaders helped convince Johnson that a lenient and swift reconstruction should take place. He harbored larger political ambitions—to create a new national party, much as Jackson had done—to which end he was quite willing to sacrifice racial and social advancements.

The new president ignored the challenges of racial equality and sectional animosity, insisting that the national government had no more authority over rebellious states than free states. His adherence to a "white man's country" philosophy and the adoption of a lenient policy toward the defeated South seemingly belied his career as military governor and politically threatened the Republican economic and social agenda. As Johnson, Edwin Stanton, and the Cabinet pondered Reconstruction policies in April and May of 1865, reports from the South gave graphic testimony to the physical violence of total war and the need for a policy of economic development. Travelers in the South, army officers, and Northern politicians found that most factories were either destroyed or ruined, railroads and moving stock were wrecked, and private property was made a desert. In Richmond, burned by the evacuating Confederates, the journalist John T. Trowbridge, a personal friend of the president, walked among the grim debris of "tall blocks, great factories, banks, railroad, freight and engine houses, two railroad bridges, and one other bridge spanning on high piers the broad [James] river" (Trowbridge 85). Petersburg, formerly the site of fifty major manufacturing establishments and six large cotton mills, was left shattered by the siege. Johnson had accompanied Lincoln on his visit to the Confederate capital, and a delegation found Johnson much moved afterward. The new president, one Virginian wrote, "spoke with much feeling in relation to the unhappy situation of Richmond and the condition of the South generally, which I think he will help as much as circumstances will allow" (Savage 407).

John Richard Dennett, another reporter, surveyed the square mile of the inner city of Atlanta, where he found twisted, rusting rails, muddy craters, and decaying carcasses of animals among "bricks and blocks of stone and other rubbish" (Dennett 268). Trowbridge noted that "every business block in Atlanta was burned, except one." Where Quartermaster George Cunningham's depot had supplied the Confederate western armies, the reporter observed that "the railroad machine shops, the foundries, the immense rolling mill, the tent, pistol, gun-carriage, shot-and-shell factories and storehouses of the Confederacy had disappeared in flames and explosions" (Trowbridge 239).

At Salisbury, North Carolina, adjacent to the large Federal cemetery, Sidney Andrews wrote that "the walls of the old factory building stand intact, but roof and floors and windows are all gone." Around the site, "the small brick buildings exist only as a half dozen irregular piles of rubbish" (Andrews 105). Robert Somers, an English journalist, visited the Martin and Weakley mill site at Cypress Creek near Florence, Alabama, and found only charred walls and twisted, rusting machinery remained where "before the war, [were] three cotton factories, of 23,000 spindles, and supporting 800 souls." At the mills, Somers wrote, "heaps of iron rods are still lying on the ground, and little bits of fine and curious mechanism are seen in the courtyards of the plantations, and in all the negro cabins of the neighborhood" (Somers 136). Sidney Andrews stopped in the neat village of Greensboro, Georgia, and noted that it "formerly had a cotton factory, which is now used as a barracks for the one hundred and fifty soldiers stationed here" (Andrews 343). At Meridian, Columbus, Selma, Fayetteville, and Columbia, the picture was repeated. The path of the war was clearly evident across the countryside, especially in the Valley of Virginia, central Alabama, and middle Georgia. In Louisiana, former Confederate governor Henry W. Allen wrote in March 1865 that "you can travel for miles in many portions of Louisiana, through once thickly settled country, and not see a man or woman." He found "the farm houses—the plantations deserted—the once smiling fields are now grown up in briars and brakes, in parasites and poisonous vines—a painful melancholy broods over the land and desolation reigns supreme" (*Army and Navy Journal*, March 16, 1865). Another journalist, Harvey M. Watterson, wrote the president from his native Raleigh, "you can scarcely have an idea of the present poverty of these people."[14] However, Johnson had witnessed such scenes in Tennessee, where Nashville was a casualty of war.

For many manufacturers, the personal and financial losses of the Civil War were truly overwhelming. At Roswell, Georgia, Barrington King found upon his return from refugeeing farther south, away from Sherman's destructive swath across the state, that "going towards the creek to see the destruction of our fine mills, '*all destroyed*,' the loss of two sons, another wounded, & one with a broken wrist, all caused by the late unnatural war, made me sad indeed."[15] Duncan Murchison, the former proprietor of the Little River factory at Fayetteville, North Carolina, lamented, "the fortunes of war have snatched away nearly the whole of my property—my cotton factory, store house, ware-houses, turpentine distillery, with all the stock on hand, were burned by Genl Sherman's army, and my grain, provisions and stock were taken by the two contending armies."[16] With six bullet wounds for himself, William H. Young of Columbus's burned Eagle factory also "suffered much & heavily in the recent war by the loss of children & property."[17] Ralph C. Brinkley, who fled the Memphis Wolfe Creek mill upon the entrance of Federal troops into Tennessee, wrote the president that he "suffered heavily by the war, and, by the loss of two lovely children" and was "weighted down with grief and affliction."[18] The psychological and economic trauma was made more acute by the uncertain political atmosphere in the North. Eli Thayer, once a confidant of John Brown, wrote Johnson that Confederate lands should quickly be confiscated and immigrants settled on them.[19] The president at times seemed to endorse treason trials and massive confiscations.

In the early summer of 1865, Southern economic recovery was problematic, with total property losses amounting to almost three-quarters of the prewar wealth. The Union blockade cost the South about $300 million a year in lost revenues from exports of tobacco, cotton, rice, hemp, and other staples, or as much as $1 billion in total specie earnings (Thomas King 4). Although speculators purchased perhaps one million bales of cotton during the conflict, most of the lint within the former Confederacy lay in an exposed, rotting, and dilapidated condition. Considering the disorganization of labor in the South following Appomattox, in the best judgment of commission merchants, not more than half a million bales were available from stocks or from the summer crop of 1865.[20] In addition, the war rendered worthless $2.7 billion of Confederate bonds and currency, while almost $.5 billion of Confederate War Department debts, much owed to manufacturers, were still outstanding.[21] All slaves were forever free, but this act represented a capital disinvestment of $2 billion for the South. An export tax of 2 1/2 cents a pound on cotton and the immediate pressing of Northern antebellum debts, amounting to over $200 million, against Southern merchants and manufacturers accentuated the chaotic economic conditions in a society where specie and bankable currency were extremely rare. Southern real property, worth $7.2 billion in 1860, was only valued at $2.05 billion in 1870, a loss of $5.56 billion.

Still greater problems lay at the very root of commerce. Robert Somers calculated that "the whole banking capital of the South, which cannot be estimated at less than two hundred millions more, was swamped in the extinction of all profitable banking business" (Somers 40). Without the foreign earnings of the annual cotton crop, no bank in the country was able to pay out specie, and in the South the situation was more dire. The remnants of North Carolina's banks contained only $800,000 in specie. Across the South, Somers found that the insurance companies, "the well-organized cotton, sugar, and tobacco plantations, mills, factories, coal and iron mines, and commercial and industrial establishments" worth hundreds of millions of dollars "sank and were engulfed in the same wave" (40). The war cost Georgia two-thirds of its taxable wealth, of which $300 million represented slave investments, $150 million was physical devaluations, and the rest was in worthless Confederate currency (Andrews 273). The total valuation of property in South Carolina fell from $489 million in 1860 to $164 million in 1870, while the decline in North Carolina over the same period was from $292 million to $131 million (Edward King 456; Schley). The fiscal policy of Johnson's Secretary of the Treasury Hugh McCulloch encouraged the contraction of the Federal greenback currency and further reduced the availability of funds across the South. In 1866, Arkansas had only 14 cents in circulating medium per capita while Rhode Island had $77 (Sharkey).

Losses to Southern manufacturers in worthless Confederate bonds and currency, prepayment certificates, and outstanding current debts reached several hundred million dollars. Prepayment certificates entitled the holder to priority in relief whenever government funds were available; they represented a pseudocurrency. By Appomattox, William Gregg held $1 million of Confederate 6 percent bonds and $350,000 of prepayment certificates.[22] Daniel Pratt held $260,000 in Confederate bonds (Evans 499). Those mills fortunate enough to survive the war held large quantities of such valueless paper. Many had also invested in state bonds. The Augusta factory held Confederate debentures from Georgia, Louisiana, Alabama, and North Carolina worth $400 million.[23] Unrealistically, William Jackson carried these on his books, "believing it possible, that at some future day, something might be realized from them."[24] The Confederate government was almost $.5 billion in arrears at the end of the war. Unpaid Confederate debts at Graniteville, South Carolina, amounted to at least $800,000.[25] At Gower, Cox, and Markley in Greenville, South Carolina, not a large company, the Confederate liability was $140,000.[26] Careful Francis Fries lost $95,755 on his military account, and the Union mill in North Carolina lost $18,405.[27]

Moreover, there were threats of other penalties of war. Under the

terms of the Federal Confiscation Act of August 6, 1861, Congress authorized Johnson to seize all factory property knowingly employed by owners in aiding and assisting the rebellion. A second confiscation act
drafted on July 17, 1862, permitted the seizure of any property owned by
residents of the Confederacy that lay within the reach of Federal courts
for debts or other encumbrances. Through these vehicles, Northern prewar debts and Federal taxes, such as the new export tax on cotton, could
be satisfied. These acts created a vexatious element in the clarification of
Southern property rights as Reconstruction unfolded.

Following the complete occupation of the former Confederacy by the
Union army in the summer of 1865, Secretary of the Treasury McCulloch
approved extensive seizures of properties that fell under the terms of
these acts. Many abandoned plantations were occupied earlier, but defeat permitted the confiscation of all Confederate national property,
including a vast array of enterprises in which the War and Navy Departments held an interest. The Confederate experiment with military socialism produced government ownership of many industries that were
normally private: saltworks, whiskey distilleries, ironworks, shoe manufactories, and chemical laboratories. Also subject to seizure were the
Quartermaster and Ordnance depots, government cotton and wool,
mines, railroads, the Macon arsenal and laboratory, the Augusta powder
works, ships and shipyards, and public buildings. In Albany, Georgia, a
startled Federal agent discovered and seized a large operation outfitted
by the Confederate navy, "a flouring & grist mill, a bakery, cooperage &
blacksmith shops, fitted up in a good manner, with steam engines,
tools &c every way suitable for the business." Located on land owned by
Confederate shipbuilder and manufacturer Nelson A. Tift, the impressive
brick buildings "with the machinery & tools belonged to the Rebel Government."[28] Tift salvaged enough of his property to commence a successful cotton mill business soon thereafter. In Alabama, the Brierfield Iron
Works went under the Federal hammer.

Secretary McCulloch, responsive to Andrew Johnson's own insistence
that treason be made odious, ruled that state and locally owned properties in the South were also alienated and liable to confiscation by virtue
of their use in the rebellion. Gustavus W. Smith's Chattanooga iron-
works, the largest rolling mill in the Confederacy, and the Charleston
gaslight company were among the properties legally attached.[29] In Texas,

Treasury agents seized the "Brazos Manufacturing Company's mill in Robinson Co. used for manufacture of cloths for C.S. Army—built by labor detailed from C.S. Army." In McClennan County, Texas, Federal occupation officers conducted a thorough investigation into the "Machinery of the Waco Manfg Co (woolen) used for making blankets & cloths for the C.S.A." Since George E. Burney and James B. Earle of Waco used the Confederate Texas Cotton Board, an agency of the Bureau of Foreign Supplies, to secure funds to purchase their machinery in England, the Federal investigating agent judged that the "machinery [was] purchased by State with proceeds of cotton sold." Initially, at least, the factory was "not under seizure—said to be built by detail from C.S. Army—but no proof as yet."[30] The very exacting system of Confederate controls in detailing factory workers, providing cotton and wool, and buying or impressing cloth threatened to alienate these properties to the Federal authorities. When the precise relationship of the Waco factory to the Confederacy became evident, a local resident wrote, "the military authorities by order General Duffin [Alfred N. Duffie] seized this company's property as government property." He added, "that closes out the company, unless they can recover from the military which might be easy enough in N.Y., but not here."[31] A strict interpretation of the confiscation acts threatened the status of nearly all remaining Southern mills.

While governmental leaders in Washington wrestled with the larger political and social issues of Reconstruction, particularly the ultimate political loyalty of the Southern civil population and the status of millions of black laborers, most Southern manufacturers were preoccupied with the probable loss of real property. The most accessible and negotiable element of their property was cotton, which sold in Augusta, Georgia, for 7 cents a pound during June 1865, while the New York asking price was $1 a pound or $300 in gold per bale.[32] In August 1865, Albert G. Browne, a Federal Treasury agent traveling by rail from Savannah, Georgia, toward the Thomasville factories—a distance of 150 miles—found "considerable quantities of cotton at almost every station." Portions of the precious lint were "in a wretched condition, some of it having been in leaky sheds." Some lots had lain in the weather for the duration of the war and the bagging was decayed, he reported, and "a great many bales have fallen to pieces, so that the marks are not to be distinguished; many of the sheds are open at the sides, and exposed to the action of the weather, and altho apparently looking fair as soon as the bale is handled, the ropes break and the bagging fails under the least touch."[33] The indistinct marking was an open invitation to seizure.

Although national cotton prices gradually fell through the summer of 1865 in anticipation of the fall harvest, they remained at historic highs. In September, Samuel Graham, proprietor of Tennessee's Pinewood factory and a staunch Unionist, paid 7 cents a pound at his mill door and sold the same cotton in New York for 40 cents a pound.[34] The fortunate manufacturers who concluded the war with either cotton, lands, or specie, rather than with Confederate bonds and currency, possessed the sinews to rebuild. Economic reconstruction depended upon Johnson's willingness to adopt a policy of accommodation that would allow manufacturers to maintain control of their real property and to rebuild. In turn, the president's policies were captive to the army officers, Treasury agents, and customs officials who flocked to the South after Appomattox to administer what they perceived as the national will, but who often succumbed to mere plunder.

Francis Fries at Salem, North Carolina, pursued a policy of cotton purchases during the war that was apparently common for most mills. With Confederate currency and goods for barter, he purchased 1,652 bales of cotton and stored them on several dozen plantations in Sumter, Chester, and Kershaw Districts, South Carolina.[35] Some of Fries's bales on outlying plantations were destroyed by floods, some were stolen, and Federal troops under Sherman burned several hundred more, but the factory's inventory during the early months of Reconstruction showed 872 bales still intact.[36] Another 153 bales were stored safely in Texas.[37] Barrington King at Roswell, Georgia, followed a similar strategy. Anticipating the worst in 1864, he stored 1,400 bales of cotton "in Augusta, Newnan, Griffin, Macon, &c."[38] Upon the evacuation of Augusta, Confederate authorities burned 1,000 of King's bales, and another 277 bales left in Savannah were seized by Federal Treasury agents swarming in the wake of Sherman's army.[39] The resourceful and renowned Federal agent R. M. Lea of Massachusetts, mixing greed with revenge, confiscated King's cotton in Savannah, marked it as his own, and dispatched the lot, worth over $100,000 dollars, to New York as part of the Treasury Department's consignment.[40] Historian Stanley Hoole estimated that in Savannah alone, 40,000 bales worth $28 million were fraudulently seized (Anderson 117ff).

A portion of King's cotton, 145 bales, was in sheds at Greensboro, Georgia, and escaped immediate detection. The manufacturer placed great confidence in the statement of General William Sherman that "no private property cotton &c would be taken after the 26 April, [1865]."[41] Nevertheless, throughout the summer arbitrary seizures on behalf of Federal authorities and private individuals continued to threaten this prized asset. The value of the contested cotton was $70,000. Daniel Augustus Tompkins of Edgefield County, later a noted mill engineer, wrote that during the war his impoverished family saved 35 bales of cotton, hidden by his mother in the garret and basement of her home, which sold for $20,000 in specie in the summer of 1865 (George Winston 16).

The farsightedness of William Gregg rivaled that of the Tompkins family. During the war, over the opposition of many stockholders, Gregg purchased 1,000 bales of cotton and stored them in several South Carolina counties and in Augusta. After Andrew Johnson officially raised the blockade and opened Savannah and the Gulf ports to foreign commerce on May 22, 1865, Gregg successfully shipped 400 bales of cloth to England.[42] While he saved a considerable portion of his cotton from Federal agents, 100 bales of cloth, amounting to about 50,000 yards, were seized as Confederate property. When Gregg protested to Secretary McCullough that this valuable material should at least be sold for the benefit of local destitute children, the secretary responded that "there is no information in the Department showing that the cloth in question is in the possession of any of its agents, and even if such were the case, he has no power to afford the desired relief."[43]

The carnival atmosphere of plunder that developed in port cities such as Memphis, Charleston, Natchez, New Orleans, and Mobile quickly engulfed Augusta and involved several manufacturers who recklessly plunged into the fray. One raft from Augusta carried 4,000 bales of cotton down river to Savannah and netted $1 million for the adventurous owners.[44] Through these speculations, Josiah Sibley, a large investor in Augusta factories, made himself "better off than before the war." Many like Sibley turned with alacrity and great skill from blockade-running to cotton speculation, and by October 1865, a reporter noted that Sibley's commission house "probably made 100m $ since 1st June on cotton, & now hold 1000 bales, which they held during the war."[45] In August 1865, another Augusta speculator, Thomas Metcalf, gave an observer the impression that he was "much richer than ever before as he had a large amt. of cotton on hand," controlling an interest in some 10,000 bales.[46] Metcalf and his partner were denied permission to ship their cotton from Augusta and "figured themselves into jail, for attempting to bribe Genl. [Charles H.] Grosvenor." The Union general exposed the affair and the culprits were convicted, but according to Gazaway Bugg Lamar, a local commission merchant and a witness to the proceedings, $200,000 of bribe money also disappeared. He wrote, "the public are tolerabley [sic] unanimous, as to its where abouts [sic]!" Afterward, Lamar believed, the Union general "retired with his plunder to Ohio."[47]

Some manufacturers and merchants went to great extremes in a desperate bid to preserve property. Gazaway Lamar successfully made a transfer of 800 bales of cotton to New York residents associated with his defunct National Bank of the Republic.[48] Another venture was not so successful. The Federal Treasury agent at Savannah was Albert G. Browne of Salem, Massachusetts, who prior to the war had achieved some notoriety as Lamar's legal counsel in the noted case involving the slave ship *Wanderer*. Browne testified that the Augusta commission merchant offered him in "one proposal, of $30–40,000, and in another proposal, of $75–100,000, to be derelict in my duty to the Government."[49] While Lamar and his Savannah partner, Solomon Cohen, went to jail, Browne claimed a fitting financial reward.

William Gregg used discretion in achieving the same ends as Lamar. He invited General Edward L. Molineux, the Federal commander at Augusta, into a partnership in the Graniteville factory in a successful bid for his patronage. Other schemes of securing influence were more direct. George Schley, owner of the Richmond factory, bought favors. In June, after Union officers seized considerable quantities of Graniteville cloth, Schley notified Gregg that "there is 290 @ 300 bales goods belonging to the Confederate government, that you still have, this can be saved, *one half for the other*."[50] Apparently an arrangement was effected, for Schley sold the contested goods in Charleston and made a division.[51] Much of the thieving at Augusta and elsewhere represented collusion between small groups of former Confederate businesspeople and adventurous Federal agents.

The legitimate owners of cotton and factories were easy prey and vulnerable to threats or intimidation. James B. Bingham, a confidant of Andrew Johnson, begged the president "to close all the cotton agencies in the South, and order the closest investigation, by responsible gentlemen, into the *acts* of the Treasury Agents." He wrote, "as a general thing, they are grossly corrupt; you would be astonished to see the large powers conferred upon irresponsible jews [*sic*] and others by roving commissions signed by McCulloch, but which I believe he never saw." Reports were common that individual agents profited by as much as $3 million. Bingham concluded, "the thieving passes all belief; no man's life is safe who should expose all."[52]

Georgia manufacturer George Schley's operations soon became enmeshed in the byzantine bureaucracy that developed among competing military and civil officials. In August 1865, Schley wrote Gazaway Lamar that "in looking after considerable lots of blockade cotton of different companies put under the executive permit I am agent for, I find considerable cotton of your company being moved, some by Govt Agents & others, and without strong & speedy efforts most of it will never be available to you." Schley, who maintained friendly connections with the occupying power, urged his usual agreement: "should you desire me to save it, I can effect it beyond doubt, one half for the other of all I realize."[53] But some of Schley's schemes went awry. In March 1866, Treasury agents claimed compensation for discovering "196 bales [of] Sea Island [cotton] which George Schley got out of Augusta Ga. by Wagons and railroad in an effort to evade the Revenue Tax." The claimants argued that "it is not necessary to inquire whether this was Confederate cotton or not, as, without going into that, the seizure was properly made, because of the attempted evasion of the Internal Revenue laws."[54] Half for half was obviously not, in every instance, a satisfactory division.

The cotton of manufacturers in Alabama was also highly vulnerable to seizure. After discovering that Barnett and Micou of the Tallassee factory had worked extensively on behalf of the Confederacy, James Q. Smith, the new Federal attorney at Montgomery, proceeded against their cotton. As Smith reported, "when hostilities ceased, B.M. & Co were in possession of not less than three thousand bales, all of which they managed to ship to Europe before the court was organized except the 600 bales [seized] being the balance." The 600 bales he "caused to be arrested." Barnett and Micou protested. They paid bond and proposed "contesting the condemnation under the pretense that the cotton was paid them by the rebel govt. for money due the Factory."[55] Since many manufacturers had purchased their cotton directly from the Confederate quartermasters who controlled all railroad transportation, its exact legal status was difficult to determine. By claiming that this cotton canceled Confederate debts, Barnett and Micou placed the Federal authorities in the difficult position of having to interpret Confederate regulations on the matter. The Federal district attorney in Montgomery also proceeded against "350 bales of cotton from 'The Planters Factory' of Autaugaville, under circumstances almost identical with the above." The cotton mill proprietors, Frederick and James Neill, contested the move, asserting that "they received the cotton from Agts. of the rebel govt. for debts of that govt. due the Factory for labor performed in Manufacturing cloth for the rebel army."[56] According to Shadrack Mims, the factory manager, the 700 bales of cotton were retrieved by stealth and dispatched to market, but "it was traced up and the U.S. Government took possession of it." A lengthy court case and a decline in cotton values deprived the Neills of much of the cotton's value (Mims 263). Similar prospects threatened every surviving factory in the South.

Attempting to forestall greater chaos, President Johnson moved with alacrity to restore civil government to the former Confederacy. First, on April 29, he opened all overland trade with the South except for contraband goods (*Papers of Andrew Johnson* 7: 669). On May 9, he requested that Cabinet members fill all vacant federal offices in Virginia and recognize the governorship of Francis H. Pierpont. All trade restrictions with the Southern states were lifted on May 22. On May 29, after the surrender of General Edmund Kirby Smith's Confederate forces in the Trans-Mississippi, Johnson announced an amnesty proclamation and a plan to organize loyal state governments in the South beginning with his native state of North Carolina. There was much in these early presidential documents for manufacturers to ponder. Johnson's amnesty pardoned all Southerners, except for fourteen classes, upon the simple affirmation of future support for the U.S. Constitution. Denied general pardons were all high-ranking Confederate civil and military personnel, governors, those who had once taken an oath to the United States Constitution before joining the Confederacy, and those owning taxable property worth $20,000 or more. The excluded classes could receive executive clemency only through a special appeal to the president, who was determined not to accept pro forma oaths. The exclusions against the property-holding class threatened to debar manufacturers from civil life under the new state governments and separate them from their estates.

A second presidential proclamation described the procedures for the reestablishment of state governments. Johnson's process was outlined in his written instructions to William W. Holden of North Carolina, his first appointed provisional governor. He required formal Southern assent to three basic principles: the doctrine of secession had to be repudiated, the emancipation of the slaves acknowledged, and all Confederate debts abrogated. On this moderate platform manufacturers and the commercial groups of the South might unite. Confronted with the possible confiscation of their estates, they represented a loyal constituency for Johnson's provisional governments and a potential bulwark against the congressional Radicals. Their skills could fashion the South's economic revival.

In this lenient policy, which favored economic reconstruction over social and political rights for freed people, Johnson had the support of many manufacturers and shippers across the North. The Boston Board of Trade, with the endorsement of the New York Chamber of Commerce, adopted a series of resolutions favoring immediate economic reconstruction. Merchant Edward Silas Tobey lectured the influential Boston body on "The Industry of the South" and concluded that "the commercial and financial interests of the United States alike demand that speedy and efficient measures be invariably employed to organize and develope [sic] industry in the Southern States in order to increase the production of their staples" (Tobey 3). A representative of the New England Cotton Manufacturing Association toured the South and returned strongly supporting the presidential plans. However, not all supported the president. Amos A. Lawrence, an eminent manufacturer at Boston who once funded John Brown, wrote Johnson that he wanted no Reconstruction without black suffrage in the South.[57]

With undisguised haste, Southern manufacturers rushed to take Johnson's prescribed oath, often with the endorsements of provisional governors or Union military officers. Manufacturers in large numbers joined the 3,000 Southerners who petitioned Johnson through the summer of 1865 for a special pardon. Most revealed a sincere, emotional desire to establish a commercial reunion with the North. A few displayed an understanding of rising Northern concerns regarding rights for freedmen, and some were less than candid about their Confederate service. On April 26, a few days after General Joseph E. Johnston's surrender in North Carolina, Barrington King quietly took the oath of loyalty in Savannah.[58] Many in the Roswell community, including the wife of the superintendent, affirmed their allegiance in a group ceremony at the local county courthouse a few months later, on August 29.[59] In Virginia, James B. Pace, a manufacturer in Danville who had staunchly supported the Confederacy, swore loyalty before a provost marshal on May 9. John D. Williams, a Fayetteville factory owner, took his oath on May 23 and was promptly enlisted as a member of the county police under the auspices of the occupying military forces.[60]

Often those needing a special pardon from Andrew Johnson reminded him of the critical role they might play in economic recovery. On September 2, Ralph C. Brinkley, of the Memphis Wolfe Creek factory, explained to the president that "he has given credit, time and labor to build Railroads in Tennessee, to develope the material resources of the State."[61] On June 29, John M. Morehead, the former governor of North Carolina and owner of two mills, wrote Johnson that "your petitioner, being limited in his resources, could not engage as extensively as he desired, in the industrial pursuits, but as far as he could he endeavored to give impulse to all industry—mining, manufacturing, mechanical & agricultural, and has employed what means he could command, to give to honest industry employment."[62] The amnesty petition of William Gregg and his sons, submitted on June 20, concluded, "should you see fit to pardon us, we will devote ourselves to developing the industrial interests of our State and aid to our ability in the reconstruction of So. Ca. upon firm Union principles."[63] If the individuals were neither under arrest nor had court cases pending against them for aid to the Confederacy, Johnson conventionally accepted such pleas.

Johnson's basic political requirement, that secession be invalidated, was one that most manufacturers could affirm. William Gregg Jr., recently a member of the Confederate army, gave a defense adopted by many Southern manufacturers when he avowed that "my father has always been a strong Union man up to time of the last troubles, was elected to the convention, without being a candidate and had to follow with the rest, although against his inclination."[64] Gregg and his family quickly received amnesty.[65] King, who took his oath in April, volunteered that "he has been all his life profoundly attached to the Union of the States and was opposed to secession, but when by almost a unanimous vote the convention of his native State passed the Ordinance of Secession, he accepted and acquiesced in it."[66] Wilfred Turner in North Carolina explained in greater detail his inward journey through the sectional crisis. Until the war, he "had always been a Whig in principle, and did not believe in the right or policy of Secession; on the contrary was esteemed and in reality a Union man." At Lincoln's call for North Carolina troops, Turner opposed the calling of a secession convention, but he "was helpless in restraining the so-called Confederate Government from its exactions." The western Carolina manufacturer "was borne along by a resistless current of events, and deemed it neither dishonor or reproach to do what . . . all men would do under like circumstances." While of necessity he cooperated with the Confederate Quartermaster Department, "not a particle of the dangerous heresy in any manner incited or controlled his social or political conduct."[67] After his pardon, Turner served as an adviser to the local military board and to Johnson's provisional governor, William W. Holden.

Charles A. Nutting, the Northern-born owner of a Georgia mill, revealed to the president that "at the time that hostilities commenced I was residing at the Seven Islands in Butts county Georgia as Superintendent and part owner of a Cotton Factory and Mills." Nevertheless, Nutting professed, "I have ever been a true and loyal citizen of the United States and never have voluntarily done any act inconsistent with my fealty and allegiance to the Old Flag."[68] John M. Worth, a brother of North Carolina manufacturer and political leader Jonathan Worth, explained that he voted against calling a secession convention in 1861 and "during the canvass I had in front of my store a large flag marked, 'United we stand and divided we fall, Union Forever.' "[69] A member of his family went to jail for distributing abolitionist literature. Jonathan Worth, an old-line Whig, noted that he voted "against the final passage of the bill, with only two other members, by which the [North Carolina Secession] Convention was assembled on the 20th May 1861."[70] The president, a refugee from Tennessee's secession, could appreciate such comments as well as the irony of having them come from former Whigs.

Archibald McIlwaine, an owner of three Petersburg factories, confided to the president that "I was very much interested and concerned in the efforts made to dissolve the Union & was resolutely and correctly opposed to them; so much so that contrary to my habits I took an active part in the canvas in a private way and in my capacity as a private citizen by my conversation and my votes I did every thing in my power to prevent a dissolution of the Union and particularly the secession of Virginia." McIlwaine, who had four sons in the Confederate service, continued, "believing that the act was wrong and that the consequences would be ruinous, at no time have I ever changed my opinion and feeling upon this subject."[71] Johnson knew that Virginians had twice rejected secession before the Fort Sumter crisis, and he pardoned McIlwaine.

Many manufacturers who requested pardons cited their opposition to the actions of the Confederate Quartermaster Department as a reason for their willingness to aid in Reconstruction. When Richard B. Baugh, manufacturer at Florence, submitted his pardon application in September 1865, he included the familiar but true refrain that he "was opposed to and voted against Secession of Alabama; and was openly opposed to the secession of the Southern States on principle and policy." Further, he credited much of his financial loss to the agency of Confederate General George W. Jones, a former congressman whom Johnson both knew and disliked. Baugh wrote, "having been engaged in manufacturing of cotton goods, the Conf. States impressed many of goods *under his* [Baugh's] *protest*, and took them for *one fourth what he could have sold them* for in the market."[72] Johnson pardoned him.

Henry Fries of Salem swore to President Johnson that "I never made a dollar out of either [Confederate or North Carolina] government and I am not well off pecuniarily now as I was before the rebellion."[73] Thomas Holt of Alamance County, North Carolina, who was better off than before the war, identified himself to the chief magistrate as the "proprietor of a small Cotton Factory" and related how "he was compelled from time to time to furnish to the Confederate Government portions of his cotton yarns, at their own price, generally about one-fourth of the market value."[74] Although of military age, young Holt had abstained from military service.

One Fayetteville manufacturer was particularly irritated at the manner in which his operations were circumscribed by Confederate policies.

John M. McDonald, who had persistently demanded exemptions from the Confederate service for employees during the war, related to Johnson that "when these difficulties assumed such organized direction as to control the legislation of the said state, the subscriber was of the opinion that no option was left him to run the said factory upon the terms required of him or suffer the whole to pass beyond the control of himself and his said sons." By cooperating with the Confederacy, McDonald was able to retain "the control of the said factory" and was "able to save his said sons or most of them and seven of his hands from taking up arms against the United States."[75] Former North Carolina governor John M. Morehead was more explicit. He noted that "in 1861 the Confederate Government required your petitioner to furnish cloth for tents, he being a manufacturer of cotton." This demand "your petitioner endeavored to avoid, until threatened with the impressment of his establishment, to avoid which he made a verbal promise to furnish some tent cloth, which he did in the latter part of 1861 & first of 1862—when he stopped its delivery." Upon the passage of the Confederate Conscription Act in 1862, "some fifteen or twenty of his hands (all subject to that law) were conscripted & taken from his employment & details to carry on his work refused." Morehead thereafter throughout the war continued "his work with old men, women & children & negroes as best he could."[76] Andrew Johnson and his provisional governors willingly counted such hostility to the Confederate bureaucracy as evidence of future loyalty.

Manufacturers of foreign or Northern birth had advantages in pressing claims of loyalty. William H. Willard of Orange County, North Carolina, a man of Northern birth, explained his embarrassment in this respect. He was compelled, "at times, to furnish the agents of the pretended Confederate Government with fabrics manufactured at this factory." Under these circumstances, he was "consequently under prejudice & danger & did allow himself to be drawn into conduct & conversations on some occasions, that might be construed into a voluntary aid to the rebellion." Like many others, he was "at heart a Union man & not a secessionist—& always cooperated cordially with what was known as the Conservative Party in North Carolina."[77] William H. Young, who was from the North, was twenty years a resident in Georgia, and presided over the remains of the Eagle factory at Columbus, explained to the president that he "fell into the current of secession in 1860 honestly & sincerely believing that it was a peaceable & constitutional remedy for all evils, & not from hostility to the institutions of the Government of the United States."[78] John A. White, owner of two Athens mills, submitted that he came from Ireland "about twenty nine years ago," engaged in manufacturing, and during the war "yielded obedience to the law of the country without questioning the right of those who had the *power* to enforce them."[79] Many genuine Yankees like Isaac Scott of the Macon factory submitted impeccable Union credentials.

Some Northerners also told strange tales. New Yorker Henry Merrell, who spent the war in Arkansas, was a well-known antebellum promoter of mills who had a Georgia-born wife. He stated that "in the beginning of the war he tried to be an Union man and did what he could do to prevent the war; but the time arrived when it became necessary for him to declare himself a rebel or sacrifice home, property, & strong personal attachments." Since he was deeply in debt for his mill, Merrell contended "it would be infamous for him to desert his condition." After selling his mill, he entered the ranks of the Confederate army as a quartermaster major, serving on the staff of General Theophilus Holmes in the Trans-Mississippi, where he "did what he was called upon to do, with fidelity."[80] In fact, Merrell accepted a commission from General Kirby Smith to buy manufacturing machinery in Europe. In his memoirs, begun during the war, Merrell explained the matter at greater length: "If any one should be disposed to deny that the Confederate Government is a Government *de facto*, I would like him to test it by placing himself under it once, & then trying to set his face against it! I think he would find it to be a very strong Government indeed" (Merrell 294).

Merrell's New York family had political influence with Senator Roscoe Conkling and Thurlow Weed, and the Arkansas miller presented a recommendation from the new Federal district attorney of eastern Arkansas that certified that he "was always opposed to secession and in favor of the Union, and his sentiments being suspected, he was severely persecuted and threatened frequently with death."[81] All true enough; indeed, early in the war Merrell sold goods for only specie and was publicly threatened. Like Merrell, in Bainbridge, Georgia, John M. Potter, a local manufacturer of New York origins, explained to President Johnson that he had resided in the South for twenty-two years and "was opposed to secession and opposed it to the extent of his ability."[82] Nevertheless, like others, he accepted local police duties during the war and served on various battlefield relief committees.

Daniel Pratt of Alabama made no mention of his Connecticut origins in his petition presented to the president's Board of Pardons in August 1865. Pratt reminded the Washington authorities that "he was a member of the Legislature of the State of Alabama at the time of the passage of the so-called ordinance of Secession, and that he continued to be a member thereof until the expiration of the term for which he had been elected."[83] The builder of Prattville opposed the secession ordinance and "did what he could to prevent its passage," although afterward he did business with the Confederate War Department. However, his nephew served through the war as a Confederate officer in Mobile.[84]

Some old Unionists, mainly former Whigs, were hard-pressed to explain their shifting political allegiance during the war years. Edward Mc-Gehee, whose Mississippi factory was burned in 1863, represented that he was "older than the Constitution of the United States and always [believed] that instrument to be sacred, in 1850 and again in 1860 exerted all the influence he possessed against secession."[85] McGehee and his brother, John Scott McGehee, owner of large estates greatly depleted by the war, suffered financial losses of over $2 million from emancipation. His family simply petitioned for the renewed rights of national citizenship. An unusual case for loyalty came from Eugenius A. and James Nisbet of Macon, Georgia. The Nisbets were also former Whigs, successful merchants, and stockholders in the Macon factory. Eugenius Nisbet attended the Georgia convention of 1861 and "in that body voted for the Secession Ordinance as a Revolutionary measure." He now explained truthfully that he was "before the secession of the State and is now opposed to the doctrine of secession."[86] However, after secession, "he was a member of the [Confederate] Provisional Congress and assisted in organizing the new government," in fact helping to draft the Confederate constitution. Both men accepted the dictates of the war and were willing in good faith to renew their allegiance to the United States.[87] Johnson quickly pardoned them.

In August 1865, Charles H. Patton, of Huntsville's Bell factory, testified that "he was a strong opponent to the secession of this state . . . and done all in his power as a civilian to prevent it."[88] A physician trained at Yale, Patton used exclusively slave labor in his mill. Patton's brother,

Robert, explained in his own case that in 1861 he "was in Montgomery during the session of the convention which passed the ordinance of secession, and though not a member of that body (being at that time President of the State Senate—and the Legislature being also in session) he exercised all his influence to prevent that fatal step." With Alabama's secession, "your petitioner in common with nearly all the Union men in Alabama fell into the current, and sided with the Rebellion."[89] Robert Patton had in fact counseled Confederate authorities on a military offensive to retake north Alabama factories.

The pardon petitions gave Andrew Johnson confidence that Southern manufacturers and their political supporters were ideological opponents of the doctrine of secession. As a skilled managerial class dependent upon presidential authority for their continued possession of factories, lands, and cotton, they offered the prospect of building a commercial foundation in the ravaged South. Several of these men served as governors during the years of Presidential Reconstruction.

A second requirement of Johnson's May 29 decree dealt with the status of former slaves. The new body politic in the South was required to give assent to all current federal legislation regarding the freedmen and to accept the Thirteenth Amendment. These demands fell far short of granting social and political equality. Probably no group in the South was so well disposed toward free labor as manufacturers, and had Johnson by policy demanded as a condition of reconstruction—as Lincoln had suggested to an early reconstruction government in Louisiana—limited political representation for educated or property-holding blacks or those with honorable military service, he would probably have secured some endorsement among them.

Practically all manufacturers, many of whom were former slave owners, acknowledged the superiority of the free labor system over slavery and welcomed the former slaves to their new but yet undefined status. Few Southern manufacturers, if any, were prepared to accept the Radical agenda of full political rights for the former slaves. In August, Wilfred Turner, the North Carolina manufacturer, wrote Johnson that "your petitioner accepts the Proclamation as to slave Emancipation and considers the Institution as ended." He pledged to never "use any means of restoring it, but on the contrary, aid the states and the General Government in regulating the status of such citizenship for its ultimate good, and in adopting all else to the necessities of their condition & conviction as the country demands." Turner's willingness to accept citizenship for blacks was undoubtedly reflective of the attitudes of many manufacturers, but he was "opposed to the present right of suffrage of the aforesaid class of population awaiting for future and necessary developments of capacity to use . . . for weal or woe the Ballot box." In a state where blacks had voted under the Constitution of 1835, he concluded, "when the proper time arrives for their entire Equality, your Petitioner will be ready for such privilege."[90]

A less benign view was explored by journalist John Trowbridge while traveling in Alabama's Black Belt in the fall of 1865. He found James Gunn, owner of a factory burned by Federal general James H. Wilson a few months previously, in a sour mood. Gunn lived deep in the Black Belt, and his dialogue was strained and facetious as Trowbridge recorded it: "I'm a foreigner. . . . I scorn to be called a citizen of the United States. . . . I shall take no oath, so help me god! . . . unless . . . it is to enable me to vote. . . . I want to vote to give the suffrage to the Negro." Gunn vented his spleen upon the plantation system: "I want this country filled up with white men. . . . I want the large plantations cut up, and manufactories established . . . we never had any manufactories for this reason . . . southern capitalists all jammed their money into niggers and land . . . as their capital increased, it was a few more niggers, a little more land" (Trowbridge 222). Apparently Gunn, having lost both slaves and mills, neither needed nor applied for a presidential pardon.

In Georgia, Barrington King, a kindly master who welcomed his own emancipation from slavery, despaired of any exaggerated political expectations for the black community, writing in August 1865 that he had "no idea that Negroes will be allowed to vote, but if it should be at the South—Negroes on a footing with the white population, when the northern states refuse that privilege—it will be time to be off."[91] King's former slaves, by the scores, were scattered across Georgia. He believed that "most of them wish to return home, but not knowing the state of affairs at Roswell about food &c advised them to try & support themselves for the present, trying the blessings of freedom, that my servants in future, must do *double the work* so as to support their children."[92] In North Georgia, King observed, as did others across the South, that many freedmen were "leaving their masters' plantations, crops ruined, no one

to do the work—all flooding to the cities & towns, expecting to be supported by Govt." Although accommodating to free labor, he believed
that "without some law compelling the Negroes to work for wages, there
will be trouble in another year, as it is the poor creatures expose themselves, become sickly & fast dying off." The high mortality rate for freed
people in the summer of 1865 convinced King and many managers that
blacks could not survive without supervision. The Radicals in Congress,
he wrote, had "the elephant & must manage him, otherwise destruction & poverty before them." He believed the state governments should
adopt laws "to make them producers, as well as others." Nevertheless,
there was some reason for optimism, for "if the Negro finds out that
Freedom is but a name, that work he must & harder than ever, it may be
no serious injury to the country after a while." The Roswell slaves, King
believed, "were an expense to me, but a great convenience among house
servants."[93] With his mills burned, King easily hired whatever black laborers he needed for rebuilding, paying only support and a $10 bonus at
Christmas. By August 1865, he wrote, "servants are coming here wanting
employment, but we refuse in all cases, have enough now."[94]

The prospect of hiring freedmen as wage laborers and selling them
essential commodities from the mill store for cash predisposed many
manufacturers and merchants to accept emancipation readily. With alacrity, Eugenius Nisbet acknowledged the extinction of slavery and kept
most of his former slaves as hirelings.[95] Others did the same. Caleb Phifer, a North Carolina manufacturer who formerly supported his state's
peace party, wrote Andrew Johnson that "his business being that of a
merchant and manufacturer, he not only acquiesces in the abolition of
slavery, but is satisfied that it is his personal interest and that of the
country that it should be abolished."[96] George Trenholm, former Confederate secretary of the treasury and an investor in a South Carolina
mill, observed the emancipation process in its early stages. He wrote in
June, "the former owners of the slaves were astonished to find with what
ease and tranquility this radical revolution was carried out." Like others,
he anticipated that "the change in the status of the negro, which to a
rich proprietor is purely economical, but the humbler class of whites
appears to be social, and prospectively political, will lead eventually to
jealousies, dissatisfaction, and bitter hostility, on the part of the laboring
whites toward the manumitted negroes." The great competition for cash

wages, as well as for political power, quickly invited racial confrontation. Like James Gunn in Alabama, Trenholm believed that the abandonment of gang labor and the subdivision of plantations into small farms set in motion strong economic forces inimical to the interests of the black community. The result would be "the gradual employment of white hirelings, the cultivation of small grain in place of cotton and the development of manufactories."[97]

The experience of manufacturers with slave workers before and during the war demonstrated that freedmen made effective mill hands. A survey of ten Savannah River factories in July 1865 revealed that all employed some black laborers. John Thompson, proprietor of Georgia's Hopewell factory, worked 45 black males and 38 black females out of a force of 120 persons. The Iron Mills, recently purchased by George H. Camp of Roswell, had 20 black workers, evenly divided by sex.[98] Altogether, 108 freedmen toiled with 1,910 whites within these factories. Traditionally, black workers were mostly used in the early stages of processing, in opening, cleaning, and carding of cotton and wool, but at some mills they were also used in spinning and weaving. No one disputed the skill and ability of black factory workers.

Francis Fries had 108 employees at the war's end, among whom were nineteen former slaves. A family member wrote that Fries employed in the wool factory "the labor of a number of young negro boys, who were growing upon my grand-father's farm, and who were not earning their board there." Many were quite proficient at making Confederate gray. One of these laborers, Ellic, was particularly accomplished: "he could read, write and cipher very well, and was trusted to lock up the mill at night and unlock in the morning." When freed, he had $400 saved, some of it perhaps stored in the family hoard of Mexican silver dollars. Upon emancipation, he immediately became a successful barber. Another freedman called Pink settled in Philadelphia and married a widow with a large family.[99] Louis Hamburger, a Georgia manufacturer, was astonished at the rapid adaptability of black workers to the new conditions. He visited Liverpool shortly after the war only to discover that a group of Macon freedmen had formed a band and contracted for their services with his elegant hotel.[100]

Sylvester S. Munger, the owner of a Houston mill, believed that the future of black factory labor was promising. Well known as a promoter of various businesses, including a fire extinguisher company, in 1867 Munger published a perceptive essay, "Manufactures in Texas," for the *Texas Almanac*. His thinking was decidedly "New South." Munger declaimed, "now that negro slavery is at an end there are many more of our white people that do not think it degrading to go into a factory and make an honest living than heretofore" (Munger 98).[101] As he noted, "add to this the disastrous consequences resulting from the war, the thousands of widows and destitute orphans, and others, all over the land, and you find the labor" (98). Manufacturers in the cotton regions could fill their mills with laborers by paying 60 cents a day. The Texan implored, take the children off the streets, the carrier-boys and store sweepers, and "put them in the factories, and make them profitable, contented, and happy" (98).

Manufacturers who employed black workers were substantially in agreement concerning their technical proficiency. Munger wrote, "I have had experience and give it: with the power of controlling them, they will do well; but without it, they can not be made profitable" (98). Henry Merrell of Arkansas believed, with some caveats, that "I never failed to make a good workman of a smart Negro, first having a care to select my man. . . . Negroes have the manipulation for anything the most difficult" (Merrell 169). Precise machinery required the most constant human care, which many whites and blacks lacked. Munger explained, "to manufacture successfully, you must work steadily and by the clock from ten to eleven hours per day" (Munger 98).[102] With the great excitement of freedom he was uncertain that blacks would accept this discipline. While welcoming freedmen to the free market economy, Munger despaired at waking up "some bright, sunny morning, with staring eyes, to find your *darkeys* all gone off to some speaking or *jubilee*, because, as they say, the *Buro*-man *saunt* for them and will *fine* them if they did not go, and you would feel *cheep*." The Houston manufacturer expected little help from either the army or the Freedmen's Bureau in bringing discipline to the black labor force: "apply to the general commanding, and he would tell you that *a negro is a white man*." But despite the Texas manufacturer's extreme displeasure with Radical political doctrine, he readily confessed that the freedmen "can spin well, card, and draw, in fact do any thing almost, and some of them quite expert; but in the cotton-factory the stopping of one hand is the breaking of a link in the chain, and does serious damage" (98).[103] He needed labor in his mill that was "regular, steady, and continuous." Reflecting upon his experience in the Houston factory, Munger believed, "it is hardly necessary for me to add in this connection, that mixed labor, that is, white and black, will not do well together" (98).

In arguments such as those advanced by Munger lay the rationalizations of a labor policy that shaped mill practices throughout Reconstruction. If controlled, the freedmen were artful and useful; if not, then the plenteous supply of white widows, fatherless children, or immigrants would be employed, and the mills would be wholly white. In this competition for factory employment, white workers possessed few advantages over blacks, and the combined pressure for jobs served to keep wages at a minimum. Such competition also served to fuel racial prejudices and impose social pressures on mill managers to hire only the traditional master class. When the British journalist Robert Somers toured Southern mills several years later, he noted that the factory hands were "all whites" (Somers 91; Beatty 169–70). Although blacks enjoyed considerable success as urban laborers, miners, and railroad workers, the factory floor, with its high technical demands and commensurate wages, became a white preserve. Blacks continued to do much of the traditional outside and heavy work, since manufacturers were perfectly willing to either segregate workers by race or banish freedmen altogether.

Other new rationalizations of work patterns also developed. Child labor was humanitarian; convict labor was vocational training at private expense. The large influx of black inmates into Southern prisons in the months after Appomattox afforded an opportunity to introduce them into the prison factory system, so artfully perfected in antebellum Texas, Louisiana, and Mississippi. There was little competition for that employment.

For Southern manufacturers in the summer of 1865, the important issue was not race or age or gender but economics. On Johnson's third dictum concerning the repudiation of all Confederate debts, manufacturers strongly dissented. Writing the president on August 14, 1865, Wilfred Turner placed racial justice and business contracts on the same plane, "giving to all their just dues." Especially in North Carolina, manufacturers opposed total repudiation of Confederate debts in hopes of being reimbursed, in part, by the state government, which owed them vast sums. This issue, which proved especially vexatious to Johnson on the national level, was placed in its best light by Turner, who wrote that commercial honor should be extended "to the idea of non-repudiation of all state or national agreements, in relying for future prosperity and greatness upon perfect integrity in the matter of contracts, whenever made in good faith & solemnity."[104] Dissent from this portion of Johnson's program became more apparent with his appointment of provisional governors and the calling of constitutional conventions.

In May, after a lengthy Washington conference, Johnson appointed his old acquaintance William W. Holden, editor of the *Raleigh Standard*, peace advocate, and son of an Orange County cotton manufacturer, as provisional governor of North Carolina.[105] In South Carolina, Johnson's provisional governor was Unionist Benjamin Perry, whose son was a partner in the Greenville factory of Grady, Hawthorn, and Perry. Former Whig judge William Sharkey was appointed the provisional governor of Mississippi in June. He came from a family that founded an antebellum cotton mill at Port Gibson in Claiborne County. Two other appointments as provisional governors, Andrew Jackson Hamilton in Texas and Lewis E. Parsons in Alabama, were also warm friends of manufacturing.[106] The commercial interest was well represented in most state assemblies as well.

The first state convention to meet gathered in Mississippi in mid-August 1865. Convened by Sharkey, the body truculently refused to repudiate debts, delegating the problem to the new state legislature (*Journal of the Proceedings of the Debates* 37, 265). Despite the governor's influence, the newly elected legislature, when convened, refused to ratify the Thirteenth Amendment as Johnson proposed and petitioned Congress to "withdraw the negro race from national and State politics."[107] A pattern developed in Mississippi that was duplicated in other states. Despite Johnson's strong suggestion that educated, property-holding, or veteran blacks be enfranchised, the state persisted in drafting black codes that punished vagrants, including disobedient household servants, permitted apprenticeship for black orphans, segregated schools and railroads, required all laborers to sign annual contracts, and prohibited miscegenation.[108] The former tailor's apprentice in the White House, who claimed that two of his slaves fled through Confederate lines to join him, made no objection.

Manufacturers were more powerful in the Alabama constitutional convention that convened on September 12. Benjamin Fitzpatrick, president of the convention, represented Daniel Pratt and Autauga County, and Robert M. Patton, whose father founded the Bell factory at Huntsville, represented Lauderdale County.[109] The convention immediately abolished slavery but debated debt repudiation for two weeks before reluctantly assenting. Then Robert Patton was chosen permanent governor under the new constitution. The South Carolina convention gathered in Charleston on September 15, followed by those of North Carolina and Georgia, which assembled in their state capitals a month later. In Charleston, Provisional Governor Benjamin F. Perry and his son, William, both now manufacturers, carefully guided the deliberations. Johnson's program was approved, with some hesitancy. The Thirteenth Amendment was promptly adopted, but neither Perry was willing publicly to go further in the direction of civil rights for blacks. On the convention floor, William Perry argued against black suffrage on the grounds that the wealthy "would be enabled to march to the polls with his two or three hundred 'freedmen' as *employees*, voting as he directed, and control all elections" (Andrews 46).

Initially, at least, the South Carolina convention refused to abrogate the state's financial obligations. The obstinacy on this point must have confused Johnson, for Secretary of State William Seward hurriedly wrote Perry that "South Carolina herself would not care to come again into the councils of the Union encumbered and clogged with debts and obligations which have been assumed in her name in a vain attempt to subvert it."[110] The emboldened Perry responded, after complaining of the federal seizure of a Greenville foundry, that "the debt is so mixed up with the ordinary expenses of the State that it cannot be separated."[111] Nevertheless, Johnson insisted that no debt incurred for the revolutionary purpose of the insurrection should be honored, and the repudiation clause finally passed. Florida repudiated all state debts incurred between January 10, 1861, and October 25, 1865, except for those incurred for building schools. Greater flexibility on the issue of debts might have produced some public support for black civil rights.

In the midst of the South Carolina convention Benjamin Perry released a letter from James D. B. DeBow, respected publisher and statistician, which encouraged the governor to foster immigration, sell off cheap public lands to the freedmen, and develop South Carolina's "infinite number of manufacturing sites."[112] Such importuning hastened the creation of a Bureau of Immigration as a means of raising land values and supplying an abundance of white laborers, a scheme that Johnson thought valuable (*New York Times*, May 21, 1866).

In the North Carolina and Georgia conventions, debt repudiation was artfully debated and a center of contention. In his proclamation calling for a North Carolina convention election, Governor Holden addressed the "brethren of the North and East and West," whom he invited to come "bring your capital, your muscle, your intelligence, your industry, your ingenuity, and settle among us" (Holden 54). Jonathan Worth, former Confederate treasurer of North Carolina, was an important leader in the convention. He was also the owner of the Cedar Falls factory, which held large war claims against the state. In campaigning for a seat in the convention, Worth confided to his brother that "I shall . . . have to take a position for repudiation or *be badly beat*."[113] This indicated that not only the president but also some of the public harbored strong opinions about war profits. Nevertheless, following Worth's successful campaign, he quickly relented and became a leading opponent of debt repudiation. When the North Carolina convention assembled in October 1865, the representatives included numerous cotton manufacturers such as Worth, Rufus Patterson, Giles Mebane, and Nathaniel Boyden. The district around the Fries factory at Salem was represented by D. H. Starbuck, a strong friend of the manufacturing interests. The convention's secretary was Richard C. Badger, son of Senator George Badger and heir to a factory interest at Raleigh.[114] Worth's reports as state treasurer provided substance for the convention's lengthy debates over finance.

In conformity with President Johnson's demands, Boyden and Patterson drafted a strong resolution for the convention, declaring secession null and void. This was approved despite the desire of a few representatives to adopt a simple repeal device. While Boyden, a Quaker abolitionist, did not advocate even limited black suffrage, his committee called upon the state to succor the freedman, "to improve and elevate him by the enactment of such laws, conceived in a spirit of fairness and liberality, as will encourage him to seek his true welfare in honest industry and the faithful discharge of the duties of his life"; however, the delicate task of codifying black civil and political rights was relegated to the state legislature, and such legislation, when adopted, was mostly based on ante-bellum laws regulating free blacks.[115]

With Worth and the mill representatives in the ascendancy, the convention questioned Governor Holden about whether he possessed correspondence with Andrew Johnson "relative to the State's assuming the debt contracted during the rebellion for the prosecution of the war, before she can be admitted again into the Union."[116] According to Holden, the state's debt rose from $10 million in 1860 to $40 million in 1865 (Holden 52). Manufacturers were large claimants against the state, which owed them at least $3.5 million.[117] When some delegates moved to nullify the war debts, Mebane, Patterson, Boyden, and Starbuck hotly argued in favor of tabling the motion. In turn, Starbuck proposed that "loyal citizens shall receive compensation for means furnished the state not in aid of the rebellion."[118] If cloth were not contraband, then this measure offered some hope of financial recovery. Only a letter from Johnson on October 15, demanding that the loyal not be taxed for the rebellion, stilled the waters; nonetheless, the debt repudiation measure was adopted by a majority of only four votes in the final hours of the convention. Sidney Andrews, a visiting journalist, believed that Jonathan Worth profited from this issue in his subsequent election to the governorship and noted in his journal that "his record for Unionism is as good, at least, as Holden's; but he favors the payment of the Rebel war debt" (Andrews 174). Upon his election as governor, Worth was replaced as state treasurer by still another manufacturer, Kemp P. Battle.[119]

The Georgia constitutional convention gathered at Milledgeville on October 21, 1865. The manufacturing interest was well represented by Andrew Jackson Hansell, of the New Manchester factory; James P. Simmons, of the Lawrenceville factory; and Charles J. Jenkins, an owner of the Augusta factory.[120] Solomon Cohen, a Savannah merchant and partner of Gazaway Lamar, was present. Journalist Andrews wrote that Charles Jenkins was "the leader of the Convention" (Andrews 242). Jenkins, a former state Supreme Court judge and manufacturer from Augusta, had opposed secession and now presided over the committee that abrogated that ordinance. The Thirteenth Amendment was quickly adopted. Then, while many delegates bestirred themselves with drafting petitions seeking a pardon for Jefferson Davis or the removal of black occupying troops, some of whom resided in the Greensboro factory, manufacturers caucused to debate the repudiation of state debts.

Much of the Georgia state debt of $17 million was held by factories. The cotton mills of Simmons at Lawrenceville and Hansell at Marietta, when burned by General Sherman, were due substantial sums by the state. Since the mills worked exclusively for Governor Joseph E. Brown, the state was also liable for their destruction. The Georgia debate over the debt was initiated by the state comptroller, who called upon the delegates to pay the war obligations "because public-spirited men furnished the provisions, clothing, and money, and took in exchange the treasury notes or bonds of the State" (261). Hansell and Simmons led the floor debates favoring the measure. James Johnson, the provisional governor, hastily telegraphed Andrew Johnson that the state had acquiesced in most of his demands, but "we are pressed on the war debt. . . . What should the convention do?"[121] On October 28, Johnson responded, as he had to the conventions in North and South Carolina, that he could not "recognize the people of any state as having resumed the relations of loyalty to the Union that admits as legal, obligations contracted or debts created in their name, to promote the rebellion."[122] Delegate James Simmons was still not swayed. A leading Unionist in the convention of 1861, by his calculation he lost "about everything but honor" in the war, despised by the Confederates and burned out by the Federals (265).

Like many manufacturers with fresh pardons, Simmons spoke with confidence: "the President stands as a wall between us and the radicalism of the North; and I am sure he would not ask us to repudiate this debt if he knew how anxious we all are to pay it, and keep the fair name of the State untarnished" (265). If necessary, Simmons proposed to reconvene the state convention after the admission of Georgia to take up the question. Solomon Cohen of Savannah astutely believed that the Northern Radicals would not accept war debts "unless joined with negro evidence, negro suffrage, negro equality, social and political" (269).

Andrew Johnson was thus presented with the option of exacting further concessions on civil rights for the freedmen in return for some concessions on contract rights. This, Cohen argued, was the test issue between the convention and the national government. After prolonged discussion, the Georgia convention voted 135 to 117 to support repudiation, with Jenkins, Simmons, Cohen, and Hansell in the minority.[123] Jenkins, the Augusta manufacturer, was then elected the permanent governor under the new constitution.

In Louisiana, Dr. Bartholomew Egan, a cotton manufacturer at Mount Lebanon, quickly endorsed Johnson's plan, believing that "either the President will be sustained, or a new rupture in which we may look for aid from those hitherto opposed to us must be the consequences."[124] Egan's son William, who entered political life soon after the Federal occupation of New Orleans, carried the family views to Washington, where he held "frequent interviews with the President and the principal members of his cabinet."[125] Another son, John C., was elected in 1865 to the Louisiana Senate, where he distinguished himself by labors on behalf of free public schools for the freedmen. John C. Egan later wrote, "all of the true people of Louisiana believed that as the slaves were emancipated, they should be educated, if they were to be fitted for free government at all, and of the measures that could be accomplished by a few true men of that Legislative period, educational interest was one of the most prominent."[126] Indeed, many educational leaders, including former Confederate officer David F. Boyd, named superintendent of the Louisiana State Seminary in October 1865, supported a practical, mechanical, and scientific education for both whites and blacks (Frost 147).

Despite being defeated on debt repudiation, Southern manufacturers and their close allies in the press and academies rallied to the support of Presidential Reconstruction. In Virginia, Alexander H. H. Stuart of Staunton, one of the first state leaders to endorse Andrew Johnson, rallied manufacturers behind the government of Francis Pierpont, formerly the governor of "loyal" Virginia (Stuart). In Texas, George E. Burney, owner of the Waco factory, entered state politics as a leader in the Democratic Party, and in Georgia, Enoch Steadman, proprietor of the Gwinette mill, stood for the state senate.[127]

Three manufacturers emerged as permanent governors in Johnson's new governments, Jonathan Worth in North Carolina, Charles Jenkins in Georgia, and Robert Patton in Alabama. Another, James Lawrence Orr of South Carolina, an outspoken defender of technological modernization, held an interest in the Batesville factory through his son's marriage. In Texas, George Washington Jones, the owner of the Bastrop mill, became lieutenant governor (*Dallas Herald*, November 10, 1866). These men strongly defended manufacturing and transportation as the best available methods of rescuing the South from its plight and were prepared to use the limited assets of the states, mostly represented by stocks in dilapidated railroads, as a vehicle of public improvement.

On January 18, 1866, as Andrew Johnson opened his debates with an increasingly radical Congress over extending the life of the Freedmen's Bureau Bill, Governor Worth charged his newly elected North Carolina legislature to accept the bureau willingly, as well as the legal and property rights of blacks. However, he conceded to the freedmen few social and political privileges not granted to free blacks before the war. Since the state economy was devastated, retrenchment and business development were his twin solutions. All banks in North Carolina contained less than $800,000 in specie, and Worth proposed that the funds be deposited in a new national bank, to be chartered by railroad and banking companies. He wished to exchange the state's $6 million of railroad stock for the state's antebellum debt, which cost $1 million in interest each year.[128] Worth conceded that "if such exchange were made, to the extent of giving the control of our Roads to non-residents, it might result in oppressive rates of freight or other regulations detrimental to the State."[129] With such extreme measures to achieve economic stability, the long process of economic reconstruction was commenced in North Carolina.

In Georgia, Charles Jenkins found the state railroads, a matter of prewar pride, operating only intermittently, with a fourth of the bridges and roadways extensively damaged by Sherman. Some operations were restored using surplus equipment purchased from the federal military. By 1866, there was no railroad service between Atlanta and Chattanooga. Jenkins encouraged a cautious policy of rebuilding the economy with tax funds and private capital, but he ignored the plight of the freedman, lecturing his legislature that "we are wholly adverse to investing him with political rights and privileges."[130] His legislature responded by chartering seventy-three manufacturing and mining companies within the following year, of which thirty-one were cotton mills.[131]

The new governor of Alabama, Robert Patton, spoke boldly about the need for a new Southern economics. At the laying of a cornerstone for a cotton mill in August 1866, he envisioned a brilliant state revival premised on manufacturing: "in the present condition of the country, a diversity of pursuits is a matter of prime necessity with us." The war and the destruction of slavery had destroyed cotton production, reducing the crop from four to one million bales a year. Immigration held little hope, in his opinion, for it remained "to be demonstrated that white labor can be successfully applied to the cultivation of cotton."[132] By Patton's calculation, the state held 20,000 widows and 60,000 orphans, who were desperate for the amenities of life. Across Alabama, "many who were formerly rich are now poor," and "many who were independent are now almost beggars."[133] The rapid establishment of mills would confer substantial benefits upon these classes. As illustrations, Patton cited his own family experience and that of the ten mill companies of Lowell. The Lowell companies, worth $10 million, consumed 100,000 bales annually and produced 100 million yards of goods. He challenged his Alabama constituents to "double the value of cotton by converting it into yarns or common osnaburgs."[134]

In June 1866, Bartholomew Egan of Louisiana lectured the student body at the Louisiana State Seminary on the new economic realities. Before the war, "the average wealth of every man, woman and child in Louisiana approximated sixteen hundred dollars," but in 1866 the average "did not amount to four hundred dollars" and was probably much less. With regard to the freedmen he cautioned, "let us extend to them every right consistent with our own well being and security; but God has never designed for them, and we can never concede to them, political or social equality." He believed a Darwinian physical law decreed that "the inferior race is destined to melt away before the energy and progressiveness of the higher race." Nevertheless, freedom for the slave fostered a new economic relationship, for "our large plantations will be broken into comparatively small holdings; our large land holders, instead of contending with debt and accumulating interest, will sell off a part of their lands and be the happier and the wealthier thereby." With the bonds of slavery broken forever, youth could energetically turn their talents to railroads, mines, and factories. To the young engineers Egan emphasized that "we have in our perennial hill streams water power sufficient for a hundred Lowells, and we must instruct our youth in and spread abroad knowledge of Mathematics and of all the applied sciences inservient to the advancement of manufactures and the arts" (Egan, *Address*).

The same economic credo echoed across South Carolina. James L. Orr, the newly elected governor, was a staunch antebellum advocate of man-ufacturing, who coveted for South Carolina "the material prosperity of New England." He advised his legislature, "I would have her acres teem with life and vigor and industry and intelligence, as do those of Massa-chusetts" (Andrews 96).

By the spring of 1866, as congressional Radicals closed with Andrew Johnson over continuing the Freedmen's Bureau and passing a civil rights bill for blacks, the Southern press mounted a drumbeat campaign in favor of the industrial agenda. The newspapers were joined by former Confederates who now remembered their troops as being half-clothed, half-shod, and half-fed, while confronted by the best equipped army in the world.[135] General David H. Hill took up this theme in his new maga-zine, *The Land We Love*, published at Charlotte, which was dedicated to the proposition that "we must make our minds correspond to the new state of things." Like the venerable *DeBow's Review*, Hill argued that the South needed "practical farmers, miners, machinists, engineers, manu-facturers, navigators, blacksmiths, carpenters, etc. etc., to develope the immense resources of our country, which war has not been able to de-stroy." He repeated prewar cotton mill slogans: the mild Southern cli-mate saved the North Carolina "operative one half at least of the expense which his Northern competition has to incur for fuel and wool-ens." With a multitude of full streams, "we ought to excel the North in this branch of industry; and we will be utterly inexcusable if we do not."[136]

Southerners, Hill wrote, had neglected the manufacturing arts because the antebellum practice was to "produce nothing, but the great staples of the South, and to import all our wants from abroad." As a result of the relative abundance of slave laborers, "the use of machinery and the study of the mechanical arts were, as a natural consequence, ignored and unheeded." Ultimately, the plantation system created a leisure class, and this privileged group, "not having to turn their thoughts into the thou-sand avenues, by which wealth is sought and gained, did not learn to prize it as a chief good."[137] In the schools, seminaries, and universities as in public life, the classics and law were emphasized over the sciences, engineering, and the mechanical arts. With slavery gone and the planta-tions breaking up, the South needed immigrants, engineers, capital, and hard work.[138]

Educators and editors agreed. A writer for the *Bainbridge Argus* wrote, "had we made arrangements for working up our own raw material previous to the war, for developing our mineral resources and for arresting the terrible stream of wealth that was flowing out of our hands and flowing into the laps of our enemies, in the first place, the war would never have been thought of at the north." The lesson of the war was that the South could never "have been conquered had the energies of the people been equally divided between the various departments of manufacturing and the labors of the field." With factories, "every interest will at once be quickened." The wages of 500 operatives, "thrown on the community in weekly installments, would increase the money circulation of our community at about the rate of three thousand dollars a week" (*Bainbridge Argus*, May 22, 1869). The energies of the Lost Cause were transformed into those creating the New South.

In the midst of Union League and Loyal League gatherings in Alabama in May 1866, Representative William Darrah "Pig Iron" Kelley of Pennsylvania lectured a receptive Montgomery audience on the mechanics of economic progress. Iron machines were the new muscle and coal the new nervous force of the world. He told his audience, "one little girl, tending a machine in a factory, will spin or weave more cotton in a day than one of your women will in a year by the ancient method of the wheel and the hand-loom" (Kelley, *South* 9, *Old South* 3). The work was suited for war orphans and widows, for "a little girl or woman watches a machine simply to see that no loose thread mars the smoothness of the fabric, and so earns good wages." He encouraged Alabama capitalists to "strive to develope and convert to immediate profit our coal and iron beds" (Kelley, *South* 9). Kelley was confident that whites would manufacture cloth, while black labor mined coal, although as a congressional Radical he advised his audience to quickly embrace black suffrage. A Tuscaloosa editor retorted, "we cheerfully welcome to our midst, Northern business men and capitalists whatever their political principles, who do not come to make a trade of politics, and to stir up hostility between the negro and the white man" (*Tuscaloosa Observer*, June 3, 1871).

In the summer of 1866, Barrington King framed a proposal to bring Northern capital to Roswell. In a broadside, he explained "the late change in the industrial system of the Southern States of American has induced the undersigned to call the attention of those wishing to Colonize and to Manufacture Cotton in All Its Forms in the midst of the Cotton growing region, to examine the advantages offered for manufacturing purposes."[139]

In no state was the "Factories to the Field" argument more avidly advanced than in reconstructed Texas. In 1866, the *Texas Almanac* noted that "the late Legislature has passed more acts of incorporation for manufacturing companies than have ever been passed by any previous legislature" (*Texas Almanac for 1867* 236). The spread of cotton culture in Texas and the failure of Confederate and Union troops to burn warehouses in the last days of the war left many investors with considerable capital for investment. The *Almanac* reported that the incorporation of "cotton and wool factories number some twenty or thirty, and if one half of these go into operation, they will confer immense benefits upon the State." The editor found "there never were before so many strong inducements for the South to embark largely, and as rapidly as possible, in manufacturing." The business climate was promising, "and the late complete revolution, nearly destroying our agricultural labor, compels thousands of our citizens to embark what little means they have left in some other pursuits, and none certainly offers such profitable returns as manufacturing." Already two factories were "nearly completed near Houston," which gave Texas "some eight or ten in operation" (236).

The restoration of civil governments under Johnson's Presidential Reconstruction gave Southern society some sense of order, and this order gave impetus to material rebuilding. While brick masons and carpenters cleared the rubble and repaired Richmond, Atlanta, and scores of other cities, the *New York Times* remarked on the large number of Southerners staying at city hotels en route to New England or Europe seeking investors and buying machinery. Despite conditions across the South, cotton was still as good as currency for the fortunate owners. Among those who made vigorous efforts at rebuilding or expanding were William Gregg, Henry Fries, George Swift, Daniel Gregg, and Bartholomew Egan.

At a board meeting at Graniteville on June 8, 1865, Gregg secured approval to buy new machinery to refurbish the mill to capture the Southern market. With assets of $116,000 from the sale of cotton in England and cloth in Baltimore, he immediately visited John C. Whitin in Massachusetts and placed a small order.[140] Then in August he traveled on to Manchester, England, finding that "the Northern men are here—thick, bankers & financiers trying to borrow money, & merchants purchasing every thing they can lay their hands on in England, France & Germany." Gregg perceptively saw that "the whole North is drunken & bloated up with the apparent wealth that has been accumulated during the war, & the bubble will be kept up as long as the Government can manufacture at will, legal tender notes, and that cannot last much longer."[141] He bought much of his new machinery at the sale of a bankrupt British factory.[142] In May 1866, when Gregg returned to South Carolina, he was accompanied by 680 crates of machinery (*Edgefield Economist*, May 23, 1866).

Henry Fries of North Carolina made his trip to England in 1867, as did Louis Hamburger on behalf of George Swift's Columbus mills.[143] Fortunate was the manufacturer who entered Reconstruction with accumulations of cotton, land, cloth, or specie.[144] Some large planters also had resources for investing. Two unburned factories at Petersburg, the Battersea and the Matoaca, held surpluses of $118,000 and $243,000, respectively, at war's end.[145] Edwin Holt of Alamance County, North Carolina, held property worth $200,000. Some other mills had equally impressive assets. George Swift and partners of Upson County, Georgia, were "immensely wealthy & good for half a million or more."[146] In January 1866, a reporter in Morgan County, Georgia, found the High Shoals factory worth $200,000 because "they hid away some of their goods & sent them North since close of war."[147] After the company sold 700 bales of cotton, he wrote, they "made money all through the war & are now enlarging & putting up new machinery in good credit & sound as ever."[148] As Johnson and the Radicals sparred over the status of Southern freedmen, Southern economic reconstruction began in earnest.

In December 1865, Barrington King at Roswell completed a new dam, "had commenced the 3rd story of the factory," and had roofed with tin "the blacksmith shop, machine building & office."[149] His son, James, was dispatched to Paterson, New Jersey, where he "purchased a small cotton mill, to make money out of the Yankees—but we fear, they are too sharp for him."[150] The Augusta factory expended $92,000 on new machinery in the fall of 1865. By June 1866, about a third of the factory was in operation and "fully equals expectation." The shipment of the remainder of the machinery was delayed, "to suit our convenience, the desire being to have it in installments of moderate size, that the changes may be made without inconvenience, or reducing our production."[151] In February 1866, the stockholders of the Columbus factory raised $150,000 in capital, rebuilt their structure in wood, and were again "ab[ou]t to commence operations."[152]

At the end of that summer an observer noted that Daniel Pratt was "receiving & putting up new machinery from Europe & the North & is going to manufacture *finer goods*."[153] Shadrack Mims, manager of Alabama's Autaugaville factory, found that "the whole machinery having worked steadily for four years, it was worn down and could not compete, either in quality or quantity of cloth, with mills that were in better condition" (Mims 263). He took 700 bales of company cotton and purchased new machinery, some of which came from William Higzaur & Sons in England. But the looms were from reliable Alfred Jenks at Bridesburg, Pennsylvania. Allen's factory in Marion County, Alabama, was rebuilt at the same time. By February 1868, the Allen brothers had "a factory in this county & one in Pickens County, besides a dry goods business in Columbus, Mississippi."[154]

New, larger mills were planned and built. The Sibley mill at Mobile, the Chattahoochee, and the Alabama and Georgia near Columbus were erected with the proceeds of cotton sales. Another mill, the Indian Hill factory, was organized at Prattville with a capital stock of $200,000, and the president reported in September 1866 that "they have just procured its machinery from Europe; it is of the most excellent kind."[155] In December 1866, James Martin began "rebuilding the Factories" at Florence with $100,000 in assets salvaged from the war.[156] The Bell factory at Huntsville undertook substantial "improvements & enlargements" in 1867 and soon thereafter engaged in "building a large factory at Nashville."[157] Ashton Butterworth of Winchester, Tennessee, went north in September 1865, and a year later his new Owl Hollow factory rose from the ashes.[158] Asa Faulkner of McMinnville, Tennessee, expended $100,000 in rebuilding his mill and buying machinery, and in October 1866, the Central factory was rated an "entirely new establishment."[159] In January 1866, another Tennessean, Thomas B. McElwee, announced the purchase of a "fine waterpower 3 miles south of Athens, and is going to purchase machinery at the North, and erect a spinning factory."[160]

In 1865, George Makepeace made two business trips north from North Carolina to refurbish historic Cedar Falls. His chief stockholder, Governor Jonathan Worth, believed "the cotton mills ought to pay very largely, all the Factories North are paying large profits."[161] In Petersburg, the Battersea mill was improved with substantial "additions of machinery."[162] William H. Powers of Richmond's Manchester factory secured $70,000, which an observer reported was "used to buy new machinery, all of wh[ich]. is now in the mill."[163] In 1866, the Fredericksburg and Falmouth factories, refugee mills at Richmond, moved their machinery back to sites on the Rappahannock.[164] In November 1865, L. D. Childs, owner of Columbia Mills in South Carolina, organized a company and purchased the remains of the old Saluda factory. With cotton saved during the war, the firm embarked upon "rebuilding their factory."[165] Its completion was noted by the *Greenville Enterprise* in June 1867. The editor also learned from "Mr. Grady [of the Grady and Hawthorne mill], and that veteran pioneer of cotton factories in this State and skillful machinist, Mr. John Bates (who was in company), that in the four cotton factories now running in Greenville, there are employed about three thousand seven hundred spindles."[166]

Evidences of the new cotton mill boom were evident in Texas. In May 1866, with assets of $35,000 in gold, Sylvester S. Munger of Houston launched the Eureka Manufacturing Company (*Texas Almanac for 1867* 237). John Murchison of Palestine, a merchant and planter, built a new mill fitted with machinery "brought from Europe." The Houston City Manufacturing Company, with capital of $100,000, bought machinery in Andover, Massachusetts, based on the same pattern used by the Texas Penitentiary (236–37). At Waco, James B. Earle's company successfully wrested control of a mill from Federal authorities and added steam power, purchasing a sixty-horsepower engine "to drive their cotton mills."[167] In 1867, Sylvester S. Munger wrote, "we have eight small factories in Texas, and we want fifty to one hundred large ones" (*Texas Almanac for 1868* 101; *Dallas Herald*, August 29, 1868). The flow of machinery continued as new mills shortly rose at Dallas and Bastrop.[168]

Neither the machinations of the Joint Committee on Reconstruction, the regional race riots of 1866, Andrew Johnson's "Swing Around the Circle," nor the fall elections of 1866 dampened Southern business optimism. In February 1867, William Gregg announced to his stockholders that Graniteville possessed "now fully double the capacity of the old establishment," with his new waterpower capable of turning 27,000 spindles.[169] Gregg also planned larger mills. He explained in March 1867, "we are about forming a company to have three millions of capital, to put up two mills on the canal at Columbus, which is to be enlarged to the capacity of 3 to 500 thousand spindles, the company to put up at once two mills with 90 thousand spindles & 1500 looms such to run on print cloth."[170] The Eagle and Phoenix Company erected a third mill a few years later. The rebuilt Eagle mill held 45,000 spindles.[171] George P. Swift's constructions at Columbus provided considerable competition for the Eagle factory. First, he completed the rebuilding of the Flint River mill. Louis Hamburger, a partner in still another mill venture, wrote in April 1867 that he "was at the Flint River Factory yesterday & found everything looking in fine order . . . it really looks like a new Factory."[172] Hamburger was dispatched to Massachusetts in June 1868 to buy machinery for the Muscogee Manufacturing Company, Swift's third new mill at Columbus.[173] The new mills, along with the Waynmanville and Franklin factories, which he also owned, placed Swift in a strong position to compete with other regional magnates, such as Holt in North Carolina and McIlwaine in Virginia. In Alamance County in North Carolina, Thomas Holt acquired several mills and, with an eye on the New Orleans market, commenced installing "considerable new machinery" that "improved our goods very much," while at Salem, Henry Fries purchased a refitting for his mill in 1867.[174]

The confidence generated by Johnson's lenient policy of reconstruction stimulated the cotton mill boom of 1865–68. Former Confederates also profited from the lessons of the war. In October 1866, the *Charlotte Western Democrat* counted that in Georgia alone "there is at this time in process of erection . . . seventy-two mills for the manufacture of cotton and woolen goods." This "astonishing fact" was but "the natural consequence of the events of the last five or six years" (*Charlotte Western Democrat*, October 10, 1866). During Presidential Reconstruction, Georgia added at least thirty-five woolen mills (Georgia Department of Agriculture 344). In South Carolina, William Gregg purchased $120,000 of new machinery and increased his production from 61,850 yards weekly in 1865 to 98,000 yards in 1867 and to 150,000 yards in 1868 (*Texas Almanac for 1867* 236–37). At the Augusta Manufacturing Company, a similar dramatic growth transpired. Between June 13, 1865, and June 30, 1868, this company "added to its machinery by $92,686.71 and paid to the stockholders the sum of $360,000, besides adding to its surplus account $124,052.27, thereby swelling that fund to $224,758.22" (*Wilmington Journal*, January 3, 1869).

By 1870, manufacturing in the Southern states approached the same level as in 1860. While Southern real property was worth less than half the 1860 value, the cotton mills of the former Confederacy now held 416,983 spindles and 11,602 looms and consumed over 90,000 bales of cotton (Grady 278). Georgia alone had 86,000 spindles. The census of the *Commercial and Financial Chronicle* in 1874 found 42 mills and 137,330 spindles in this state (cited in *Charlotte Observer*, September 30, 1874). Thus the phoenix commenced to rise from the ashes.

On December 3, 1866, Andrew Johnson addressed Congress on the course of his Reconstruction. Fifty representatives and twenty senators, representing ten state governments of Johnson's creation, were absent from the chamber. The president reported that the "animosities engendered by the war are rapidly yielding to the beneficent influence of our free institutions, and to the kindly effects of unrestricted social and commercial intercourse."[175] He had restored the Southern postal service and local courts, customs were again collected, and blacks were free to contract for their services. Across the South businesses stirred: newspapers circulated, railroads ran, and mills rose. The president wanted to go further, to build a Southern transcontinental railroad and raise levies on the Mississippi River, but his edifice was a house built on sand. Unmentioned were the condition and status of Southern freed people. Any Reconstruction that ignored the great mass of Southern black laborers, the cornerstone of the Southern economy, was flawed. The Radicals seized upon this defect, defeated the president's supporters in the fall elections of 1866, and launched a new Reconstruction program in March 1867. The Radicals would brook no compromise, but Southern white yeomanry violently opposed racial equality. Thereafter, Southern political life was characterized by violence and uncertainty, much engendered by the Ku Klux Klan and kindred organizations, which brought to an end Johnson's false spring.

8

Forging the New South

Radical Reconstruction began the process of political integration anew.[1] The Radicals reestablished new military districts, created new state constitutions on the basis of the Fourteenth Amendment, and replaced Andrew Johnson's officialdom with new biracial legislatures and governments. However, the attempt by Thaddeus Stevens, Charles Sumner, and their congressional supporters to force racial equality upon the South was short-lived in most states, ending in 1870 in Virginia and 1877 in South Carolina. When the last Federal troops were withdrawn, the new industrial order was clearly taking shape upon the earlier foundations. After Redemption, or restoration of home rule, American manufacturing dramatically moved southward, until half of the cotton spindles in the United States lay within the former Confederacy. Southern manufacturers who attempted to stay secession, who gave reluctant support to the Confederate war, and who strongly endorsed Andrew Johnson's Presidential Reconstruction finally claimed a predominant role in the intellectual and political leadership of the South. The rise of the cities, the extension of railroad networks, and the development of extraction industries, banks, and commerce found them at the forefront of Southern development. One of their number, Henry Grady, formalized the credo of the New South: that the Southerners must diversify, must manufacture, must join the modern world of industry or be hewers of wood and drawers of water for those who did.[2] The Confederacy perished, in part, for want of a single horseshoe factory, and the omnipresent poverty and deprivation of the region could be cured only by economic development. The message harkened back to the great cotton mill campaigns of the antebellum era but took on new rationalizations as Radical Reconstruction rose and waned. Many New South advocates saw a sense of racial uplift in this message, for by common efforts all boats would be lifted by the rising tide, but Henry Grady and most of his followers firmly endorsed the world of Jim Crow, premised on a permanent, but paternalistic, racial divide.

In the South, the Radicals reversed the policy of retrenchment espoused by Johnson's governments and expanded educational and social services; however, many Radical programs resembled those of their predecessors: they sought immigration and capital investment and fostered railroads and schools but, due to the rising hard times, the cries to open the mines, lay the railroads, raise the mills, and clear the forest were often mere slogans. National excesses created a backdrop for Radical financial scandals in the South: the "Black Friday" attempt by Jay Gould and Jim Fisk to corner the national gold market in 1869; the reckless efforts to expand and control railroad routes such as the struggle between Cornelius Vanderbilt and Daniel Drew in New York; the hasty contraction of the federal currency by the withdrawal of large quantities of greenbacks from circulation; and the onset of a worldwide panic and a four-year depression in 1873. As national trunk lines pushed South, each state seemed to have its own microcosmic version of the Credit Mobilier scandal, in which congressmen were bribed to aid the Union Pacific Railroad.

The years of Radical Reconstruction in the South were tumultuous ones and characterized by considerable violence between the Ku Klux Klan and kindred organizations against the Loyal League, the Union League, the occupation army, and state militia. The Klan was especially active in some mill communities such as Alamance County, North Carolina, and Greenville, South Carolina, where blacks sought skilled, mechanical jobs.[3] The turbulence of Radical politics often came to the factory door. Several Southern mills burned. After a conflagration destroyed portions of the Vaucluse factory in South Carolina, Federal troops intervened on behalf of James J. Gregg and "arrested certain parties & with pistols & threats & required parties to say as nearly as they would what he wished them to say."[4] The steady decline of cotton prices, the growth of sharecropping, and the overbuilding of railroads did as much to undermine the stability of these governments as violence. By the time the Panic of 1873 fully subsided, the Reconstruction experiment was over.

Even during the Radical era, the gospel of wealth and the creed of Social Darwinism found Southern disciples. This was evident at a Southern commercial convention that met in Norfolk in October 1868. Alexander H. H. Stuart, an Upper South advocate of manufacturing, General William "Billy" Mahone, recent hero of the battle of the Crater, and Colonel William Lamb, mayor of Norfolk and former commander of Fort Fisher at Wilmington, organized the gathering to promote direct trade with Europe via Liverpool steam lines and the establishment of a Virginia and Pacific railroad to tap the interior. While Lamb spoke at length about his wartime experiences in organizing blockade runners and the Southern struggle for economic survival, Jeremiah R. Clapp of Memphis pleaded with the body to coin wealth from science and technology, "We have a grand country here; but down-trodden as it is now, thank God there are elements of greatness and prosperity which even the hate or venom of man cannot rob us of. (Applause). . . . If we turn our attention to manufactures, where are the people who can compete with us? We have the raw material at our doors—we have all the elements of the most successful manufacturing people on earth. (Applause)."[5]

Across the South, others took relief from the constant political broils with Radicals to reflect on New South possibilities. A Texas editor penned an editorial, "Bring the Factories to the Field." After surveying the costs of labor, land, and raw materials, he argued "that cloth can be made better and more cheaply in the South than anywhere else in the world" (*Texas Almanac for 1870* 167). The *Tuscaloosa Observer* invited Northern investments, insisting that there was no prejudice "against Northern capitalists, in Alabama," except, perhaps, during debates over the Reconstruction Acts of 1867 (*Tuscaloosa Observer*, June 3, 1871). In North Carolina, Jasper Stowe, a former Whig newly minted as a Conservative Democrat, presented the industrial creed to a convocation of the Patrons of Husbandry, whom he boldly invited to purge their minds of the "great and formidable prejudice" against manufacturing interests and invest in cotton mills. After reciting to this group of farmers the familiar statistical advantages of Southern manufacturing based on the costs of transportation and raw materials, he argued, "there never was a time in the history of the country when machinery of every kind could be purchased at rates so low as now, and the time is in every respect, most opportune for Patrons to open up the way to wealth."[6] In fact, throughout the South, the Patrons of Husbandry were among the warmest advocates of the industrial gospel.[7] That Stowe's advice was generally accepted was demonstrated at each succeeding census (Grady 278).

Only a token number of Southern manufacturers braved the threats of violence and participated in the new Radical state governments. In North Carolina, William W. Holden won election as a Radical governor, supported by Nathaniel Boyden, the Quaker manufacturer (Holden 149).[8] George Swepson, an opportunist created by the confused politics of Reconstruction, amassed a large collection of North Carolina factory stocks and plunged into Radical politics with disastrous results for himself and others. In 1871, he was arrested and arraigned for bribing state officials.[9] Noah B. Cloud, editor of the Montgomery *American Cotton Planter*, a friend of Daniel Pratt, and a strong antebellum proponent of manufacturing, served as the superintendent of education in the Radical government of Alabama. The list was short.

Manufacturers and their allies were an important element in challenging the Radicals and ushering in the restored governments under local white control; they were quintessential "redeemers." Alexander H. H. Stuart in Virginia, Jonathan Worth in North Carolina, James Chesnut, Jr., in South Carolina, Nelson Tift in Georgia, Bartholomew Egan in Louisiana, and George Burney in Texas all played leading roles in marshaling the Conservative political forces of their states against the Radical Republicans.

In Virginia, Stuart, who had taken the lead in securing President Johnson's favor during Presidential Reconstruction, was largely responsible for organizing a Conservative movement. In December 1868, he and Francis G. Ruffin, the former Confederate assistant commissary general and a cousin of "fire-eater" Edmund Ruffin, called a convention to form an opposition party. Stuart, despite his mountain Whiggist antecedents, looked "with extreme aversion on negro suffrage," while Frank Ruffin was a prominent negrophobe (Stuart 22). In 1869, Stuart established a Committee of Nine who lobbied Congress and President Grant for submission to a public referendum of the clause in the Radical Underwood Constitution, which disfranchised former Confederates (22). The voters rejected the clause, and the resulting election effectively returned Virginia to Conservative control.

In the North Carolina gubernatorial election of 1868, held under the auspices of the Radicals, Jonathan Worth unsuccessfully opposed William Holden, but he gathered an impressive array of men into his movement. On behalf of Worth and the Conservatives, Daniel R. Goodloe and Hinton Rowan Helper, who authored popular antebellum pamphlets on slavery's debilitating effects upon manufacturing, mounted a blatantly racial campaign in a newspaper facetiously called the *Holden Herald*.[10] Kemp P. Battle, an ardent advocate of manufacturing, joined the affair as a Conservative candidate for state treasurer. Holden's subsequent administration was marred by violence. In 1870, following several murders by the Ku Klux Klan, he declared martial law in two mill counties, Alamance and Caswell, and brought in the east Tennessee militia to restore order. The arrests of over 100 men brought little peace to these communities, for those charged were quickly freed by the courts.[11] The affair provided a pretext for Holden's subsequent impeachment (Holden 81).

Jasper Stowe, an old-line Whig, judged these events sufficient cause to join the Conservative effort "to throw off the yoke of Radical Robbery and oppression." The political violence compelled him to make peace with his bitter enemies, the old states' rights Democrats. Now, finally, he abjured further "unwarranted invective against the Secessionist[s]" and wrote graciously that they "preserved the honor and manhood of a great people," and, further, he pledged himself to wage perpetual political war against Radicalism.[12] In 1876, Thomas Holt, scion of a prominent manufacturing family, began his ascent toward the governorship by winning a seat as a Conservative in the North Carolina Senate.

In South Carolina in September 1867, James Chesnut, son of a pioneer manufacturer, presided over the convention that organized the Conservative Party (Reynolds 75). Other cotton manufacturers prominent in the Conservative organization included Gabriel Cannon, a local leader at Spartanburg; Benjamin and William Perry of Greenville; and James G. Gibbes at Columbia (38, 88). Gibbes, who lost a mill to Sherman's army, was secretary of the party. Francis Dawson's staunchly New South organ, the *Charleston News and Courier*, promoted the movement (313). Often in parallel columns, Dawson noted the founding of new mills and charges of financial irregularity against the Radical government.

In Georgia, Nelson A. Tift took the leadership in organizing the Conservative movement.[13] A former merchant and shipbuilder in the Confederacy, in the New South Tift turned to cotton manufacturing. The Conservative movement was organized at Macon in December 1867, with Tift and other manufacturers playing a leading role.[14] The Conservative Party in Georgia, like those of other states, adhered to the twin policies of the Johnson administration: racial stratification and economic progress. The Macon proceedings were organized by John J. Gresham, a former president of the Macon factory, and James A. Nisbet, former Macon mayor and a partner in the factory. Charles A. Nutting, a Vermont native and the president of the Planter's factory, and Methvin S. Thompson, a Scot and the president of the Macon mill, were prominent among the delegates. Former quartermaster general Alexander Lawton of Savannah was a firm supporter. The central executive committee of the new party included Tift, Gresham, and Eugenius Nisbet. The Conservative convention baited the Radicals by offering to adopt for Georgia any Northern constitution that met congressional approval.

In 1869, Tift published a popular anti-Radical pamphlet, "The Condition of Affairs in Georgia." He was highly critical of former Confederate governor Joseph E. Brown, then in league with the Radicals (Brown 3–4). In an attempt to foster congressional support, Tift solicited testimony from across Georgia on the consequences of "military rule and black supremacy."[15] Augustin H. Hansell, of the Marietta factory; James P. Simmons, of the Lawrenceville mill; and William Schley, of the Richmond mill, contributed essays. Hansell, who held a judgeship in southern Georgia, insisted that racial violence doomed the Radical experiment at equality.[16]

Simmons linked economic development with racial peace, writing Tift that "as an original, consistent, and uncompromising Union man, one who was not and is not in any way responsible for secession or any of its consequences, I take this occasion to say that if the people of Georgia, white and black, are allowed to adjust our future relations for ourselves, the general government interfering with us by special legislation no more, the relations of capital and labor will, within a very few years, become as well regulated here as in any other state."[17]

William Schley, an Augusta manufacturer, noted sardonically that "progress of a people depends more upon intelligent industry than legislative enactments on the equality of race."[18] For himself, he was "heart-ily sick of the insecurity and instability of the government," and he believed that people in Georgia, "for the first time in her history, are fully alive to the importance of a proper development of her many valuable resources, and with an almost unanimous desire to ignore politics and tax their intellects and energies in developing agriculture, manufactures, and mining, and to resuscitate their lost fortunes."[19]

Other Georgia manufacturers shared these views. Enoch Steadman, proprietor of the Gwinette mill, in an unsuccessful campaign for the Georgia Senate in 1870, advocated the basic Conservative credo: "re-trenchment and reform" and measures "to advance the prosperity of the State."[20] After much effort, the Conservatives successfully ousted Rufus Brown Bullock, the Radical governor, in 1871, whereupon he promptly became secretary of a new Atlanta cotton factory.

Elsewhere across the South, Conservatives were equally influential. Bartholomew Egan, a Louisiana cotton manufacturer, had two sons serv-ing as officeholders in the Radical government. However, in 1874 the family worked within the Louisiana Democratic Central Committee to overthrow "carpet bag governments."[21] With the support of the Redeem-ers, William Egan was appointed to the Louisiana Supreme Court in 1876. Farther west, in 1868, George E. Burney, owner of the Waco Factory, ad-vanced to the Texas Democratic State Executive Committee, the center of redemptionist activity within that state (*Dallas Herald*, September 19, 1868).

The Conservative movement, with its allied press, fully endorsed the Compromise of 1877, which ended the Reconstruction experiment.[22] With Rutherford Hayes inaugurated as president in March 1877 and Fed-eral occupation troops removed from the South, political control was effectively returned to native sons.

Despite considerable effort, Radical Reconstruction did little to im-prove the overall economic condition of Southern freed people either by the distribution of land or the acquisition of jobs, and in some areas, such as convict leasing, it perpetuated a system of forced labor. Through-out Reconstruction, blacks were systematically excluded from many oc-cupations involving mechanical skills and the artisan trades. Radical congressman William Darrah "Pig Iron" Kelley of Pennsylvania, after several tours of the South, wrote that he was satisfied that the region stood on the threshold of considerable development, but manufacturing would be racially segregated, with blacks in the new iron and mining industries and whites in the cotton mills. The journalist Edward King visited the numerous mills at Richmond and Petersburg, which before and during the war employed hundreds of slaves working machinery, and found 5,000 freedmen working in the tobacco factories while "in the cotton-mills white labor exclusively is employed" (Edward King 582).[23]

Yet some cotton manufacturers kept blacks at work toiling on company plantations, hauling and cleaning cotton and doing much of the manual labor outside the mills. Some former factory slaves simply maintained their old jobs. In 1867, the Waynmanville factory employed blacks to make general repairs, expecting in turn for the company store to get "all the funds in the Freedmen's hands."[24] Mississippi manufacturer Edward McGehee hired a freedman to manage his large plantation.[25] In Alabama, factories employed freedmen to grow cotton on shares, as did the planters.[26] Daniel Pratt, like many manufacturers, kept skilled former slaves at work in his shops.

However, the Conservatives came to power as apostles of continued economic growth, which would build manufacturing cities and improve the lives of both whites and blacks. Although the Panic of 1873 bankrupted many mills and turned others into Northern hands, the new spindles continued to increase under Conservative rule. In 1874, six states in the Cotton Belt with 148 factories held 416,837 spindles and processed 130,000 bales of cotton.[27] Georgia, now often called the "Empire State" with 137,330 spindles, was the most advanced, while South Carolina had 62,872 spindles. In 1880, there were 714,078 spindles and 15,222 looms in the South, and thereafter the quantity of machinery doubled every decade (Grady 278). There was a comparable growth in railroad mileage and in products of the extraction industries. A student of the period has noted that with the end of Radical Reconstruction "there was an explosion of industrial activity," as the number of manufacturing firms rose from 30,000 to nearly 69,000 by the turn of the century (Doyle 9). The remarkable growth in cities, manufacturing, mining, and transportation was celebrated. A jovial correspondent wrote manufacturer Enoch Steadman in Georgia, "I am almost inclined to believe that 'King Cotton' is about to regain his lost scepter, and he will yet rule the world."[28] The youthful Henry W. Grady, editor of the *Atlanta Constitution*, beguiled rapt audiences with the vision that more than railroads, or mines, or foundries, cotton manufacturing was the main source of Southern wealth. With its flower for beauty, its seed for oil, and its stalk for wood pulp, "not the fleeces that Jason sought can rival the richness of this plant, as it unfurls its banners in our fields" (Grady 107). In Grady's oratory, the Old South of plantations and slavery—the South of the Lost Cause—had heroically failed; the New South of cities and factories was rising.

In October 1881, *Harper's Magazine* took cognizance of Southern developments by publishing Henry Grady's article, "Cotton and Its Kingdom," an initial presentation before a national audience of the New South doctrine. The Atlanta editor, who spent his childhood at the Grady, Hawthorn, and Perry factory at Greenville, South Carolina, and matured amid the spinning mills of Athens, Georgia, articulated themes widely used since the antebellum period. Like Andrew Carnegie, he espoused laissez-faire economics and popular democracy, and, like Alexander Hamilton and Henry Clay, he extolled national banking, tariffs, and hard money. These, along with cheap lands and labor, opened the South to unparalleled opportunities for economic growth. Like Andrew Johnson, Grady also espoused black racial inferiority and a creed of paternalism that easily meshed with rising Northern racist assumptions in the age of Darwin. According to the Georgian, the premise of the dominant Conservative Democratic movement was that black tenant farmers would raise cotton while white Anglo-Saxons fabricated it.

Henry Grady became the prophet of the new business aristocracy. Like the Old South manufacturing advocate James D. B. DeBow, he painted word pictures of old cities rebuilt from Civil War wreckage and of new towns rising on the landscape. Atlanta, Nashville, Mobile, Charleston, Anniston, Memphis, Charlotte, Norfolk, Columbia, and Birmingham were among the urban showplaces of his New South.

Some of his evidence was statistical. The census of 1880 validated that the quantities of Southern livestock, mules, and horses were again at their antebellum levels, and in 1885 Georgia's assessment of real property finally equaled that of 1860, rising to $368 million. Most of the growth in this New South was urban, for farm lands were still valued at $50 million less than before the war (Grady 167). Despite the depletion of the land by single-crop planting, cotton was again in ascendancy, aided by the new fertilizer industry. The cotton crop of 1880 was larger by half than that of 1860, and 8 million bales were grown by 1888 (263). There was no note in these word pictures of economically depressed farmers, declining staple prices, sharecropping, railroad freight rate discrimination, or a dependent credit relationship with the Northeast, issues that later were to fuel the Populist upheaval against the Conservatives.

Henry Grady's article for *Harper's* in 1881, like his newspaper columns and speeches, invoked the recent census as evidence that cotton mill spindles were swiftly moving South. At Augusta, "in the past two years two new mills, the Enterprise and Sibley, with 30,000 spindles each, have been established; and a third, the King, has been organized, with a capital of $1,000,000 and 30,000 spindles" (278). This addition gave Augusta 170,000 new spindles. The Atlanta factory, with 1,618 looms fabricated at the Lowell machine shop, was hardly completed "before the second was started; a third is projected; and two companies have secured charters for the building of a forty mile canal to furnish water-power and factory fronts to capital in and about that city" (278–79).[29] Across Georgia at Columbus, William H. Young's new mill, now styled the Eagle and Phoenix, increased consumption of cotton from 1,927 bales in 1870 to 19,000 bales in 1880 (278).

Throughout the Black Belt, Grady's optimistic views were seconded by others. Edward King, in *The Great South*, serialized in *Scribner's Magazine* in 1874, found a "dozen prosperous cotton factories in Alabama" and predicted that "Northern capital will find one of its most profitable fields in the very region which, ten years ago, was hardly counted among the cotton and woolen producing sections of the South" (Edward King 334–35, 110). Charles Nordhoff, in *The Cotton States in the Spring and Summer of 1875*, interviewed "the largest planter in the State," who established "a cotton-factory in Southern Mississippi, where he now employs two hundred and fifty hands." This endeavor was "so successful that he is about to double its capacity" (Nordhoff 84). Such ventures were highly profitable.

Grady reminded audiences that inexpensive labor and materials gave these mills an advantage, for "the earnings of sixty Southern mills, large and small, selected at random, for three years, averaged fourteen per cent per annum" (Grady 279). Even Robert L. Dabney, late chaplain to General Thomas "Stonewall" Jackson, succumbed to the vision. In 1882, like college presidents at military schools and universities across the South, he advised the students at Hampden-Sydney College, that " 'a new South' is inevitable, and therefore it will be right for you to accept it, though it was our duty to fight to prevent it" (Dabney 3).

Grady found a chorus of allies in the press. His articles in the *Atlanta Constitution* were endorsed by Henry Watterson in the *Louisville Courier-Journal*, Francis Dawson in the *Charleston News and Courier*, and Daniel Tompkins, an engineer and mill promoter, of Charlotte. The New South creed found ready acceptance in pulpits, convention halls, and national trade publications such as Richard H. Edmonds's *Manufacturer's Record* (Ide 131–40; Chew 85, 94; Straker iv; Bullock 11). The theme was circulated across the North by men like William "Pig Iron" Kelley, industrialists looking for investment opportunities (Kelley). In 1886, the Philadelphia editor Alexander K. McClure promoted Grady's views with a laudatory book on the South's "industrial, financial, and political condition" (McClure 62).

With considerable gusto, Henry Grady carried this message to the merchant princes of New England, including the Lawrence and Appleton families, at the Boston Merchants' Association and the Bay State Club in 1889. In this symbolic reconciliation with the North, the Georgia editor pleaded his brand of compromise: "we wrested our State government from Negro supremacy when the Federal drumbeat rolled closer to the ballot-box and Federal bayonets hedged it deeper about than will ever again be permitted in this free government" (194). If the Yankee Republicans would acquiesce in the social demands of the politically solid Democratic Conservative South, then the erstwhile Rebels would cooperate with Northern capitalists in building mills and railroads. These were the terms for an economic rapprochement.

Grady's compromise was endorsed by the movement of Northern men and capital into the South. He estimated that three-quarters of the capital invested in the Augusta factories by 1880 came from the North (Grady 278). Other examples abounded. In 1868, Samuel and Thomas Nicholson came from Boston to Gallatin, Tennessee, and erected a cotton mill.[30] Bernhard Friedman, from Hungary, settled in Tuscaloosa, Alabama, in 1866 and soon purchased a cotton mill, which he ran until 1887, when he became a vice president of the Tennessee Coal, Iron, and Land Company (Owen 3: 616). John McDougal, a Scotsman, settled in Tallahassee in 1870 and shortly thereafter organized a company that built a successful cotton mill (Rerick 1: 611). The flow of men and materials was richer than before the war. Cornelius Vanderbilt, Thomas Scott, Jay Gould, John Pierpont Morgan, and Henry Fricks, along with practically the whole directory of Matthew Josephson's "Robber Barons," saw rich financial opportunities in the South and took them (Woodward).

However, many of the larger capitalists in the New South were native men with rich experience in antebellum manufacturing. Samuel Morgan, a brother of the Confederate cavalry raider, organized a new mill at Nashville and along with Vernon K. Stevenson, the former western quartermaster, helped to rebuild that city. James Wesson raised a new factory and town in Mississippi, while Stephen Duncan, previously one of Mississippi's largest slaveholders, along with several merchants, organized the Natchez Cotton Mills Company.[31] In North Carolina, Henry Fries, brother and heir of Francis, built a third factory in 1880 and expanded into flouring and banking.[32] Thomas Holt in North Carolina's Alamance County launched several new mill enterprises. Bartholomew Egan of Louisiana organized the Mount Lebanon Manufacturing Company in 1869.[33] Many of the new manufacturers came from the countryside to make their fortunes in the new cities: men such as James Buchanan Duke and Richard Joshua Reynolds in North Carolina. Edwin W. Marsh, an heir of the Trion Manufacturing Company in north Georgia, diversified his holdings and became an important builder of the new Atlanta (Doyle 101–2). Mark A. Cooper, proprietor of a rural antebellum cotton mill, became in the New South one of Georgia's "more prominent iron entrepreneurs" (Lichtenstein 110). Henry F. DeBardeleben, an associate of Daniel Pratt of Alabama, expanded into coal and iron mines, sometimes using convict laborers, and helped establish the modern city of Birmingham (91–93).

The *Textile Manufacturer's Directory* of 1880 gave a clear indication of the ability of Southern mill men to survive and thrive (Wyckoff). The Bell factory was spinning again at Florence. Jacob Bonsack ran a new mill at Salem, Virginia. The Georgia factories at Athens, Milledgeville, Flint River, Houston County, Roswell, Trion, and Troup County were all again in successful operation under old hands. The peripatetic New Yorker Henry Merrell and his partners were again ensconced at Camden, Arkansas. Familiar names were spinning in Tennessee: Nicholson, Brient,

McElwee, Simonton, Lenoir, Faulkner, Oakley, Graham, Landis, and Orr. In South Carolina, Converse, Cannon, Bates, Fingers, and Hickman presided over the industrial revival. North Carolina river valleys were again populated with familiar mills: Cedar Falls, Rockfish, Franklin, Randolph, Homesley, Leaksville, Mountain Island, Orange, Battle, and Fries. In Virginia, the Mount Vernon, Falmouth, Battersea, Etrick, Matoaca, and Merchants mills were again turning. In addition, between 1880 and 1894, 245 new cotton factories rose in the South (Edmonds, *Facts* 25).

Each successive census seemingly validated the growing expectations. Richard Edmonds estimated that the South had 1.7 million spindles in 1890 and 3 million by 1894, by which date the region wove most of the national cotton crop (Edmonds, *Facts* 25, *Southern Redemption* 29). By 1903, 300 mills within a radius of 100 miles of Charlotte, North Carolina, turned 3 million spindles (Tompkins 183). A generation later, Southern mills consumed two-thirds of all American cotton while possessing half of the nation's spindles and 10 percent of the spinning capacity of the world (Edmonds, *Blue Book* 142–43). There was equally impressive growth in the development of railroads, mining, tobacco, and petroleum extraction, but manufacturing was the backbone of Southern economic development. The Southern Commercial Congress, held at Atlanta in 1910, validated this impressive growth.[34] Manufacturing incident to tobacco, minerals, and lumber was also in the ascendancy. A cigarette-making machine invented by John Bonsack, a son of the cotton and woolen manufacturer at Salem, Virginia, gave the South a virtual monopoly in this industry and made princely fortunes.

The great economic progress did not disguise the fact that Southern capitalism had an underside. Many antebellum social patterns of factory life persisted into the New South. In the pleadings for rebuilding, Grady and his supporters ignored the plight of rural black and white tenant farmers, child laborers in the factories, the prison convict lease system, and the discriminatory wage system under which women labored.[35] The antebellum use of leased convicts in the penitentiary factories of Mississippi, Texas, and Louisiana spawned a New South practice of leasing prisoners, usually blacks, for such private enterprises as building railroads, clearing swamps, and tending plantations. By 1886, 9,699 Southern prisoners out of 64,349 in the country worked under the convict lease system (Lichtenstein 19). Within the factory towns in the Gilded Age, with company-made rules, the family labor system kept 25,000 white children under fifteen years of age in the cotton mills (Flynt 49). Mines and tobacco factories employed others. Mill work hours remained like those in antebellum agriculture, from dawn to dusk, while the ten-hour day reigned across the North. In the Southern mills, blacks were generally excluded or relegated to menial tasks.

Thus the New South legacy of manufacturers was not unalloyed. Within a sea of regional poverty, they diversified the economy and planted their mills and paternalistically controlled villages across the landscape. Their bitter Civil War experiences engendered in them an almost maniacal fear of state regulation and red tape. They were the paladins of conservatism who opposed labor legislation (Evans 617–21). And they were instruments of Jim Crow. Within the political ranks of the ruling Conservative Party, manufacturers positioned themselves at the center of opposition to the emerging Populists and their biracial politics and economic war against monopolistic railroads, Wall Street bankers, and cotton speculators. They engineered the industrialization and urbanization of the New South and structured it around their own historical values. Their great strengths were that they imported or invented new technologies and introduced them into the South; they engendered transportation, modernization, and urbanization and, in cooperation with allies from the North, they aided capital formation. They also underwrote large humanitarian measures throughout the region, bequeathing to the New South not only an entrepreneurial mind-set but a stirring number of hospitals, universities, libraries, museums, and art galleries.

Southern progress had a price, one too high for the Populists, who vented an agrarian rage against the new industrialism. In a land characterized by vast poverty and its consequences, New South manufacturers were certainly not without critics, for their very successes created a glaring inequality of fortunes. A former Confederate officer wrote, "the loom is no longer heard in the home; vast factories, owned by monopolists for whom the cant of the age has already found their appropriate name of 'Kings of Industry' now undersell the home products everywhere" (Dabney 6). The list of popular economic grievances lengthened as the South became increasingly subservient to the financial interests of the Northeast. In stark contrast to the growing prosperity of new cities, the New South farm economy languished. The slow decline of the market price of cotton to 4 cents a pound in 1894 left desperate poverty among tenant farmers in much of the rural South, which also meant poor education and poor health. Populist leaders such as Thomas Watson of Georgia, Benjamin Tillman of South Carolina, Leonidas Polk of North Carolina, and Jeff Davis of Arkansas attacked the most visible symbols of the new wealth: factories, railroads, and banks.[36]

Rather than declare war on insurance companies, railroads, and industries, the Progressives sought to regulate the excesses of the new economics, to balance more carefully the interests of labor, race, and class. Appearing before the Southern Commercial Congress in 1910, Progressives Woodrow Wilson and Theodore Roosevelt condemned the political influence of national railroads that enforced discriminatory freight rates in the South, the growth of the trusts that violated the practices of the free market economy, the lack of credit for farmers, and the failure of the states to properly control working conditions.[37] As grievous as these problems were, they were far more amenable to solution than had been the slavery controversy.

Whatever the difficulties wrought by Southern capitalism, the New South movement brought positive rewards: an impressive amount of technological modernization, the generation of new wealth, and the unleashing of an enormous outburst of philanthropy. However, above all it demonstrated the realization of an Old South vision that commerce and manufacturing, railroads, and banking would bring economic balance to the agrarian way of life. Many of the Old South mill pioneers never lived to witness the rise of the new order. Francis Fries and Edwin M. Holt of North Carolina, William Gregg of South Carolina, Daniel Pratt of Alabama, and James D. B. DeBow of New Orleans were survived by a new generation of manufacturers who formed an integral part of the Southern political hierarchy. Many men who served their tutelage in the mills, such as Thomas Turner and Thomas Holt in North Carolina and Braxton Bragg Comer in Alabama, became popular New South governors.

Former Confederate quartermasters played a modest role in building Henry Grady's new order.[38] Abraham C. Myers returned from exile in England soon after the war and retired to a quiet life near Washington.[39] His military successor in Richmond, Alexander Lawton, was elected to the Georgia Senate as a Conservative during Reconstruction, helped to establish the American Bar Association in 1879 and served as its president, and at the end of his career was appointed by President Grover Cleveland as American minister to Austria-Hungary (*National Cyclopaedia of American History* 2: 148–49). William Crenshaw, the Richmond manufacturer who labored arduously on behalf of the Confederate Bureau of Foreign Supplies in England, returned from exile to establish a successful fertilizer company whose product was much in demand to replenish depleted cotton lands (36: 203). George Cunningham, Confederate quartermaster at Atlanta, made his postwar home in Nashville and rebuilt his hardware business with the proceeds of cotton smuggled abroad during the conflict.[40]

A generation after the war, as the old soldiers of the North and South met in reunion on the once bloody battlefields, the men who made the blue and the gray gathered regularly at their annual meetings in the American Textile Association and at the international fairs held in Philadelphia, Chicago, St. Louis, New Orleans, and Atlanta. There they had much to share: the desperate struggle to establish manufacturing in the antebellum period, the crises wrought by the Civil War years, the uncertainties of Reconstruction, and an unalloyed confidence in the future of American capitalism. At last, the eagle and the phoenix had joined. On this new field, Southern and Northern manufacturers alike were allies in pursuing economic progress through technological innovation; they formed an important cord in the emerging national tapestry.

ABBREVIATIONS

AHR – *American Historical Review*

Ala A – Manuscript Division, Alabama Department of Archives and History, Montgomery

Baker, Harvard – Baker Library, Harvard University, Cambridge

Boston Pub. – Boston Public Library, Boston

CSA – Confederate States of America

Duke – Perkins Library Duke University, Durham, N.C.

EHCRLMA – Early Handwritten Credit Reporting Ledgers of the Mercantile Agency, R. G. Dun Collection, Baker Library, Harvard University

Emory – Manuscript Division, Emory University, Atlanta, Ga.

ESTU – East Tennessee State University, Johnson City

Fla A – History and Research Division, Florida State Archives, Gainesville

Ga A – Georgia Department of Archives and History, Atlanta

GMfgCo – Graniteville Manufacturing Company Archives, Graniteville, S.C.

HPL – Huntsville Public Library, Huntsville, Ala.

Indiana – Manuscript Division, Lilly Library, Indiana University, Bloomington

JAH – *Journal of American History*

JNH – *Journal of Negro History*

JSH – *Journal of Southern History*

LC – Manuscript Division, Library of Congress, Washington, D.C.

LSU – Manuscript Division, Louisiana State University, Baton Rouge

Mass HS – Massachusetts Historical Society, Boston

Miss A – Mississippi Department of Archives and History, Jackson

Mor HS – Moravian Historical Society, Old Salem, N.C.

Ms. Census-1850 – Manuscript Returns of the Seventh Census, 1850, consisting of schedules of population, slaves, and industry

Ms. Census-1860 – Manuscript Returns of the Seventh Census, 1860, consisting of schedules of population, slaves, and industry

MVHM – Merrimac Valley Textile Museum, North Andover, Mass.

NA – National Archives of the United States, Washington, D.C.

NCA – North Carolina Department of Archives and History, Raleigh

Niles – *Niles' National Register* (Baltimore), old series

NWSU of La – Northwest State University of Louisiana, Natchitoches

ODU – Old Dominion University, Norfolk, Va.

Old Colony HS – Old Colony Historical Society, Taunton, Mass.

OR – *Official Records of the War of the Rebellion*

OR-Atlas – Atlas accompanying the *Official Records of the War of the Rebellion*

ORN – *Naval Records of the War of the Rebellion*

SHSP – Southern Historical Society Papers, Old Series

Tenn A – Tennessee State Library and Archives, Nashville

THR – *Textile History Review*

Tusc – President Andrew Johnson Museum and Library, Tusculum College, Greenville, Tenn.

Tx A – Archives Division, Texas State Library, Austin

U Ala – University of Alabama, Tuscaloosa

UGA – University of Georgia, Athens

UK – University of Kentucky, Lexington

UN Ala – University of North Alabama, Florence

UNC – University of North Carolina, Chapel Hill

USC – Caroliniana Library, University of South Carolina, Columbia, SC

USC, Aiken – University of South Carolina, Aiken, SC

U Tenn – University of Tennessee, Knoxville

U TX – University of Texas, Austin

UVa – University of Virginia, Charlottesville

Va HS – Virginia Historical Society, Richmond

VSL – Archives Branch, Virginia State Library, Richmond

Widener, Harvard – Widener Library, Harvard University, Cambridge

WM – College of William and Mary, Williamsburg, Va.

Abstract of Confederate Census of Major Lower South Factories—May 1864

Name of Factory	State	Cotton Looms	Wool Looms	Cotton Spindles	Cotton Goods Monthly	Woolen Goods Monthly	Cotton Sales to the CSA (6 months)	Woolen Sales to the CSA (6 months)
Alcova	Ga			840				
Alguandon	Ga			1,120				
Athens	Ga	60		1,800	31,791	3,079	88,293	12,958
Augusta	Ga	462		14,280	460,892		2,074,014	
Columbus	Ga	38		1,678	20,500	10,380		
Covington	Ga			2,272				
Eagle	Ga	196	86	9,596	109,000	55,000	110,200	296,000
Georgia	Ga	66		5,000	20,000		116,049	
Graniteville	SC	334		9,120	280,000		140,000	
Grant	Ga	52		2,150	36,000		144,000	
Gwinette	Ga	72		5,000	30,000			
High Shoals	Ga	27	3	2,616	22,222	1,118	60,000	
Ivy	Ga		24			12,789		69,314
Macon	Ga	100		5,200	89,369		123,125	
Manchester	Ga	40		2,556	13,482		67,141	
Montour	Ga	50	50	4,608	31,452		120,721	
Newton	Ga	12		2,160	62,625	13,943	10,413	
Oconee	Ga	90		4,336	10,130	9,207		
Planters	Ala	25		3,000	12,200	4,800	20,561	
Prattville	Ala	70	36	2,580	38,547	9,635	175,310	
Princeton	Ga	34		2,000	19,285	1,283	69,000	

Name	State							
Rock	Ga	16	4	1,188	17,646	1,100		
Roswell	Ga	166		2,600	71,698		408,750	
Saluda	SC							
Scottsville	Ala	25	6	2,016	25,149	2,736	105,205	8,826
Scull Shoals	Ga	5		2,000				
Tallassee	Ala	114	30	3,892	102,196	15,290	307,997	49,271
Thomaston	Ga	24		1,418	25,000			
Tuscaloosa	Ala	40	8	2,700	34,116	5,200	92,893	11,580
Vaucluse	SC	50		1,800	76,000		38,000	
Waynmanville & Franklin	Ga	24		2,992	33,600			
Totals:		2,192	247	102,518	1,672,900	145,560	4,271,672	496,024

The cotton and woolen goods figures are in yards, and the machinery totals include some looms and spindles not in use. The May survey revealed that Cunningham drew three-quarters of the Confederate woolen production in the Lower South from the Eagle factory at Columbus, while the Augusta factory provided half of his cotton goods. Twenty-four of the mills produced 370,152 pounds of yarn monthly, of which Cunningham received only 3,022 pounds. The largest yarn manufacturers were Roswell (47,208), Newton (47,000), New Manchester (32,140), Gwinette (28,125), Montour (26,000), and Saluda (22,700). Other significant producers were Waynmanville (18,500), New High Shoals (15,665), Athens (15,552), Georgia (15,000), Oconee (13,255), Tuscaloosa (13,000), and Covington (12,400). Extracted from Statement of Factories Inspected by G. W. Cunningham, Q.M., Entry 453, General Information Index, Miscellaneous Factories No. 2, Box 2, RG 109, NA.

APPENDIX B

Abstract of Confederate Census of North Carolina Factories—November 1864

Name of Factory	Looms Cotton (Wool)	Cotton Spindles	Wool Spindles	Cotton Goods Monthly	Woolen Goods Monthly	Cotton Yarns Monthly	Sales to	
							N.C.	QM
Alamance	30	1,400		10,000		9,750	1/5	1/3
Beaver Creek	80	3,000		25,000		5,000	1/2	
Big Falls		650				5,000	1/10	1/3
Blount Creek	9	1,280		13,000		3,700		
Buck Shoal		396				4,500	Little	1/3
Catawba Mills		532				4,500	1/6	1/3
Cedar Falls	50	2,406		30,000		5,000	1/3	1/3
Christian's		250				2,500	None	
Clover Orchard	14					10,000	All	
Concord	52	2,200		26,000		9,000	None	
Cross Creek		1,000				11,000	1/3	
Deep River	20	1,024		12,000		3,500	1/3	1/3
Eagle	10	528		5,000		4,000	Little	
Elkin	10	700		5,000		7,500	None	
Enterprise		250				3,000	1/6	1/2
Fayetteville Mills	48	2,000		28,000			1/3	
Granite Factory		528				9,000	Lit.	1/3
Granite Shoals		528				7,800	1/3	1/3
Hamburg		600				6,000	None	1/3
Homesly's	(6)	500	200			6,000	All	
Ivy Shoals	20	800				7,500	None	1/3
James Town	(12)		120		4,000		1/2	1/2

Johnson Little Riv.	5	1,320				12,000	Little	1/3
Jones, Mendenhall & Gardner								
Laurel Falls		568				6,000	1/8	
Leaksville								
Little River	21	1,024		8,500		5,000	Little	
Long Island	12	528		8,000		3,750	1/3	1/3
Mountain Island	52 (26)	3,000	627	8,000	8,000	6,500	9/10	
Orange					5,000		All	
Patterson's		625		4,800		9,000	1/9	1/3
Randolph	25	1,170		15,000		5,625	1/3	1/3
Richmond	30			10,686		16,250	1/3	1/3
Rockfish	119	4,200		70,000			1/8	
Rock Island	(70)		1,880		18,000		5/6	
Rocky River		700				7,500	None	
Salem	(26)	500	546		9,300	4,000	9/10	
Saxapahaw	20	1,300		12,800		7,500	3/4	
Stowe's	24	1,150		8,000		14,000	None	1/3
Swift Island								
Taylorsville		500				6,000	1/3	1/3
Turner's	10	650		4,000		6,000	Little	
Union Factory	20			15,000		2,800	1/3	1/3
Union Mills		1,000				9,500		
Wachovia		600				8,000	1/4	
Wood Lawn	42	1,400		10,000		3,500	1/3	1/3
Totals	723 (140)	40,807	3,373	328,786	44,300	257,175		

Yarn figures are in pounds, and cloth is in yards. Sales to the state of North Carolina or to Major Chisman of the Quartermaster Department are given as separate ratios. Data abstracted from Tabular Statement of Cotton & Woolen Factories in North Carolina inspected by Wm. A. Miller, bonded agent in Q.M. Deptmt 1864, Entry 453, General Information Index, Miscellaneous Factories No. 1, Box 2, RG 109, NA.

Statistical Survey of Workers in Ten Savannah River Mills—June 1864–June 1865

Mill Residents Community	White Male Workers	White Female Workers	Black Male Workers	Black Female Workers	Child (10–15)	Youth (15–20)	Adult (20–30)	Older (30–60)	Deaths (yr.)	In Mill
Athens	48	65	1		12	30	40	32	1	290
Augusta	350	450		1	200	350	200	51	7	2,500
Georgia	50	50	2		25	25	30	20		306
Graniteville	188	199	1		80	80	100	128	15	900
Hopewell	21	16	45	38	15	20	60	25	1	242
Iron Mills	31	60	8	12	40	3	37	11	3	250
Princeton	36	39	3		20	20	35	23	1	200
Richmond	35	57		1	12	30	30	21		
Scull Shoals	29	33	3		19	13	23	10	1	150
Vaucluse	45	77	3		27	30	33	38	12	300
Totals	833	1,046	66	52	450	621	588	359	47	5,417

There is an apparent miscalculation in the Princeton factory figures, which probably understates by 20 the number of female or slave workers. The daily wages earned by the 2,018 workers in June 1865 reflected the prewar income levels. Children earned daily from US 17 cents to US 35 cents, with US 20 cents being the most common wage, except for the Princeton factory, which paid only US 10 cents. Scull Shoals had not yet established a free wage scale in U.S. funds. The highest daily wage paid to experienced operatives was US$1.50 at four mills, US$2.00 at three mills, and US$2.50 at the Augusta factory. The mortality figures reflect a typhoid epidemic that struck the Savannah River region in February 1865. Among the deaths were 18 children, 16 youths, 7 adults, and 6 older workers. Twenty-seven persons succumbed at Vaucluse and Graniteville alone. The mills surveyed daily produced 45,120 yards of cotton goods and 3,480 pounds of yarn from 16,850 pounds of raw cotton. Data extracted from J. M. Bigney to W. G. Provost, July 10, 1865, GMfgCo Ms., GMfgCo.

APPENDIX D

Assets of Selected Mills in the Summer of 1865

Principal	Factory	Cotton Bales	Cash Assets
James Wesson[1]	Enterprise, Miss.	375	$100,000
A. P. Allgood[2]	Tryon, Ga.	700–800	
John White[3]	Athens, Ga.		$300,000
John Potter[4]	Bainbridge, Ga.		$105,230
Joseph Tooke[5]	Houston, Ga.	600	
Ephraim Hopping[6]	High Shoals, Ga.	700	
Enoch Steadman[7]	Gwinette, Ga.		(50,000 acres)
George Swift[8]	Flint River, Ga.		$500,000
David Jewell[9]	Rock Mills, Ga.	400–500	
Richard Baugh[10]	Florence, Ala.	3,000	
James Kirkman[11]	Tuscaloosa, Ala.	4,000	
Henry Fries[12]	Salem, NC	1,025	
Edward McGehee[13]	Woodville, Miss.	900	$100,000
William Gregg[14]	Graniteville, SC	1,000	
Jonathan Worth[15]	Cedar Falls, NC	over 100	
Frederick Neill[16]	Autaugaville, Ala	700	
William H. Young[17]	Eagle and Phoenix, Ga.		$600,000

Sources:

1. EHCRLMA, October 18, 1865, Miss.-Choctaw, V, 128.
2. EHCRLMA, February 27, 1866, Ga.-Chattooga, VI, 12.
3. EHCRLMA, November 12, 1866, Ga.-Clark, VI, 93.
4. EHCRLMA, August 1, 1866, Ga.-Decatur, IX, 79.
5. EHCRLMA, February 9, 1866, Ga.-Houston, XVII, 303.

6. EHCRLMA, January 23, 1866, Ga.-Morgan, XXII, 179; EHCRLMA, January 23, 1866, Ga.- Walton, XXII, 179.

7. EHCRLMA, January 23, 1866, Ga.-Newton, XXV, 11.   ·

8. EHCRLMA, January 29, 1867, Ga.-Upson, XXXIII, 191.

9. EHCRLMA, December 8, 1865, Ga.-Warren, XXXV, 116.

10. EHCRLMA, October 28, 1865, Ala.-Lauderdale, XIII, 27.

11. EHCRLMA, December 28, 1865, Ala.-Tuscaloosa, XXIV, 110.

12. Jos. Martin's Statement of Investigation of Cotton Stored in South Carolina 1866, 1866, Fries Ms., Mor HS; John Fries, Reminiscences of Confederate Days, April 14, 1923, Private Papers, NCA.

13. EHCRLMA, October 31, 1867, Miss.-Wilkinson, XXII, 144.C.

14. Minutes of the Board of Directors, April 26, 1865, GMfgCo Ms., GMfgCo.

15. Jonathan Worth to George Makepeace, September 19, 1865, *The Correspondence of Jonathan Worth* 1: 427.

16. Mims 263.

17. Memorandum of Business Thought, September 1874, Mill Account Book, 1856–57, Stowesville Cotton Factory Ms., Duke.

NOTES

Preface

1. Among monographs on manufacturing within single Southern states, Mary A. DeCredico emphasizes the pecuniary motives of Confederate business leaders, scarcity of raw materials, and ineffective leadership in *Patriotism for Profit*. A more detailed study relating planters to business interests is Ernest Lander's *The Textile Industry in Antebellum South Carolina*. Jerrell H. Shofner and William W. Rogers's "Textile Manufacturing in Florida during the Civil War" has good data on that state. Much literature is found in dissertation form. Richard Griffin's "North Carolina: The Origin and Rise of the Cotton Textile Industry, 1830–1880" has a valuable list of individuals and mills. Other useful studies are Laurel E. Janke Wilson's "Textile Production in Nineteenth Century Orange, Alamance, and Durham Counties, North Carolina," and Percy Love Guyton's "The Government and Cotton to 1862." The latter has extensive and valuable tables on the flow and consumption of the annual crop. Maurice K. Melton's "Major Military Industries of the Confederate Government" and John R. DeTreville's "The Little New South: Origins of Industry in Georgia's Fall Line Cities, 1840–1865," reveal the strengths of urban communities. Randall M. Miller's "The Cotton Mill Movement in Ante-Bellum Alabama" presents a solid treatment of early industry in that state.

An excellent biography of an important Alabama leader, carefully built on manuscripts, local government records, and newspapers, is Curt John Evans's "Daniel Pratt of Prattville." Evans interprets Pratt in a much more favorable light than the earlier studies of Randall Miller, Wayne Flynt, or Jonathan Weiner, but he also describes an aggressive entrepreneur who both opposed secession and supported slavery.

2. Beatty's careful study describes slaveholding protocapitalists being transformed into a bourgeoisie, with worker class conflicts and a colonial type dependency upon the Northeast.

Introduction

1. In 1852, the entire country had 23,283 miles of telegraph lines, which swelled to 83,000 miles by 1865 (Thompson 243).

2. See Richard W. Griffin's provocative essay, "Textile Industry," 1227–29.

3. Cotton processing employed the largest number of laborers in the Western world: perhaps one-third of the British workforce and 130,000 in the United States. For a fuller discussion of the contemporary cotton trade, see Christy's article in Elliott, *Cotton Is King*, and Mitchell, *European Historical Statistics*, 429.

4. England had 2,650 mills and 30 million spindles.

5. See *An Exposition of the Property of the Etowah Manufacturing and Mining Company* (1). The Confederate government later valued the whole at $1 million and purchased it (Adjutant General to M.S. Temple, January 24, 1864, Etowah Manufacturing and Mining Company, Confederate Papers, M346, reel 287. Company listings within these papers are alphabetical and chronological.).

6. These were established in 1832, in 1838, and in the 1840s, respectively (Pollock 34; Will Book, January 1, 1878, Va.-Petersburg, 310–15; Ms. Census-1860, Pop., Va.-Dinwiddie, 294/2879). In using population schedules for 1860, the page is cited first and the household number second. There is wide variation in the spelling of local place names in the nineteenth century, but those accepted as standard are found in Fisher's *A New and Complete Statistical Gazetteer of the United States of America*.

7. John Fries, Reminiscences of Confederate Days, April 4, 1923, Private Papers Ms., NCA; Tabular Statement of Cotton & Woolen Factories North Carolina Inspected by Wm. A. Miller, bonded agent in Q.M. Deptmt 1864, Entry 453, General Information Index, Miscellaneous Factories No. 1, Box 2, RG 109, NA (hereafter Miscellaneous Factories No. 1); Statement of Factories Inspected by G. W. Cunningham, Q.M., Entry 453, General Information Index, Miscellaneous Factories No. 2, Box 2, RG 109, NA (hereafter Miscellaneous Factories No. 2).

8. Both Holt and Fries may be referenced in Bess Beatty's able study *Alamance* (14–31); The Mercantile Agency, The Early Handwritten Reporting Ledgers of the Mercantile Agency, N.C.-Alamance, II, 8.h, R. G. Dun Collection, Baker, Harvard (hereafter EHCRLMA, state, locality, volume, and page).

9. EHCRLMA, II, 5; Ms. Census-1860, Pop., N.C.-Alamance, 191/1400.

10. The principal biographies of Gregg are Broadus Mitchell's *William Gregg, Factory Master of the Old South*, and Tom Downey's well-cast essay, "Riparian Rights and Manufacturing in Antebellum South Carolina," 77–108. Downey demonstrates that the South Carolina legislature, whether "capitalist" or "precapitalist" in mind-set, strongly encouraged the development of manufacturing at Horse Creek in Edgefield District.

11. William Gregg to Theodore D. Wagner, July 27, 1863, Theodore D. Wagner Ms., South Carolina Historical Society; see Steadman (42) for a list of stockholders.

12. Steadman 41; EHCRLMA, February 1880, S.C.-Barnwell, III, 158; EHCRLMA, April 1871, S.C.-Edgefield, IX.a, 78.

13. EHCRLMA, March 26, 1858, IX.a, 71.

14. One of King's managers left a rich autobiographical account of his experiences at Roswell (Merrell 143, 150, 192–201).

15. Ms. Census-1850, Indus., Ala.-Autauga; for a recent biography of Pratt, see Evans, "Daniel Pratt of Prattville."

16. *Southern Cultivator*, November 1861, 291, cited in Parrish and Willingham (9).

Chapter 1. The Advent of Abraham C. Myers, Quartermaster General of the Confederacy

1. For a manufacturer's hostile response, see Merrell (296). Robert Barnwell Rhett successfully urged the Confederate convention to adopt the "true doctrines of political economy" and to deny all bounties, taxes, or duties "to promote or foster any branch of industry" (Ball 201–2).

2. By contrast, Gorgas developed long-range plans, established uniform production standards, instituted a system of quality control, administered qualifying examinations, trained a bureaucracy, or, in a word, created a modern business system within the Ordnance Bureau (Collins 517–44). In some measure, Myers and Gorgas were both captives of Christopher Memminger's failed financial policies, of which Charles Ball writes, "The root cause of these [currency and funding] disasters was a complete absence of effective executive management and leadership" (Ball 267).

3. Duff Green to General George Goldwaite, March 21, 1861, A. B. Moore Ms., Ala A.

4. This sum was periodically raised and was $25 by August 1861. Abraham C. Myers to Leroy P. Walker, July 3, 1861, Letters Sent to the Confederate Secretary of War, April 1861–January 1864, Quartermaster General's Office ms., ch. 5, vol. 157, RG109, NA (hereafter Letters Sent, CSA QM Ms.).

5. A. C. Myers to G. W. Randolph, August 16, 1862, ibid.

6. Pierre T. G. Beauregard to Leroy P. Walker, February 27, 1861, "Abraham Myers File." Compiled Service Records of Confederate Generals and Staff Officers, and Nonregimental Enlisted Men, M331, reel 185, NA (hereafter Compiled Service Records); A. C. Myers to C. M. Conrad, February 8, 1861, ibid.

7. A. C. Myers to C. M. Conrad, February 8, 1861, ibid.; A. C. Myers to W. P. Miles, February 7, 1861, William P. Miles Ms., UNC.

8. P. T. G. Beauregard to L. P. Walker, February 27, 1861, Compiled Service Records, M331, reel 185.

9. A. C. Myers to W. P. Miles, March 14, 1861, William P. Miles Ms.

10. A. C. Myers to D. E. Twiggs, May 16, 1861, *The War of the Rebellion: A Compilation of the Official Records of the Union and Confederate Armies* (128 vols.), series I, vol. 15: 501 (hereafter OR).

11. George Davis to James A. Seddon, April 26, 1864, OR, IV, 3: 318–22. The Confederate Senate did not approve Myers's rank of lieutenant colonel until February 1862; by contrast, Josiah Gorgas was confirmed in March 1861 and Lucius Northrop three months later.

12. A. C. Myers to W. P. Miles, March 14, 1861, William P. Miles Ms.

13. A. C. Myers to W. L. Cabell, April 24, 1861, War Department Collection of Confederate Records, T131, reel 7, NA (hereafter War Department Collection).

14. Circular, April 2 and 30, 1861, ibid.

15. A. C. Myers to J. P. Benjamin, February 28, 1862, Letters Sent, CSA QM Ms.

16. United States, Department of the Navy, *Official Records of the Union and Confederate Navies in the War of the Rebellion* (30 vols.), series I, vol. 4: 22–48 (hereafter ORN).

17. "Report of the Quartermaster General," Message of the President (Richmond, Va., February 19, 1865); Myers to James A. Seddon, April 23, 1863, Letters Sent, CSA QM Ms.

18. The Clothing Bureau employed 2,000 employees within two years and had expenditures "amounting to a little less than ten millions of dollars" (Richard P. Waller to Abraham Myers, June 23, 1863, Letters Received by the Confederate Quartermaster General, 1861–1865, M469, reel 5, NA [hereafter Letters Received by CQG]).

19. William G. Ferguson to Alexander R. Lawton, September 15, 1863, reel 6, ibid.

20. Ibid.

21. "Remarks of Major Julius Hessee, read before the Court of Inquiry, February 3d, 1862" (Mobile, 1862), 5, Parrish #4881.

22. Some field commanders and civilians took exception to these appointments and intrigued to keep the Confederate Congress from confirming them. Winnemore was not confirmed by the Confederate Senate until March 9, 1865 (Alexander R. Lawton to Jefferson Davis, February 29, 1865, "J. T. Winnemore File," Compiled Service Records, M331, reel 271).

23. A. C. Myers to Vernon K. Stevenson, September 10, 1861, OR, I, 52, pt. 2: 142–43.

24. Ibid.

25. A. C. Myers to J. M. Galt, June 5, 1861, War Department Collection, T131, reel 7.

26. "Memoranda Book Relating to Agents and Supplies," CSA QM Ms., ch. V, vol. 227, 3; "Report of Quarter Master General," OR, IV, 1: 884; A. C. Myers to James Seddon, January 26, 1863, Letters Sent, CSA QM Ms.

27. Alexander H. Stephens to George W. Randolph, September 2, 1862, Letters Received by the Confederate Secretary of War, 1861–1865, M437, reel 34, NA (hereafter Letters Received by CSW); W. H. J. Walker to Joseph E. Brown, March 21, 1861, Joseph E. Brown Ms., Ga A.

28. George Schley to Joseph E. Brown, March 20, 1861, Joseph E. Brown Ms., Ga A.

29. A. C. Myers to George Schley, April 22, 1861, War Department Collection, T131, reel 7; see also George Schley to J. E. Brown, March 20, 1861, Joseph E. Brown Ms., Ga A; George Schley to Alexander Stephens, August 28, 1862, Letters Received by CSW, M437, reel 34; Alexander Stephens to G. W. Randolph, September 2, 1862, ibid.

30. A. R. Lawton to Judah P. Benjamin, OR, I, 6: 307.

31. Maryland troops were clothed and equipped through such an initiative by Mrs. Bradley Johnson, wife of the general (Davis 21–22, 136).

32. OR, IV, 1: 496.

33. Myers to Benjamin, November 18, 1861, Letters Sent, CSA QM Ms. The bureau's official count of regiments was 100 (April 1861), 198 (July 1861), 400 (November 1861), 475 (February 1862), 547 (October 1862), 713 (October 1863), and 1,000 (April 1865).

34. Douglas Ball is highly critical of the inability of Secretary of the Treasury Christopher Memminger to secure specie, reliably fund the Confederate debt, create a viable currency, and control inflation. These problems became more acute as the war progressed (Ball 113–19).

35. Confederate regulations stipulated reduced issues for the second and following years of service:

Clothing Issues	For Three Years			Total
	1st	2nd	3rd	
Cap	2	1	1	4
Cover	1	1	1	3
Coat (Jacket)	2	1	1	4
Trousers	3	2	2	7
Flannel Shirts	3	3	3	9

Flannel Drawers	3	2	2	7
Boots	4	4	4	12
Stockings	4	4	4	12
Great Coat	1			1
Blanket	1		2	3

Confederate States of America, War Department, *Regulations for the Army of the Confederate States*, 108; South Carolina, *Journal of the Convention of the People of South Carolina*, 633. Union army regulations were about the same. *New York Herald*, January 13, 1862.

36. A. C. Myers to J. M. Galt, April 19, 1861, War Department Collection, T131, reel 76.

37. Circular, May 16, 1861, ibid., reel 7.

38. George H. Camp to J. M. Selkink, April 25, 1861, Barrington King Ms., Ga A; Camp to I. Bryan, April 25, 1861, ibid.

39. George H. Camp to President, April 16, 1861, ibid.

40. Isaac Scott to E. A. Nisbet, March 2, 1861, Confederate Papers Relating to Citizens or Business Firms, M346, reel 910, NA (hereafter Confederate Papers).

41. George H. Camp to Hay & McDevitt, April 23, 1861, Barrington King Ms., Ga A; Camp to Van Waganer & Washburn, July 18, 1861, ibid. Two Connecticut owners of the Graniteville mill had dividends sequestered (J. J. Ryan to William Gregg Jr., March 5, 1863, Graniteville Manufacturing Co. Ms., Graniteville Manufacturing Company Archives, Graniteville, S.C. [hereafter GMfgCo. Ms.]).

42. William Gregg to John C. Whiten, November 26, 1860, John C. Whiten Ms., Baker, Harvard; J. J. Gregg and Co. to Hay, McDevitt and Co., November 17, 1860, J. J. Gregg and Co. Ms., USC.

43. George H. Camp to William Gregg, July 25, 1861, Barrington King Ms., Ga A.

44. F. and H. Fries to W. Turner, July 12, 1861, Fries Ms., Mor HS.

45. *Richmond Enquirer*, October 17, 1861.

46. Francis Fries to H. W. Fries, October 24, 1861, Fries Ms., Mor HS.

47. Barrington King to A. Low & Co., May 24, 1861, Barrington King Ms., Ga A.

48. James Gregg to Hay and McDevitt, November 19, 1860, GMfgCo. Ms., GMfgCo.

49. George H. Camp to Stephens & Moore, July 23, 1861, Barrington King Ms., Ga A.

50. Barrington King to W. E. Baker, May 4, 1861, ibid.

51. Barrington King to W. R. Gignilliat, May 4, 1861, ibid.

52. George H. Camp to Tate, Stephen, & Co., May 21, 1861, ibid.

53. G. H. Camp to N. I. Bryan, July 2, 1861, ibid.

54. Francis Fries to Lewis Thomas, July 15, 1861, Fries Ms., Mor HS.

55. George Camp to John W. Pratt, August 13, 1861, Barrington King Ms., Ga A.

56. James Gregg to Mr. Duncan, December 18, 1860, GMfgCo. Ms., GMfgCo.

57. G. H. Camp to Kent, Paine, & Co., July 6, 1861, Barrington King Ms., Ga A.

58. *Richmond Enquirer*, October 17, 1861.

59. G. H. Camp to J. M. Selkin, May 14, 1861, Barrington King Ms., Ga A.; Camp to N. I. Bryan, July 23, 1861, ibid.

60. By 1860, some Virginia mills exported osnaburgs to South America, and Graniteville goods were sold in China. Consequently, Gregg believed that "the spinners and manufacturers could throw their surplus stock upon foreign markets, and thus preserve their home or domestic trade from injury" (*Proceedings 6*).

61. John Schley, of the Richmond factory, advocated that the Confederacy buy cotton at 11 cents a pound, issue notes based on this collateral, and levy an export tax to pay the interest. The notes would then constitute the circulating medium. Duff Green's proposal was similar. See Schley; *Proceedings of the Convention of Cotton Planters, held in Macon, Ga., July 4, 1861 with a Communication on the Proposed Issue of Treasury Notes by the Confederate Government, by Duff Green, Esq.*, 2.

62. Ball argues that the seizure of all available specie was a simpler and more practicable route to financial stability (147–48, 79–93).

63. *The Rebellion Record*, 2: 407–11. The Confederate Currency Act of May 16, 1861, provided for the issuance of treasury notes.

64. William [sic] Pratt to John K. Wrenn, April 18, 1861, Milner, Wood & Co. Ms., UN Ala.

65. Francis Fries to William Steel, April 5, 1861, Fries Ms., Mor HS.

66. Circular, May 14, 1861, War Department Collection, T131, reel 7, NA.

67. *DeBow's Review* 31 (July 1861): 87ff; *Augusta Daily Constitutionalist*, July 9, 1861; Ball 203–4.

68. *Public Laws of the Confederate States of America*, 130.

69. William Gregg to John C. Whiten, March 31, 1861, John C. Whiten Ms., Baker, Harvard.

70. Two Georgia supporters of Constantine Baylor's ideas on direct trade, Thomas Butler King and Gazaway Bugg Lamar, became major blockade-runners (*Augusta Daily Constitutionalist*, August 11, 1861).

71. Georgia, *Journal of the House of Representatives of the State of Georgia*, 142–43.

72. C. G. Baylor to J. E. Brown, June 14, 1861, Joseph E. Brown Ms., Ga A.

73. In fact, Baylor sailed to New York in October 1864 and before Unionist meetings attacked the Confederate government as "a fraud and a despotism,"

much to the embarrassment of Governor Brown and cotton manufacturers who had assumed he was embarking on a legitimate foreign mission (*New York Times*, October 15 and 18, November 8, 1864).

74. Georgia, *Journal of the House of Representatives of the State of Georgia*, 346.

75. James Gregg to L. P. Walker, March 14, 1861, GMfgCo. Ms., GMfgCo.

76. A. C. Myers to J. J. Gregg, July 15, 1861, War Department Collection, T131, reel 7.

77. A. C. Myers to Martin, Weakley & Co., July 3, 1861, ibid.

78. George Camp to C. G. Memminger, July 23, 1861, Barrington King Ms., Ga A; George Camp to John H. Reagan, August 8, 1861, ibid.

79. *Democrat* (Huntsville, Ala.), September 11, 1861.

80. A. B. Moore to L. P. Walker, July 21, 1861, OR, IV, 1: 493.

81. A. C. Myers to Larkin Smith, May 26, 1861, Compiled Service Records, M331, reel 230.

82. Ibid.

83. A. C. Myers to T. R. R. Cobb, June 7, 1861, War Department Collection, T131, reel 7.

84. A. C. Myers to L. P. Walker, August 12, 1861, Letters Sent, CSA QM Ms.

85. Green and Scott, July 2, 1861, "Falmouth Cotton Mill—Letterpress Book—1859–1867," Duff Green Ms., Duke.

86. OR, I, 51, pt. 2: 588.

87. J. B. Ferguson to R. P. Waller, August 8, 1861, Letters Received by CQG, M469, reel 1.

88. J. B. Ferguson to R. P. Waller, August 7, 1861, ibid.

89. George Camp to J. B. Ferguson Bros & Co., August 15, 1861, Barrington King Ms., Ga A.

90. Adam Johnson, contract with J. B. Ferguson, August 1, 1861, Confederate Papers, M346, reel 863.

91. J. B. Ferguson to R. P. Waller, August 8, 1861, Letters Received by CQG, M469, reel 1.

92. George Camp to J. B. McClellan, August 10, 1861, Barrington King Ms., Ga A.; J. B. Ferguson to Barnett, Micou & Co., August 27, 1861, Confederate Papers, M346, reel 44.

93. Foster, Fant, and Porter to J. B. Ferguson, November 2, 1861, Confederate Papers, M346, reel 318.

94. F. and H. Fries to John L. Martin, April 29, 1862, Fries Ms., Mor HS. Some of these establishments fell behind Union lines in the spring of 1862 and redirected their goods elsewhere.

95. A. C. Myers to L. P. Walker, August 24, 1861, Letters Sent, CSA QM Ms.

96. S. H. Oliver to J. B. Ferguson, January 22, 1862, Confederate Papers, M346, reel 270.

97. Alexander H. H. Stuart thought that 100,000 sheep were clipped in Augusta County alone during the first winter of the war (Stuart to George W. Randolph, April 29, 1862, OR, I, 51, pt. 2: 550).

98. A. C. Myers to L. P. Walker, May 13, 1861, ibid., IV, 1: 314–15.

99. A. C. Myers to L. P. Walker, August 10, 1861, Letters Sent, CSA QM Ms.

100. L. P. Walker to G. B. Lamar, OR, IV, 1: 557.

101. J. A. Rice to W. B. Wood, April 19, 1861, Milner, Wood & Co. Ms., UN Ala.

102. F. M. Rogers to Joseph W. Stewart, May 22, 1861, ibid.

103. John O. Noble to Milner, Wood, & Wren, May 8, 1861, ibid.; Thomas W. Jones to Milner, Wood and Co., May 8, 1861, ibid.; W. B. Miller & Co to Milner, Wood & Wren, ibid.; Dr. William R. Holt to William A. Carrigan, September 24, 1861, James Wilson White Ms., UNC.

104. George H. Camp to R. M. McPherson, September 3, 1861, Barrington King Ms., Ga A.

105. Barrington King to Rev. W. E. Baker, March 22, 1862, ibid.

106. Ibid.

107. John McVea to Major General Stephen Lee, June 24, 1864, OR, IV, 3: 590.

108. Ibid., 1: 506.

109. "Memoranda Order Book Relating to Agents and Supplies," Confederate Quartermaster Ms., ch. V, vol. 127, 3, RG 109, NA.

110. OR, VI, 1: 538. In February 1862, Benjamin wrote Davis that "the supplies of clothing, shoes, tents, and other articles embraced within the scope of the Quartermaster's Bureau, could not possibly have been furnished in time for the wants of the present winter had not the entire population aided with common accord the efforts of the government" (Benjamin to Davis, February 1862, ibid., 959).

111. Ibid., IV, 1: 534.

112. Gen. George Goldthwaite to Duff C. Green, March 22, 1862, ibid., 1012.

113. Ibid., 349.

114. Ibid., I, 51, pt. 2: 557.

115. Ibid., 588.

116. "Report by Lucius J. Dupree," March 29, 1862, War Department Collection, T131, reel 8.

117. Richmond Enquirer, October 17, 1861.

118. V. K. Stevenson to W. W. Mackall, October 4, 1861, Compiled Service Records, M331, reel 236.

119. George W. Cunningham, Voucher, January, February 1862, ibid., reel 68.

120. W. J. Anderson to R. F. Jones, July 25, 1864, ibid., reel 7.

121. J. Alexander to Jefferson Davis, March 19, 1862, OR, IV, 1: 1008.

122. W. J. Anderson to L. Polk, October 6, 1861, Compiled Service Records, M331, reel 7.

123. John S. Besser to Francis R. Lubbock, December 10, 1861, Lubbock Ms., Tx A.

124. "Message of Gov. F. R. Lubbock to the Extra Session of the Ninth Legislature of the State of Texas, Delivered, Feb. 5th, 1863," *State Gazette* (Austin), 1863, 7. In some items, this was about 10 percent of Federal procurement for eight months of 1861, which was 1.5 million shirts and drawers, 250,000 jackets, but 700,000 frock coats (*New York Herald*, January 13, 1863).

125. Young, Wriston, and Orr to James Sloan, October 2, 1861, Civil War Military Collections, NCA.

126. F. Fries to H. W. Fries, October 7, 1861, Fries Ms., Mor HS.

127. F. Fries to James Sloan, December 27, 1861, ibid.

128. R. L. Patterson to F. Fries, December 8, 1861, ibid.

129. Barrington King to Stephen Elliott, August 13, 1861, Barrington King Ms., Ga A.

130. A. C. Myers to J. F. Minter, December 6, 1861, War Department Collection, T131, reel 7.

131. A. P. Allgood to G. W. Randolph, April 22, 1862, Letters Received by CSW, M437, reel 24.

132. Young, Wriston, and Orr, to James Devereux, March 12, 1862, Civil War Military Collections, NCA.

133. A. R. Homesley to Charles W. Garrett, June 12, 1862, ibid.

134. F. and H. Fries to Gov. H. F. Clark, April 18, 1862, Fries Ms., Mor HS.

135. S. T. Wilder to J. & J. H. Webb, March 28, 1862, James Webb Ms., UNC; F. & H. Fries to McMillan, April 6, 1862, Fries Ms., Mor HS.

136. Young, Wriston, and Orr to H. A. Dowd, May 23, 1863, Civil War Military Collections, NCA.

137. F. and H. Fries to John Linton, January 5, 1862, Fries Ms., Mor HS; R. P. Waller to L. Smith, November 7, 1862, Compiled Service Records, M331, reel 258.

138. J. B. Ferguson to Larkin Smith, June 25, 1862, Compiled Service Records, reel 92.

139. A. C. Myers to G. W. Randolph, May 24, 1862, Letters Sent, CSA QM Ms.

140. A. C. Myers to G. W. Randolph, July 5, 1862, ibid.

141. *Dallas Herald*, November 29, 1862; Voucher of James B. Earle, December 22, 1862, Confederate Papers, M346, reel 271.

142. F. and H. Fries to Adam Butner, December 29, 1862, Fries Ms., Mor HS; also F. and H. Fries to Adam Butner, December 30, 1862, ibid.

143. The Mexican border state of Nuevo Leon y Coahuila, with two power mills and cotton factories holding 14,500 spindles, did a large Confederate trade (Tyler 100, 110).

144. George W. Kendall to D. Richardson, November 6, 1864, in *Texas Almanac for 1865*, 39.

145. F. and H. Fries to H. A. Dowd, April 28, 1863, Fries Ms., Mor HS.

146. F. Fries to J. R. McLean, February 9, 1863, ibid.

147. J. P. Benjamin to Davis, February 1862, OR, IV, 1: 959.

148. A. C. Myers to W. H. Haynes, March 30, 1863, War Department Collection, T131, reel 9; A. C. Myers to Vance and Brother, March 31, 1863, ibid.; A. C. Myers to T. J. Washington, June 9, 1863, ibid.

149. A. C. Myers to G. W. Randolph, May 23, 1862, ibid., reel 8.

150. R. P. Waller to Larkin Smith, November 7, 1862, Compiled Service Records, M-331, reel 258.

151. Winnemore expended $2.6 million in the six weeks before the Crescent City fell (A. C. Myers to G. W. Randolph, April 24, 1862, Letters Sent, CSA QM Ms.).

152. *Mobile Advertiser and Register*, June 13, 1861.

153. L. B. Northorp to G. W. Randolph, April 1, 1862, OR, IV, 1: 1035.

154. A. S. Johnson to J. P. Benjamin, February 27, 1862, "Gen. A. S. Johnston's Command, Sept. 1861–April 1862," Confederate States of America, Letters and Telegrams Sent Ms., Chapter II, vol. 217, RG 109, NA; W. J. Anderson to R. F. Jones, July 25, 1864, Compiled Service Records, M331, reel 7.

155. OR, IV, 1: 1038.

156. A. C. Myers to T. J. Jackson, June 16, 1862, War Department Collection, T131, reel 8.

157. A. C. Myers to G. W. Randolph, April 2, 1862, Letters Sent, CSA QM Ms.; A. C. Myers to J. E. Johnston, May 21, 1862, War Department Collection, T131, reel 8; A. C. Myers to Beauregard, May 21, 1862, Compiled Service Records, M-331, reel 185.

158. R. E. Lee to A. C. Myers, June 10, 1862, Letters Received by CQG, M469, reel 2; R. E. Lee to A. C. Myers, September 21, 1862, OR, I, 19, pt. 2: 614.

159. F. & H. Fries to Young, Wriston & Orr, March 17, 1862, Fries Ms., Mor HS; EHCRLMA, N.C.-Guilford, XI, 518; F. & H. Fries to R. P. Waller, October 7, 1862, Fries Ms., Mor HS.

160. Francis Fries to G. W. Garrett, October 17, 1862, Fries Ms., Mor HS.

161. F. Fries to R. P. Waller, October 23, 1862, ibid.

162. Edward Willis to L. D. Childs, February 2, 1864, Edward Willis Ms., LC; Willis to A. R. Lawton, February 3, 1864, ibid.; G. S. Crafts to William B. B. Cross, November 6 and 7, 1864, Letters Received by CQG, M469, reel 11.

163. E. Willis to Thomas Jordan, January 16, 1864, Edward Willis Ms., LC.

164. William A. Finger to George W. Cunningham, December 1, 1864, Letters Received by CQG, M469, reel 12.

165. William Browne to Jefferson Davis, December 23, 1862, Jefferson Davis Ms., Duke.

166. Ibid.

167. Ibid.

168. I. T. Winnemore to A. C. Myers, August 28, 1862, Letters Received by CQG, M469, reel 2.

169. William Browne to Jefferson Davis, December 23, 1862, Jefferson Davis Ms., Duke.

170. R. P. Waller to Larkin Smith, November 7, 1862, Compiled Service Records, M331, reel 258.

171. Ibid. Upon his occupation of New Orleans, General Benjamin Butler took a large interest in Ed. Gautherin and Co. (OR, III, 2: 766–75; Parton 377–82).

172. R. P. Waller to Larkin Smith, November 7, 1862, Compiled Service Records, M331, reel 258.

173. F. W. Dillard to A. C. Myers, January 6, 1863, ibid., reel 76.

174. G. W. Cunningham to William P. Johnston, April 9, 1863, OR, I, 23, pt. 2: 767.

175. R. P. Waller to A. C. Myers, April 24, 1863, Letters Received by CQG, reel 5.

176. Richmond's monthly receipts of Virginia woolens in early 1862 amounted to: Danville (5,000 yards), Manchester (10,000 yards), Crenshaw (25,000 yards), Scottsville (several thousand yards), Kelly, Tackett and Ford (several thousand yards). The cotton mills of Richmond and Petersburg consumed 600 bales, or 300,000 pounds, of cotton a month and plentifully supplied "cotton shirting for linings, & cotton drillings and osnaburgs for drawers." In September 1862, Waller manufactured "from eight to ten thousand suits of pants & jackets per week," but continued work depended upon obtaining large supplies of woolens from such Georgia mills as the Eagle factory at Columbus and the Ivy mill at Roswell. While cotton production was up over the prewar period, woolen production fell below the 600,000 pounds processed in 1853 (Richard P. Waller to Larkin Smith, September 30, 1862, Compiled Service Records, M331, reel 258; Ms. Census-1860, Industry, Va.-Henrico; *DeBow's Review* 32 [March–April 1862]: 328; Fisher 724).

177. "Abstract, Goods Recd by R. P. Waller," February 7, 1863, Compiled Service Records, M331, reel 258.

178. A. C. Myers to J. A. Seddon, January 7, 1863, Letters Sent, CSA QM Ms.

179. F. and H. Fries to H. A. Dowd, April 28, 1863, Fries Ms., Mor HS.

180. A. C. Myers to H. Lee, July 21, 1863, OR, IV, 2: 254.

181. R. P. Waller to L. Smith, June 11, 1863, Compiled Service Records, M331, reel 258.

182. John W. Leak to H. A. Dowd, December 18, 1863, Civil War Military Collections, NCA; John Milton, November 1863, "Letterbook, 1861–1863," Milton Ms., U. Fla.

183. "Memoranda Book Relating to Agents and Supplies," 1864, CSA QM Ms., ch. V, vol. 227, 17, RG 109, NA.

184. I. T. Winnemore to A. C. Myers, April 4, 1863, Letters Received by CQG, M469, reel 5.

185. "Memoranda Book Relating to Agents and Supplies," 1864, CSA QM Ms., ch. V, vol. 227, p. 17, RG 109, NA.

186. John Milton, November 1863, "Letterbook, 1861–1863," Milton Ms., U. Fla.

187. F. and H. Fries to Thomas and Son, August 4, 1863, Fries Ms., Mor HS.

188. F. and H. Fries to P. A. Wilson, September 17, 1863, ibid.; Illegible to H. A. Dowd, August 17, 1863, Civil War Military Collections, NCA; R. M. Stafford to H. A. Dowd, May 30, 1863, ibid.

189. A. R. Lawton to J. M. McCue, October 12, 1863, War Department Collection, T131, reel 9.

190. Major Thornton A. Washington to General H. P. Bee, December 4, 1862, "Thornton Washington File," Compiled Service Records, M331, reel 260.

191. Thornton A. Washington to James A. G. Dickerson, January 19, 1863, ibid.; Washington to E. K. Smith, November 23, 1863, ibid.

192. A. C. Myers to J. A. Seddon, March 30, 1863, Letters Sent, CSA QM Ms.

193. John S. Cobb to A. R. Lawton, October 17, 1863, Letters Received by CQG, M469, reel 6.

Chapter 2. The Reign of Quartermasters

1. The act of April 16, 1862, drafted able-bodied men between eighteen and thirty-five; that of October 1862 extended the age to forty-five.

2. "Time Book—Cedar Falls Manufacturing Co., 1846–1865, Sept.–June," Private Papers, NCA.

3. J. G. Gibbes and Co. to D. F. Jamison, January 6, 1862, *Journal of the Convention of the People of South Carolina*, 355–56, 380.

4. Isaac Powell to J. E. Brown, April 25, 1862, Joseph E. Brown Ms., Ga A.

5. A. P. Allgood to J. E. Brown, February 18, 1862, ibid.

6. "Statement of Hands &c Employed by F. & H. Fries," November 6, 1862, Letterbook April 62–February 63, Fries Ms., Mor HS.

7. J. J. Gresham to G. W. Randolph, May 2, 1862, Letters Received by CSW, M437, reel 27.

8. A. Chase to G. W. Randolph, May 9, 1862, ibid.

9. Atwood and Rokenbaugh to G. W. Randolph, May 21, 1862, ibid.

10. Thomas N. Cooper to G. W. Randolph, May 14, 1862, ibid.

11. Ibid.

12. Petition to the Secretary of War, May 1863, Letters Received by CSW, M437, reel 27.

13. J. J. Gregg to G. W. Randolph, May 21, 1862, ibid.

14. Atwood and Rokenbaugh contract with J. B. Ferguson, July 2, 1862, Confederate Papers, M346, reel 753; W. E. Jackson contract with J. B. Ferguson, June 25, 1862, ibid., reel 28.

15. A. C. Myers to G. W. Randolph, June 2, 1862, Letters Sent, CSA QM Ms.; L. Smith to I. T. Winnemore, July 30, 1862, War Department Collection, T131, reel 8. Josiah Gorgas did not have to report monthly.

16. J. B. Ferguson to William Gregg, September 19, 1862, Gregg Ms., GMfgCo.

17. L. Smith to I. T. Winnemore, July 30, 1862, War Department Collection, T131, reel 8.

18 J. B. Ferguson to William Gregg, September 19, 1862, Gregg Ms., GMfgCo.

19. A. C. Myers to G. W. Randolph, May 23, 1862, Letters Sent, CSA QM Ms.

20. A. C. Myers to J. P. Benjamin, October 10, 1861, ibid.

21. F. Fries to W. W. Holden, August 17, 1862, Fries Ms., Mor HS.

22. C. T. Haigh to C. W. Garrett, July 3, 1862, Civil War Military Collections, NCA.

23. F. and H. Fries to James Chesnut Sr., October 23, 1862, Fries Ms., Mor HS.

24. Ibid.

25. Francis Fries to W. W. Holden, November 7, 1861, ibid.

26. Ibid.

27. Francis Fries to W. W. Holden, August 27, 1862, ibid.

28. Ibid.

29. Ibid.

30. Ibid.

31. Thomas M. Holt to H. A. Dowd, September 15, 1863, Civil War Military Collections, NCA.

32. George Camp to N. I. Bayard, September 3, 1861, Barrington King Ms., Ga A.

33. *Macon Telegraph*, February 26, 1862; Circular, "Office—Roswell Manufacturing Company," March 12, 1862, Confederate Imprints, 1861–1865, microfilm edition, number 2938 in Crandall.

34. Young, Wriston, and Orr to James Devereux, March 24, 1862, Civil War Military Collections, NCA.

35. D. F. Ramseur to Z. B. Vance, n.d., Governor's Papers, NCA.

36. J. B. Ferguson to L. Smith, June 25, 1862, Compiled Service Records, M331, reel 92.

37. Z. B. Vance to W. N. Edwards, September 18, 1862, OR, IV, 1: 85–86.

38. Conscription Act, October 11, 1862, ibid., 166–67.

39. This act included the "20 Negro" provision, which excluded one white male for each twenty slaves.

40. H. Atwood to J. A. Seddon, December 6, 1862, Letters Received by CSW, M437 reel 30.

41. M. Holt to William A. Carrigan, November 5, 1862, James Wilson White Ms., UNC; George Camp to N. I. Bayard, September 3, 1862, Barrington King Ms., Ga A.

42. "Minutes of the Graniteville Manufacturing Company," July 15, 1862, GMfgCo Ms., GMfgCo.

43. "Augusta Factory Record Book, 1858–1911," June 30, 1862, GMfgCo Ms., USC, Aiken.

44. Expenses for the same period amounted to $34,288.56 (ibid., December 31, 1862).

45. Robert M. Patton to John G. Shorter, September 9, 1862, Shorter Ms., Ala A.

46. F. & H. Fries to R. P. Waller, October 9, 1862, Fries Ms., Mor HS.

47. F. & H. Fries to Charles W. Garrett, October 13, 1862, ibid.

48. Zebulon Vance to J. & H. Fries, October 10, 1862, Copies of Letters and Telegrams Sent and Received by Governor Zebulon B. Vance of North Carolina, 1862–1865, T781, NA (hereafter Copies of Letters and Telegrams).

49. F. and H. Fries to Z. Vance, October 13, 1862, Fries Ms., Mor HS.

50. Governor's Report, November 17, 1862, OR, IV, 1: 183.

51. F. & H. Fries to James Sloan, November 28, 1862, Fries Ms., Mor HS.

52. F. & H. Fries to Z. Vance, December 2, 1862, ibid.

53. "Statement of Cost of Goods Manufactured by Us for the State of North Carolina," November 5, 1862, ibid.

54. F. & H. Fries to J. Sloan, November 28, 1862, ibid.

55. T. M. Holt to H. A. Dowd, January 13, 1864, Civil War Military Collections, NCA.

56. E. M. Holt to W. A. Carrigan, November 5, 1862, James Wilson White Ms., UNC; T. M. Holt to H. A. Dowd, January 13, 1864, Civil War Military Collections, NCA.

57. Charles T. Haigh to C. W. Garrett, October 30, 1862, Civil War Military Collections, NCA.

58. G. O'Neill to C. W. Garrett, October 28, 1862, ibid.

59. Ibid.

60. C. T. Haigh to C. W. Garrett, October 30, 1862, ibid.

61. Ibid.

62. T. R. Tate to C. W. Garrett, November 7, 1862, ibid.; John Shaw to C. W. Garrett, November 1, 1862, ibid.; John Newlin to C. W. Garrett, n.d., ibid.; John W. Leak to Peter A. Wilson, March 12, 1863, ibid.

63. Virginia, General Assembly, "Testimony before the Committee on Extortion, 1863" (January 26, 1863), Confederate Imprints, 1861–1865, microfilm edition, doc. 22, 3, number 2281 in Crandall.

64. Ibid.

65. Osnaburgs, worth 17 cents in January 1862, advanced to 21 cents in June, 33 cents in November, and 40 cents in December. When the Bureau paid 33 cents, "a few bales were sold at auction, in order to test their market value, and brought 66 cents per yard." There was also a heavy appreciation in the price of canvas, from 17 cents in June 1861 to 22 cents in January 1862, 35 cents in November 1862, and 45 cents in December 1862 (ibid., 4).

66. Ibid.

67. Ibid., 5.

68. It was founded in 1849; the mill proprietors claimed five profitless years before the war and an average of only 7 percent dividends thereafter (ibid.).

69. Ibid. Canvas duck sold in May 1861 for 12 1/2 cents a yard and advanced to 35 cents in September 1862, an average monthly increase of over 7 percent (ibid.).

70. Ibid.

71. Ibid.

72. Like others before him, McIlwaine claimed his mill earned no dividends between July 1854 and January 1860 (ibid.).

73. Ibid., 4.

74. Virginia, General Assembly, "Testimony before the Committee on Extortion, 1863" (January 26, 1863), Confederate Imprints, 1861–1865, microfilm edition, doc. 22, 4, number 2281 in Crandall.

75. "Proceedings of the First Confederate Congress, Third Session in Part, March 20–May 1, 1863," April 2, 1863, in Southern Historical Society Papers 53: 82.

76. F. & H. Fries to R. P. Wilson, February 6, 1863, Fries Ms., Mor HS.

77. F. Fries to W. T. Dortch, April 3, 1863, ibid.

78. Henry Atwood to J. A. Seddon, December 6, 1862, Letters Received by CSW, M437, reel 30.

79. F. Fries to J. R. McLean, March 10, 1863, Fries Ms., Mor HS.

80. A. C. Myers to I. T. Winnemore, July 21, 1863, War Department Collection, T131, reel 9.

81. "Augusta Factory Record Book, 1858–1911," August 8, 1862, GMfgCo Ms., USC, Aiken.

82. Ibid., December 31, 1862.

83. A. C. Myers to W. E. Jackson, March 26, 1863, War Department Collection, T131, reel 9.

84. "Augusta Factory Record Book, 1858–1911," February 16, 1863, GMfgCo ms., USC, Aiken. The company had previously declined to sell Rev. Joseph R. Wilson, father of Woodrow Wilson, forty bales of cloth on behalf of the Georgia Relief and Hospital Association, inviting him instead to buy at the pubic auctions (ibid., June 18, 1861).

85. T. M. Holt to H. A. Dowd, January 13, 1864, Civil War Military Collections, NCA.

86. Jasper Stowe to E. M. Holt, November 15, 1864, Archibald A. T. Smith Ms., UNC.

87. "Remarks of Major Julius Hessee, read before the Court of Inquiry, February 3d, 1862" (Mobile, 1862), 2–40, Parrish 4881.

88. Ibid., 3–18.

89. A. C. Myers to G. W. Jones, April 14, 1863, June 20, 1863, War Department Collection, T131, reel 9. "Junius" was the pseudonym of a patriot writer in the Revolutionary period.

90. Ibid., April 15, 1863.

91. Ibid., April 21, 1863.

92. Ibid., May 2, 1863.

93. A. C. Myers to G. W. Randolph, April 24, 1862, Letters Sent, CSA QM Ms.

94. The problem was a common one suffered by other retreating quartermasters. James Walker to A. C. Myers, July 22, 1862, Letters Received by CQG, M469, reel 3.

95. I. T. Winnemore to Jefferson Davis, February 29, 1864, Compiled Service Records, M331, reel 271.

96. A. C. Myers to W. J. Anderson, February 16, 1863, War Department Collection, T131, reel 9; A. C. Myers to W. J. Anderson, June 1, 1863, ibid.

97. I. T. Winnemore to Jefferson Davis, February 29, 1864, Compiled Service Records, M331, reel 271.

98. Endorsement by A. R. Lawton in ibid.

99. A. C. Myers to H. Hirsch, February 16 and March 3, 1863, War Department Collection, T131, reel 9.

100. Ibid., June 4, 1863.

101. H. W. Mercer to G. W. Randolph, September 20, 1862, Letters Received by CQG, M469, reel 3.

102 A. C. Myers to H. Hirsch, March 3, 1863, War Department Collection, T131, reel 9.

103. E. McLean to S. Cooper, November 29, 1964, Letters Received by CQG, M469, reel 13. Howell Cobb later ordered Hirsch out of Savannah, but the order was countermanded by the secretary of war (Herman Hirsch to A. R. Lawton, March 8, 1865, ibid., reel 14).

104. Robert Kean, then chief of the Bureau of War, found nothing admirable in this "official execution," for there was "no moral wrong in this act, no direct injury to the country." He observed a "great clamor . . . against other quartermasters, and as soon as a man is found who owns his transaction, believing it harmless, his head goes off—sacrifice to public wrath and official purity" (Kean 48). Benjamin Bloomfield at Yorktown and James Glover at Knoxville faced similar charges (L. Smith to B. Bloomfield, July 17, 1862, War Department Collection, T131, reel 8; A. R. Lawton to J. Glover, March 2, 1864, ibid., reel 10).

105. A. R. Lawton to C. W. Styron, January 25, 1864, War Department Collection, T131, reel 9.

106. J. Blue Moore to A. C. Myers, April 24, 1862, Letters Received by CQG, M469, reel 2.

107. Cash Book of A. M. Barbour, QM CSA, September 19, 1862, Records of the Confederate States of America (Pickett Papers), reel 117, microcopy in LC. Barbour purchased horses and wagons from John W. Coyle for $18,000 and 16,680 sacks, mostly from Lynch and Callendar. He hired his own forage agents, teamsters, blacksmiths, and free black laborers. On February 6, 1862, he paid out $200,000 in bounty money and on April 6 and 7 sold 244 horses at Charlottesville for $11,474, leaving no receipts.

108. A. R. Lawton to J. E. Johnston, October 27, 1863, War Department Collection, T131, reel 9.

109. Ibid.; A. R. Lawton to L. Polk, February 9, 1864, ibid., reel 10.

110. A. R. Lawton to A. M. Barbour, February 11, 1863, ibid., reel 9. Barbour in turn delayed in distributing the army payroll, owing Braxton Bragg's forces $2 million in October 1863.

111. A. M. Barbour to J. E. Johnston, October 5, 1863, OR, I, 30, pt. 4: 729.

112. A. M. Barbour to W. H. Browne, January 4, 1863, Letters Received by CQG, M469, reel 4; special order of J. E. Johnston and A. M . Barbour, in William Barnwell File, August 13, 1864, Compiled Service Records, M331, reel 15. Beauregard authorized this practice in May 1862, after his retreat to Corinth (George W. Brent to Eugene E. McLean, May 25, 1862, OR, I, 10, pt. 1: 544).

113. A. C. Myers to A. M. Barbour, July 22, 1863, War Department Collection, T131, reel 9.

114. A. R. Lawton to J. E. Johnston, October 27, 1864, ibid.

115. In an attempt to refurbish his army after the loss of Vicksburg, Barbour sent identical telegrams to Livingston Mims at Enterprise, J. L. Calhoun at Montgomery, Isaac Winnemore at Augusta, George Cunningham at Atlanta, and F. W. Dillard at Columbus: "How many blankets, shoes, and tents can you furnish immediate to this army?" Mims promised 6,000 suits of clothing and ordered "osnaburgs from Choctaw factory made into tents rather than shirts and drawers, if you think best." Dillard offered 8,000 uniforms and 7,000 pairs of shoes, and Cunningham offered 16,200 pairs of shoes. Deeming this insufficient, Barbour moved to secure his own supplies (Alfred M. Barbour to J. E. Johnston, October 5, 1863, OR, I, 30, pt. 4: 729–30).

116. J. E. Johnston to J. E. Seddon, December 1863, in Johnston (266).

117. A. R. Lawton to E. E. McLean, December 10, 1863, War Department Collection, T131, reel 9.

118. E. McLean to A. R. Lawton, March 15, 1864, Letters Received by CQG, M469, reel 9.

119. Ibid.

120. J. L. Morgan to A. M. Barbour, June 23, 1863, ibid., reel 8.

121. C. W. Robertson to D. H. Toole, September 8, 1863, ibid.

122. E. McLean to A. R. Lawton, March 15, 1864, ibid., reel 9.

123. But about 1,700 of these were payroll accounts (ibid.).

124. Agreement between A. M. Barbour and G. W. Bagby, May 2, 1864, G. W. Bagby Ms., Va HS.

125. Ibid.

126. A. R. Lawton to D. H. Maury, January 15, 1863 [1864], War Department Collection, T131, reel 9.

127. Agreement between A. M. Barbour and G. W. Bagby, May 2, 1864, G. W. Bagby Ms., Va HS.

128. "Statement of Differences Arising upon the Settlement of the Account of A. M. Barbour," February 15, 1865, Barbour File, Compiled Service Records, M331, reel 15.

129. B. S. Gaither to J. A. Seddon, December 22, 1863, ibid., reel 185; J. Devereux to A. Myers, October 3, 1861, ibid.

130. His contractors included Isaac Shiver, Jacob Levy, Alfred Moses, R. Becher, Ulm Frishman, David Wiell, A. Cohen and Son, and Horah and Ramsay ("Abstract of Articles Purchased by A. Myers, Capt. and A.Q.M. for 3d Quarter ending, September 30th, 1861," September 30, 1861, Compiled Service Records, M331, reel 185). One of the first to complain of this practice was Francis Fries, who told James Sloan that he was "exceedingly annoyed by the Jews who came to buy

the fine jeans, who claim to have contracts with you for caps etc" (F. and H. Fries to James Sloan, July 22, 1862, Fries Ms., Mor HS).

131. Solomon A. Myers to James G. Martin, January 20, 1862, Civil War Military Collections, NCA; Henry C. Jenks to J. A. Martin, December 13, 1861, ibid.

132. Henry C. Jenks to J. A. Martin, December 13, 1861, ibid.

133. L. O'B. Branch to J. G. Martin, December 20, 1861, ibid.

134. "Affidavit of T. W. Allison and N. R. Mendenhall," December 10, 1862, Compiled Service Records, M331, reel 185; "Affidavit of D. R. Newsom," December 10, 1862, ibid.

135. A. Myers to L. B. Northrop, February 23, 1864, ibid.

136. W. F. Alexander to W. W. Peirce, War Department Collection of Confederate Records, T131, reel 9.

137. Inspection by illegible, January 20, 1865, Letters Received by CQG, M469, reel 13.

138. Ibid.

139. The Richmond bureau itself often encouraged smuggling. Philip Whitlock, a detailed cutter, went north in March 1863 to replenish his purse and the depot's supplies of thimbles, needles, and tailoring necessities (Herman Whitlock, September 8, 1860, EHCRLMA, Va.-Richmond 43, 256; "Account by Whitlock," 1909, Philip Whitlock Ms., Va HS). Josiah Gorgas also sent men across the Potomac for supplies and profit (John Jones 2: 114). In 1864, Braxton Bragg investigated the Richmond Clothing Depot and court-martialed eight men (Braxton Bragg to William M. Gardner, September 16, 1864, OR, IV, 3: 725).

140. "Proceedings of the First Confederate Congress, Third Session in Part, January 29– March 19, 1863," in *Southern Historical Society Papers* 48: 144.

141. "Proceedings of the First Confederate Congress, Fourth Session, Dec. 7, 1963–Feb. 18, 1864)," in *Southern Historical Society Papers* 50: 38.

142. In March 1862, as the permanent government was seated, the *Richmond Examiner* railed, "the representation of the Synagogue is not diminished; it remains full" (March 20, 1862).

143. A. C. Myers to L. P. Walker, August 26, 1861, Letters Sent, CSA QM Ms.; J. P. Benjamin to A. R. Lawton, September 29, 1861, OR, IV, 1: 624.

144. G. A. Wallace to Secretary of War, September 15, 1862, Letters Received by CSW, M437, reel 78.

145. A. C. Myers to A. B. Barbour, March 1, 1862, War Department Collection, T131, reel 8.

146. Henry A. Wise to Judah P. Benjamin, March 22, 1862, OR, IV, 1: 1015.

147. A. C. Myers to R. E. Lee, July 14, 1862, ibid.

148. A. C. Myers to J. A. Seddon, November 22, 1862, Letters Sent, CSA QM Ms.

149. The troops from other states were better supplied. An officer in the Twenty-first North Carolina from Salem wrote, "our regiment are better prepared for the winter than almost any other troops that I have seen in the service" (J. C. James to F. Fries, December 10, 1862, Fries Ms., Mor HS).

150. A. C. Myers to J. P. Benjamin, January 6, 1862, Letters Sent, CSA QM Ms.

151. A. C. Myers to J. A. Seddon, December 11, 1862, ibid.

152. A. C. Myers to J. A. Seddon, November 22, 1862, ibid.

153. A. C. Myers to J. A. Seddon, December 11, 1862, ibid.

154. William G. Ferguson to *Richmond Whig*, November 18, 1862, ms. in Compiled Service Records, M331, reel 92.

155. A. C. Myers to G. W. Randolph, November 12, 1862, Letters Sent, CSA QM Ms.

156. Ibid.

157. By contrast, Confederate supply problems in Virginia and the Trans-Mississippi contributed to the dismissal of Secretary of War George Wythe Randolph in the fall of 1862 (*Richmond Whig*, November 19, 1862). Randolph also unwisely endorsed a scheme proposed by Myers and Lucius B. Northrop to trade cotton through the lines at Memphis for bacon and blankets. Jefferson Davis abrogated the scheme and fired Randolph (Kean 32; John Jones 1: 224–25).

158. Thomas N. Waul inspected Myers's bookkeeping without result (*Journal of the Congress of the Confederate States of America* 1: 720).

159. A. C. Myers to J. A. Seddon, February 14, 1863, Letters Sent, CSA QM Ms.

160. A. C. Myers to A. F. Cone, February 19, 1863, War Department Collection, T131, reel 9.

161. A. C. Myers to F. W. Dillard, March 3, 1863, Ibid.

162. Colonel Cone was later brought before a court martial by General Braxton Bragg, who found thirty-two violations of Confederate statutes in the operations of the Richmond Clothing Depot (Braxton Bragg to William M. Gardner, September 16, 1864, OR, IV, 3: 725–27; John Jones 2: 301).

163. A. C. Myers to J. A. Seddon, December 9, 1862, Letters Sent, CSA QM Ms.

164. "Act to Prevent Fraud in the Quartermaster's and Commissary's Departments, and the Obtaining under False Pretense Transportation for Private Property," *Public Laws of the Confederate States of America*, 159–60.

165. The Richmond depot alone employed fifty-one quartermasters and assistants and a commensurate number of clerks (ibid., 114–15; John Jones 1: 244, 2: 118).

166. A. C. Myers to L. Smith, April 14, 1863, OR, IV, 2: 483; J. A. Seddon to Jefferson Davis, January 3, 1863, Letters Sent by the Confederate Secretary of War to the President, 1861–1865, M523, reel 1, NA.

167. Circular, March 21, 1863, War Department Collection, T131, reel 9. The quartermasters were Larkin Smith (Virginia), William W. Peirce (North Carolina), Hutson Lee (South Carolina), Isaac Winnemore (Georgia), J. L. Calhoun (Alabama), James Glover (Tennessee), and Livingston Mims (Mississippi).

168. A. C. Myers to L. Smith, April 14, 1863, OR, IV, 2: 483. Dillard was given control of all hides in the Lower South, and Major Charles S. Carrington was allowed to draw forage in the Upper South (Circular, March 21, 1863, War Department Collection, T131, reel 9). There were strong protests against the new policy. Cunningham at Atlanta and Leonidas Polk opposed it. Cunningham was denied permission "to retain an Agent at Charleston to purchase articles imported by Frazer & Co." (A. C. Myers to C. W. Cunningham, May 11, 1863, ibid.). Polk, who along with Beauregard and Maury Dabney proceeded to ignore the whole procedure, questioned the propriety of drawing supplies through a government agency "which is 1,000 miles off" while manufacturing depots were at hand (L. Polk to J. A. Seddon, February 29, 1984, OR, I, 30, pt. 4: 815).

169. Richard Waller administered the depot's $10 million budget, and O. T. Weisiger was placed in charge of the Manufacturing Department with sixty cutters and trimmers and 2,000 seamstresses. A separate Shoe Department was established. William Ferguson served as Waller's assistant "in all Contracts, Purchases, and general supervision of the whole" (R. P. Waller to A. C. Myers, June 23, 1863, Letters Received by CQG, M469, reel 5).

170. A. C. Myers to J. A. Seddon, January 26, 1863, OR, IV, 2: 372.

171. E. V. Early to Unknown, August 5, 1863, Letters received by CQG, M469, reel 8.

172. A. C. Myers to R. E. Lee, March 19, 1863, War Department Collection, T131, reel 9.

173. A. C. Myers to J. L. Corley, March 3, 1863, ibid.

174. Ibid., May 13, 1863. The sinking of the *Leopard*, "having 40,000 pairs of shoes, etc. on board," created considerable concern at the Clothing Depot (John Jones 1: 291).

175. A. C. Myers to G. F. Maynard, June 30, 1863, War Department Collection, T131, reel 9.

176. A. C. Myers to J. L. Corley, July 8, 1863, ibid.

177. "Letter from Major-General Henry Heth, of A. P. Hill's Corps, A. N. V.," SHSP 4: 157.

178. Lee originally anticipated fighting his crucial battle on the rolling hills around Cashtown, two days' march from the Potomac, with General Stuart's independent cavalry command available for action.

179. A. C. Myers to J. L. Corley, July 8, 1863, War Department Collection, T131, reel 9.

180. A. C. Myers to Hutson Lee, July 8 and 18, 1863, ibid.; A. C. Myers to J. L. Corley, July 17, ibid.

181. Kilpatrick to Alfred Pleasonton, July 5, 1863, OR, I, 27, pt. 1: 988; Lee to S. Cooper, July 31, 1863, ibid., pt. 2: 309.

182. Lee to J. A. Seddon, July 16, 1863, *The Wartime Papers of R. E. Lee*, 553.

183. Jefferson Davis to Confederate Senate, January 27, 1864, OR, IV, 3: 49–50.

184. J. B. Hope to Annie, August 12, 1863, J. B. Hope Ms., WM.

185. Stephen Mallory, June 12, 18, 1861, Diary (Typed Copy), vol. 1, Mallory Ms., UNC.

186. Illegible to W. P. Miles, February 24, 1862, William P. Miles Ms., ibid.; Richard S. North to W. P. Miles, February 24, 1862, ibid.

187. Henry Gourdin to W. P. Miles, February 23, 1862, ibid.

188. Jefferson Davis to Miles, February 27, 1862, ibid.; J. B. Jones to Miles, April 16, 1862, ibid.

189. Confederate States of America, Congress, House of Representatives, "Report of the Committee on Military Affairs on the Message of the President, Transmitting a Communication from the Secretary of War, Relative to the Quartermaster General," 2.

190. Ibid., 4–12; James Richardson 1: 262.

191. George Davis to J. A. Seddon, April 26, 1864, OR, IV, 3: 319; "Proceedings of the First Confederate Congress, Third Session" (January 29–March 19, 1863), in *Southern Historical Society Papers* 48: 153.

192. William P. Miles et al. to Jefferson Davis, April 28, 1863, Compiled Service Records, M331, reel 185; "Proceedings of the First Confederate Congress, Fourth Session, Dec. 7, 1963–Feb. 18, 1864," in *Southern Historical Society Papers* 50: 111.

193. A. R. Lawton to J. A. Seddon, July 28, 1863, Compiled Service Records, M331, reel 154.

194. See "Alexander Robert Lawton"; DeCredico 59.

195. Gilbert Moxley Sorrel, a fellow Georgian, found Lawton to be "an admirable, well-rounded character, with many friends" (Sorrel 190).

196. J. B. Hope to Annie, August 8, 1863, J. B. Hope Ms., WM.

197. Ibid.; also J. B. Hope to Annie, August 10, 1863, ibid.

198. The newspaper argued that while many quartermasters got rich, few were cashiered, and the issue of an "an honest and diligent administration" was more important than the appointment of either Myers or Lawton.

199. Kean 126; "Proceedings of the First Confederate Congress, Fourth Session, Dec. 7, 1863–Feb. 18, 1864," in *Southern Historical Society Papers* 50: 109–12.

200. "Proceedings of the First Confederate Congress, Fourth Session, Dec. 7, 1863–Feb. 18, 1864," in *Southern Historical Society Papers* 50: 109.

201. Ibid., 273, 274; *Journal of the Congress of the Confederate States* 3: 604.

202. Confederate States of America, Congress, House of Representatives, "Report of the Committee on Military Affairs on the Message of the President," 10, 12.

203. Davis's prime congressional foe, Henry S. Foote, defeated the effort with an exhaustive debate on frauds within the bureau ("Proceedings of the First Confederate Congress, Fourth Session, Dec. 7, 1863–Feb. 18, 1864," in *Southern Historical Society Papers* 50: 38–39; John Jones 2: 124, 135, 151; Kean 133).

204. In frustration, Davis and Seddon ordered Myers to resume his station and serve as a colonel under General Lawton, a service he refused.

205. A. R. Lawton to J. A. Seddon, March 4, 1864, A. R. Lawton Ms., UNC.

206. *Journal of the Congress of the Confederate States of America* 2: 812; George Davis to J. A. Seddon, April 26, 1864, OR, IV, 3: 322. Myers's version of these events, that he was an innocent victim of Davis's maliciousness, can be followed in A. C. Myers to Braxton Bragg, June 13, August 1864, Braxton Bragg Ms., Western Reserve Historical Society, Cleveland, cited in Burke (34–36). The Senate, which defended Myers, also authorized local attorney generals to indict army quartermasters charged with corruption ("Proceedings of the First Confederate Congress, Fourth Session, Dec. 7, 1863–Feb. 18, 1864," in *Southern Historical Society Papers* 50: 283–84).

207. G. A. Trenholm to R. E. Lee, March 11, 1863, Lee's Headquarters Papers, A.N.VA., Va HS.

208. A. C. Myers to J. A. Seddon, June 21, 1863, OR, IV, 2: 755, 599. This amount reached $128 million in December 1864 (A. R. Lawton to J. A. Seddon, December 29, 1864, OR, IV, 3: 974; A. R. Lawton to E. D. Fry, January 17, 1865, War Department Collection, T131, reel 10).

Chapter 3. Confederate Mobilization

1. Historians have been highly critical of Memminger's attempt to finance an expensive modern war with credit rather than taxation (Ball 238–41; Todd 130–34).

2. A. R. Lawton to R. E. Lee, September 7, 1863, War Department Collection, T131, reel 9.

3. J. Longstreet to S. Cooper, December 16, 1863, OR, I, 31, pt. 3: 837.

4. Endorsement in Longstreet to Cooper, December 16, 1863, ibid.

5. F. W. Sims to Lawton, February 22, 1864, ibid., IV, 3: 92–93; Lawton to Seddon, October 24, 1863, ibid., 2: 883; F. W. Sims to Lawton, October 3, 1863, ibid., 881–82.

6. Endorsement in Longstreet to Cooper, December 16, 1863, ibid., I, 31, pt. 3: 837–38.

7. Ibid., January 2, 1864; ibid., 32, pt. 2: 508–9.

8. Lawton to Davis, January 7, 1864, War Department Collection, T131, reel 9.

9. Lawton to Joseph E. Johnston, February 9, 1864, ibid., reel 10.

10. A. R. Lawton to J. Davis, January 7, 1864, ibid., reel 9.

11. Cross to Cone, December 12, 1863, ibid.

12. Lawton to Longstreet, March 9, 1865, ibid., reel 10.

13. At this time, John W. Mallett and Josiah Gorgas were instituting a uniform system of production in the Ordnance Department (Collins 517).

14. Wartime Atlanta is ably described in DeCredico (35–39).

15. Lawton to Cunningham, December 19, 1863, War Department Collection, T131, reel 9.

16. Cunningham to William Preston Johnston, April 9, 1863, OR, I, 23, pt. 2: 767, 769.

17. Livingston Mims to J. R. Waddy, February 5, 1863, ibid., 24, pt. 3: 616–17.

18. Lawton to Cunningham, December 19, 1863, War Department Collection, T131, reel 9.

19. Ibid.

20. Cunningham to Lawton, January 29, 1864, Compiled Service Records, M331, reel 68.

21. Cunningham to Lawton, May 2, 1864, Letters Received by CQG, M469, reel 8.

22. Ibid.

23. Cunningham to Lawton, January 29, 1864, Compiled Service Records, M331, reel 68.

24. Miscellaneous Factories No. 1.

25. Cunningham to Lawton, January 29, 1864, Compiled Service Records, M331, reel 68.

26. Lawton to James R. Mallory, September 3, 1864, War Department Collection, T131, reel 10.

27. Cunningham to Lawton, January 29 1864, Compiled Service Records, M331, reel 168.

28. Cunningham to Lawton, May 2, 1864, Letters Received by CQG, M469, reel 8.

29. Miscellaneous Factories No. 2.

30. Ibid.

31. Ibid.

32. E. E. McLean to A. R. Lawton, March 15, 1864, Letters Received by CQG, M469, reel 9.

33. William Barnwell to A. R. Lawton, June 5, 1864, Letters Received by CQG, M469, reel 10.

34. A. R. Lawton to A. F. Cone, March 11, 1864, War Department Collection, T131, reel 10.

35. W. B. B. Cross to G. W. Cunningham, June 4, 1864, ibid.

36. W. B. B. Cross to A. F. Cone, August 12, 1864, ibid.

37. "Abstract, Goods Recd. by R. P. Waller, Maj. & Q.M. from Jany. 1st 1863 to Feby 7th 1863," February 7, 1863, Compiled Service Records, M331, reel 258.

38. Voucher, William G. Ferguson, July 12, 1864, ibid., reel 92.

39. Lynch and Callender to W. G. Ferguson, February 1, 1864, Letters Received by CQG, M469, reel 8.

40. Endorsement by W. B. B. Cross, W. G. Ferguson to A. F. Cone, February 2, 1864, ibid.

41. Voucher, W. G. Ferguson, July 12, 1864, Compiled Service Records, M331, reel 92.

42. Lawton to Cunningham, April 9, 1864, War Department Collection, T131, reel 10.

43. Circular, April 23, 1864, Compiled Service Records, M331, reel 68.

44. W. B. B. Cross to John de Bree, April 14, 1864, ORN, II, 2: 645–46.

45. Lawton to A. L. Reves, April 1, 1864, Compiled Service Records, M331, reel 154.

46. "Resources of the Confederacy in February, 1865," in *Southern Historical Society Papers* 2: 127.

47. John de Bree to Lawton, April 16, 1864, ORN, II, 2: 646.

48. John de Bree to S. R. Mallory, April 28, 1864, ibid., 644–45.

49. "Estimated Wants of the Diffe. Bureaux in the Way of Cotton Goods," April 1864, Letters Received by CQG, M469, reel 9.

50. Enclosure, "Bureau Estimates," in W. B. B. Cross to G. W. Cunningham, April 1864, ibid.

51. Cunningham to Lawton, January 29, 1864, Compiled Service Records, M331, reel 68.

52. Josiah Gorgas to Lawton, April 4, 1864, Letters Received by CQG, M469, reel 8.

53. "Bureau Estimates," in W. B. B. Cross to Cunningham, April 1864, ibid., reel 9.

54. O. T. Weisiger to W. B. B. Cross, April 29, 1864, ibid.

55. Cunningham to Lawton, January 29, 1864, Compiled Service Records, M331, reel 68; Cunningham to Lawton, May 2, 1864, Letters Received by CQG, M469, reel 8.

56. John de Bree to S. R. Mallory, April 28, 1864, ORN, II, 2: 644–45.

57. "Resources of the Confederacy in February, 1865."

58. Ibid. The head of the army hospital in Columbia, South Carolina, despaired of getting, under his own signature, any bedding material on government requisition, "in consequence of the factories being engaged in making it for other depts." He invited General P. T. G. Beauregard to request 60,000 yards from the Graniteville factory for his use (J. J. Chisholm to P. T. G. Beauregard, April 18, 1864, Letters Received by CQG, M469, reel 8).

59. Lawton to Cunningham, July 9, 1864, War Department Collection, T131, reel 10.

60. W. B. B. Cross to Cunningham, June 4, 1864, ibid., reel 10.

61. G. W. Cunningham to A. R. Lawton, May 2, 1864, Letters Received by CQG, M469, reel 8.

62. W. G. Ferguson to A. F. Cone, April 13, 1864, ibid.

63. Ibid.

64. G. W. Cunningham to A. R. Lawton, May 12, 1864, Compiled Service Records, M331, reel 68; A. R. Lawton to G. W. Cunningham, July 9, 1864, War Department Collection, T131, reel 10.

65. In September 1861, the governor telegraphed the Confederate authorities that "a resolution of our Legislature now in session directs me to inquire of you what provision has been made for the clothing of our troops, and if our State can assist by receiving the commutation and providing clothes" (Henry T. Clark to L. P. Walker, September 11, 1861, OR, IV, 1: 604).

66. Jonathan Worth to W. J. Yates, December 25, 1863, *Correspondence of Jonathan Worth* 1: 277–78.

67. Z. B. Vance to General Assembly, November 17, 1862, OR, IV, 2: 183.

68. A. C. Myers to Z. B. Vance, March 17, 1862, Copies of Letters and Telegrams, T781.

69. David A. Barnes to A. C. Myers, ca. September 20, 1862, ibid.

70. J. B. Ferguson to L. Smith, June 25, 1862, Compiled Service Records, M331, reel 92.

71. Ibid.

72. A. C. Myers to J. G. Martin, June 5, 1862, War Department Collection, T131, reel 8.

73. A. C. Myers to Henry T. Clark, June 12, 1862, ibid.

74. A. C. Myers to Z. B. Vance, December 8, 1862, Copies of Letters and Telegrams, T781.

75. Jonathan Worth to W. J. Yates, December 25, 1863, *Correspondence of Jonathan Worth* 1: 277–78.

76. W. W. Peirce to A. C. Myers, March 25, 1863, Letters Received by CQG, M469, reel 5.

77. P. A. Wilson to W. W. Peirce, March 25, 1863, ibid.

78. S. R. Chisman to J. B. Hope, May 26, 1863, James B. Hope Ms., WM.

79. W. W. Peirce to S. R. Chisman, May 25, 1863, ibid.

80. Ibid.

81. S. R. Chisman to J. B. Hope, June 11, 1863, ibid.

82. A. C. Myers to Z. B. Vance, June 29 1863, War Department Collection, T131, reel 9.

83. W. B. B. Cross to W. W. Peirce, October 22, 1863, ibid.

84. Z. B. Vance to J. A. Seddon, January 7, 1864, OR, IV, 3: 10.

85. W. W. Peirce to A. R. Lawton, January 25, 1864, Letters Received by CQG, M469, reel 7.

86. A. R. Lawton to Z. B. Vance, January 21, 1864, OR, IV, 3: 38.

87. Jefferson Davis to Z. B. Vance, ca. February 29, 1864, Letters and Telegrams Sent and Received by Governor Zebulon B. Vance, T781, NA.

88. A. R. Lawton to W. H. Whiting, April 1, 1864, War Department Collection, T131, reel 10.

89. A. R. Lawton to W. W. Peirce, February 25, 1864, ibid.

90. A. R. Lawton to W. W. Peirce, March 22, 1864, ibid.

91. R. C. Gatlin to W. W. Peirce, April 14, 1864, Letters Received by CQG, M469, reel 8.

92. W. W. Peirce to R. C. Gatlin, June 2, 1864, ibid., reel 11.

93. W. W. Peirce to A. R. Lawton, July 12, 1864, ibid.

94. Alex W. Vick, "Report of Clothing Received in Heth's Division from October 1st 1863 to March 1st 1864," March 11, 1864, ibid., reel 9.

95. Ira B. Foster to Quartermaster Office, November 12, 1863, Georgia Q.M. General Ira R. Foster Ms., Ga A.

96. Enoch Steadman to J. E. Brown, December 9, 1862, Joseph E. Brown Ms., ibid.

97. Isaac Brown to J. E. Brown, December 1, 1863, ibid.

98. Georgia, General Assembly, *Acts of the General Assembly . . . 1862*, 101–3; Georgia, Senate, *Journal of the Senate*; Ira R. Foster to J. A. Seddon, January 30, 1864, OR, IV, 3: 64–65.

99. W. B. B. Cross to Ira R. Foster, November 12, 1863, War Department Collection, T131, reel 9.

100. A. R. Lawton to John W. C. Watson, February 15, 1864, Civil War Papers, Miss A.

101. John Milton to G. W. Cunningham, June 13, 1864, Commissary Activities and Correspondence, 1863–65, Ms., Fla A.

102. OR, IV, 3: 500.

103. G. W. Cunningham to John Milton, June 21, 1864, Commissary Activities and Correspondence, 1863–1865, Ms., Fla A; see also William Bailey to John Milton, June 15, 1864, OR, IV, 3: 500; G. W. Cunningham to A. R. Lawton, August 18, 1864, Letters Received by CQG, M469, reel 10.

104. A. R. Lawton to T. H. Watts, July 27, 1864, War Department Collection, T131, reel 10.

105. G. W. Cunningham to A. R. Lawton, August 18, 1864, Letters Received by CQG, M469, reel 10.

106. Virginia, Governor, Message of the Governor of Virginia and Accompanying Documents, Executive Document 41, "Report of the Virginia Quartermaster," February 3, 1863 (Richmond, 1863), 1–3.

107. Ibid., Executive Document No. 19, "Report of the Commercial Agent of Virginia, with the Accompanying Documents" (Richmond, 1864), 9.

108. S. Bassett French to Governor, May 25, 1864, OR, IV, 3: 557.

109. Virginia, Governor, Message of the Governor of Virginia and Accompanying Documents, Executive Document No. 19, "Report of the Commercial Agent of Virginia," 10; ibid., Executive Document No. 23, "Supplemental Report of the Commercial Agent of Virginia, 1864" (Richmond, 1864), 3.

110. A. R. Lawton to J. A. Seddon, July 26, 1864, OR, IV, 3: 556.

111. Z. B. Vance to J. A. Seddon, September 19, 1864, ibid., 671–72.

112. W. B. B. Cross to S. R. Chisman, August 2, 1864, War Department Collection, T131, reel 10.

113. S. R. Chisman to A. R. Lawton, August 6, 1864, Letters Received by CQG, M469, reel 11.

114. S. R. Chisman to A. R. Lawton, August 15, 1864, ibid.

115. Ibid., August 16, 1864, reel 10; Beatty 79–80.

116. A. R. Lawton to W. A. Miller, September 2, 1864, War Department Collection, T131, reel 10.

117. James Sloan to W. B. B. Cross, September 1, 1864, Letters Received by CQG, M469, reel 11.

118. Miscellaneous Factories No. 1.

119. Ibid.

120. W. A. Miller to A. R. Lawton, September 12, 1864, Letters Received by CQG, M469, reel 11.

121. Ibid., September 17, 1864.

122. A. R. Lawton to McDonald and Sons, September 21, 1864, War Department Collection, T131, reel 10.

123. W. A. Miller to A. R. Lawton, September 12, 1864, Letters Received by CQG, M469, reel 11.

124. W. A. Miller to A. R. Lawton, September 19, 1864, ibid.

125. Ibid.

126. Vance to General Holmes, October 25, 1864, OR, IV, 3: 746.

127. Jasper Stowe to E. M. Holt, November 15, 1864, Archibald A. T. Smith Ms., UNC.

128. Ibid.

129. F. and H. Fries to R. P. Waller, February 20, 1863, Fries Ms., Mor HS.

130. W. B. B. Cross to S. R. Chisman, November 14, 1864, War Department Collection, T131, reel 10.

131. A. R. Lawton to S. R. Chisman, November 28, 1864, ibid.

132. Z. B. Vance to J. A. Seddon, September 19, 1864, OR, IV, 3: 671–72.

133. A. R. Lawton to J. A. Seddon, September 1864, ibid., 692.

134. W. B. B. Cross to S. R. Chisman, November 14, 1864, War Department Collection, T131, reel 10.

135. Cunningham to Lawton, May 2, 1864, Letters Received by CQG, M469, reel 8.

136. Cunningham to Lawton, May 12, 1864, Compiled Service Records, M331, reel 68.

137. Cunningham to Lawton, May 2, 1864, Letters Received by CQG, M469, reel 8.

138. Cunningham to Lawton, May 12, 1864, Compiled Service Records, M331, reel 68; J. M. Wesson's contract with Livingston Mims, June 1, 1864, Wesson File, Confederate Papers, M346, reel 1091.

139. In May 1864, the Commissary Department was due 66,335 pounds of yarn, 850 pounds of rope, and 35,000 yards of osnaburgs from the Alcora, Alguadon, Amiss, Covington, Princeton, Scull Shoals, and Gwinette mills, while the Grant and Troup factories sold directly to the army 39,000 yards of osnaburgs and 4,000 pounds of yarns. Vaucluse, under the rules, owed the navy 53,000 yards of osnaburgs (Cunningham to Lawton, May 12, 1864, Compiled Service Records, M331, reel 68).

140. Ibid.

141. Ibid.

142. Miscellaneous Factories No. 1.

143. Ibid.

144. Cunningham to Lawton, May 2, 1864, Letters Received by CQG, M469, reel 8.

145. William G. Ferguson, voucher, July 12, 1864, Compiled Service Records, M331, reel 92. In January 1863, the depot received 552,127 yards of cottons, 5,691 gross of buttons, 1,140 pounds of thread, and 6,301 pounds of warps (Richard Waller, Abstract, February 7, 1863, ibid., M331, reel 258).

146. List of Contracts Remaining Unfilled, February 9, 1863, Confederate Papers, M346, reel 625.

147. Vouchers, June 30, 1863, ibid.

148. Livingston Mims to James Hamilton, October 14, 1863, Letters Received by CQG, M469, reel 9; George W. Jones to Larkin Smith, December 15, 1863, ibid. Depots at Wytheville, Greensboro, Salisbury, Raleigh, Charleston, and Montgomery also operated on a large scale.

149. The mills were Ettrick (256,830), Battersea (776,081), and Matoaca (464,101) (William G. Ferguson, voucher, July 12, 1864, Compiled Service Records, M331, reel 92).

150. G. W. Cunningham to A. R. Lawton, May 2, 1864, Letters Received by CQG, M469, reel 8.

151. A. R. Lawton to R. E. Lee, February 5, 1864, War Department Collection, T131, reel 10.

152. Ibid.

153. A survey of Kershaw's division showed that 790 men were without shoes, and another 1,480, including 159 from artillery batteries, were nearly so (Report of Barefooted Men in Kershaw's Division, September 21, 1864, Letters Received by CQG, M469, reel 11).

154. A. R. Lawton to J. L. Corley, December 12, 1864, OR, I, 42, pt. 2: 1268–69.

155. A. R. Lawton to J. L. Corley, December 12, 1864, War Department Collection, T131, reel 10; Lawton to Corley, OR, I, 42, pt. 3: 1268–69.

156. Lawton to Corley, December 12, 1864, War Department Collection, T131, reel 10; Lawton to Corley, OR, I, 42, pt. 3: 1268–69.

157. G. W. C. Lee to Lawton, February 9, 1864, OR, I, 52, pt. 2: 615.

158. Endorsement in ibid.

159. Ibid.

160. E. McLean to S. Cooper, April 28, 1864, Letters Received by CQG, M469, reel 9.

161. McLean found the books and papers "in good order," with "no objectional [sic] accounts" while Landis's duties were "energetically performed" (Orders, June 1, 1863, Compiled Service Records, M331, reel 152).

162. "Recordbook of Maj. A. L. Landis, Quartermaster in the Army of Tennessee," ch. V, vol. 226, Confederate Quartermaster Ms., RG 109, NA.

163. A. R. Lawton to W. F. Ayer, November 18, 1864, War Department Collection, T131, reel 10.

164. W. B. B. Cross to F. W. Dillard, October 18, 1864, ibid.

165. A. R. Lawton to W. F. Ayer, November 18, 1864, ibid.

166. Ibid. Cavalryman Basil W. Duke recalled that on June 26, 1863, General

John Hunt Morgan's command of 2,800 men received "new and excellent cloth-ing," an event "unprecedented in the history of the command" (Duke 404).

167. A. R. Lawton to S. A. Miller, January 27, 1865, OR, IV, 3: 1041.

168. A. R. Lawton to S. A. Miller, December 12, 1864, War Department Collec-tion, T131, reel 10.

169. Lawton to J. L. Corley, December 12, 1864, ibid.

170. House of Representatives, Confederate Congress, "Report of the Special Committee on the Pay and Clothing of the Army" (February 11, 1865) 4, Confeder-ate Imprint no. 600, in Crandall.

171. Lawton to Miller, January 27, 1865, OR, IV, 3: 1040.

172. House of Representatives, Confederate Congress, "Report of the Special Committee on the Pay and Clothing of the Army." (February 11, 1865), 4, Confed-erate Imprint no. 600, in Crandall.

173. Vance estimated the state's issues during the war at 250,000 uniforms, 50,000 blankets, and 12,000 overcoats (Dowd 489).

174. Lawton to Miller, January 27, 1865, OR, IV, 3: 1040.

175. Lawton to Breckinridge, February 16, 1865, ibid., 1089–90.

Chapter 4. Factories under Siege

1. He continued, "we particularly need, just now, all the power and influence that association can give us in procuring machinery and supplies that must come from foreign countries" (*Daily South Carolinian*, June 4, 1864).

2. F. & H. Fries to J. Fisher, September 27, 1862, Fries Ms., Mor HS.

3. Merrell's nom de guerre during the war, and the spelling most frequently used for him, is "Merrill."

4. "Art. IX.—How Our Industry Profits by the War. Responses from Georgia," *DeBow's Review* 32 (May–August 1862): 78.

5. George Camp to Mr. Leslie, July 11, 1861, Barrington King Ms., Ga A; Edwin M. Holt to William A. Carrigan, August 1861, James Wilson White Ms., UNC; Beatty 89.

6. James Watson to Green and Scott, June 11, 1861, Duff Green Ms., Duke.

7. F. & H. Fries to C.R. Bishop, October 24, 1862, Fries Ms., Mor HS; F. & H. Fries to George Makepeace, September 28, 1862, ibid.

8. F. & H. Fries to Thomas H. Liddall, September 28, 1862, ibid.

9. F. & H. Fries to J. G. Gibbes and Co., April 6, 1862, ibid.

10. F. & H. Fries to J. L. Fremont, September 23, 1862, ibid.

11. F. & H. Fries to F. C. & B. G. Worth, June 16, 1862, ibid. Makepeace experi-

mented with lard to make wool more manageable (George Makepeace to C. W. Garrett, April 14, 1862, Civil War Military Collections, NCA).

12. George Camp to N. I. Bryan, September 3, 1861, Barrington King Ms., Ga A.

13. F. & H. Fries to Thomas Liddall, September 28, 1862, Fries Ms., Mor HS.

14. George Camp to Green and Scott, September 10, 1861, Duff Green Ms., Duke.

15. George Camp to Hugh Bone, September 17, 1861, Barrington King Ms., Ga A.

16. George H. Camp to Benjamin C. Gray, May 11, 1861, ibid.; Camp to Burnett and Canter, July 23, 1861, ibid.

17. J. Rhodes Browne to W. S. Downer, June 25, 1862, Eagle Factory File, Confederate Papers, M346, reel 270.

18. F. & H. Fries to George Makepeace, December 5, 1862, Fries Ms., Mor HS.

19. H. T. Nelson to editor, *Augusta Daily Constitutionalist*, July 10, 1861.

20. George H. Camp to H. J. Nelson, July 25, August 13, and August 29, 1861, Barrington King Ms., Ga A.

21. E. J. McCall to James Montgomery, December 26, 1862, Receipt Book, 1862–1863, GMfgCo, USC Aiken.

22. January 2, 1863, Deed Book 14, Ala.-Autauga County, 780.

23. Orders for Bobbins, November 28, 1864, Daniel Pratt Ms., Ala A.

24. "Art. IX," 79; George W. Evans to Green and Scott, September 26, 1861, Duff Green Ms., Duke.

25. George Camp to A. D. Brown, September 17, 1861, Barrington King Ms., Ga A.

26. George W. Evans to Green and Scott, September 26, 1861, Duff Green Ms., Duke.

27. George Makepeace to W. W. Peirce, October 5, 1863, Cedar Falls File, Confederate Papers, M346, reel 155.

28. H. W. Fries to W. H. Powers, September 30, 1863, Fries Ms., Mor HS.

29. George Camp to N. I. Bryan, September 3, 1861, Barrington King Ms., Ga A.

30. June 30, 1864, Augusta Factory Record Book, 1858–1911, GMfgCo Ms., USC Aiken.

31. George Camp to John Scott, August 10, 1861, Barrington King Ms., Ga A; George Camp to W. J. Small, September 3, 1861, ibid.

32. George Camp to J. & R. Winship, July 23, 1861, ibid. Camp also recommended to Winship the services of a "young man here who has for some years been in Rogers Shop and Machinist Association, in Paterson" (ibid.).

33. OR, I, 26, pt. 2: 308.

34. F. & H. Fries to J. Fisher, September 27, 1862, Fries Ms., Mor HS.

35. Barrington King to J. A. Hayden, December 24, 1863, Barrington King Ms., Ga A.

36. James M. Wesson to General, January 14, 1863, May 9, 1864, Confederate Papers, M346, reel 1091.

37. James Harolson to John G. Shorter, March 14, 1863, Shorter Ms., Ala A.

38. Charles S. Lucas to John G. Shorter, November 5, 1863, ibid. In June 1864, the Louisiana legislature appropriated funds to provide 20,000 cards for public use (John McVea to Maj. Gen. Stephen Lee, June 24, 1864, OR, IV, 3: 1097). In Texas, at least one private manufacturer of cards, Eubanks of Williamson County, received public acclaim for the quality of his product (*Austin Texas Star Gazette*, February 18, 1863). Samuel Bassett French, the Virginia commercial agent, was enjoined by the legislature on March 9, 1864, to undertake the purchase and distribution of cards (Gov. William Smith to Gentlemen of Senate and House of Delegates, December 7, 1864, OR, IV, 3: 919).

39. Joseph E. Brown to Z. B. Vance, February 4, 1863, Copies of Letters and Telegrams, T731, 120–21.

40. Ibid., March 14, 1863, 176–77.

41. Z. B. Vance to John White, July 10, 1863, ibid., 298.

42. Vance to James Seddon, January 7, 1864, ibid., 401–2.

43. Francis Fries to J. L. Fulkerson, June 25, 1862, Fries Ms., Mor HS.

44. F. & H. Fries to John C. Washington, August 6, 1862, ibid.

45. F. & H. Fries to Thomas H. Liddall, September 28, 1862, ibid.

46. F. & H. Fries to C. Phifer, September 6, 1862, ibid.

47. E. N. Candler to Milner & Wrenn, May 17, 1861, Milner, Wood & Co. Ms., UN Ala.

48. W. K. Hill to Milner, Wood, and Co., May 18, 1861, ibid.

49. Unknown to J. and J. H. Webb, January 30, 1863, James Webb Ms., UNC.

50. John T. Bellamy to J. and J. H. Webb, January 26, 1863, ibid.

51. Unknown to J. and J. H. Webb, January 30, 1863, ibid.

52. Lieutenant Maxwell Clarke was charged with managing the Naval Rope Works factory. Voucher, A. G. McIlwaine File, January 2, 1865, Confederate Papers, M346, reel 632.

53. "An Act Making an Appropriation for the Removal and Erection of the Naval Rope-Walk," *Acts and Joint Resolutions Passed at the Second Session of the Second Confederate Congress* (Holmes Beach, Fla., 1970), 12; A. R. Lawton to A. F. Cone, January 28, 1864, War Department Collection, T131, reel 9. After commencing operations in January 1863, the Navy Rope Walk at Petersburg produced "cotton cordage of excellent quality" for the armed forces, as well as for "coal miners, and private parties upon public work" (ORN, II, 2: 534). Stephen Mallory's report

of April 3, 1864, stated that the facility was self-supporting and producing about 500 pounds of rope per day, having provided the navy with 84,259 pounds "from the 1st of April, 1863, to the 30th of September, 1864 [1863]" (ibid., 638).

54. Item by George Schley, May 20, 1862, Letters Received by CSW, M437, reel 49; DeCredico 53.

55. Voucher, Garland Goode File, October 15, 1863, Confederate Papers, M346, reel 360.

56. W. G. Ferguson to A. F. Cone, June 20, 1864, Letters Received by CQG, M469, reel 10.

57. J. B. Pace to A. R. Lawton, June 7, 1864, ibid., reel 11.

58. George Camp to John White, August 8, 1861, Barrington King Ms., Ga A; George Camp to President, Augusta Mills, August 1, 1861, ibid.; George Camp to N. P. Gignilliat, August 22, 1861, ibid.

59. William Amis to James H. Seddon, n.d., Letters Received by CSW, M437.

60. F. & H. Fries to H. G. McCray, April 18, 1862, Fries Ms., Mor HS.

61. H. W. Fries to John Shortridge, December 24, 1863, ibid.

62. F. & H. Fries to George W. Read, May 5, 1862, ibid.

63. Thomas M. Holt to Robert Baird, December 20, 1864, Robert Baird Ms., Duke. Beatty states that Edwin M. Holt bought the Cane Creek factory in 1857 and sold it in 1860 to son Thomas, who renamed it the Granite factory (Beatty 27).

64. March 11 and February 1, 1865, Robert Baird Ms., Duke.

65. John M. Johnston to Baird, January 13, 1865, ibid.

66. George Camp to N. P. Gignilliat, July 13, 1861, Barrington King Ms., Ga A.

67. E. Lafitte to William Gregg, February 2, 1863, GMfgCo Ms., USC Aiken; Theodore D. Wagner to Gregg, March 2, 1863, ibid.

68. South Carolina, House of Representatives, the Committee on Incorporation, "A Bill to Incorporate the Batesville Manufacturing Company" (December 3, 1863), in Confederate Imprints, microform reel 19, number 2044 in Crandall. Another spinning and weaving mill was chartered in South Carolina with an approved capital first of $150,000 and then of $1 million (South Carolina, House of Representatives, The Committee on Incorporation and Engrossing Acts, "A Bill to Incorporate the Carolina Cotton and Woolen Factory" [December 5, 1862], ibid., reel 22).

69. F. Fries to J. Fisher, November 13, 1861, Fries Ms., Mor HS.

70. F. and H. Fries to Fraser & Co., October 24, 1861, ibid.

71. Fraser Account Sheet, December 15, 1862, ibid.

72. F. & H. Fries to J. Fisher, August 12, 1862, ibid.

73. B. King to Rev. W. E. Baker, August 8, 1863, Barrington King Ms., Ga A.

74. "What We Are Gaining by the War," *DeBow's Review* 32 (March–April 1862): 327.

75. F. & H. Fries to Fraser and Co., October 7, 1861, Fries Ms., Mor HS.

76. Young, Wriston, and Orr to P. A. Wilson, February 17, 1863, Civil War Military Collections, NCA.

77. F. & H. Fries to George Schley, June 22, 1863, Fries Ms., Mor HS.

78. John G. Shorter to James Seddon, May 1, 1863, Records of the Confederate States of America (Pickett Papers), microform reel 35, LC.

79. OR, I, 52, pt. 2: 481.

80. Lancaster & Co. to John H. Winder, August 13, 1863, ibid.

81. September 23, 1863, ibid.

82. Samuel R. Chisman to W. W. Peirce, August 30, 1864, Letters Received by CQG, M469, reel 11.

83. Jones, Mendenhall, and Gardner was located at Jamestown, in Guilford County (Miscellaneous Factories No. 1).

84. C. L. Bauner to Benjamin, November 14, 1863, Records of the Confederate States of America (Pickett Papers), microform reel 35, LC.

85. William W. Boyce to Secretary of State, September 24, 1863, ibid.

86. Warren Aken to Benjamin, December 9, 1863, ibid.

87. John Sherrill, "Report of Acting Master Sherrill, U.S. Navy, commanding U.S. bark Roebuck, regarding capture of the British schooner Kate," January 23, 1864, ORN, I, 17:633.

88. A. R. Lawton to T. L. Bayne, January 5, 1864, War Department Collection, T131, reel 9.

89. J. D. C. Atkins to Judah Benjamin, June 18, 1864, William W. Clark Ms., Duke.

90. Orville Jennings, Statement, September 30, 1865, Pardon Petitions and Related Papers Submitted in Response to President Andrew Johnson's Amnesty Proclamation of May 29, 1865 (hereafter Pardon Petitions), M1003, reel 14, RG 94, NA.

91. William H. Haynes to Henry Merrill [Merrell], December 1, 1864, Pardon Petitions, M1003, reel 14.

92. Henry Merrill [Merrell], Petition, October 26, 1865, ibid.

93. Henry Merrill [Merrell] File, January 1865, Confederate Papers, M436, reel 680.

94. Commission of John White and Thomas M. Crossan, ca. November 1862, Copies of Letters and Telegrams, T731, 52–54.

95. Joseph H. Flanner and Francis T. Lawley were also appointed.

96. Zebulon B. Vance to C. G. Memminger, November 13, 1862, Copies of Letters and Telegrams, T731.

97. Vance to White, July 10, 1863, ibid.

98. Ibid.

99. There were also 18,000 blankets, 18,000 yards of wool cloth, and assorted uniform materials (Abstract Z V, ca. April 1864, Letters Received by CQG, M469, reel 9).

100. Vance to Seddon, January 7, 1864, OR, IV, 3: 10.

101. Vance to White, July 10, 1863, Copies of Letters and Telegrams, T731.

102. Vance to James Mason, March 11, 1863, OR, IV, 3: 165.

103. H. W. Fries to H. A. Dowd, January 26, 1864, Civil War Military Collections, NCA.

104. J. H. Foust to H. A. Dowd, n.d., ibid.

105. Dennis Curtis to Henry A. Dowd, May 4, 1864, ibid.

106. Records of the Union Manufacturing Company, January 19, 1865, 94ff., Union Mfg. Co. Ms., Duke.

107. Thomas Holt to H. A. Dowd, n.d., Civil War Military Collections, NCA.

108. Cloth Made for Maj. S. R. Chisman QM Confederate States, April 1865, Fries Ms., Mor HS; John Fries, "Reminiscences of Confederate Days," unpublished ms. (April 4, 1923), Private Papers, NCA.

109. "An Act to Raise Two Million Dollars," December 10, 1863, *General Laws of the Tenth Legislature of the State of Texas* (Houston, 1864), 9.

110. "An Act [for] . . . the Erecting of Certain Machinery . . . ," December 15, 1863, *General Laws of the Tenth Legislature of the State of Texas* (Austin, 1864), 22.

111. OR, I, 26, pt. 2: 308.

112. Haynes to Boggs, January 18, 1864, ibid., 32, pt. 2: 1135, and June 10, 1864, 34, pt. 4: 656.

113. Haynes to Boggs, January 18, 1864, ibid., 32, pt. 2: 1135.

114. Haynes to Boggs, June 10, 1864, ibid., 34, pt. 4: 656, 656–57.

115. Herman H. Runge to Andrew Johnson, August 19, 1865, Petition Pardons and Related Papers, M1003, reel 54; Henry Runge to Andrew Johnson, ibid.

116. "Proceedings of the First Confederate Congress, Third Session in Part, March 20–May 1, 1863," April 4, 1863, in *Southern Historical Society Papers* 44: 89.

117. The mill began regular operations only on October 1, 1865 (*Texas Almanac for 1868* [Galveston, Texas, 1867], 169–80).

118. Haynes to Boggs, June 10, 1864, OR, I, 34, pt. 4: 657.

119. December 29, 1864, Grantee Index to Deeds, Texas-Bastrop, Book B, 89.

120. A. R. Lawton to Simeon Hart, March 9, 1864, War Department Collection, T131, reel 10.

121. OR, I, 26, pt. 2: 308.

122. John Lee to H. A. Dowd, December 7, 1863, Civil War Military Collections,

NCA; June 3, 1864, "Memoranda Book Relating to Agents and Supplies," ch. V, vol. 227, RG 109, NA.

123. The quartermaster also paid $10 a dozen for them ("Memoranda Book Relating to Agents and Supplies").

124. January 3, 1862, Francis Fries Memorabilia Book, 1854–1862, Francis Fries Collection, Mor HS.

125. May 25 and July 10, 1861, "Time Book—Cedar Falls Manufacturing Company, 1846–1865, Sept.–June," Private Papers, NCA.

126. May 1864, ibid.

127. J. M. Bigney to W. G. Provost, July 10, 1865, GmfgCo Ms., GMfgCo.

128. Fries—Silas's Quarters Time Book (1862–1865), July 1862, Francis Fries Collection, Mor HS.

129. Fries—Silas's Quarters Time Book (1862–1865), August 1863, ibid.

130. Fries Memorabilia Book, 1854–1862, January 3, 1862, ibid.

131. December 18, 1861–April 26, 1865, Time Book—Cedar Falls Manufacturing Company, 1846–1865, Sept.–June, Private Papers, NCA.

132. Winter hours were slightly reduced (J. M. Bigney to W. G. Provost, July 10, 1865, GmfgCo. Ms., GmfgCo; Time Book—Cedar Falls Manufacturing Co., 1846–1865, Private Papers, NCA.

Chapter 5. The Bureau of Foreign Supplies and the Crenshaw Line

1. Stephen Wise, in his major study of blockade-running, argues that "the Confederacy was able to supply their troops because of a reliance on a system based on steam vessels, carrying essential goods through the Federal Navy's blockade" (Wise 7).

2. Thomas E. McNeill to Jefferson Davis, February 20, 1865, OR, IV, 3: 1098.

3. He was posted to Manchester in October 1862 (Myers to Benjamin, October 10, 1862, Letters Sent, CSA QM Ms.).

4. Myers to G. W. Randolph, October 4, 1862, ibid.

5. F. & H. Fries to J. B. Ferguson, September 7, 1862, Fries Ms., Mor HS.

6. James B. Ferguson to Lawton, September 1863, Compiled Service Records, M331, reel 92.

7. He arrived in June 1863. The Navy Department posted Felix Senac to European service for the Clothing and Provisions Bureau.

8. Lawton to Seddon, October 1, 1863, Letters Sent, CSA QM Ms.

9. Lawton to McRae, October 13, 1863, War Department Collection, T131, reel 9.

10. Myers to L. P. Walker, May 13, 1861, Letters Sent, CSA QM Ms.

11. L. Smith to G. W. Randolph, July 31, 1862, ibid.

12. Lawton to McRae, October 13, 1863, War Department Collection, T131, reel 9.

13. The steamers were the *Columbia*, the *R. E. Lee*, the *Merrimac*, and the *Eugenie*. The *Phantom* was later acquired. Huse purchased the *Columbia* and 157,000 stand of arms by December 5, 1862 (Gorgas to Seddon, December 5, 1862, OR, IV, 2: 227–28). In the year ending September 30, 1863, department vessels imported 113,504 small arms (Gorgas to Seddon, November 15, 1863, OR, IV, 2: 955–56). Although Gorgas claimed that these vessels made fifty round trips through the blockade without a loss up to August 2, 1863, five of the seven steamers were lost in the next few months (Vandiver, ed. xxxii, 52–54; Wise 95–100, 141). In May 1862, the U.S. consul at Liverpool reported that thirty additional small English steamers were being prepared to run the blockade (Gideon Welles, Letter from the Sec. of the Navy, May 27, 1862, ORN, I, 7: 432). Two years later the same Liverpool consul estimated that sixty blockade-runners were under construction (Extracts Received by Acting Rear-Admiral S. P. Lee, May 11, 1864, Despatches of the United States Consuls in Bermuda, 1818–1906, T262, RG 57, NA (hereafter Despatches). The War Department vessels, purchased when freightage rose to $2 million for each trip through the blockade, fully reimbursed the government their original cost with each trip. The *Flora*, which sank after only three successful voyages from Bermuda to Wilmington, left a profit of £173,000 (Charles Maxwell Allen to William H. Seward, ibid.). A single cargo, like that of the *Justitia* in January 1862, was valued at £93,000 (Vandiver, ed. 34).

14. Seddon to Davis, November 26, 1863, OR, IV, 2: 1015.

15. Ibid.; Louise Hill 3.

16. Lawton to Bayne, May 4 and 5, 1864, War Department Collection, T131, reel 10.

17. W. G. Ferguson to Aurelius F. Cone, October 1, 1863, Letters Received by CQG, M469, reel 6.

18. OR, III, 1: 583–86.

19. J. B. Ferguson to Lawton, October 31, 1863, Compiled Service Records, M331, reel 92.

20. Ferguson to Lawton, October 31, 1863, ibid.

21. Myers to Seddon, April 22, 1863, Letters Sent, CSA QM Ms.

22. Ferguson to Lawton, October 31, 1863, Compiled Service Records, M331, reel 92.

23. A general source of complaint was that the Austrian rifles had a smaller bore than the Enfield—.54 caliber rather the standard .57—and ammunition was difficult to secure. Some also had weak lock springs. Union officers complained that the weapon was "not fit for a soldier" and that "the guns furnished us are

of poorest description, being Austrian rifles, .54 caliber" (OR, I, 26, pt. 1: 800; ibid., 34, pt. 3: 373). After battlefield gleanings increased Confederate stocks of the coveted Enfield, Gorgas withdrew the Austrian rifle (SHSP 16: 287). Nevertheless, VMI cadets and Forrest's cavalry rendered effective service with this arm.

24. Gorgas to Seddon, May 22, 1863, OR, IV, 2: 564.

25. Ferguson to Lawton, September 1863, Compiled Service Records, M331, reel 92.

26. Ferguson to Myers, April 18, 1863, OR, IV, 2: 556.

27. North to Ferguson, April 1, 1863, ibid., 558.

28. Ferguson to Myers, April 18, 1863, ibid., 557.

29. W. G. Crenshaw to J. A. Seddon, July 10, 1863, ibid., 625. In his memoir, Huse attacked government contractors such as Crenshaw as men on the make: "that was their business, and they pursued it eagerly, for the profits were large" (Huse 34).

30. Seddon to McRae, December 29, 1863, OR, IV, 2: 1067.

31. Benjamin, in sending Huse $1.2 million on March 10, 1862, wrote that "I now take pleasure in assuring you of the full approval to your Government of your conduct in the business intrusted to your charge." He further elaborated that "the responsibility you have assumed in making purchases of army supplies, not directly authorized by your instructions, is also approved," and "your assumption of it under the circumstances was judicious and proper" (Benjamin to Huse, March 10, 1862, ibid., 1: 985).

32. Gorgas to Seddon, May 22, 1863, ibid., 2: 564.

33. Huse to Gorgas, June 13, 1863, ibid., 645; Crenshaw to Seddon, July 10, 1863, ibid., 624–25; Myers to Gorgas, April 21, 1863, War Department Collection, T131, reel 9.

34. Seddon to McRae, December 29, 1863, OR, IV, 2: 1067–68.

35. McRae to Seddon, July 4, 1864, ibid., 3: 525–30. Secretary Benjamin was a supporter of Saul Isaac within the administration, writing that company in March 1862, "I shall continue my remittances by every favorable opportunity, but shall probably not send them otherwise than in cash, as we prefer leaving to the merchants the very large profits from shipping produce," and concluding, "our demands for supplies from England will continue quite large, and we trust you may find your connection with our young Government equally profitable and agreeable" (Benjamin to Isaac, Campbell and Co., March 17, 1862, ibid., 1: 1007–8).

36. McRae to Seddon, July 4, 1864, ibid., 3: 525–30; Myers to Seddon, May 16, 1863, ibid., 2: 555–56; Myers to Gorgas, April 21, 1863, War Department Collection, T131, reel 9.

37. McRae to Seddon, August 4, 1864, Letters Received by CQG, M469, reel 11.

38. Ferguson to Lawton, October 31, 1863, Compiled Service Records, M331, reel 92; Myers to Seddon, July 29, 1863, Letters Sent, CSA QM Ms.

39. Ferguson to Lawton, September 1863, Compiled Service Records, M331, reel 92.

40. Ferguson to Lawton, September 1863, ibid. John Jones wrote that military stores at Wilmington could not be brought to Richmond for lack of railroad transportation (2: 317).

41. Ruffin was the former editor of the *Farmer's Register* and a relation of secessionist Edmund Ruffin.

42. In January 1863, when Lee's chief commissary officer, Major Charles S. Carrington, sought to impress 30,000 bushels of offal from local flour mills, including Haxall, Crenshaw and Company, the Crenshaws vigorously protested, knowing that Ruffin would support their position (Haxall, Crenshaw and Company to Maj. Charles S. Carrington, January 6, 1863, Letters Received by CQG, M469, reel 4).

43. Francis Gildart Ruffin, ca. January 20, 1865, Testimony (copy) 1865, of Francis Gildart Ruffin before the [Joint Committee on Quartermasters and Commissaries of the] Confederate States Congress Concerning the Confederate States Subsistence Department, 14, Francis G. Ruffin Ms., Va HS (hereafter Testimony 1865). A brief account of this affair can be found in Wise (101–4).

44. Ruffin, Testimony 1865.

45. Seddon to McRae, September 26, 1863, OR, IV, 2: 826.

46. Seddon to William G. Crenshaw, June 21, 1863, ibid., 601.

47. Ruffin, Testimony 1865, 15, 29.

48. Lewis Dabney Crenshaw, Memorandum, 1864, Francis G. Ruffin Ms., Va HS; John Slidell, Caleb Huse, and Colin McRae opposed the entire cooperative venture (W. G. Crenshaw to Seddon, June 6, 1863, OR, IV, 2: 587–88).

49. Seddon to W. G. Crenshaw, June 21, 1863, OR, IV, 2: 601.

50. Ferguson to Lawton, October 31, 1863, Compiled Service Records, M331, reel 92.

51. The blockade created serious problems for the Crenshaw Woolen Mill (*Richmond Enquirer*, October 17, 1861).

52. Ferguson to Lawton, October 31, 1863, Compiled Service Records, M331, reel 92.

53. According to Lucius Northrop, William Crenshaw was advanced $100,000 in gold by the War Department, but, if so, it was expended mostly on military items (Northrop, "Report on Subsistence," November 20, 1863, OR, IV, 2: 970).

54. The *Flora, Hebe, Kate, Don, Dee, Ceres, Vesta, Annie,* and *Edith* were among these vessels (Extracts, enclosed in Allen to Seward, March 10, 1864, Despatches, T262, RG 57).

55. Lewis D. Crenshaw, Memorandum, 1864, Francis G. Ruffin Ms., Va HS.

56. Virginian Beverly Tucker contracted with William S. Lindsay and Company to send out a vessel in April 1862, which was lost (Beverly Tucker to G. W. Randolph, September 19, 1862, OR, IV, 2: 87). A year later Tucker formed a partnership with George N. Saunders, then in London, to build steamers "to convey public supplies, not contraband of war, from Europe, to the West Indies, for shipment thence to a Confederate port" (A. C. Myers to George N. Saunders, May 19, 1863, War Department Collection, T131, reel 9).

57. Crenshaw to Seddon, July 10, 1863, OR, IV, 2: 624–25.

58. Winnemore to Lawton, October 17, 1863, Compiled Service Records, M331, reel 271. The Augusta brokers T. S. Metcalf and Phinizy and Company were the sources for most of the cotton, which cost $500,000 (Myers to J. M. Seixas, August 6, 1863, War Department Collection, T131, reel 9). The Phinizy firm also operated blockade-runners out of Bermuda.

59. Ferguson to Lawton, October 31, 1863, Compiled Service Records, M331, reel 92.

60. Ibid.

61. McRae to Seddon, July 4, 1864, OR, IV, 3: 525.

62. Bullock to Mallory, January 24, 1864, ORN, II, 2: 577.

63. Seddon to James R. Crenshaw, May 23, 1863, OR, IV, 2: 567.

64. Ferguson to Lawton, October 31, 1863, Compiled Service Records, M331, reel 92.

65. Joseph B. Breck, "Report of Acting Master Breck, U.S. Navy, commanding U.S.S. Niphon," August 18, 1863, ORN, I, 9:174. The cargo probably resembled that of the *Hebe*, which carried in 8,000 pairs of shoes and 10,000 yards of flannels in June (Invoice, June 1, 1863, Compiled Service Records, M331, reel 92). The *Leopard*, taken by the Federals in April 1863, was loaded with 40,000 pairs of shoes (John Jones 1: 291; Lamson to Lee, October 25, 1863, ORN, I, 9: 250).

66. Lamson to Lee, October 25, 1863, ORN, I, 9: 250.

67. Lawton to A. F. Cone, September 10, 1863, War Department Collection, T131, reel 9.

68. Benjamin F. Sands, "Report of Captain Sands, U.S. Navy," October 21, 1863, ORN, I, 9: 248–50.

69. Lawton to Ferguson, October 12, 1863, OR, IV, 2: 870, 895.

70. William Whiting, "Report of Major-General Whiting, C.S. Army," August 24, 1863, ORN, I, 9: 174.

71. Lewis Dabney Crenshaw, Memorandum, 1864, Francis G. Ruffin Ms., Va HS.

72. Ruffin, Testimony 1865, 15.

73. Whiting, "Report." In Bermuda, the U.S. consul Allen reported on November 20, 1863, that "the blockade runners here are in much trouble, having recently sustained heavy losses"; he continued, "they report the blockade at Wilmington very strong"(C. M. Allen to William H. Seward, November 20, 1863, Despatches, T262, RG 57).

74. Sidney P. Lee, "Report," January 11, 1863, ORN, I, 9: 402.

75. Allen to Seward, July 13, 1864, Despatches, T262, RG 57.

76. Lewis D. Crenshaw, Memorandum, 1864, Francis G. Ruffin Ms., Va HS.

77. Sidney P. Lee, "Report," December 17, 1863, ORN, I, 9: 337–38, 402. Several Ordnance Bureau steamers, including the *Phantom*, the *Lee*, and the *Merrimac*, were lost as well. With considerable self-restraint, in February General Lawton explained to General Joseph E. Johnston that "the loss of nearly one hundred thousand prs of shoes & as many blankets off Wilmington since Sept. has left us in a sad condition in reference to these all important items." Since the *Ceres* and the *Vesta* alone carried over 50,000 pairs of shoes, the total losses were far greater (Lawton to Johnston, February 9, 1864, War Department Collection, T131, reel 10).

78. Lawton to Lee, January 20, 1864, ibid., reel 9.

79. Allen to Seward, February 20, 1864, Despatches, T262, RG 57.

80. Lawton to Bayne, December 7, 1863, War Department Collection, T131, reel 9. Some of the bales, valued at £40 each, were destroyed going through the blockade.

81. Bayne to Seddon, March 22, 1864, OR, IV, 2: 240–41.

82. Lawton to Waller, April 28, 1864, War Department Collection, T131, reel 10.

83. Ruffin, Testimony 1865, 18, Francis G. Ruffin Ms., Va HS.

84. Thomas L. Dudley to Francis G. Ruffin, December 6, 1864, ibid.

85. Allen to Seward, July 13, 1864, Despatches, T262, RG 57.

86. Lewis D. Crenshaw, Memorandum, 1864, Francis G. Ruffin Ms., VA HS.

87. Ibid.; Allen to Seward, March 10, 1864, Despatches, T262, RG 57.

88. Crenshaw, Memorandum, 1864, Francis G. Ruffin Ms., Va HS.

89. Ibid.

90. Ruffin, Testimony 1865, 20.

91. Ibid., 20–21.

92. Lawton to Seixas, March 1864, War Department Collection, T131, reel 10.

93. Seddon to McRae, August 1, 1864, OR, IV, 3: 567.

94. Under the Confederate law, "An Act to Facilitate Transportation for the Government," of May 1, 1863, Lawton secured authority to limit passenger trains to one per day on each of the fifty Southern lines; he could impress trains, rolling stock, or entire railroads if companies refused to cooperate with the government. He could require railroads to link with each other in the cities. Lawton was the

sole government contractor, at a standard rate, with railroads for the transport of troops, mails, and military stores. He had authority to make common schedules, establish through trains in any district, and control military details of skilled workers. With the Transportation Office restored to his authority, on September 15, 1864, he established a uniform bill of lading for all military shipments within the Confederacy. One congressman estimated that the quartermaster general employed 5,000 provost marshals at Southern depots watching civilians, military personnel, and official cargo. At the suggestion of Southern railroad presidents, Lawton established a trunk line between Richmond and Augusta, and at the urging of F. W. Sims, Alexander Lawton, and Secretary of War John C. Breckinridge, on February 15, 1865, the Confederate Congress debated whether total control should be exercised over transportation. Finally, on February 28, 1865, Jefferson Davis overcame his earlier reluctance and authorized Lawton's impressment of all railroads, steamboats, canals, and telegraph lines within the Confederacy (SHSP 41: 174–78; 52: 356–57; 46: 72; 52: 121; OR, IV, 3: 258, 643; ibid., I, 42, pt. 3: 1348–49). Ranking Confederates such as Vernon L. Stevenson (quartermaster for the western district), Alexander Lawton, and William Mahone, like George B. McClellan for the Union, were former railroad presidents and intimately familiar with the powerful role exerted by railroads on military affairs. A contemporary historian writes, "taken together, this network of routes cultivated by the Confederacy may have been the rebellion's most lasting geographical and physical legacy" (Nelson 45).

95. McCue mistook the *Hebe* for the *Nassau*, which was lost the previous year.

96. Alexander Collie to James Mason, December 10, 1863, James Mason Ms., LC, cited in Wise (137).

97. Catastrophe eventually overtook this fleet. Wise writes that "by December [1863], the Confederacy had lost all the blockade runners operated by the Ordnance Bureau and a large number of the private vessels that they had depended upon to deliver goods" (Wise 141).

98. Vance to Seddon, January 7, 1864, OR, IV, 3: 10. In the midst of this controversy, perhaps because of it, the Navy Department seized Crenshaw's most successful ship, the *Atalanta*, as it lay in the Cape Fear River at Wilmington. The vessel was appraised at £46,500, and the navy paid Crenshaw and Collie £12,500 each for their half shares (Crenshaw, Memorandum, 1864, Francis G. Ruffin Ms., Va HS). After being rechristened the CSS *Tallahassee*, this vessel was armed with three cannon and 120 men and made a cruise from Wilmington in August 1864, destroying twenty-six prizes off the East Coast ("Cruise of the CSS Tallahassee," August 31, 1864, ORN, I, 3: 701).

99. McRae to Seddon, July 4, 1864, OR, IV, 3: 525–30.

100. Allen to Seward, October 24, 1864, December 15, 1864, Despatches, T262, RG 57.

101. Lawton to Waller, September 28, 1863, OR, IV, 2: 828–29. After the earlier loss of the *Hebe*, Lawton wrote Waller that "the heavy losses experienced by this Department of late, especially in connection with the 'Lee,' the 'Ceres,' and the 'Banshee' make it more important than ever that we should draw speedily from Nassau whatever that market may afford" (Lawton to Waller, December 17, 1863, War Department Collection, T131, reel 9).

102. Ferguson to Lawton, December 5, 1863, Compiled Service Records, T131, reel 92.

103. Lawton to Waller, September 28, 1863, War Department Collection, T131, reel 9.

104. Waller used fifteen different ships, of which nine were captured or sunk between August and March 4, 1864: *Antonica, Banshee, Bendigo, Dee, Don, Fanny, Hebe, Margaret and Jessie*, and *Venus* (Waller to Lawton, December 16, 1863, Letters Received by CQG, M469, reel 7).

105. This assumes that the clothing bales held 550 yards of cloth and that the blanket bales contained 25 pairs each. The *Dee* in October had a typical cargo of 2,500 pairs of shoes and 3,200 blankets (Lawton to Cone, October 1863, War Department Collection, T131, reel 9).

106. Ruffin, Testimony 1865, 22. The profits for such merchants represented an enormous expense to the Confederacy. An accounting in August 1864 showed that two contracts, with Collie and Rosenberg, alone cost the Quartermaster Department £175,000, or $17.5 million in Confederate currency (Lawton to Seddon, August 26, 1864, Compiled Service Records, M331, reel 154).

107. Ruffin, Testimony 1865, 22.

108. Lawton to Seixas, March 3, 1864, War Department Collection, T131, reel 10.

109. Lawton to F. W. Sims, January 16, 1864, ibid.; Lawton to Seixas, March 3, 1864, ibid.

110. July 29, 1864, Memoranda Book Relating to Agents and Supplies, ch. V, vol. 227, RG 109, NA.

111. January 1864, ibid.

112. March 18, 1864, ibid., 24.

113. Frank Ruffin, Testimony 1865, 23.

114. Trenholm to Seddon, August 12, 1864, OR, IV, 3: 588.

115. Memoranda Book Relating to Agents and Supplies, ch. V, vol. 227, 42, RG 109, NA.

116. William H. Haynes to W. R. Boggs, January 18, 1864, OR, I, 22, pt. 2: 1135.

117. Lawton to Seddon, August 5, 1864, Compiled Service Records, M331, reel 154.

118. Ferguson to Lawton, January 15, 1864, Letters Received by CQG, M469, reel 7.

119. Memoranda Book Relating to Agents and Supplies, ch. V, vol. 227, 42, RG 109, NA.

120. June 30, 1864, ibid., 47.

121. Waller to Lawton, Compiled Service Records, M331, reel 258.

122. Lawton to McRae, September 21, 1864, War Department Collection, T131, reel 10.

123. Lawton to Sharp, March 12, 1864, OR, IV, 3: 210–11.

124. Lawton to Waller, March 13, 1864, War Department Collection, T131, reel 10.

125. June 20, 1864, Memoranda Book Relating to Agents and Supplies, ch. V, vol. 227, 46, RG 109, NA.

126. Lawton to Ferguson, September 3, 1864, OR, IV, 3: 684.

127. June 20, 1864, Memoranda Book Relating to Agents and Supplies, ch. V, vol. 227, 46, RG 109, NA.

128. Lawton to Sharp, September 23, 1864, War Department Collection, T131, reel 10.

129. Bullock to Mallory, September 15, 1864, ORN, II, 2: 720.

130. D. L. Braine to Gideon Welles, October 10, 1864, ibid., I, 10: 548.

131. W. B. B. Cross to Bridewell, December 21, 1864, War Department Collection, T131, reel 10.

132. January 6, 1865, Memoranda Book Relating to Agents and Supplies, ch. V, vol. 227, 58, RG 109, NA.

133. McRae to Seddon, August 4, 1864, Letters Received by CQG, M469, reel 11.

134. Memoranda Book Relating to Agents and Supplies, ch. V, vol. 227, 56–58, RG 109, NA.

135. Items are computed at 100 shoes per case, 76 blankets per bale, and 576 yards of woolens per bale. In contrast, for the entire year of 1863 Bayne received 420,000 pairs of shoes and 292,000 blankets (G. A. Trenholm to Jefferson Davis, December 12, 1864, OR, IV, 3: 955).

136. Seddon to Davis, December 10, 1864, ibid., 930. From June 1864 until January 15, 1865, Frank Ruffin estimated that he received at Wilmington some 3 million pounds of meat, about ten days' rations for the army, of which 1.5 million pounds were delivered by Crenshaw, 57,300 pounds by government steamers, and the rest by private vessels (Ruffin, Testimony 1865, 30).

Chapter 6. The Coming of Total War

1. The transformation of the Civil War into a rapacious and destructive contest is ably chronicled in Charles Royster's *The Destructive War* and John B. Walter's *Merchant of Terror*.

2. W. L. Calhoun to Head Quarters, December 24, 1863, Confederate Papers, M346, reel 317.

3. Voucher, Ira G. Foster, August 31, 1864, ibid. The Federal army used the Mount Vernon factory in Alexandria, Virginia, as a military prison.

4. OR, II, 3: 682.

5. John H. Burton and C. P. Bolles to Josiah Gorgas, ca. May 1864, Confederate Papers, reel 1005; Charles G. Wagner to Gorgas, May 12, 1864, ibid.

6. Burton and Boles to Gorgas, ca. May 1864, ibid.

7. Benjamin Micou to Gorgas, May 5, 1864, ibid.

8. Halleck to George McClellan, February 12, 1862, OR, I, 17: 153.

9. LeRoy Fitch, "Report of Lieu.-Commander Fitch, U.S. Navy," ORN, I, 24: 63.

10. Ibid.

11. Dodge to Henry Binmore, April 2, 1863, ibid., 70.

12. "Report of Lieutenant-Commander Phelps," ibid., 25: 130.

13. Robert B. Mitchell, "Report of Robert B. Mitchell," OR, I, 17, pt. 1: 29.

14. See Surby's *Grierson Raids*. "Chickasaw, the Scout," or L. H. Naron, wrote the narrative of these escapades.

15. Sumner to Slaughter, November 21, 1862, cited in Longstreet (294).

16. Slaughter to Sumner, ibid., 295.

17. Tillson explained to a Federal commission that "when the rebellion broke out I stopped all operations entirely, and before I commenced this was carried by special orders to Quartermaster [Aurelius F.] Cone, and then notified that I was either to go to work with my establishment or go to Richmond jail, and they would take possession of my property" (OR, I, 12, pt. 1: 88).

18. Expenses of Moving Machinery, April 22, 1864, Falmouth Cotton Mill—General Journal, 1860–1865, in Duff Green Ms., Duke.

19. Robert M. Patton to Gov. John G. Shorter, September 19, 1862, Shorter Ms., Ala A.

20. R. B. Baugh to Andrew Johnson, September 15, 1865, Pardon Petitions, M1003, reel 1.

21. Patton to Shorter, September 9, 1862, Shorter Ms., Ala A.

22. Lawton to E. C. McLean, December 4, 1864, War Department Collection, T131, reel 10.

23. Baugh to Andrew Johnson, September 15, 1865, Pardon Petitions, M1003.

24. Myers to Mims, June 15, 1863, War Department Collection, T131, reel 9. Jones's free-wheeling activities soon got him into trouble. After hearing persistent reports that the quartermaster was "conducting his business in a most scandalous manner, & using his office entirely for his own benefit," General Richard Taylor assigned a detective to investigate the situation and found overwhelming evidence that the major was doing business for himself at Chattanooga with government goods (A. R. Lawton to E. C. McLean, December 4, 1864, ibid., reel 10).

25. Instructions for the Government of Armies of the United States in the Field, April 24, 1863, OR, III, 3: 148–64.

26. Lieber spent twenty-one years at the University of South Carolina, where he shaped the tenets of German idealism into a defense of slavery. Later in the North during the Civil War, he wrote on guerrilla warfare and martial law (Friedel 333).

27. Instructions for the Government of Armies of the United States in the Field, April 24, 1863, OR, III, 3: 150.

28. Ibid., 151.

29. Ibid., 150.

30. Halleck to Stanton, November 15, 1863, ibid., 1040.

31. Halleck to Sherman, September 28, 1864, in Sherman 1: 128.

32. Gen. James A. Garfield to Gen. David S. Stanley, April 16, 1863, OR, I, 23, pt. 2: 242.

33. Gen. James Garfield to Col A. D. Streight, April 8, 1863, ibid., pt. 1: 282. See Colvin (53–54).

34. A. D. Streight to J. A. Garfield, April 9, 1863, OR, I, 23, pt. 2: 224. In early May, after a race across northern Alabama, General Nathan Bedford Forrest captured Streight and 1,300 of his men near Rome, Georgia (Speed 4: 414).

35. Florence M. Cornyn to Brig. Gen. Grenville M. Dodge, June 2, 1863, OR, I, 23 pt. 1: 349, 350.

36. EHCRLMA, April 6, 1866, Tn.-Hardin, XV, 211.

37. EHCRLMA, November 6, 1868, Tn.-Franklin, X, 158.

38. Items, November 22 and December 10, 1861, Samuel D. Weakley File, Confederate Papers, M346, reel 1081; James Martin to Seddon, June 5, 1862, April 12, 1861, and December 20, 1863, ibid., reel 661.

39. The debate over the legal status of these mills went on for a generation and may be followed in OR, I, 7: 684, 692–93, 695, 738, 752, 769, and in Report in Case of James Martin, S.D. Weakley, Alex D. Coffee, & Saml. J. Dyas, July 30, 1908, Confederate Papers, M346, reel 1082.

40. Owen 4: 1733; James Martin to Seddon, December 20, 1863, Confederate Papers, M346, reel 661.

41. R. B. Baugh to Andrew Johnson, September 15, 1865, Pardon Petitions, M1003, reel 1.

42. Cornyn to Dodge, June 2, 1863, OR, I, 23, pt. 1: 350.

43. These included Martin and Weakley, Baugh and Kennedy, and Milner and Wood (EHCRLMA, December 14, 1866, December 1866, and January 11, 1868, Ala.-Lauderdale, XIII, 20, 27, 26).

44. Datus Coon, "Report of Col. Datus Coon, Second Iowan Cavalry," January 20, 1865, OR, I, 45, pt. 1: 582.

45. LeRoy Fitch to David D. Porter, April 25, 1863, ORN, I, 24: 87.

46. Ellet to Stanton, April 30, 1863, ibid., 90.

47. Seddon to Joseph E. Johnston, July 25, 1863, OR, I, 24: 233.

48. W. T. Sherman to John Sherman, January 25, 1863, in Thorndike (185).

49. General Paine reported that "Colonel Grierson burned the cotton-mill, railroad depot, and railroad bridge" (Gen. Halbert E. Paine to Col. Richard B. Irwin, June 9, 1863, OR, I, 26, pt. 1: 126–28). Henry Merrell noted "the fine Cotton Factory at Baton Rouge which had supplied West Louisiana had been burned at the fall of that place" (Merrell 306).

50. Gen. Halbert E. Paine to Col. Richard B. Irwin, June 9, 1863, OR, I, 26, pt. 1: 126–28.

51. F. D. Conrad to Members of Congress, October 5, 1863, ibid., IV, 1: 854–55.

52. John Burrus McGehee to James S. McGehee, March 28, 1908, vol. 1, 380, James S. McGehee Ms., LSU.

53. Eve Brower to James S. McGehee, April 4, 1904, ibid., 381.

54. John B. McGehee to James S. McGehee, March 28, 1904, ibid., 380–81.

55. Vouchers, April 1863, Confederate Papers, M346, reel 629.

56. John B. McGehee to James S. McGehee, March 28, 1904, James S. McGehee Ms., vol. 1, 380–81, LSU.

57. John B. McGehee, Reminiscences of the Fight, Destruction of the Residence, on Bowling Green Plantation, October 6, 1864, and February 10, 1903, ibid., part 1, 52–53.

58. Seddon to Johnston, July 24, 25, 1863, OR, I, 24: 232–33.

59. John D. Ashmore, writing in the manufacturing district of South Carolina at this time, believed, "if the tramp of the enemy's cavalry were heard in every farm-yard throughout the land, and in every tan-yard, shoe shop, mill, cotton factory, wool-carding machine, store yard, salt depot, and slaughter pen, and they were to come with purses in their hands instead of drawn swords and loaded weapons, they could and would demand whatever they wanted" (John D. Ashmore to C. D. Melton, August 7, 1863, ibid., IV, 2: 771).

60. William T. Sherman, "Report of Maj. Gen. William T. Sherman," May 24, 1863, ibid., I, 24: 754.

61. John J. Pettus, "Report to the Mississippi Senate and House of Representatives," November 3, 1863, ibid., IV, 2: 920.

62. Sherman, "Report," May 24, 1863, ibid., I, 24: 754.

63. Ibid. Grant later wrote that "the proprietor visited Washington while I was president to get pay for his property, claiming that it was private. He asked me to give him a statement of the fact that his property had been destroyed by National troops, so that he might use it with Congress where he was pressing, or proposed to press, his claim. I declined" (Grant 1: 507).

64. Sherman, "Report," May 24, 1863, OR, I, 24: 754.

65. Myers to Mims, June 3, 1863, War Department Collection, T131, reel 9.

66. Confederates estimated Union losses to be 1.8 million cartridges, 100,000 uniforms, 5,000 barrels of flour, 1,000 bales of cotton, and vast quantities of other stores.

67. According to the scout, L. H. Naron, this action occurred on December 30, 1864.

68. See also EHCRLMA, October 18, 1864, Miss.-Choctaw, V, 128.

69. J. H. Gillis to S. P. Lee, June 6, 1863, ORN, I, 9: 60.

70. See also J. H. Gillis to S. P. Lee, February 1, 1864, ibid., 430; Josiah Pickett, "Report," April 19, 1864, OR, I, 33: 274–75.

71. Lawton to Cone, January 28, 1864, War Department Collection, T131, reel 9.

72. Col. John G. Foster to Gen. H. W. Halleck, July 24, 1863, OR, I, 27 pt. 2: 964, 968.

73. Pratt to Andrew B. Moore, July 10, 1861, A. B. Moore Ms., Ala A.

74. Pratt to Watts, July 22, 1864, Thomas Hill Watts Ms., Ala A.

75. Micou to Benjamin, August 26, 1863, Records of the Confederate States of America (Pickett Papers), reel 25, LC.

76. J. Rhodes Browne to Seddon, December 31, 1863, Confederate Papers, M346, reel 270.

77. James Martin, "Report of Evidence Taken Before a Joint Special Committee of Both Houses of the Confederate Congress to Investigate the Affairs of the Navy Department," September 17, 1862, ORN, I, 1: 507.

78. Browne to Seddon, December 31, 1863, Confederate Papers, M346, reel 270.

79. M. J. Crawford to Lamar Cobb, May 10, 1864, OR, IV, 3: 461.

80. James W. Atwood to J. E. Brown, February 25, 1864, Joseph E. Brown Ms., Ga A.

81. Thomas M. Turner to J. E. Brown, August 12, 1863, ibid.

82. D. A. Jewell to Adj. and Insp. General, June 3, 1863, Adjutant and Inspector General Ms., Ga A.

83. A. P. Allgood to J. E. Brown, July 20, 1863, Joseph E. Brown Ms., Ga A.

84. A. V. Brumby to J. E. Brumby, January 20, 1864, ibid.

85. Stephen B. Marshall to James Seddon, March 1, 1864, Letters Received by CSW, M437, reel 45; John Thompson to J. E. Brown, June 18, 1863, Joseph E. Brown Ms., Ga A.

86. George Schley to Adjutant and Inspector General, July 12 and September 5, 1864, Adjutant and Inspector General Ms., Ga A.

87. William Gregg to Seddon, July 10, 1863, Letters Received by CSW, M437.

88. William Gregg to Brig. Gen. E. L. Molineux, May 13, 1865, GMfgCo Ms., GMfgCo.

89. Exempts List, March 15, 1862, Letters Received by CQG, M469, reel 1.

90. William G. Bentley to William G. Ferguson, ibid., reel 10.

91. Time Book—Cedar Falls Manufacturing Co., 1846–1865, Private Papers, NCA.

92. J. M. Bigney to W. G. Provost, July 10, 1865, GMfgCo ms., GMfgCo.

93. Barrington King to W. E. Baker, May 23, 1862, Barrington King Ms., Ga A.

94. King to Baker, May 1, 1862, ibid.

95. King to Baker, May 23, 1862, ibid.

96. Ibid.

97. Pixley & Childs to P. A. Wilson, January 13, 1863, Civil War Military Collections, NCA.

98. L. D. Childs to Z. B. Vance, December 15, 1862, Governor's Papers, NCA.

99. Myers to R. P. Walker, War Department Collection, T131, reel 9.

100. M. D. Holmes to Peter A. Wilson, March 3, 1863, Civil War Military Collections, NCA.

101. Samuel L. Graham to John N. Graham, May 24, 1865, in John N. Graham, The Graham Family History, 24, Eleanor Graham Ms., Tenn A.

102. John M. Carmack to John E. Tooke, January 27, 1862, OR, II, 1: 879.

103. John D. Ashmore to C. D. Melton, August 17, 1863, ibid., IV, 2: 774.

104. J. P. Strant, A.A. G., Special Order 33, March 13, 1864, ibid., I, 32, pt. 3: 621.

105. Enclosure in J. A. Seddon to Jefferson Davis, November 8, 1864, ibid., IV, 3: 810.

106. A. Thomas to Andrew Johnson, August 29, 1865, Pardon Petitions, M1003, reel 69.

107. EHCRLMA, July 6, 1866, Ga.-Gwinette, XVI, 116; Hennig Accounts, Memoranda Book Relating to Agents and Supplies, ch. V, vol. 227, 11.

108. A. K. Seago to Enoch Steadman, February 7, 1863, Enoch Steadman Ms., Duke.

109. Report of the President and Treasurer of the Graniteville Manufacturing Company Made to a Called Meeting of the Stockholders, April 8, 1867, Augusta, Ga., April 18, 1867, GMfgCo Ms., GMfgCo.

110. Brumby to Brown, January 30, 1864, Joseph E. Brown Ms., Ga A.

111. William Gregg to T. D. Wagner, July 27, 1863, T. D. Wagner Ms., UNC.

112. Barrington King to W. E. Baker, December 14, 1863, Barrington King Ms., Ga A.

113. In the winter campaign in east Tennessee, as Burnside fell back on Knoxville, he ordered White's division to destroy "the cotton factory at Lenoir's" (James H. Wilson to U.S. Grant, November 14, 1863, OR, I, 31, pt. 3: 146).

114. Halleck to Sherman, September 28, 1864, in Sherman 2: 128–29.

115. Barrington King to W. E. Baker, May 30, 1864, Barrington King Ms., Ga A.

116. Item, January 17, 1879, William King Ms., UNC.

117. Charles H. Cox to Frank Lord, July 13, 1864, Charles H. Cox Ms., microform, Emory.

118. A copy of this report, without date, is in the Barrington King Ms., Ga A.

119. W. T. Sherman to H. W. Halleck, July 7, 1864, OR, I, 38, pt. 5: 73. In an article by "B" on "Sherman's Method of Making War," reprinted in the *Southern Historical Society Papers* in 1885, a commentator suggested, "How much franker it would have been to have added to his last sentence, 'and thus get rid of so many competitors to the factories of the North' " (SHSP 13: 444).

120. William King, July 9, 1864, Diary, William King Ms., UNC.

121. Ibid. In September 1864, William King served Sherman as a peace emissary to Joseph E. Brown and Alexander Stephens, and after the war he worked for the Freedmen's Bureau and the Southern Claims Commission.

122. Barrington King to Ralph B. King, July 22, 1865, Barrington King Ms., Ga A.

123. OR, I, 39, pt. 2: 416–23.

124. Halleck to Sherman, September 28, 1864, in Sherman 2: 128–29.

125. Memoranda Book Relating to Agents and Supplies, ch. V, vol. 227, 11.

126. William B. B. Cross to Cunningham, October 20, 1864, War Department Collection, T131, reel 10.

127. P. T. G. Beauregard to Lawton, January 24, 1865, OR, I, 49, pt. 1: 390.

128. August 12, 1864, Augusta Factory Record Book, GMfgCo Ms., USC-Aiken.

129. Lawton to Cunningham, July 28 and August 24, 1864, War Department Collection, T131, reel 10.

130. January 18, 1865, Minutes of the Board of Directors, GMfgCo Ms., GMfgCo.

131. Jonathan Worth to J. M. Odell, January 18, 1865, in *The Correspondence of Jonathan Worth* 1: 341.

132. August 17, 1864, Minutes of Board of Directors, GMfgCo Ms., GMfgCo.

133. By August 1864, the Treasury Department payments to the Quartermaster

Department were in arrears over $89 million (Lawton to Seddon, Letters Sent, CSA QM Ms.; Lawton to Seddon, November 2, November 15, 1864, Compiled Service Records, M331, reel 154).

134. C. C. Platter, November 19, 1864, C. C. Platter Ms., UGA.

135. Peter J. Osterhaus, "Report of Peter J. Osterhaus," December 26, 1864, OR, I, 44: 82; Oliver O. Howard, "Report of Gen. Oliver O. Howard," December 28, 1864, ibid., 67.

136. John W. Geary, "Report of Brig. Gen. John W. Geary," January 6, 1865, ibid., 271.

137. William B. B. Cross to F. W. Dillard, August 19, 1864, War Department Collection, T131, reel 10.

138. Rowell, *Yankee Cavalryman* 209; OR, I, 44: 368.

139. EHCRLMA, Ga.-Baldwin, II, 83 and 104.14.

140. A. C. Myers to Capt. Michaeloffoki, March 9, 1863, War Department Collection, T131, reel 9.

141. In March 1864, Baylor opened a correspondence with General Lawton with the prospect of delivering army supplies from abroad (Lawton to Baylor, February 13, 1864, March 11, 1864, War Department Collection, T131). At this time, Frank Ruffin also made an agreement for supplies with a confidential agent "at the instance of the President, as I was authoritatively informed, who was expected to go to Canada" (Ruffin, Testimony 1865, 21). Baylor also made agreements with manufacturers and secured an appointment as a commercial commissioner from the Georgia legislature.

142. *New York Times*, July 17, 1864; J. E. Brown to Jefferson Davis, May 9, 1864, OR, IV, 3: 402.

143. Baylor's open letter on this subject appeared in the *New York Times* but was disavowed by the Georgia political leadership. Governor Joseph Brown's embarrassed disclaimer in the *Times* reflected a deep suspicion of the manufacturing interest (*New York Times*, November 27, 1864).

144. See also OR, I, 44: 211.

145. Sherman's entire army captured or slaughtered 100,000 hogs, 20,000 head of cattle, and 15,000 horses and mules (Henry W. Slocum, "Report of Henry W. Slocum," January 9, 1865, ibid., 159; Willis 332). This compares favorably with the spoils extracted from Kentucky by General Braxton Bragg in 1862 of 50,000 barrels of pork and "a great number of hogs," 8,000 beeves, 15,000 horses, and 1 million yards of cloth (John Jones 1: 176). Of course, Sherman left much of middle Georgia a barren wasteland.

146. Joseph Wheeler, "Report of Major General Joseph Wheeler," December 24, 1864, OR, I, 44: 408; George W. Rains to Seddon, July 23, 1863, ibid., IV, 2: 661.

147. June 30, 1865, Augusta Factory Record Book, 1858–1911, GMfgCo Ms., USC-Aiken.

148. Nora Winder to Sherman, February 12, 1865, OR, I, 47, pt. 2: 395–96.

149. Minutes of the Board of Directors, March 1, 1865, GMfgCo Ms., GMfgCo.

150. Ibid., March 23, 1865.

151. Ibid., March 1, 1865.

152. Ibid., March 23, 1865.

153. Ibid., March 1, 1865.

154. Gregg to Brig. Gen. E. L. Molineux, May 13, 1865, ibid.

155. Lawton to Miles, November 14, 1865, War Department Collection, T131, reel 10.

156. Cunningham to Lawton, March 17, 1865, Letters Received by the CQG, M469, reel 14.

157. Minutes of the Board of Directors, March 20, 1865, GMfgCo Ms., GMfgCo.

158. Ibid., March 23, 1865.

159. Augusta Factory Record Book, 1858–1911, June 10, 1865, GMfgCo Ms., USC-Aiken.

160. Minutes of the Board of Directors, April 20, 1865, GMfgCo Ms., GMfgCo.

161. Gen. James S. Robinson to Capt. E. K. Buttrick, OR, I, 47, pt. 1: 659.

162. William T. Sherman, "Report of Maj. Gen. William T. Sherman," February 15, 1865, ibid., 21.

163. Minutes of the Board of Directors, August 17, 1864, GMfgCo Ms., GMfgCo.

164. Military details in North Carolina factories in Memoranda Book Relating to Agents and Supplies, ch. V, vol. 227, 51; Confederate Quartermaster Department Ms., RG109, NA; Richmond County Manufacturing Company—Account Book, 1863–1865, August 1864, Private Papers, NCA; John Jones (August 12, 1864) 2: 263.

165. December 1864 and January 1865, Richmond County Manufacturing Company—Account Book, 1863–1865, Private Papers, NCA.

166. Petition to R. P. Waller, ca. February 1863, Letters Received by CQG, M469, reel 4.

167. SHSP 51: 369–70.

168. By December 1, 1862, a single calico dress cost $30 in Richmond. John B. Jones thought that "a portion of the people look like vagabonds." He saw "men and women and children in the streets in dingy and dilapidated clothes; and some seem gaunt and pale with hunger—the speculators, and thieving quartermasters and commissaries only, looking sleek and comfortable." In the North, he heard "they are without shirts—cotton being unattainable" (John Jones 1: 200).

169. J. M. Bigney to W. G. Provost, July 10, 1865, GMfgCo Ms., GMfgCo.

170. Marie to Gen. Edward L. Molineux, June 15, 1865, ibid.

171. W. H. Day, "Report of W. H. Day," OR, I, 47, pt. 1: 864.

172. Ray was particularly chagrined that under Federal occupation no one could get married without first taking an oath of allegiance (Ray Diary, March 1865, Cumberland County Public Library, N.C.).

173. EHCRLMA, September 25, 1865, NC-Cumberland, VI, 358.M, 372.A, 338, 334, 338, 369; C. C. Platter, March 13, 1865, Diary, C. C. Platter Ms., UGA.

174. E. J. Hale Jr. to James H. Lane, July 31, 1865, SHSP 12: 427.

175. C. K. Mallory, Monthly Reports, December 23, 1862 [1863], Records of the Confederate States of America (Pickett Papers), reel 117, LC.

176. Alfred N. Duffie to Charles G. Halpine, July 9, 1864, OR, I, 37, pt. 1: 143.

177. Jacob Bonsack, notarized statement, July 13, 1864, Confederate Papers, M346, reel 79.

178. Alfred N. Duffie to Charles G. Halpine, July 9, 1864, OR, I, 37, pt. 1: 144.

179. EHCRLMA, August 1, 1865, Va.-Augusta, V, 23.

180. J. W. Overby to W. G. Ferguson, July 4, 1864, Letters Received by CQG, M469, reel 11.

181. Shriser's Report, June 27, 1864, ibid.

182. Lewis served as lieutenant governor of Virginia during Reconstruction (Cheney 225).

183. Wesley Merritt, "Report of Wesley Merritt," OR, I, 43, pt. 1: 37.

184. J. A. S. Lightburn to S. F. Adams, November 18, 1864, ibid., pt. 2: 643.

185. Philip Sheridan to John A. Rawlins, February 27–March 28, 1865—Expedition from Winchester to the Front of Petersburg, Va., March 14, 1865, ibid., 46, pt. 1: 477–78.

186 Thomas C. Devin, February 27–March 28, 1865—Expedition from Winchester to Petersburg, Va., ibid., 490.

187. Ibid. Devin claimed the destruction of 3,000 Confederate uniforms, 2,000 drawers and shirts, 1,000 shelter tents, and "1 cloth mill, filled with machinery and in full operation, containing an immense amount of Confederate gray cloth and 1,500 pounds of wool; 2 cotton mills with 35 bales of cotton, 1 candle factory" (ibid., 494).

188. P. H. Sheridan, "Report of P. H. Sheridan from February 27 to March 28, 1865," July 16, 1865, ibid., 481.

189. William G. Bentley to William G. Ferguson, Letters Received by CQG, M469, reel 10.

190. William Ferguson, voucher, July 12, 1864, Compiled Service Records, M331, reel 92; see also Orders of Company B, 39th Va. Militia, March 13 to April 13, 1862, Compiled Service Records of Confederate Soldiers Who Served in Organizations from the State of Virginia, M324, reel 851.

191. Endorsement, William G. Bentley to William G. Ferguson, June 2, 1864, Letters Received by CQG, M469, reel 10.

192. W. G. Ferguson, voucher, July 12, 1864, Compiled Service Records, M331, reel 92.

193. Thirty-ninth Virginia Militia, Compiled Service Records of Confederate Soldiers Who Served in Organizations from the State of Virginia, M324, reel 851; Seddon to Lee, June 15, 1864, OR, I, 40, pt. 2: 686. On April 4, 1865, an astonished Federal lieutenant commanding the Fifth New York Artillery dashed into Petersburg to secure a bridge but found himself dodging snipers located in a large building on the south side of the river; he then "took possession of the house, which was a cotton factory containing some one hundred and forty bales of spun yarn and fifty bales of cotton" (Valentine H. Stone, "Report of Valentine H. Stone," April 4, 1865, ibid., 46, pt. 1: 1091).

194. Gen. George A. Sharpe to Gen. George G. Meade, March 18, 1865, ibid., 56, pt. 3: 29.

195. EHCRLMA, December 28, 1865, Ala.-Tuscaloosa, XXIV, 110; EHCRLMA, October 1867, ibid.; EHCRLMA, February 16, 1866, ibid., IV, 94.

196. John T. Croxton, "Report of John T. Croxton," May 1865, OR, I, 49, pt. 1: 424, 429, 418.

197. Francis L. Cramer, "Report of Maj. Francis L. Cramer, First Alabama Cavalry (Union), of Operations," August 11–15, 1865, ibid., 52, pt. 1: 106.

198. This is a useful abridgement of John T. Trowbridge, *The South: A Tour of Its Battlefields and Ruined Cities*.

199. Edward F. Winslow to E. B. Beaumont, April 9, 1865, OR, I, 49, pt. 1: 480–87.

200. James H. Wilson to William D. Whipple, June 29, 1865, ibid., 369.

201. George P. Swift to Louis Hamburger, April 11, 1865, Louis Hamburger Ms. Duke.

202. Edward P. Winslow to E. B. Beaumont, April 18, 1865, OR, I, 49, pt. 1: 487.

203. William H. Young to Andrew Johnson, August 3, 1865, Pardon Petitions, M1003, reel 24.

204. Francis Salter, "Report of Surg. Francis Salter, U.S. Army," May 3, 1865, OR, I, 49, pt. 1: 352.

205. Edward P. Winslow to E. B. Beaumont, April 18, 1865, ibid., 487.

206. James H. Wilson, "Reports of Bvt. Maj. Gen. James H. Wilson," May 3, 1865, ibid., 352.

207. EHCRLMA, January 6, 1866, Ga.-Muscogee, XXIII, 30, 24; Edward F. Winslow to E. B. Beaumont, April 18, 1865, OR, I, 49, pt. 1: 484–87; Van Horne 355.

208. EHCRLMA, February 15, 1865, Ga.-Muscogee, XXIII, 41; Fontaine 96. A

refugee free Negro, Arthur Greer, gave Federal officers a graphic description of manufacturing activities in Columbus in November 1863: "Says the Government has all kinds of manufactories at Columbus. Rolling mill, foundries, gun shops, sword & pistol manufacturers, nail factory, army comb manufactory &c that on the majority of Gov't shops they work day & night that Negroe workmen are employed as far as possible" (Arthur Greer—General Statement, November 6, 1863, Union Provost Marshall's File of Papers Relating to Individual Civilians, M345, reel 111).

209. Wilson, "Reports."

210. Robert H. G. Minty, "Report of Col. Robert H. G. Minty, Fourth Michigan Cavalry," ibid., 442.

211. EHCRLMA, September 20, 1865, Ga.-Upson, XXXIII, 191.

212. As almost solitary examples of oversight or good fortune, two factories within the Federals' grasp escaped the torch: Prattville and Waynmanville. The New England origins of their owners, Daniel Pratt and George Swift, may have saved them.

213. Col. Orville E. Babcock to Gen. Burnside, November 7, 1863, OR, I, 31, pt. 3: 77.

214. Cannon to Memminger, November 22, 1863, Letters Received by CSW, M437.

215. A. Thomas to Andrew Johnston, Pardon Petitions, M1003, reel 69.

216. Scott and Angel 234; Alvan C. Gillem, "Report of Brig. Gen. Alvan C. Gillem," April 24, 1865, OR, I, 49, pt. 1: 330.

217. Jefferson Davis to R. E. Lee, March 30, 1865, ibid., pt. 2: 1174.

218. Gillem, "Report," 332.

219. List of Property Taken at the Close of the War, April 1865, Fries Ms., Mor HS.

220. John Fries, Reminiscences of Confederate Days, April 4, 1923, Private Papers, NCA.

221. List of Property Taken at the Close of the War, April 1865, Fries Ms., Mor HS.

222. W. D. Turner, n.d., Notley D. Tomlin Ms., Duke.

223. Ibid.

224. Gillem, "Report," 334.

225. George Stoneman to George H. Thomas, April 13, 1865, ibid., 324; Tenney 698.

226. By January 25, General Lawton was distraught over the irreparable loss of quartermaster stores between Greensboro and Charlotte (Lawton to R. J. Echols, January 25, 1865, War Department Collection, T131, reel 10).

227. After the war, a North Carolina official questioned whether these raids in part were motivated "with an eye also to the suppression of the rivalry which might grow formidable after the restoration of peace, with the advantages possessed by the South in climate, in the cost of living, in the savings of the cost of transportation, and the more decided advantage in the proximity of the cotton field" (North Carolina, State Board of Education, *North Carolina and Its Resources* [Raleigh, 1896], 188).

228. Lawton to Beauregard, January 12, 1864, A. R. Lawton Ms., UNC.

Chapter 7. The Tortuous Course Toward Economic Reconstruction

1. The most comprehensive modern biography of Johnson is Trefousse, *Andrew Johnson*.

2. *The Papers of Andrew Johnson* 6: 224; Hall 155, 165. In Tennessee, Johnson was prepared to introduce black suffrage gradually, "first, those who had served in the army; those who could read or write, and perhaps a property qualification for others, say $200 or $250" (Savage appendix, 102).

3. OR, I, 4: 512; ibid., 52, pt. 2: 159.

4. Ibid., 4: 396; ibid., 22, pt. 2: 760; ibid., 54, pt. 2: 134.

5. Ibid., 47, pt. 3: 708; ibid., 52, pt. 2: 176.

6. Charles P. Mellon to Charles A. Fuller, September 5, 1864, Records of the Civil War Special Agencies of the Treasury Department (1st Special Agency—Nashville District—Letters Received by Asst Spec. Agent: December 1863–June 1865).

7. Pitzer Miller to Andrew Johnson, November 29, 1862, *The Papers of Andrew Johnson* 6: 78.

8. Pitzer Miller to Andrew Johnson, March 7, 1863, ibid., 6: 166–67.

9. Ibid.

10. Williams to William P. Campbell, February 13, 1864, Records of the Civil War Special Agencies of the Treasury Department (1st Special Agency—Franklin District, Letters Received by Asst Spec. Agent: December 1863–June 1865).

11. Charles P. Mellon to Charles A. Fuller, September 6, 1864, Records of the Civil War Special Agencies of the Treasury Department (1st Special Agency—Nashville District, Letters Received by Asst Spec. Agent: Dec 1863–June 1865).

12. A Johnson family history notes, "In the late eighteen fifties Andrew Johnson invested heavily in the Holston Cotton Factory in Union, Tennessee, now known as Bluff City. It was located at the present site of the now defunct Bluff City Mill. After Johnson's death, his daughter Mary . . . came to Union to oversee the cotton factory" (The Johnson, Stover, and Bachman Connection Ms., based

on Mary E. Bachman Richards papers in possession of Elizabeth Bachman Carrier, Bluff City, Tenn.). This is plausible. Johnson's early account books indicate that he ran a sundry store in connection with his tailor's trade and did a fair business in cloth and thread; he may have had prewar investments in manufacturing (Andrew Johnson, Account Books, 1831–1842, Andrew Johnson Museum, Tusculum College, Greenville, Tenn.). Later, as governor and senator, he had a substantial income available for investments and built an estate of $100,000. His relationship with the Prather and Snapp cotton mill is clear. The company was established in 1873, and the proprietor borrowed funds from "late prest. Johnson wh[ich] he has been unable to pay back & we understand that Mrs. Stover has taken an int[erest] in the cotton fac[tory] to that am[oun]t" (EHCRLMA, June 6, 1878, Tenn.-Sullivan, XXVII, 228). This investment of $15,500 can be followed in John Maloney to Mary. J. Stover, February 6, 1878, Andrew Johnson Papers, Andrew Johnson Museum, Tusculum College, Tusculum, Tenn.

13. Edward Ayers, in *The Promise of the New South* (104–31), emphasizes the social consequences of economic reconstruction, while James C. Cobb, in *Industrialization and Southern Society, 1877–1984*, analyzes the promotional psychology; Robert P. Sharkey's *Money, Class, and Party* remains one of the most useful economic studies of the period.

14. Harvey M. Watterson to Andrew Johnson, June 29, 1865, *The Papers of Andrew Johnson* 8: 319.

15. Barrington King to Ralph B. King, July 22, 1865, Barrington King Ms., Ga A.

16. Duncan Murchison to Andrew Johnson, July 10, 1865, Pardon Petitions, M1003, reel 41.

17. William H. Young to Andrew Johnson, August 3, 1865, ibid., reel 24.

18. R. C. Brinkley to Andrew Johnson, ibid., reel 48.

19. Eli Thayer to Andrew Johnson, June 6, 1864, *The Papers of Andrew Johnson* 6: 714– 15.

20. *Nation* 1, no. 10 (September 1865): 294.

21. John C. Breckenridge to Jefferson Davis, February 18, 1865, OR, IV, 3: 1094. Several studies of the economic costs of the war are analyzed in Ball (300–301).

22. Minutes of the Board of Directors, September 21, 1864, GMfgCo Ms., GMfgCo; E. C. Elmore, 1864, Confederate Papers, M346, reel 282.

23. Report of the President of the Augusta Factory at the Annual Meeting of the Stockholders, on 30th June, 1873, June 30, 1873, GMfgCo Ms., GMfgCo.

24. Augusta Factory Records Book, 1858–1911, June 30, 1866, GMfgCo Ms., USC, Aiken.

25. Gregg later said that the accounting for the whole war showed a deficiency of $221,000 for his company (Report of the President & Treasurer of the Graniteville Manufacturing Co., April 18, 1867, GMfgCo Ms., GMfgCo).

26. Arthur G. Gower to George E. Bowman, April 10, 1936, Markley Family Ms., USC.

27. State of North Carolina in Account with F & H Fries, April 1865, Fries Ms., Mor HS; Record of the Union Manufacturing Company—1848, July 13, 1865, 96, Union Mfg. Co. Ms., Duke.

28. Albert G. Browne to Hugh McCulloch, September 13, 1865, Letters Relating to Claims Received in the Office of the Secretary of the Treasury, 1864–1887, RG56, NA (hereafter Letters Relating to Claims).

29. The rolling mill at Chattanooga was later sold to a Northern purchaser for $170,000. A. O. Anderson to Andrew Johnson, April 1866, Letters Relating to Claims.

30. George W. Dent to Treasury Dept., March 14, 1866, ibid.

31. EHCRLMA, August 12, 1867, Tx.-McLennan, XXI, 10.Q, Baker, Harvard. In October 1865, a Northern journalist visiting New Braunfels found a cotton mill in operation, started within the previous three weeks. The mill, which operated from early dawn until eleven o'clock at night, was "stated to have come from England; but I discovered it was from New York, smuggled across the border, just before the close of the war, from Mexico" (*Letters from the Commercial Correspondent of an Association of Cotton Manufacturers* [Boston: George C. Rand & Avery, 1865], 14). Federal authorities did not seize this mill. Apparently the local German owners offered substantial proof of wartime loyalty to the Union.

32. W. Stevenson to Gen. Edward L. Molineux, June 30, 1865, GMfgCo ms., GMfgCo.

33. Albert G. Browne to Hugh McCullough, August 15, 1865, Letters Relating to Claims.

34. S. L. Graham to John N. Graham, September 1865, Graham Family History, Eleanor Graham Ms., Tenn A.

35. Jos. Martin's Statement of Investigation of Cotton Stored in South Carolina 1866, 1866, Fries ms., Mor HS.

36. Disposition of Cotton Stored in South Carolina, 1866, ibid.

37. John Fries, Reminiscences of Confederate Days, April 4, 1923, Private Papers, NCA.

38. King expected that with these bales and "other property—should the vandals not destroy, hope yet to make a good division to stockholders; if the factory should be lost, will have something left of the wreck" (King to Rev. W. E. Baker, August 10, 1864, Barrington King Ms., GSA).

39. Mrs. R. B. King to Uncle Marshall, February 2, 1865, ibid.

40. Barrington King, Disposition, August 12, 1865, ibid. Mrs. King wrote her uncle, "Oh, Uncle Marshall! it is such a dreadful thing after beginning life so

happily & living in such ease & comfort to have everything swept away at one blow" (Mrs. R. B. King to Uncle Marshall, February 2, 1865, ibid.).

41. B. King to Eva, May 3, 1865, ibid.

42. William Gregg, Minutes of the Board of Directors, June 8, 1865, GMfgCo Ms., GMfgCo.

43. George Hunnington to William Gregg, July 10, 1865, ibid.

44. W. Stevenson to Gen. Edward L. Molineux, June 30, 1865, ibid.

45. EHCRLMA, October 18, 1865, Ga.-Augusta, Ib, 105.

46. EHCRLMA, August 5, 1865, Ga.-Augusta, Ib, 8.

47. Gazaway B. Lamar to Brother, September 22, 1865, Letters Relating to Claims.

48. C. S. Marshall to Hugh McCullough, July 27, 1866, ibid.

49. A. G. Browne to Hugh McCulloch, March 31, 1866, ibid.

50. E. Willis to William Gregg, June 25, 1865, GMfgCo Ms., GMfgCo.

51. See Schley's voucher with ibid.

52. James B. Bingham to Andrew Johnson, February 19, 1866, Letters Relating to Claims.

53. George Schley to Gazaway B. Lamar, August 16, 1865, ibid.

54. Hughes, Denver, and Peck to Hugh McCulloch, March 26, 1866, ibid.

55. James Q. Smith to Hugh McCullough, March 7, 1866, ibid.

56. He also claimed sixty-nine bales of cotton belonging to Chattanooga's Direct Trade and Importing Company (ibid.).

57. Amos A. Lawrence to Andrew Johnson, July 1, 1865, *The Papers of Andrew Johnson* 8: 336.

58. Barrington King to Andrew Johnson, Pardon Petitions, M1003, reel 20.

59. August 29, 1865, Green County Citizens: Amnesty, Miscellaneous Ms., UGA.

60. James B. Pace to Andrew Johnson, July 30, 1865, Pardon Petitions, M1003, reel 59; John D. Williams to Andrew Johnson, May 23, 1865, ibid., reel 43.

61. R. C. Brinkley to Johnson, September 2, 1865, ibid., reel 50.

62. John M. Morehead to Johnson, June 29, 1865, ibid., reel 41.

63. William Gregg, Jr. to Johnson, June 20, 1865, ibid., reel 45.

64. Ibid.

65. Pardon document, June 28, 1865, GMfgCo Ms., GMfgCo.

66. Barrington King to Johnson, August 23, 1865, Pardon Petitions, M1003, reel 20.

67. Wilfred Turner to Johnson, August 24, 1865, ibid., reel 43.

68. Charles A. Nutting to Johnson, July 18, 1865, ibid., reel 21.

69. J. M. Worth to Johnson, June 30, 1865, ibid., reel 43.

70. Jonathan Worth to Johnson, ca. July 22, 1865, ibid.

71. Archibald G. McIlwaine to Johnson, July 5, 1865, ibid., reel 64.

72. R. B. Baugh to Johnson, September 15, 1865, ibid., reel 1.

73. Henry W. Fries to Johnson, July 22, 1865, ibid., reel 38.

74. Thomas M. Holt to Johnson, June 27, 1865, ibid., reel 39; Beatty 108–9.

75. John M. McDonald to Johnson, June 28, 1865, Pardon Petitions, M1003, reel 40.

76. John M. Morehead to Johnson, June 29, 1865, ibid., reel 41.

77. William H. Willard to Johnson, June 7, 1865, ibid., reel 43.

78. William H. Young to Johnson, August 3, 1865, ibid., reel 24; Isaac Scott to Johnson, August 15, 1865, ibid.

79. John A. White to Johnson, July 14, 1865, ibid.

80. Henry Merrill [Merrell], petition, October 26, 1865, ibid., reel 14.

81. Orville Jennings, statement, September 30, 1865, ibid.

82. John M. Potter to Johnson, August 11, 1865, ibid., reel 22.

83. Daniel Pratt to Johnson, August 2, 1865, ibid., reel 9.

84. Benjamin Fitzpatrick, a Prattville politician and Johnson supporter, wrote Lewis Parsons, Alabama's provisional governor, that the federal government was after the manufacturers' cotton and he coveted a pardon to secure his property (Benjamin Fitzpatrick to Lewis E. Parsons, September 8, 1865, ibid.).

85. Word missing in the original (E. M. McGehee to Johnson, July 22, 1865, ibid., reel 33).

86. E. A. Nisbet to Johnson, July 22, 1865, ibid., reel 21.

87. James I. Nisbet to Johnson, August 1865, ibid.

88. Charles H. Patton to Johnson, August 8, 1865, ibid., reel 8.

89. Robert M. Patton to Johnson, ca. August 8, 1865, ibid.

90. Wilfred Turner to Johnson, August 24, 1865, ibid., reel 43.

91. Barrington King to R. B. King, August 12, 1865, Barrington King Ms., Ga A.

92. Barrington King to Eva, June 7, 1865, ibid.

93. Barrington King to R. B. King, August 12, 1865, ibid.

94. Barrington King to C. B. King, July 24, 1865, ibid.; Barrington King to Eva, June 7, 1865, ibid.

95. E. A. Nisbet to Johnson, July 22, 1865, Pardon Petitions, M1003, reel 21.

96. Caleb Phifer to Johnson, July 25, 1865, ibid., reel 41.

97. George A. Trenholm to W. W. Royce, June 4, 1865, Trenholm Ms., LC.

98. J. M. Bigney to W. G. Provost, July 10, 1865, GMfgCo. Ms, GMfgCo.

99. John Fries, Reminiscences of Confederate Days, April 4, 1923, Private Papers, NCA.

100. Hamburger wrote, "I met up with some Macon negroes, who have a

troupe of slave minstrels here & I tell you I am very glad to see a negro from Georgia" (Hamburger to wife, June 26, 1867, Louis Hamburger Ms., Duke).

101. Henry Merrell of Arkansas agreed with this, complaining that before the war, "I have been told by young gentlemen from the low country of Georgia that, until they saw me, they had never seen a white man do a hand's turn of work . . . even the overseers and Negro drivers rode on horse-back" (Merrell 166).

102. Mark M. Smith poses some intriguing consequences of "time conscious-ness" and "time discipline" in the South. He argues, for example, that antebel-lum planters "modernized" their agricultural routines by essentially applying the new technology of time and motion studies to slave workers. Therefore in the New South, "there was no new time consciousness simply because southerners had already developed an understanding of time both compatible with and complementary to the type of time essential to the new bourgeois social and economic order demanded by emancipation" (Smith 154, 215 note 44). Manufac-turers took a dissenting view of this time-seasoning process, finding workers, white and black, generally lacking an understanding of the technical require-ments of maintaining an integral group of machines in harmonious operation. Free workers, like slaves, might have feigned ignorance, however, in order to profit from time disobedience. Henry Merrell, who managed both whites and blacks, coined a common plaint, "Mechanics & work-people we had to unlearn much they already knew, & teach them what we knew ourselves, & there keep them at work, until, swelled up in their own opinion by what we ourselves had taught them, they took the notion that we could not get on without them, put on airs, & struck for unreasonable wages, leaving us to begin over again and teach new hands" (Merrell 264). Of course, factories pioneered the use of the clock, bell, and whistle in the antebellum South and did likewise in the chaos of the New South.

103. Black laborers were employed in the Texas prison factory. In 1863, Thomas Carothers petitioned John B. Magruder that "if you can spare me as many as twenty prisoners (negroes would be preferred) to work in the factory, I will most gladly receive them, and after being placed in my charge I would relieve the military department of all expense in relation to them" (Carothers to Ma-gruder, September 20, 1863, OR, II, 6: 306).

104. Wilfred Turner to Andrew Johnson, August 24, 1865, Pardon Petitions, M1003, reel 43.

105. According to Holden, Johnson said that "he expected to confiscate the estates of the large slave owners, who were traitors and proscribed, and divide them among the woolhat boys of the South, who had been impoverished and had been compelled to fight for slavery against their will" (Holden, *Memoirs*, 54).

106. Writing of the postwar period, Dan R. Frost persuasively argues that "Southern academics who hoped to rectify the South's material and technological inferiority within the reconstructed Union believed higher education could eventually transform the south into a dynamo of industry and science," and they "pointed to the Confederate experiment as both proof of the efficacy of industrialization and the South's ability to industrialize" (Frost 148).

107. U.S. Congress, Senate, "Provisional Governors of States," Executive Documents, no. 26, 79, series 1237, 39th Congress, 1st Session, March 6, 1866.

108. Andrew Johnson to William L. Sharkey, August 15, 1865, *The Papers of Andrew Johnson* 8: 599–600; U.S. Congress, Senate, 39th Congress, 2nd Session, Executive Documents, no. 6, 1–10, series 1276.

109. Alabama, *Journal of the Proceedings of State of Alabama, Held in the City of Montgomery, On Tuesday, September 12, 1865* (Montgomery, 1865), 7.

110. W. H. Seward to Benjamin F. Perry, November 20, 1865, in Andrew Johnson, "Message from the President of the United States . . . in Regard to Provisional Governors of States," March 6, 1866, 39th Congress, 1st Session, Senate Executive Documents, no. 43, 200, series 1238.

111. Ibid., 201.

112. J. D. B. DeBow to Benjamin Perry, October 12, 1865, in *New York Times*, October 15, 1865; "Future of the South," *DeBow's Review* 1 (January 1866): 6.

113. Jonathan Worth to J. M. Worth, August 20, 1865, Jonathan Worth Ms., UNC.

114. North Carolina, *Journal of the Convention of the State of North Carolina, at Its Session of 1865* (Raleigh, 1865), 7.

115. The North Carolina "black code" later adopted by the legislature legitimized black testimony before the courts and black marriages but sanctioned other legislation that inhibited free economic and political activity by blacks (Andrews 160).

116. North Carolina, *Journal of the Convention of the State of North Carolina*, 15.

117. H. A. Dowd to P. H. Winston, January 28, 1865, Compiled Service Records, M331, reel 78.

118. North Carolina, *Journal of the Convention of the State of North Carolina*, 47, 87.

119. A general bill to tax retailers was amended to exclude an "owner of a cotton or woolen factory . . . when such factory has been destroyed" (North Carolina, *The Journal of the Session of 1865* [Raleigh, 1865], 78).

120. Georgia, "Journal of the Proceedings of the People of Georgia Held in Milledgeville in October and November 1865 Together with Proclamations and Resolutions Adopted," in Allen P. Chandler, *The Confederate Records of the State of*

Georgia, Compiled and Published Under Authority of the Legislature (Atlanta, 1910), 4: 138.

121. James Johnson to W. H. Seward, October 27, 1865, in Andrew Johnson, "Message . . . in Regard to Provisional Governors of States," March 6, 1866, 39th Congress, 1st Session, Senate Executive Documents, no. 43, 81, series 1238.

122. W. H. Seward to James Johnson, October 28, 1865, ibid.; "Journal of the Proceedings of the People of Georgia," 4: 222.

123. "Journal of the Proceedings of the People of Georgia," 4: 284.

124. Bartholomew Egan to Theodore O. Moore, August 17, 1866, Moore Ms., LSU.

125. Bartholomew Egan to Theodore O. Moore, May 25, 1866, ibid.

126. J. C. Egan, Hon. David F. Boyd, n.d., Walter L. Fleming Ms., LSU; Slave ownership papers, December 24, 1868, Egan Ms., NWSU of La.

127. In the period of Radical Reconstruction, Steadman advocated "retrenchment and reform" and other measures "to advance the prosperity of the State" (*Dallas Herald*, September 19, 1868); Enoch Steadman to J. W. Stroud, L. F. Livingston, and V. H. Crowley, in *Covington Georgia Enterprise*, November 11, 1870.

128. Governor's Address, January 18, 1866, Jonathan Worth Ms., UNC.

129. Ibid. Scott Nelson argues that Worth and another North Carolina manufacturer, John M. Morehead, wanted to build up Morehead City, where Morehead held property (Nelson 61–62). It should be noted that the Southern states were not recognized by Congress, could market bonds in New York or London for only pennies on the dollar, had a severely limited tax base, and held as the main asset for development only stocks in railroads.

130. Georgia, *Journal of the House of Representatives of the State of Georgia, at the Annual Session of the General Assembly, Commenced at Milledgeville, December 4th, 1865* (Milledgeville: Nisbet, Barnes, & Moore, 1866), 95–96.

131. Ibid., 321ff; Georgia, *Journal of the House of Representatives of the State of Georgia at the Annual Session of the General Assembly, Commenced at Milledgeville, November 15, 1866* (Milledgeville: J. W. Bruce, 1866), index.

132. *DeBow's Review* 3 (January 1867): 56.

133. Ibid., 64.

134. Ibid., 56.

135. Frost cogently argues that Southern academics quickly espoused this rationalization of defeat as a way to preserve a sense of honor, then to insist "that defeat required Southerners to embrace science and industrialization in order to lift the South out of its poverty and economic dependence on the North" (Frost 152).

136. *The Land We Love* 1, no. 1 (May 1866): 1–5.

137. Ibid.

138. Ibid., 4, no. 6 (February 1869): 303–16.

139. Broadside, 1866, Barrington King Ms., Ga A.

140. Minutes of the Board of Directors, June 8, 1865, GMfgCo Ms., GMfgCo.

141. William Gregg to James Jones, October 7, 1865, Gregg Ms., LC.

142. The looms cost $28 each (Report of the President & Treasurer of the Graniteville Manufacturing Co. Made to a Called Meeting of the Stockholders, April 18, 1867, April 18, 1867, GMfgCo Ms., GMfgCo; William Gregg to James Jones, August 28, 1865, Gregg Ms., LC).

143. Louis Hamburger to wife, September 9, 1867, Louis Hamburger Ms., Duke.

144. See appendix 4.

145. EHCRLMA, March 31 and May 26, 1868, Va.-Dinwiddie, XI, 457.

146. EHCRLMA, January 19, 1867, Ga.-Upson, XXXIII, 191.

147. EHCRLMA, January 23, 1866, Ga.-Walton, XXII, 179.

148. EHCRLMA, December 24, 1866, ibid.

149. Barrington King to W. E. Baker, December 30, 1865, Barrington King Ms., Ga A.

150. King to W. E. King, October 12, 1865, ibid.

151. June 30, 1865, Augusta Factory Record Book, 1858–1911, GMfgCo Ms., USC, Aiken.

152. EHCRLMA, February 15, 1866, Ga.-Muscogee, XXIII, 41.

153. EHCRLMA, September 10, 1866, Ala.-Autauga, II, 5.

154. EHCRLMA, February 29, 1868, Ala.-Marion, XVI, 144; EHCRLMA, July 11, 1866, ibid.

155. EHCRLMA, September 10, 1866, Ala.-Autauga, II, 26.

156. EHCRLMA, December 14, 1866, Ala.-Lauderdale, XIII, 20.

157. EHCRLMA, July 31, 1874, and May 18, 1870, Ala.-Madison, XV, 195.

158. EHCRLMA, September 22, 1865, and November 6, 1868, Tn.-Franklin, X, 158.

159. EHCRLMA, October 13, 1866, Tn.-Warren, XXXIII, 6.

160. EHCRLMA, January 9, 1866, Tn.-McMinn, XXIII, 17.

161. J. M. Worth to Jonathan Worth, December 14, 1865, Jonathan Worth Ms., UNC.

162. EHCRLMA, March 31, 1868, Va.-Dinwiddie, XI, 554.F.

163. EHCRLMA, December 1, 1868, Va.-Chesterfield, X, 290.1.

164. George B. Scott to Duff Green, February 10, 1866, Duff Green Ms., Duke; EHCRLMA, October 19, 1866, Va.-Chesterfield, X, 290.G.

165. EHCRLMA, November 25, 1865, SC-Richland, XII, 1.

166. Cited in *DeBow's Review* 3 (June 1867): 570.

167. Earl and Moss to Blanton Duncan, January 19, 1867, Graves-Earle Family Ms., Baylor University.

168. *Dallas Herald*, May 7, 1850; Deed Book K, Texas-Bastrop County, 39.

169. William Gregg to Stockholders, February 1867, Letterbook, 1867, GMfgCo Ms., GMfgCo; Gregg to H. H. Hickman, April 15, 1867, ibid.

170. William Gregg to O. G. Lynch, March 25, 1867, ibid.

171. Jasper Stowe, Memorandum of Business Thought, September 1874, Mill Account Book, 1856–57, Stowesville Cotton Factory Ms., Duke; Fontaine 100–102.

172. Louis Hamburger to George P. Swift, April 18, 1867, Louis Hamburger Ms., Duke.

173. Henry U. Perry to Louis Hamburger, June 29, 1868, ibid.; Hamburger to wife, June 22, 1869, ibid.; George P. Swift to Hamburger, July 1, 1876, ibid.

174. William E. Holt to Uncle, May 1870, James Wilson White Ms., UNC. Thomas Holt wrote at the time, "the new cotton mill is running, is a magnificent mill, & I expect making money fast, on checks . . . I intend to put in looms this summer, there is more money in checks than anything else, & no end to the demand" (Thomas Holt to William A. Carrigan, March 8, 1870, James W. White Ms., UNC).

175. United States, Congress, House of Representatives, "Message of the President," Executive Documents Doc. No. 1, Series 1281, 1–2, 39th Congress, 2nd Session, December 3, 1866.

Chapter 8. Forging the New South

1. Although Congress attempted in 1871 to satisfy selected claims of Southern Unionists for the wanton destruction of their property by the Federal armies, the Southern Claims Commission established such stringent requirements for proving loyalty that no Southern corporation or manufacturer received funds. Both Barrington King of Roswell and James Martin of Florence were unsuccessful petitioners (Klingberg 134, 179). General Order No. 100 became the basis of modern American military conduct against belligerents and was followed during the Philippine insurrection, the two world wars, and later military actions.

2. An analysis of the New South business ideology may be found in Doyle (314–16).

3. Two recent studies are Beatty's *Alamance* (110–16) and Nelson's *Iron Confederacies* (95–114, 115–38).

4. William Gregg to H. H. Hickman, February 7, 1867, GMfgCo Ms., GMfgCo.

5. *Proceedings of the Convention Held for Establishing Direct Trade Between Norfolk and Liverpool; and for Completing the Connections of Norfolk with the Ohio and Missis-*

sippi Rivers, and the Pacific Coast, Held in the City of Norfolk on the 14th, 15th, and 16th Days of October, 1868, 9.

6. Jasper Stowe, Memorandum of Business Thought, September 1874, Mill Account Book, 1856–57, Stowesville Cotton Factory Ms., Duke.

7. In 1875, the Texas Grange established a manufacturing company at Jefferson to make ironware (EHCRLMA, November 5, 1875, Tx.-Marion County, XXII, 426).

8. Like many Radicals, Holden was largely concerned with railroad development (Harris 246–47).

9. A. J. Newlin to Maria Franck, August 4, 1868, Maria Franck Ms., UNC; *Fayetteville Eagle*, January 12, 1871.

10. Helper, March 19 and April 2, 1868.

11. William Holt to Wm. A. Carrigan, August 9, 1870, James Wilson White Ms., UNC.

12. Jasper Stowe to Matt W. Ransom, August 21, 1876, Matt Ransom Ms., UNC.

13. Although Hill opposed the secession of Georgia, he sat in the Confederate Senate. In March 1865, at LaGrange, Hill told an audience that the Radical Republicans "will not see that this disciplined labor, while it protects society, and keeps the negro in contented, happy subjection, is furnishing food and raiment to millions all over the world" (Benjamin Hill 3).

14. *Proceedings of the Conservative Convention of the People of Georgia, Held in the City of Macon, December 5th, 1867.*

15. Ibid.

16. U.S. Congress, House of Representatives, "Condition of Affairs in Georgia: Evidence Before the Committee on Reconstruction Relating to the Condition of Affairs in Georgia," Miscellaneous Documents No. 52, pt. 1 (1869), 180–81, Series 1385, 40th Congress, 3rd Session (1868–1869).

17. Ibid., 173–74.

18. Ibid., 187.

19. Ibid., 186–87.

20. Enoch Steadman to J. W. Stroud, L. F. Livingston, and V. H. Crowley, in *Covington Georgia Enterprise*, November 11, 1870.

21. The Action of the Democratic Central Committee, 1876, Egan Ms., NWSU of La.; William Egan to Unknown, August 2, 1874, ibid.

22. The Southern press was filled with evidence of this. For example, Judge T. J. Mackey of South Carolina, a supporter of Radical governor Daniel Henry Chamberlain, worked for Wade Hampton and Rutherford Hayes, believing this would bring increased immigration and capital to South Carolina (*Savannah Morning News*, January 1, 1877).

23. Doyle finds, as do many other historians, that in the postwar cities "modern forms of competition and segregation between the races appeared earliest" (262–64). Beatty writes that in the rural areas of North Carolina, "in several southern mills white workers threatened to strike if blacks joined their ranks" (170).

24. James Woods to Louis Hamburger, September 10, 1867, Louis Hamburger Ms., Duke.

25. Edward McGehee Papers, vol. II, 35, LSU; James S. McGehee Ms., LSU.

26. In 1867, Simpson and Moore contracted with N. E. Lackey, and Benjamin H. Micou of Tallassee factory made a labor contract with Scott Micou and five other individuals in 1872. For one-third of the proceeds of the cotton crop, Micou obligated the signatories "not [to] leave the said premises without permission first obtained [and] that they will labor faithfully on all week days during such hours as said B. H. Micou or his agent may prescribe" (Deed Book J, January 13, 1872, Ala.-Elmore County, 496; Deed Book M, August 15, 1867, Ala.-Coosa County, 99).

27. *Commercial and Financial Chronicle*, cited in *Charlotte Observer*, September 30, 1874.

28. S. P. Sanford to E. Steadman, March 13, 1868, Enoch Steadman Ms., Duke.

29. See also December 1870–August 1871, Loom Book, 1898, Lowell Machine Shop Ms., Baker, Harvard.

30. EHCRLMA, December 30, 1868, Tenn.-Sumner, XXXII, 50.

31. EHCRLMA, May 27, 1870, Tn.-Davidson, VII, 75; EHCRLMA, November 23, 1866, Miss.- Copiah, VII, 236.J.; EHCRLMA, July 1877, Miss.-Adams, II, 169.

32. Catalogue of the Products of the Woolen Mills, Cotton Mills, Flouring Mills of F. & H. Fries, 1884, Henry E. Fries Ms., Duke.

33. Incorporation Papers of Mount Lebanon Manufacturing Company, November 5, 1869, Egan Ms., NWSU of LA.

34. In the previous thirty years, coal production rose from 6 million tons to 108 million tons, and pig iron manufacturing grew from 397,000 tons to 3.4 million tons. Southern petroleum extraction, which commenced with the discovery of Texas reserves in 1866, was 179,000 barrels in 1880 and 23.9 million barrels in 1910 (Hodge 64, 65, 159).

35. Alexander Lichtenstein writes that "the convict lease was not the persistence of a 'precapitalist' form of labor coercion, but the extension and elaboration of a new forced-labor system wholly compatible with regional industrial development and the continuation of racial domination" (13). In fact, prewar prison cotton factories in Mississippi, Louisiana, and Texas operated with little concern for racial domination since inmates were mostly white. The individuals who leased the Baton Rouge prison occasionally put prisoners to work on the

levies. The procedure allowed antebellum Louisiana to save money, a fact that appealed to other states as well. However, the vast growth of the Southern prison population in Reconstruction, swollen mostly by the incarceration of freedmen convicted of property crimes, propelled "demand" beyond available space, thus presenting a rationale for extensive private leasing off prison property. A noble penal idea, that prisoners should be reformed by learning helpful skills, was transmogrified into a system of exploitation for personal profit, but the process began before emancipation.

36. William J. Cooper writes that "the advent of Tillmanism caused little change in the attitude toward industry [in South Carolina] . . . he did nothing to inhibit industrial growth, which exploded in the decade between 1890 and 1900" (124–25). Yet Tillman presented himself as an instrument of Jeffersonian agrarianism throughout a long tenure in office.

37. As a Progressive president confronted with war, Woodrow Wilson and his intimate Southern advisers adopted many of the same tactics of mobilization utilized by the Confederacy (Wilson, *The Papers of Woodrow Wilson* 45: 170–71, 225, 283–85, 324, 358–59, 448–51.

38. William Hesseltine found that thirty-four former Confederate officers "became prominent industrialists in the New South," in comparison to seventy-four who entered upon railroading (Hesseltine 22).

39. Myers to Andrew Johnson, June 24, 1865, Pardon Petitions, M1003; Myers to Johnson, March 13, 1866, Miller, Chesnut, Manning Ms., USC.

40. EHCRLMA, May 21, 1865, Tn.-Davidson, VI, 51.

BIBLIOGRAPHICAL ESSAY ON SELECTED SOURCES

The primary sources for this study have been original documents found in university, state, and national archives, as indicated by the notes. The most useful guides to these sources have been Kenneth W. Munden and Henry Putner Beers's *Guide to Federal Archives Relating to the Civil War* (Washington, D.C.: Government Printing Office, 1962) and Henry Putner Beers's *Guide to the Archives of the Government of the Confederate States of America* (Washington, D.C.: Government Printing Office, 1968), which are enhancements of internal guides used within the National Archives. Most Confederate government documents are housed within the National Archives Record Group 109. John R. Sellers has compiled *Civil War Manuscripts: A Guide to the Collections in the Manuscript Division of the Library of Congress* (Washington, D.C.: Government Printing Office, 1986), a similar list of holdings in the Library of Congress.

Among many guides to university archives, one that stands out for its completeness and detail is Richard C. Davis and Linda Angle Miller's *Guide to the Cataloged Collections in the Manuscript Department of the William R. Perkins Library, Duke University* (Santa Barbara, Calif.: Clio Books, 1980). Also useful are Susan Sokil Blosser and Clyde Norman Wilson Jr.'s *The Southern Historical Collection: A Guide to Manuscripts* (Chapel Hill: University of North Carolina Library, 1970) and Allen H. Stokes Jr.'s *A Guide to the Manuscript Collection of the South Caroliniana Library* (Columbia: South Caroliniana Library, 1982).

Several useful guides to the historical literature of the period stand out. Allan Nevins, James I. Robertson Jr., and Bell I. Wiley's *Civil War Books: A Critical Bibliography* (Baton Rouge: Louisiana State University Press, 1967) is brilliantly supplemented by Steven E. Woodworth, ed., *The American Civil War: A Handbook of Literature and Research* (Westport, Conn: Greenwood Press, 1996), which has forty-seven essays and bibliographies on various chapters of the war. David J. Eicher's edition of *The Civil War in Books: An Analytical Bibliography* (Urbana: University of Illinois Press, 1997) essentially updates the Nevins volume. T. Michael Parrish and Robert M. Willingham Jr.'s *Confederate Imprints: A Bibliography of Southern Publications from Secession to Surrender* (Austin: Jenkin; Katonah, N.Y.: Foster, [ca.1987]) is an excellent guide to Confederate publications; it is useful for following the fine pamphlet collection in the Rare Book Room of the Library of Congress.

General literature on cotton manufacturing can be surveyed in Charles J. H. Woodbury's *Bibliography of the Cotton Manufacture* (2 vols., Waltham, Mass.: Press of E. L. Barry, 1909–10) and in Julia Card Bonham's dissertation, "Cotton Textile Technology in America: Three Centuries of Evolutionary Change" (University of Pennsylvania, 1969), which explores the interrelation of machinery parts in their peculiarly American settings. Among the rich literature on New England and mid-Atlantic cotton mills is Anthony F. C. Wallace's *Rockdale: The Growth of an American Village in the Early Industrial Revolution* (New York: Alfred A. Knopf, 1978), which is filled with technical and social details about manufacturing in Pennsylvania's Delaware valley.

The political economy of the wartime Confederacy has generally been neglected, but valuable peripheral studies include Robert R. Russell's *Economic Aspects of Southern Sectionalism, 1840–1861* (New York: Russell and Russell, c. 1924, 1960), which is based on a careful reading of Old South journals such as *Niles' Register* and *DeBow's Review*; the autobiography of James G. Blaine, *Twenty Years of Congress: From Lincoln to Garfield* (2 vols., Norwich, Conn.: Henry Bill, 1884–86); and Ellis P. Oberholtzer's biography of Jay Cooke, *Jay Cooke, Financier of the Civil War* (2 vols., Philadelphia.: G. W. Jacobs, 1907). The latter two are filled with useful details of the nuances of Civil War currency transactions. Robert P. Sharkey's *Money, Class, and Party: An Economic Study of Civil War and Reconstruction* (Baltimore: Johns Hopkins University Press, 1959) ably examines the gyrations of tariff, national banking, and currency policies under Treasury Secretary Hugh McColloch.

Confederate financial policy is usefully analyzed in Richard C. Todd's *Confederate Finance* (Athens: University of Georgia Press, 1954) and Douglas B. Ball's *Financial Failure and Confederate Defeat* (Urbana and Chicago: University of Illinois, 1991), which fault Memminger for the collapse of fiscal stability in the South. John C. Schwab's older study, *The Confederate States of America, 1861–1865: A Financial and Industrial History of the South during the Civil War* (New York: B. Franklin, c. 1901, 1968), is an overview of Confederate policy. Richard I. Lester's *Confederate Finance and Purchasing in Great Britain* (Charlottesville: University of Virginia Press, 1975) examines the Erlanger loan, Huse's career (which he finds credible), and Confederate shipbuilding and concludes that England replaced the North as a Southern supplier to a much greater extent than is generally recognized. Caleb Huse's own book, *The Supplies for the Confederate Army, How They Were Obtained in Europe and How Paid For* (Boston: T. R. Marvin and Son, 1904), is literate but disingenuous with regard to his financial manipulations. On Confederate logisti-cal support, Richard D. Goff's *Confederate Supply* (Durham, N.C.: Duke University Press, 1969) excels, although it has little about the clothier generals. Based on a careful reading of the documents of the Cotton Bureau, James Lynn Nichols's *The Confederate Quartermaster in the Trans-Mississippi* (Austin: University of Texas Press, 1964) fills, in part, a great void for that region, but still many aspects of Texas business and border trade remain to be clarified. Samuel B. Thompson's *Confederate Purchasing Operations Abroad* (Chapel Hill: University of North Caro-lina Press, 1935) is strong on Confederate operations in Canada, a generally ne-glected area of study, and Edward C. Anderson's *Confederate Foreign Agent*, edited by Stanley Hoole (University, Ala.: Confederate Publishing House, 1976), is filled with valuable information on goods skirting the Federal blockade.

Three especially provocative essays on the Confederate government's tenuous relations with manufacturers are Charles Ramsdell's "The Control of Manufactur-ing by the Confederate Government," *Mississippi Valley Historical Review* 8, no. 3 (December 1921); Elizabeth Yates Webb's "Cotton Manufacturing and State Regu-lations in North Carolina, 1861–1865," *North Carolina Historical Review* 9, no. 2 (April 1932); and Louise B. Hill's *State Socialism in the Confederate States of America* (Charlottesville, Va.: Historical Publishing Company, 1936). Charles B. Dew ex-plored an important Confederate business endeavor in *Ironmaker to the Confeder-acy: Joseph R. Anderson and the Tredegar Iron Works* (New Haven, Conn.: Yale University Press, 1966). Hartwell T. Bynum's "Sherman's Expulsion of the Roswell Women in 1864," *Georgia Historical Quarterly* 54, no. 2 (summer 1970), explores an aspect of the Union's war against civilian laborers.

Civil War travelers to the South included William Russell, the *London Times* correspondent, whose *My Diary, North and South* (Philadelphia: Temple University Press, 1987) reveals much of Confederate psychology. The rich travel collection for Reconstruction happily includes many writers concerned with the physical consequences of the war. Carl Schurz's *The Condition of the South: Extracts from the Report of Major-General Carl Schurz, on the States of South Carolina, Georgia, Alabama, Mississippi, and Louisiana* (Washington, D.C., 1866) finds former slave owners yearning for capital.

Books with graphic materials on the destruction of Southern property include Sidney Andrews's *The South since the War: As Shown by Fourteen Weeks of Travel and Observations in Georgia and the Carolinas* (New York: Houghton Mifflin, 1971); John Richard Dennett's *The South As It Is: 1865–1866*, edited by Henry M. Christ-man (New York: Viking Press, 1965); and John T. Trowbridge's *The Desolate South, 1865–1866*, edited by Gordon Carroll (New York: Duell, Sloan and Pearce; Boston: Little, Brown, 1956), which is a slight abridgement of the original work published in 1866. Other authors observant of social conditions are Robert Somers in *The Southern States since the War, 1870–71*, edited by Malcolm C. McMillan (University: University of Alabama Press, 1965); Edward King in *The Great South*, edited by W. Magruder Drake and Robert R. Jones (Baton Rouge: Louisiana State University Press, 1972); Whitelaw Reid in *After the War: A Southern Tour* (New York: Harper and Row, 1965); and Charles Nordhoff in *The Cotton States in the Spring and Summer of 1875* (New York: D. Appleton, 1876).

Howard K. Beale's injunction in "On Rewriting Reconstruction History," *American Historical Review* 45 (July 1940), was to study the continuity of economic causation in the Civil War period without undue distraction by the political and racial violence. Several historians have attempted this. Peter Wallenstein's *Public Policy in Nineteenth Century Georgia* (Chapel Hill: University of North Carolina Press, 1987) discovers a strong commitment to development within an important state, especially with regard to infrastructure such as railroads, towns, schools, and penitentiaries, and Mark W. Summers in *Railroads, Reconstruction, and the Gospel of Prosperity* (Princeton, N.J.: Princeton University Press, 1984) corrects many misconceptions about the Radical political leaders and makes a splendid case that their principal mission was to develop the South, although this zeal contributed to egregious financial errors in funding railroads with grants of money and lands. Northern finance is viewed in a more predatory light by Scott Reynolds Nelson in *Iron Confederacies: Southern Railways, Klan Violence, and Reconstruction* (Chapel Hill: University of North Carolina Press, 1999). Jonathan M. Wiener's *Social Origins of the New South: Alabama, 1860–1885* (Baton Rouge: Louisiana State University Press, 1978) presents valuable comparative data on Northern and Southern economic development.

Lincoln's views on confiscation, slavery, and Reconstruction are synthesized well by David Herbert Donald in *Lincoln* (London: Jonathan Cape, 1995), while Eric L. McKitrick ably chronicles his successor's choices in *Andrew Johnson and Reconstruction* (New York: Oxford University Press, 1960). Harold Woodman's *King Cotton and His Retainers: Financing and Marketing the Cotton Crop of the South, 1800–1925* (Columbia: University of South Carolina Press, c. 1968, 1990) is a focused economic study of the alliance between cotton planters and Northern factors. Particularly important is his analysis of the reestablishment of this network during Reconstruction.

The New South campaign for industry is insightfully surveyed by Don H. Doyle's *New Men, New Cities, New South: Atlanta, Nashville, Charleston, Mobile, 1860–1910* (Chapel Hill: University of North Carolina Press, 1990) and by James C. Cobb's *Industrialization and Southern Society, 1877–1984* (Lexington: University of Kentucky Press, 1984). Patrick H. Hearden's *Independence and Empire: The New*

South's Cotton Mill Campaign (DeKalb: University of Northern Illinois Press, 1982) argues that nationalism and economic development were not particularly integrated in Southern thinking; rather, the tools of business afforded only a means to contend with the Yankees on a new and bloodless field. The Conservative economic policy is discussed by William J. Cooper Jr. in *The Conservative Regime: South Carolina, 1877–1890* (Baltimore: Johns Hopkins University Press, 1968). Paul M. Gaston's *The New South Creed: A Study in Southern Mythmaking* (New York: Knopf, 1970) emphasizes a reconciliation theme of national bonding through business, while George R. Woolfolk in *The Cotton Regency: The Northern Merchants and Reconstruction, 1865–1880* (New York: Bookman Associates, 1958) finds the New South in an imperial relationship with the North. Robert E. Perry's "Middle Class Townsmen and Northern Capital: The Rise of the Alabama Cotton Textile Industry, 1865–1900" (Ph.D. diss., Vanderbilt University, 1986) stresses the benevolent role of Yankee entrepreneurs in creating the New South, and Yoshimitsu Ide's "The Significance of Richard Hathaway Edmonds and His *Manufacturer's Record* in the New South" (Ph.D. diss., University of Florida, 1959) details the career of an important promoter of the postwar mill boom.

New South labor issues have been insightfully dealt with by J. Wayne Flynt in several studies, including *Dixie's Forgotten People: The Southern Poor Whites* (Bloomington: University of Indiana Press, 1979), which postulates that a white underclass persisted into the New South and populated the mill villages. Alexander C. Lichtenstein focuses on the private exploitation of the black prison class in the extraction industries in *Twice the Work of Free Labor: The Political Economy of Convict Labor in the New South* (London and New York: Verso, 1996). These are supplemented by Gavin Wright's "Cheap Labor and Southern Textiles before 1880," *Journal of Economic History* 39 (September 1979).

As notes of this volume indicate, to a considerable extent this study has been based on the original source materials housed in university, state, or national archives. Since so many documents were destroyed in the war, it has been necessary, in part, to reconstruct the course of industrial growth from sources outside the South. Massachusetts collections in particular hold many valuable manuscript and newspaper materials. Harvard's Baker Library houses the R. G. Dun Collection of "Early Handwritten Credit Reporting Ledgers of the Mercantile Agency," which consists of hundreds of folio volumes of credit reports. These records cover most geographical areas of the South from the mid-1840s to the late 1870s, the war years excluded. Small companies, and those in urban areas, were more inclined to use this service than were large or rural mills. Ledger entries usually consist of letter extracts, often two or three a year, about mill financial conditions.

The Amos A. Lawrence papers at the Massachusetts Historical Society represent the social and financial correspondence of a major manufacturing family and cover practically all aspects of antebellum investment, including the South. The collections of the Merrimac Valley Textile Museum at North Andover hold papers of several companies doing business in the South. The Gustavus Vasa Fox papers in the New York Historical Society give details on Fox's career as a mill manager in New England and hold some Southern correspondence. The papers of Hamilton Smith at the University of Indiana at Bloomington are especially valuable on the topic of Southern mill activity, including several thick clipping books filled with materials from the 1845–60 period. These archives also house the rich Indiana Cotton Mills Collection, which shows fully the problems faced by frontier manufacturers.

The Flowers Collection at Duke University is splendidly indexed and covers most phases of Southern manufacturing. This collection holds papers related to James D. B. DeBow, Enoch Steadman, William Gregg, George E. Badger, William H. Holden, Charles J. Jenkins, Jefferson Davis, Jesse Turner, Amory Fisher, Henry E. Fries, Louis Hamburger, Augustin H. Hansell, John Carrigan, Robert Baird, Duff Green, John Bonsack, Eugenius A. Nisbet, and many others. Duke also has the factory papers of the Cane Creek, Staunton Woolen, Union, and Shoals mills.

The Southern Historical Collection at the University of North Carolina, Chapel Hill, has the papers of Alexander R. Lawton and Edwin M. Holt, among many others. The Moravian Historical Society in Old Salem houses the extensive collection of the Fries mills as well as Francis Fries's personal papers. The North Carolina Division of Archives and History at Raleigh has some mill records and valuable correspondence in both the Governors' and Private Papers collections.

In the Caroliniana Library at the University of South Carolina, Columbia, are the papers of James Gregg, Vardry McBee Sr., and James Chesnut. Most of the Graniteville Manufacturing Company papers and some records of the Augusta Manufacturing Company are now housed at the University of South Carolina, Aiken. These were previously housed at the company archives in Graniteville, which still has supplemental materials. The Georgia Department of Archives and History at Atlanta holds the facsimiles of the Barrington King manuscript collection, and the Alabama Department of Archives and History has a collection of the papers of Daniel Pratt, the Winter family papers, and a rich archive related to Alabama's antebellum economic development. The Robert Jemison Jr. Collection is located at the University of Alabama, Tuscaloosa, and the Patton, Donegan, and Company manuscripts are at the Huntsville Public Library. The University of North Alabama at Florence has the Milner and Wood Collection, Louisiana State University has the James Stewart McGehee Collection, and the Northwest State

University of Louisiana has the Bartholomew Egan family papers. Various supplemental collections were consulted at the University of Kentucky, the University of Texas, Baylor University, the Library of Congress, the University of Virginia, and state archives in Tennessee, Texas, Louisiana, Mississippi, Florida, and Virginia.

There are diverse and rich resources in the physical remains of Southern mills. The resplendent factory buildings at Graniteville give a visual testimony of the manner of their construction. Portions of Francis Fries's Salem mills have been preserved. Many factory buildings were lost at Athens, although their foundations remained until modern times. Mill locations are often indicative of the manner in which waterpower was harvested. Especially instructive are the mill locations at Cypress Creek (Florence), the Rip Raps (Richmond), Saluda (Columbia), Wolf Creek (Memphis), and Dog River (Mobile). The Merrimac Valley Textile Museum at North Andover, Massachusetts, has complete sets of some antebellum machinery as well as a rich collection of manufacturers' catalogs, manuals, and technical studies.

The largest collection of Confederate administrative documents, thanks to Union captures, are those now housed in the National Archives at Washington, D.C. Many of these are available only in microform and in many instances are difficult to read and incomplete. The War Department Collection of Confederate Records, Record Group 109, has the Compiled Service Records of Confederate Generals and Staff Officers, and Nonregimental Enlisted Men, M331, for which there is a supplemental series; the Union Provost Marshall's File of Papers Relating to Individual Civilians, M345; and the immense and largely unexploited Confederate Papers Relating to Citizens or Business Firms, M346. Unfortunately, there has been no general study of the Confederate Quartermaster Department, but the bureau papers in RG 109, although technical, are useful. These include the Letters Received by the Confederate Quartermaster General, 1861–1865, M469; the Letters Sent by the Confederate Secretary of War to the President, 1861–1865, M523; the Letters and Telegrams Sent by the Confederate Quartermaster General, 1861–1865, M900; and the War Department Collection of Confederate Records, Chapter V, Quartermaster Department, 1861–65, T131. Record Group 94, which holds the valuable Pardon Petitions and Related Papers Submitted in Response to President Andrew Johnson's Amnesty Proclamation of May 29, 1865 (the "Pardon Petitions"), M1003, is a large collection of material from several thousand contrite Southerners explaining their wartime behavior. Regrettably, related materials from the executive branch no longer exist.

Correspondence of the Confederate Secretary of War and the Adjutant and Inspector General, both in RG 109, have long needed an authoritative reorganization. These are, respectively, the Letters Received by the Confederate Secretary of War, M437, and Letters Received by the Confederate and Adjutant and Inspector General, 1861–1865, M474. This correspondence may be supplemented by the Records of the Confederate States of America, 1859–1872, the "Pickett Papers," and the Alexander Stephens manuscripts held by the Library of Congress. The papers of General P. T. G. Beauregard's Charleston quartermaster problems are also in the Library of Congress. The Headquarters Papers of the Army of Northern Virginia reside in the Virginia Historical Society in Richmond.

Industrial census materials for 1850 and 1860 were returned to the states many years ago, but now, fortunately, the University of North Carolina has accumulated microforms of most extant materials. The National Archives holds census returns for population and slaves. A Confederate census of North Carolina and large Lower South mills is in RG 109, and an incomplete postwar census of Georgia mills is in the Georgia state archives.

WORKS CITED

Primary Sources—Manuscripts

Adjutant and Inspector General Ms., Ga A.

G. W. Bagby Ms., Va HS.

Robert Baird Ms., Duke.

Joseph E. Brown Ms., Ga A.

Civil War Military Collections, NCA.

Civil War Papers, Miss A.

William W. Clark Ms., Duke.

Commissary Activities and Correspondence, 1863–65, Ms., Fla A.

Compiled Service Records of Confederate Generals and Staff Officers, and Non-regimental Enlisted Men, M331, RG 109, NA (cited as Compiled Service Records).

Compiled Service Records of Confederate Soldiers Who Served in Organizations from the State of Virginia, M324, RG 109, NA.

Confederate Papers Relating to Citizens or Business Firms, M346, RG 109, NA (cited as Confederate Papers).

Confederate Quartermaster Ms., RG 109, NA.

Confederate States of America. Letters and Telegrams Sent Ms., Chapter II, vol. 217, RG 109, NA.

Copies of Letters and Telegrams Sent and Received by Governor Zebulon B. Vance of North Carolina, 1862–1865, T781, NA (cited as Copies of Letters and Telegrams).

Charles H. Cox Ms., microform, Emory.

Jefferson Davis Ms., Duke.

Deed Book 14, Ala.-Autauga County.

Deed Book J, Ala.-Elmore County.

Deed Book K, Texas-Bastrop County.

Deed Book M, Ala.-Coosa County.

Despatches of the United States Consuls in Bermuda, 1818–1906, T262, RG 57, NA.

Egan Ms., NWSU of La.

Walter L. Fleming Ms., LSU.

Georgia Q.M. General Ira R. Foster Ms., Ga A.

Maria Franck Ms., UNC.

Francis Fries Collection, Mor HS.

Henry E. Fries Ms., Duke.

Fries Ms., Mor HS.

GMfgCo Ms., USC, Aiken.

Governor's Papers, NCA.

Eleanor Graham Ms., Tenn. A.

Graniteville Manufacturing Co. Ms., Graniteville Manufacturing Company Archives, Graniteville, S.C. (cited as GMfgCo. Ms.).

Grantee Index to Deeds, Texas-Bastrop, Book B.

Graves-Earle Family Ms., Baylor University.

Duff Green Ms., Duke.

J. J. Gregg and Co. Ms., USC.

Gregg Ms., GMfgCo.

Gregg Ms., LC.

Louis Hamburger Ms. Duke.

J. B. Hope Ms., WM.

Johnson, Andrew. Account Books, 1831–1842. Andrew Johnson Museum, Tusculum College, Greenville, Tenn.

Andrew Johnson Papers, Andrew Johnson Museum, Tusculum College, Tusculum. Tenn.

Barrington King Ms., Ga A.

William King Ms., UNC.

A. R. Lawton Ms., UNC.

Lee's Headquarters Papers, A.N.VA., Va HS.

Letters and Telegrams Sent and Received by Governor Zebulon B. Vance, T781, NA.

Letters Received by the Confederate Quartermaster General, 1861–1865, M469, RG 109, NA.

Letters Received by the Confederate Secretary of War, 1861–1865, M437, RG 109, NA.

Letters Relating to Claims Received in the Office of the Secretary of the Treasury, 1864–1887, RG56, NA (cited as Letters Relating to Claims).

Letters Sent by the Confederate Secretary of War to the President, 1861–1865, M523, RG 109, NA.

Letters Sent to the Confederate Secretary of War, April, 1861–Jan., 1864. Quartermaster General's Office Ms., ch. V, vol. 157, RG 109, NA (cited as Letters Sent, CSA QM Ms.).

Lowell Machine Shop Ms., Baker, Harvard.

Lubbock Ms., Tx A.

Mallory Ms., UNC.

Markley Family Ms., USC.

Edward McGehee Papers, LSU.

James S. McGehee Ms., LSU.

Memoranda Book Relating to Agents and Supplies, ch. V, vol. 227, RG 109, NA.

Mercantile Agency. Early Handwritten Credit Reporting Ledgers of the Mercantile Agency. R. G. Dun Collection, Baker Library, Harvard University (cited as EHCRLMA).

William P. Miles Ms., UNC.

Miller, Chesnut, Manning Ms., USC.

Milner, Wood & Co. Ms., UN Ala.

Milton Ms., U. Fla.

Miscellaneous Ms., UGA.

A. B. Moore Ms., Ala A.

Moore Ms., LSU.

Ms. Census-1850, Indus., Ala.-Autauga.

Ms. Census-1860, Industry, Va.-Henrico.

Ms. Census-1860, Pop., N.C.-Alamance.

Ms. Census-1860, Pop., Va.-Dinwiddie.

Pardon Petitions and Related Papers Submitted in Response to President Andrew Johnson's Amnesty Proclamation of May 29, 1865, M1003, RG 94, NA (cited as Pardon Petitions).

C. C. Platter Ms., UGA.

Daniel Pratt Ms., Ala A.

Private Papers, NC A.

Matt Ransom Ms., UNC.

Ray, Melinda. The Diary of Melinda Ray. Cumberland County Public Library, NC.

Records of the Civil War Special Agencies of the Treasury Dept., A-R, RG366, NA.

Records of the Confederate States of America (Pickett Papers), microcopy in LC.

Francis G. Ruffin Ms., Va HS.

Shorter Ms., Ala A.

Archibald A. T. Smith Ms., UNC.

Statement of Factories Inspected by G. W. Cunningham, Q.M., Entry 453, General Information Index, Miscellaneous Factories No. 2, Box 2, RG 109, NA.

Enoch Steadman Ms., Duke.

Stowesville Cotton Factory Ms., Duke.

Tabular Statement of Cotton & Woolen Factories North Carolina Inspected by Wm. A. Miller, bonded agent in Q.M. Deptmt 1864, Entry 453, General Information Index, Miscellaneous Factories No. 1, Box 2, RG 109, NA.

Tillinghast, Sarah Ann. "Memoirs" (n.d.). Ms. in Cumberland County Public Library, Fayetteville, NC.

Notley D. Tomlin Ms., Duke.

Trenholm Ms., LC.

Union Mfg. Co. Ms., Duke.

Virginia. Governor. Message of the Governor of Virginia and Accompanying Documents. Richmond, 1863, 1864.

T. D. Wagner Ms., UNC.

Theodore D. Wagner Ms., South Carolina Historical Society.

War Department Collection of Confederate Records, T131, RG 109, NA (cited as War Department Collection).

Thomas Hill Watts Ms., Ala A.

James Webb Ms., UNC.

John C. Whiten Ms., Baker, Harvard.

Philip Whitlock Ms., Va HS.

Will Book, Va.-Petersburg.

Edward Willis Ms., LC.

James Wilson White Ms., UNC.

Jonathan Worth Ms., UNC.

Primary Sources—Printed

Alabama. *Journal of the Proceedings of State of Alabama, Held in the City of Montgomery, On Tuesday, September 12, 1865.* Montgomery, 1865.

Andrews, Sidney. *The South since the War: As Shown by Fourteen Weeks of Travel and Observations in Georgia and the Carolinas.* Boston: Houghton Mifflin, c: 1866, 1971.

Beaumont, B[etty]. *Twelve Years of My Life: An Autobiography of Mrs. B. Beaumont of Woodville, Mississippi.* Philadelphia: T. B. Peterson and Bros., 1887.

Brown, Joseph E. "Ex-governor Brown Replies to B. H. Hill's Notes on the 'Situation.' " Augusta: Georgia Printing Company, 1867.

Chesnut, Mary Boykin. *Mary Chesnut's Civil War.* Ed. C. Vann Woodward and Elizabeth Muhlenfeld. New Haven: Yale University Press, 1981.

Confederate States of America, Congress, House of Representatives. "Report of the Committee on Military Affairs on the Message of the President, Transmitting a Communication from the Secretary of War, Relative to the Quartermaster General." Richmond, 1864.

Confederate States of America, War Department. *Regulations for the Army of the Confederate States, 1862.* Richmond: J. W. Randolph, 1862.

Egan, Bartholomew. *Address Delivered at the Commencement of the Louisiana State Seminary and Military Academy on the 29th June, 1866.* Alexandria, La., 1866.

Georgia. General Assembly. *Acts of the General Assembly of the State of Georgia Passed in Milledgeville at the Annual Session in November and December, 1862.* Milledgeville, 1863.

Georgia. *Journal of the House of Representatives of the State of Georgia at the Annual Session of the General Assembly Commenced at Milledgeville, December 4th, 1865.* Milledgeville: Nisbet, Barnes, & Moore, 1866.

Georgia. *Journal of the House of Representatives of the State of Georgia at the Annual Session of the General Assembly, Commenced at Milledgeville, November 6th, 1862.* Milledgeville, 1862.

Georgia. *Journal of the House of Representatives of the State of Georgia at the Annual Session of the General Assembly Commenced at Milledgeville, November 15, 1866.* Milledgeville: J. W. Bruce, 1866.

Georgia. "Journal of the Proceedings of the People of Georgia Held in Milledgeville in October and November 1865 Together with Proclamations and Resolutions Adopted." In Allen P. Chandler, *The Confederate Records of the State of Georgia, Compiled and Published Under Authority of the Legislature.* Atlanta, 1910.

Georgia. Senate. *Journal of the Senate.* Milledgeville, 1863.

Grady, Henry Woodfin. *Joel Chandler Harris' Life of Henry W. Grady, Including His Writings and Speeches.* Ed. Joel Chandler Harris. New York: Cassell, 1890.

Grant, Ulysses S. *Personal Memoirs of U.S. Grant.* 2 vols. New York: Charles L. Webster, 1885.

Hill, Benjamin H. *Speech on the Means of Success, the Source of Danger, And the Consequences of Failure in the Confederate Struggle for Independence.* Atlanta: Economical Book and Job Printing, 1874.

Holden, William Woods. *Memoirs of W. W. Holden.* John Lawson Monographs of the Trinity College Historical Society. Durham: Seeman Printery, 1911.

———. "Message from the President of the United States . . . in Regard to Provisional Governors of States." Senate Executive Documents. Doc. No. 43. Series 1238. 39th Congress, 1st Session. March 6, 1866.

———. *The Papers of Andrew Johnson.* Ed. LeRoy Graf, Ralph W. Haskins, and Paul H. Bergeron. 16 vols. Knoxville: University of Tennessee, 1967–2000.

Jones, Joseph. "Agricultural Resources of Georgia: Address Before the Cotton Planters' Convention of Georgia at Macon, December 13, 1860." *Augusta Chronicle & Sentinel* (1861): 11.

Journal of the Congress of the Confederate States of America, 1861–1865. 7 vols. Washington, D.C.: Government Printing Office, c. 1904, 1905, 1968.

Journal of the Proceedings of the Debates in the Constitutional Convention of the State of Mississippi, August 1865. Jackson, 1865.

King, Edward. *The Great South.* Ed. W. Magruder Drake and Robert R. Jones. Baton Rouge: Louisiana State University Press, 1972.

King, Thomas Butler. *Speech of Thomas Butler King, Delivered in the Hall of the House of Representatives at Milledgeville, Ga., November 10th, 1863.* Milledgeville: Boughton, Nisbet, Barnes, & Moore, 1863.

"Letter from Major-General Henry Heth, of A. P. Hill's Corps, A.N.V." In *Southern Historical Society Papers* 4, no. 4 (July–December 1877): 157.

Letters from the Commercial Correspondent of an Association of Cotton Manufacturers. Boston: George C. Rand & Avery, 1865.

Lubbock, Francis R. *Six Decades in Texas: The Memoirs of Francis Richard Lubbock.* Ed. C. W. Raines. Austin and New York: Pemberton Press, c. 1900, 1968.

Maxwell, James Robert. *Autobiography of James Robert Maxwell of Tuskaloosa, Alabama.* New York: Greenbert, 1926.

McCue, J. Marshall. *Speech of Mr. McCue, of Augusta, Delivered in the House of Delegates, on the 16th and 17th October, 1863, on the Bill to Protect Sheep and Increase the Production of Wool.* Richmond, 1863.

Merrell, Henry. *The Autobiography of Henry Merrell: Industrial Missionary to the South.* Ed. James L. Skinner. Athens: University of Georgia Press, 1991.

"Message of Gov. F. R. Lubbock to the Extra Session of the Ninth Legislature of the State of Texas, Delivered, Feb. 5th, 1863." *State Gazette* (Austin), 1863.

Morgan, Mrs. Irby. *How It Was: Four Years Among the Rebels.* Nashville: Methodist Episcopal Church Publishing House, 1892.

Nichols, George Ward. *The Story of the Great March from the Diary of A Staff Officer by Brevet Major George Ward Nichols, Aid[e]-de-Camp to General Sherman.* New York: Harper and Brothers, 1866.

North Carolina. *Journal of the Convention of the State of North Carolina, at Its Session of 1865.* Raleigh, 1865.

———. *The Journal of the Session of 1865.* Raleigh, 1865.

Proceedings of Manufacturing and Direct Trade Association of the Confederate States. Atlanta, 1861 (cited as *Proceedings*).

Proceedings of the Conservative Convention of the People of Georgia, Held in the City of Macon, December 5th, 1867. Macon: Telegraph Steam Printing House, 1867.

Proceedings of the Convention Held for Establishing Direct Trade Between Norfolk and Liverpool; and for Completing the Connections of Norfolk with the Ohio and Mississippi Rivers, and the Pacific Coast, Held in the City of Norfolk on the 14th, 15th, and 16th Days of October, 1868. Norfolk, Va: Journal Job Office, 1868.

Proceedings of the Convention of Cotton Planters, held in Macon, Ga., July 4, 1861 with a Communication on the Proposed Issue of Treasury Notes by the Confederate Government, by Duff Green, Esq. [Macon]: 1861.

"Proceedings of the First Confederate Congress, Fourth Session [various dates], 1864." In *Southern Historical Society Papers*, vol. 50. Richmond: Virginia Historical Society, 1943.

"Proceedings of the First Confederate Congress, Third Session in Part [various dates], 1863." In *Southern Historical Society Papers*, vols. 43, 44, 48. Richmond: Virginia Historical Society, 1941, 1943.

Schley, John. *Our Position and Our True Policy*. Augusta, 1863.

Sherman, William T. *Memoirs of General W. T. Sherman*. 2 vols. New York: C. L. Webster, 1891.

South Carolina. *Journal of the Convention of the People of South Carolina, held in 1860, 1861 and 1862, together with the Ordinances, Reports and Resolutions, etc.* Columbia, S.C.: R. W. Gibbes, 1862.

Texas. Legislature. *General Laws of the Tenth Legislature (Second Extra Session) of the State of Texas*. Austin: State Gazette Office, 1865.

Tobey, Edward S. *The Industry of the South: Its Immediate Organization Indispensable to the Financial Security of the Country, A Speech Delivered Before the Boston Board of Trade, November 7th, 1865, by Edward S. Tobey*. Boston: J. H. Eastburn's Press, 1865.

United States. Congress. House of Representatives. "Condition of Affairs in Georgia: Evidence Before the Committee on Reconstruction Relating to the Condition of Affairs in Georgia." Miscellaneous Documents No. 52, pt. 1 (1869). Series 1385. 40th Congress, 3rd Session. 1868–1869.

United States. Congress. House of Representatives. "Message of the President." Executive Documents Doc. No. 1. Series 1281, 1–2. 39th Congress, 2nd Session. December 3, 1866.

United States. Congress. Senate. "Provisional Governors of States." Executive Documents Doc. No. 26. Series 1237. 39th Congress, 1st Session. March 6, 1866.

United States. Department of the Navy. *Official Records of the Union and Confederate Navies in the War of the Rebellion*. 30 vols. plus index. Washington, D.C.: Government Printing Office, 1894–1927 (cited as ORN).

The War of the Rebellion: A Compilation of the Official Records of the Union and Confederate Armies. 70 vols. in 130 serials, index, atlas. Washington, D.C.: Government Printing Office, 1881–1901 (cited as OR).

The Wartime Papers of R. E. Lee. Ed. Clifford Dowdey. New York: Bramhall, 1961.

Willis, Charles Wright. *Army Life of an Illinois Soldier, Including a Day by Day Record of Sherman's March to the Sea—Letters and Diary of the Late Charles W. Willis,*

Compiled and Published by His Sister, Mary E. Kellogg. Washington, D.C.: Globe Printing Company, 1906.

Wilson, Woodrow. *The Papers of Woodrow Wilson.* Ed. Arthur Link et al. 69 vols. Princeton, N.J.: Princeton University Press, 1966–1994.

Secondary Sources

Adams, Ephraim Douglass. *Great Britain and the American Civil War.* 2 vols. New York: Russell and Russell, 1925.

Alexander, Edward Porter. *Military Memoirs of a Confederate.* Ed. T. Harry Williams. Bloomington: Indiana University Press, c. 1907, 1935, 1962.

"An Act [for] . . . the Erecting of Certain Machinery . . ." December 15, 1863. *General Laws of the Tenth Legislature of the State of Texas.* Austin, 1864.

"An Act Making an Appropriation for the Removal and Erection of the Naval Rope-Walk." *Acts and Joint Resolutions Passed at the Second Session of the Second Confederate Congress.* Holmes Beach, Fla., 1970.

"An Act to Raise Two Million Dollars. December 10, 1863." *General Laws of the Tenth Legislature of the State of Texas.* Houston, 1864.

Anderson, Edward C. *Confederate Foreign Agent.* Ed. Stanley Hoole. University, Ala.: Confederate Publishing Company, 1976.

Appletons' Cyclopaedia of Applied Mechanics: A Dictionary of Mechanical Engineering and the Mechanical Arts. Ed. Park Benjamin. 2 vols. New York: D. Appleton, 1886.

Appleton's [sic] Dictionary of Machines, Mechanics, Engine-Work for Engineering. 2 vols. New York: D. Appleton, 1867.

Armes, Ethel Marie. *The Story of Coal and Iron in Alabama.* Birmingham, Ala.: Chamber of Commerce, 1910.

"Art. IX.—How Our Industry Profits by the War. Responses from Georgia." *DeBow's Review* 33 (May–August 1862): 78.

Ayers, Edward L. *The Promise of the New South.* Oxford: Oxford University Press, 1992.

Ball, Douglas B. *Financial Failure and Confederate Defeat.* Urbana and Chicago: University of Illinois Press, 1991.

Beatty, Bess. *Alamance: The Holt Family and Industrialization in a North Carolina County, 1837–1900.* Baton Rouge: Louisiana State University Press, 1999.

Bullock, Rufus. *Letter from His Excellency Governor Bullock of Georgia in Reply to the Honorable John Scott, United States Senator.* Atlanta, 1871.

Burke, Walter E., Jr., Quartermaster. *A Brief Account of the Life of Colonel Abraham*

Charles Myers, Quartermaster General CSA. Fort Myers: Southwest Florida Historical Society, 1976.

Chase, Henry, and Charles W. Sanborn. *The North and the South: A Statistical View of the Condition of the Free and Slave States*. New York: Sheldon, Blakeman, 1856.

Cheney, Newell. *History of the Ninth Regiment, New York Volunteer Cavalry: War of 1861 to 1865, Compiled from Letters, Diaries, Recollections and Official Records*. Poland Center, N.Y., 1901.

Chew, Morris R. *History of the Kingdom of Cotton and Cotton Statistics of the World*. New Orleans, 1884.

Cleveland, Henry. *Alexander H. Stephens, in Public and Private, with Letters and Speeches, Before, During, and Since the War*. Philadelphia: National Publishing, 1866.

Cobb, James C. *Industrialization and Southern Society, 1877–1984*. Lexington: University of Kentucky Press, 1984.

Collins, Steven G. "System in the South: John W. Mallet, Josiah Gorgas, and Uniform Production at the Confederate Ordnance Department." *Technology and Culture* 40 (July 1999): 517–44.

Colton, Matthias Baldwin, and William Francis Colton. *Column South with the Fifteenth Pennsylvania Cavalry: From Antietam to the Capture of Jefferson Davis*. Compiled by Suzanne Colton Wilson. Ed. J. Ferrell Colton and Antoinette G. Smith. Flagstaff, Ariz.: J. F. Colton, 1960.

Colvin, Roland E. "The Just Objects of War; Conduct of Union Troops Toward Non-Combatants and Private Property in Alabama, 1862–1865." Master's thesis, College of William and Mary, 1983.

[Colwell, Stephen]. *The Five Cotton States and New York: or, Remarks on the Social and Economical Aspects of the Southern Political Crisis*. N.p., 1861.

Cooper, William J. *The Conservative Regime: South Carolina, 1877–1890*. Baltimore: Johns Hopkins University Press, 1968.

The Correspondence of Jonathan Worth. Ed. J. G. de Roulhac Hamilton. 2 vols. Raleigh: Edwards and Broughton, 1909.

Coulter, E. Merton. *The Confederate States of America, 1861–1865*. Baton Rouge: Louisiana State University Press, 1950.

Crandall, Marjorie L., ed. *Confederate Imprints*. 2 vols. Boston: Boston Athenaeum, 1955.

Crandall, Warren D., and Isaac D. Newell et al. *History of the Ram Fleet and the Mississippi Marine Brigade in the War for the Union on the Mississippi and Its Tributaries: The Story of the Ellets and Their Men*. St. Louis: Buschart Brothers, 1907.

Dabney, Robert L. *The New South*. Raleigh: Edwards, Broughton, 1883.

Davis, William C. *Battle at Bull Run: A History of the First Major Campaign of the Civil War*. Baton Rouge: Louisiana State University Press, 1977.

DeCredico, Mary A. *Patriotism for Profit: Georgia's Urban Entrepreneurs and the Confederate War Effort*. Chapel Hill: University of North Carolina Press, 1990.

DeLeon, Thomas Cooper. *Four Years in Rebel Capitals: An Inside View of Life in the Southern Confederacy, from Birth to Death; from Original Notes, Collated in the Years 1861 to 1865*. Mobile: Gossip Printing, 1892.

Dennett, John Richard. *The South As It Is: 1865–1866*. Ed. Henry M. Christman. New York: Viking Press, 1965.

DeTreville, John R. "The Little New South: Origins of Industry in Georgia's Fall Line Cities, 1840–1865." Ph.D. diss., University of North Carolina, 1985.

Dew, Charles R. *Ironmaker to the Confederacy: Joseph R. Anderson and the Tredegar Iron Works*. New Haven, Conn.: Yale University Press, 1966.

Dowd, Clement. *Life of Zebulon B. Vance*. Charlotte, N.C.: Observer Printing and Publishing House, 1897.

Downey, Tom. "Riparian Rights and Manufacturing in Antebellum South Carolina: William Gregg and the Origins of the 'Industrial Mind.'" *JSH* 65: 77–108.

Doyle, Don H. *New Men, New Cities, New South: Atlanta, Nashville, Charleston, Mobile, 1860– 1910*. Chapel Hill: University of North Carolina Press, 1990.

Duke, Basil W. *A History of Morgan's Cavalry*. Ed. Cecil Fletcher Holland. Bloomington: Indiana University Press, 1960.

Edmonds, Richard H. *Blue Book of Southern Progress*. Baltimore: Manufacturers' Record Publishing Company, 1926.

———. *Facts About the South*. Baltimore: Manufacturers' Record Publishing Company, 1895.

———. *The Southern Redemption: From Poverty to Prosperity. In 1860 the Richest Part of the Country—in 1870 the Poorest—in 1880 Signs of Improvement—in 1889 Regaining the Position of 1860*. Baltimore: Manufacturers' Record Publishing Company, 1890.

Elliott, E. N. *Cotton Is King, and Pro-Slavery Arguments: Comprising the Writings of Hammond, Harper, Christy, Stringfellow, Hodge, Bledsoe, and Cartwright, on This Important Subject*. Augusta, Ga.: Prichard, Abbot & Loomis, 1860.

Evans, Curt J. "Daniel Pratt of Prattville: A Northern Industrialist and a Southern Town." Ph.D. diss., Louisiana State University, 1998.

An Exposition of the Property of the Etowah Manufacturing and Mining Company, at Etowah, Cass County, Georgia, and Testimonials of its Value. New York, 1860.

Finlay, George P., and D. E. Simmons, compilers. *Index to Gammel's Laws of Texas, 1822–1904*. Austin: H. P. N. Gammel, 1906.

Fisher, Richard S. *A New and Complete Statistical Gazetteer of the United States of America, Founded on and Compiled from Official Federal and State Returns, and the Seventeenth National Census*. New York: J. H. Colton, 1853.

Flint, Charles L., C. F. McCay, J. C. Merriam, and Thomas P. Kettell. *Eighty Years' Progress: The United States from the Revolutionary War to the Great Rebellion*. New York: L. Stebbins, 1864.

Flynt, J. Wayne. *Dixie's Forgotten People: The Southern Poor Whites*. Bloomington: Indiana University Press, 1979.

Fogel, Robert William, and Stanley L. Engerman. *Time on the Cross: The Economics of American Negro Slavery*. Boston and Toronto: Little, Brown, 1974.

Fontaine, Francis (State Commissioner of Land and Immigration). *The State of Georgia: What It Offers to Immigrants, Capitalists, Producers and Manufacturers, Fruit and Vegetable Growers, and Those Desiring to Better Their Condition*. Atlanta, 1881.

Friedel, Frank. *Francis Lieber: Nineteenth-Century Liberal*. Baton Rouge: Louisiana University Press, 1947.

Frost, Dan R. "A Confederate Education in the New South: Southern Academia and the Idea of Progress in the Nineteenth Century." Ph.D. diss., Louisiana State University, 1994.

Georgia. Department of Agriculture. *Georgia: Historical and Industrial*. Atlanta, 1901.

Gibbes, James G. *Who Burnt Columbia?* Newberry, S.C.: E. H. Aull, 1902.

Goff, Richard D. *Confederate Supply*. Durham, N.C.: Duke University Press, 1969.

Griffin, Richard W.. "North Carolina: The Origin and Rise of the Cotton Textile Industry, 1830–1880." Ph.D. diss., Ohio State University, 1954.

———. "Textile Industry." In *Encyclopedia of Southern History*. Ed. David C. Roller and Robert W. Twyman. Baton Rouge: Louisiana State University Press, 1979.

Guyton, Percy Love. "The Government and Cotton to 1862." Ph.D. diss., Duke University, 1952.

Hall, Clifton. *Andrew Johnson: Military Governor of Tennessee*. Princeton, N.J.: Princeton University Press, 1916.

Hamersly, Thomas H. S., compiler. *Complete Army and Navy Register of the United States of America from 1776 to 1887*. New York: T. H. S. Hamersly, 1888.

Harris, William C. *William Woods Holden, Firebrand of North Carolina Politics*. Baton Rouge: Louisiana State University Press, 1987.

Helper, Hinton Rowan, ed. *The Holden Record*. Raleigh: The Register, March 19 and April 2, 9, 16, 1868.

———. *The Impending Crisis of the South: How to Meet It*. New York: A. B. Burdick, 1860.

Hesseltine, William B. *Confederate Leaders in the New South*. Westport, Conn.: Greenwood Press, c. 1950, 1970.

Hill, Louise Biles. *State Socialism in the Confederate States of America*. Charlottesville, Va.: Historical Publishing Company, 1936.

Hitchcock, Henry. *Marching with Sherman: Passages from the Letters and Campaign Diaries of Henry Hitchcock, Major and Assistant Adjutant General of Volunteers, November 1864–May 1865*. Ed. Mark Anthony DeWolfe Howe. New Haven, Conn.: Yale University Press, 1927.

Hodge, LeRoy, ed. *The South's Physical Recovery Described in One Hundred Addresses by National Leaders: Proceedings of the Third Annual Southern Commercial Congress, Atlanta, Ga., March, 1911*. Washington, D.C.: Southern Commercial Congress, 1911.

Huse, Caleb. *The Supplies for the Confederate Army, How They Were Obtained in Europe and How Paid For, Personal Reminiscences and Unpublished History*. Boston: T. R. Marvin & Son, 1904.

Ide, Yoshimitsu. "The Significance of Richard Hathaway Edmonds and His *Manufacturer's Record* in the New South." Ph.D. diss., University of Florida, 1959.

Johnston, J. E. *Narrative of Military Operations Directed During the Late War Between the States*. New York: D. Appleton, 1874.

Jones, James Pickett. *Yankee Blitzkrieg: Wilson's Raid Through Alabama and Georgia*. Athens: University of Georgia Press, 1976.

Jones, John B. *A Rebel War Clerk's Diary at the Confederate States Capital*. Ed. Howard Swiggett. 2 vols. New York: Old Hickory Bookshop, 1935.

Kean, Robert G. H. *Inside the Confederate Government: The Diary of Robert Garick Hill Kean*. Ed. Edward Younger. New York: Oxford University Press, 1957.

Kelley, William D. *The Old South and the New: A Series of Letters*. New York and London: G. P. Putnam, 1888.

———. *The South—Its Resources and Wants*. Washington, D.C.: Union Republican Congressional Executive Committee, 1866.

Kennedy, Joseph C. G. *Preliminary Report on the Eighth Census, 1860*. Washington, D.C.: Government Printing Office, 1862.

Kettell, Thomas J. *Southern Wealth and Northern Profits, as Exhibited in Statistical Facts and Official Figures*. New York: George W. & John A. Wood, 1860.

Klingberg, Frank W. *The Southern Claims Commission*. Berkeley: University of California Press, 1955.

Lander, Ernest. *The Textile Industry in Antebellum South Carolina*. Baton Rouge: Louisiana State University Press, 1969.

Lichtenstein, Alexander C. *Twice the Work of Free Labor: The Political Economy of Convict Labor in the New South*. London and New York: Verso, 1996.

Longstreet, James. *From Manassas to Appomattox*. Ed. James I. Robertson. Bloomington: Indiana University Press, 1960.

McClure, Alexander K. *The South: Its Industrial, Financial, and Political Condition*. Philadelphia: J. B. Lippincott, 1886.

Melton, Maurice K. "Major Military Industries of the Confederate Government." Ph.D. diss., Emory University, 1978.

Miller, Randall M. *The Cotton Mill Movement in Ante-Bellum Alabama*. New York: Arno Press, 1978.

Mims, Shadrack. "History of Autauga County." *Alabama Historical Quarterly* 8 (fall 1946).

Mitchell, B. R. *European Historical Statistics, 1750–1970*. New York: Columbia University Press, 1975.

Mitchell, Broadus. *William Gregg, Factory Master of the Old South*. Chapel Hill: University of North Carolina Press, 1928.

Mordecai, Samuel. *Virginia, Especially Richmond, in By-gone Days; With a Glance at the Present: Being Reminiscences and Last Words of an Old Citizen*. 2nd ed. Richmond: West & Johnston, 1860.

Munger, S. S. "Manufacturers in Texas." *Texas Almanac for 1868*. Galveston, 1867.

The National Cyclopedia of American Biography. 63 vols. New York: J. T. White, 1898–1984.

Nelson, Scott Reynolds. *Iron Confederacies: Southern Railways, Klan Violence, and Reconstruction*. Chapel Hill: University of North Carolina Press, 1999.

Nichols, James L. *The Confederate Quartermaster in the Trans-Mississippi*. Austin: University of Texas Press, 1964.

Nordhoff, Charles. *The Cotton States in the Spring and Summer of 1875*. New York: D. Appleton, 1876.

North Carolina. State Department of Education. *North Carolina and Its Resources*. Raleigh, 1896.

Owen, Thomas McAdory. *History of Alabama and Dictionary of Alabama Biography*. 4 vols. Chicago: S. J. Clarke, 1921.

Owsley, Frank Lawrence. *King Cotton Diplomacy*. Chicago: University of Chicago Press, c. 1931, 1959.

Parrish, T. Michael, and Robert M. Willingham Jr. *Confederate Imprints: A Bibliography of Southern Publications from Secession to Surrender; Expanding and Revising the Earlier Works of Marjorie Crandall & Richard Harwell*. Austin, Tex., and Katonah, N.Y.: Jenkins Publishing Company (ca. 1984).

Parton, James. *General Butler in New Orleans, History of the Administration of the Department of the Gulf in the Year 1862*. New York: Mason Brothers, 1864.

Pollard, Edward A. *Life of Jefferson Davis*. Philadelphia: National Publishing Company, 1869.

Pollock, Edward. *Historical and Industrial Guide to Petersburg, Virginia*. Petersburg: T. S. Beckwith, 1884.

Public Laws of the Confederate States of America, Passed at the Third Session of the

First Confederate Congress, 1863. Ed. James M. Matthews. Richmond, Va.: R. M. Smith, 1863.

Putnam, Sallie A. Brock. *In Richmond during the Confederacy.* New York: R. M. McBride, 1961.

Ramsdell, Charles W. *Behind the Lines in the Southern Confederacy.* Baton Rouge: Louisiana State University Press, 1944.

———. "The Control of Manufacturing by the Confederate Government." *Mississippi Valley Historical Review* 8, no. 3 (December 1921): 231–49.

The Rebellion Record: A Diary of American Events, with Documents, Narratives, Illustrative Incidents, Poetry Etc. Ed. Frank Moore. 12 vols. New York: G. P. Putnam, 1862.

Rerick, Rowland H. *Memoir of Florida.* Ed. Francis P. Fleming. 2 vols. Atlanta: Southern Historical Association, 1902.

"Resources of the Confederacy in February, 1865." *Southern Historical Society Papers.* Vol. 2. Richmond, 1876.

Reynolds, John S. *Reconstruction in South Carolina, 1865–1867.* Columbia: State Company, 1905.

Richardson, Albert D. *The Secret Service, the Field, the Dungeon, and the Escape.* Hartford, Conn.: American Publishing, 1866.

Richardson, James D. *A Compilation of the Messages and Papers of the Confederacy.* 2 vols. Nashville: United States Publishing Company, 1906.

Robertson, James I., ed. *Proceedings of the Advisory Council of the State of Virginia: April 21– June 19, 1861.* Richmond: State Library, 1977.

Rowell, John. *Yankee Artillerymen: Through the Civil War with Eli Lilly's Indiana Battery.* Knoxville: University of Tennessee Press, 1976.

———. *Yankee Cavalryman: Through the Civil War with the Ninth Pennsylvania Cavalry.* Knoxville: University of Tennessee Press, 1971.

Royster, Charles. *The Destructive War: William Tecumseh Sherman, Stonewall Jackson, and the Americans.* New York: Alfred A. Knopf, 1991.

Savage, John. *The Life and Public Service of Andrew Johnson, Seventeenth President of the United States.* New York: Derby and Miller, 1866.

Scott, Samuel W., and Samuel P. Angel. *History of the Thirteenth Regiment Tennessee Volunteer Cavalry U.S.A.* Philadelphia, 1973.

Sharkey, Robert P. *Money, Class, and Party: An Economic Study of Civil War and Reconstruction.* Baltimore: Johns Hopkins University Press, 1959.

Shofner, Jerrell H., and William W. Rogers. "Textile Manufacturing in Florida during the Civil War." *Textile History Review* 4, no. 3 (July 1963): 118–25.

Smith, Mark M. *Mastered by the Clock: Time, Slavery, and Freedom in the American South.* Chapel Hill: University of North Carolina Press, 1997.

Somers, Robert. *The Southern States since the War, 1870–71.* Intro. Malcolm C. Mc-Millan. University: University of Alabama Press, 1965.

Sorrel, G. Moxley. *Recollections of a Confederate Staff Officer.* New York and Washington, D.C.: Neale, 1905.

Speed, Thomas. "Cavalry Operations in the West Under Rosencrans and Sherman." In *Battles and Leaders of the Civil War.* 4 vols. New York: Thomas Yoseloff, 1956.

Standard, Diffee William. *Columbus, Georgia, in the Confederacy[:] The Social and Industrial Life of the Chattahoochee River Port.* New York: William Frederick Press, 1954.

Steadman, Enoch. *The Southern Manufacturer.* Gallatin, Tenn.: Gray and Boyers, 1858.

Straker, David Augustus. *The New South Investigated.* Detroit, 1888.

Stuart, Alexander Hugh Holmes. *A Narrative of the Leading Incidents of the Organization of the First Popular Movement in Virginia in 1865 to Re-establish Peaceful Relations Between the Northern and Southern States, and of the Subsequent Efforts of the "Committee of Nine," in 1869, to Secure the Restoration of Virginia to the Union.* Richmond: William Ellis Jones, 1888.

Superintendent of the Census. *Manufactures of the United States in 1860; Compiled from the Original Returns of the Eighth Census, under the Direction of the Secretary of the Interior.* Washington, D.C.: Government Printing Office, 1865.

Surby, Richard W. *Grierson Raids, and Hatch's Sixty-four Days March, with Biographical Sketches, and the Life and Adventures of Chickasaw, the Scout.* Chicago: Round and James, 1865.

Tenney, William Jewett. *The Military and Naval History of the Rebellion in the United States with Biographical Sketches of Deceased Officers.* New York: D. Appleton, 1865.

Texas Almanac for 1864. Austin: D. Richardson, 1864.

Texas Almanac for 1865. Austin: D. Richardson, 1864.

Texas Almanac for 1867. Galveston, 1866.

Texas Almanac for 1868. Galveston, 1867.

Texas Almanac for 1870. Galveston, 1870.

Thomas, Emory. *The Confederacy as a Revolutionary Experience.* Englewood Cliffs, N.J.: Prentice-Hall, 1971.

Thompson, Robert Luther. *Wiring a Continent: The History of the Telegraph Industry in the United States, 1832–1866.* Princeton, N.J.: Princeton University, 1847.

Thorndike, Rachel Sherman, ed. *The Sherman Letters: Correspondence Between General Sherman and Senator Sherman from 1837 to 1897.* New York: Da Capo, c. 1894, 1969.

de Tocqueville, Alexis. *Democracy in America*. Ed. Phillips Bradley. 2 vols. New York: Alfred A. Knopf, 1945.

Todd, Richard Cecil. *Confederate Finance*. Athens: University of Georgia Press, 1954.

Tomlinson, Charles, ed. *Cyclopaedia of Useful Arts, Mechanical and Chemical, Manufactures, Mining and Engineering*. 2 vols. London and New York: George Virtue, 1852–54.

Tompkins, Daniel A. *A History of Mecklenburg County and the City of Charlotte from 1740 to 1903*. Charlotte: Observer Printing House, 1903.

Trefousse, Hans L. *Andrew Johnson: A Biography*. New York and London: W. W. Norton, 1989.

Trowbridge, John Townsend. *The Desolate South, 1865–1866*. Ed. Gordon Carroll. New York: Duell, Sloan, and Pearce; Boston: Little, Brown., 1956.

————. *The South: A Tour of Its Battlefields and Ruined Cities*. Hartford, Conn.: L. Stebbins, 1866.

Tyler, Ronnie C. *Santiago Vidaurri and the Southern Confederacy*. Austin: Texas State Historical Association, 1973.

Upson, Theodore F. *With Sherman to the Sea*. Ed. Oscar Osburn Winther. Baton Rouge: Louisiana State University Press, 1943.

Vandiver, Frank E. *Ploughshares into Swords: Josiah Gorgas and Confederate Ordnance*. Austin: University of Texas Press, 1952.

Vandiver, Frank E., ed. *Confederate Blockade Running through Bermuda, 1861–1865: Letters and Cargo Manifests*. Austin: University of Texas Press, 1947.

Van Horne, Thomas Budd. *History of the Army of the Cumberland: Its Organization, Campaigns, and Battles, Written at the Request of Major General George H. Thomas Chiefly from His Private Military Journal and Official and Other Documents*. Cincinnati: R. Clarke, 1875.

Walter, John B. *Merchant of Terror: General Sherman and Total War*. Indianapolis: Bobbs-Merrill, 1973.

Webb, Elizabeth Yates. "Cotton Manufacturing and State Regulations in North Carolina, 1861–1865." *North Carolina Historical Review* 9, no. 2 (April 1932).

Weigley, Russell F. *Quartermaster General of the Union Army: A Biography of M. C. Meigs*. New York: Columbia University Press, 1959.

"What We Are Gaining by the War." *DeBow's Review* 32 (March and April 1862): 327.

White, George. *Historical Collections of Georgia: Contains the Most Interesting Facts, Traditions, Biographical Sketches, Anecdotes, etc. Relating to Its History and Antiquities from Its First Settlement to the Present Time*. New York: Pudney and Russell, 1854.

Wilson, Laurel E. Janke. "Textile Production in Nineteenth Century Orange, Ala-
    mance, and Durham Counties, North Carolina." Ph.D. diss., University of
    North Carolina, Greensboro, 1986.
Winston, George Tayloe. *A Builder of the New South: Being the Story of the Life Work
    of Daniel Augustus Tompkins*. Garden City, N.J.: Doubleday, Page, 1920.
Winston, Robert. *Andrew Johnson, Plebeian and Patriot*. New York: Barnes and
    Noble, 1928.
Wise, Stephen. *Lifeline of the Confederacy: Blockade Running during the Civil War*.
    Columbia: University of South Carolina Press, 1988.
Woodward, C. Vann. *The Origins of the New South*. Baton Rouge: Louisiana State
    University Press, c. 1951, 1971.
Wyckoff, William C., ed. *Textile Manufacturers' Directory*. New York, 1880.

Newspapers and Periodicals

Athens Southern Watchman, 1862
Augusta Daily Constitutionalist, 1861
Austin Texas Star Gazette, 1863
Bainbridge Argus, 1869
Charleston Mercury, 1862
Charlotte Observer, 1874
Charlotte Western Democrat, 1866
Covington Georgia Enterprise, 1870
Daily South Carolinian, 1864
Dallas Herald, 1862
DeBow's Review, 1861, 1862
Democrat (Huntsville, Ala.), 1861
Edgefield Economist, 1866
Fayetteville Eagle, 1871
Macon Telegraph, 1862
Mobile Advertiser and Register, 1861
Natchitoches Union, 1862
New York Herald, 1862, 1863
New York Times, 1864
Richmond Enquirer, 1861
Richmond Whig, 1862
Savannah Morning News, 1877

Texas State Gazette, 1864
Tuscaloosa Observer, 1871
Washington Telegraph, 1862
Wilmington Journal, 1869
Winston-Salem People's Press, 1863

INDEX

towards Abraham C. Myers, 66; on Huse, 162; and passport office, 87; on profits, 55–56; on Union raid, 194
Jones, Dr. Joseph, 17

Kean, Robert, 89; on Abraham C. Myers and Jefferson Davis, 86
Kelley, Tackett, and Ford, 43; and blanket supply, 24
Kelley, William Darrah, 266; on segregation of labor, 279
Kershaw, General Joseph, 125
Kettell, Thomas P., xiii, xiv
Keyes, General Edward D., 194
Kilpatrick, General Hugh Judson, 85, 209
King Cotton diplomacy, 156
King, Edward, 282; on segregation, 280
King, James Barrington, xx, 136, 198–99, 203, 205, 234, 266–68; cotton purchases of, 239; fear of Sherman, 203–04; on freedmen, 252–53; and machinery imports, 142; oath of, 245, 246; and orders from England, 15; on postwar rebuilding, 268; and postwar resources, 358n 38; and secession panic, 16, 25
King, Thomas Butler, 20
King, William, 209; negotiations with Sherman, 204; peace emissary with Freedmen's Bureau, 350n 121
King's Mountain iron works, xvii
Kirkman and Hays (Tuscaloosa), 134
Knight, Jacob B. and Benjamin, 221
Knoxville, Tenn., siege at, 96–98

Labor: in Athens factory, 44–45; in Cedar Falls, 152–53; in Columbus, 222–23; and costs, 62; and cotton industry, 248, 300n 3; at Crenshaw Woolen Mill, 61; in depots, 9; at Fries's mill, 44; in Macon, 44; in Petersburg siege, 219–20; wages, 215
  conditions of, 151–52, 198; Georgia's repeal of regulations, 21; hours, xv, 198; and mortality, 216; and residencies, 215; work days, 152–53
  military: exemptions for workers, 44; losses to, 62–63
  workers: black, 62, 65; black prisoners, 361n 103; children, 61, 151, 216; and contracts with factories, 367n 26; and deportation, 204–05; foreign, 61, 64; in Reconstruction, 254–56, 266,

279–80; seamstresses, 69, 74, 81, 126, 191; slave, 75, 151–52, 226; women, 151, 204, 214–16, 225
Lafone, Henry, 175
Lamar, Gazaway Bugg, 175, 241, 242, 260; and contracts with bureau, 24
Lamb, Colonel William, 169; postwar political career of, 275
Lancashire cotton famine, 160
Landis, Major Absalom L., 126, 230
Lauderdale County, Ala., destruction of factories in, 188
Lawlin Excelsior Gas (Charlotte), 75
Lawrence, Amos A., 244
Lawrenceburg factory, 231; burning of, 201
Lawton, Alexander R., 77, 88–89, 98, 212, 278; and Florida, 115; and New South career, 287–88; problems, 91, 93–94; and Stoneman's raid, 355n 226; and strategic planning, 95; and Vance, 109–14, 119–21; and Virginia, 117
  mobilization, 100; full, 123–25; orders for Cunningham to control Lower South mills, 105; railroads, 98, 341n 94; and rational procurement, 102, 108–09
  supply issues: to armies (1864), 125, 127; and debt problems, 208; and imports, 156, 157, 165–66, 169, 174, 176; in Lee's army, 95; and Longstreet debacle, 98; and rationed military cloth, 105–08
  system of production: and idle machinery survey, 141; importations of machines, 177–78; impressment of machinery, 140; plans for, 98–99; and uniform contracts, 108
Lea, R. M., Federal Treasury agent, 239
Leach and Avery, 220
Leak, John W., 60
Lebanon factory, 230
Lee, Hutson, 10, 71, 85; wool impressment in Charleston, 38
Lee, General Robert E., 35, 36, 37, 224; controversy with Abraham C. Myers, 46, 47; and Knoxville campaign, 95, 98; and quartermaster losses, 170; on winter supply (1862–1863), 83
Leman, W., 212
Lenoir, William, 230, 350n 113
Lester's factory, 200

Price, General Sterling, 183; and property destruction, 180–81
Prices: actions of Henry Atwood, 65; and concern of Gregg, 65; and control of profits, 47, 59; debate over, 52–53; inflation of, 27, 314n 65; and Lawton's calculation, 120–21; in North Carolina, 56–57. *See also* Cotton mills: profits and losses; Profits
Prisoners, 180, 226
Private aid, for soldiers, 12–13
Production: at Atlanta depot, 100; Lawton's controls of, 108–09; in Lower South mills, 103; in north Alabama mills, 185; in North Carolina mills, 118; Richmond Clothing Bureau, 310n 176; Trans-Mississippi, 148
Profits: in Augusta, 56, 66, 213; and blockade-runners, 175–76; and charges of excess, 64; at Crenshaw Woolen Mill, 64; and English commission merchants, 343n 106; at Fries's factory, 59; at Graniteville, 56; in James River factory, 314n 6; in Richmond and Petersburg mills, 61–64. *See also* Prices
Putnam, Sallie, 203

Quarles, General William, 126
Quartermaster Department, 4, 8, 187; agreements with Commissary and Navy over rationing, 106; and fraud, 68–74; lack of planning of, 39, 76–77, 78; reform efforts of, 82–83; and Trans-Mississippi, 32, 39–40, 148–50. *See also* Lawton, Alexander R.; Myers, Abraham C.
  personnel, 8, 9, 10; support for Abraham C. Myers's promotion, 87–88
  problems, 13, 27, 66–67, 70, 78, 91, 95; arson, 199; and foreign competition with Ordnance, 159; opposition to reorganization, 320n 168; with state quartermasters, 320n 167
  productivity, 28, 81, 83–84; importation of supplies, 343n 105; and losses by blockade-runners, 170; payments below market prices, 63; percentage of Lower South goods taken, 103; receipts (1862), 310n 176; and resistance to importations of machinery, 153

Radical Republicans, 273
Railroad Bureau: Lawton's assumption of control, 96–97, 341n 94; as precedent for later actions, 341n 94, 368n 37
Railroads, 104, 245, 257, 263, 273, 280, 366n 8; decline of, 94; limited capacity of, 98, 172; mechanical systems, 98–99; reconstruction issue, 363n 129; seizure of, 341n 94; threat of seizure, 237; uniform schedules and through trains, 97. *See also individual railroads*
Randolph, Secretary George Wythe, 44; supply problems and dismissal, 319n 157; support of Lee on details issue, 46
Randolph Manufacturing Company, 147
Rawhide, Hardin County, Tenn., destruction of mill in, 187
Ray, Melinda, 217
Reagan, Secretary John H., 22
Reconstruction: efforts at rebuilding, 267; and influence of technology on, 362n 106, 363n 135
Regiments, official count of, 303n 33
Rentch, Daniel S., 218
Reynolds, General Joseph J., 189
Reynolds, Richard Joshua, 284
Richmond Enquirer, 61, 77; Abraham C. Myers's assistant, relationship to, 9; on Myers-Davis controversy, 89; on secession panic, 16; and supply dilemma, 92; support for Abraham C. Myers, 79
Richmond Examiner, 172; and endorsement of profit controls, 60–61; on Myers-Davis controversy, 89–90
Richmond factory (Ga.), 11, 140, 197, 215
Richmond, Va., prices compared with Fayetteville, 61
Richmond Whig, 61, 81; attack on Quartermaster Department, 78–79; and campaign for price controls, 60–61; criticism of manufacturers, 50
Ritchie, Thomas, 9
Roanoke Island, 77
Robinson, General James S., 213
Rock factory, 197
Rock Island factories, 117
Rockfish Creek factory, 59–60
Rockfish factory, 48, 217
Rockingham cotton mill, 217
Rome, Ga.: burning of factory in, 206; raid on, 187